THE LONG-DISTANCE RUNNER

THE LONG-DISTANCE RUNNER

An Autobiography

TONY RICHARDSON

WILLIAM MORROW AND COMPANY, INC.
New York

Copyright © 1993 by Woodfall America, Inc.

Introduction copyright © 1993 by Joan Didion

Publisher and author are grateful to acknowledge the use of the following
copyrighted material: "Many Happy Returns" from *Collected Poems*
by W. H. Auden (Vintage, 1991) reprinted with permission.
Copyright © 1976, 1991 by The Estate of W. H. Auden.

It is the policy of William Morrow and Company, Inc., and its imprints
and affiliates, recognizing the importance of preserving what has been
written, to print the books we publish on acid-free paper, and we exert
our best efforts to that end.

Library of Congress Cataloging-in-Publication Data

Richardson, Tony, 1928–1991.
    The long-distance runner : a memoir / Tony Richardson.
        p.   cm.
    ISBN 0-688-12101-2
    1. Richardson, Tony, 1928–1991. 2. Motion picture producers and
directors—Great Britain—Biography. 3. Theatrical producers and
directors—Great Britain—Biography. I. Title.
PN1998.3.R53A3   1993
791.43′028′092—dc20   93-6250
[B]   CIP

Printed in the United States of America

First Edition

1 2 3 4 5 6 7 8 9 10

BOOK DESIGN BY PAUL CHEVANNES

Foreword

Dear Reader,

My father, Tony Richardson, died of AIDS on November 14, 1991. We discovered this book on the day of his death, hidden away at the back of a dark and dusty disused cupboard, where he also kept his Oscars. Until finding it that day we had little knowledge of its existence. All I knew was that several years before I would come across him, lying on the sofa in the late LA afternoons, scribbling away on yellow legal pads. I asked him what he was writing and he said something like, "I'm having a go at my life, a sort of memoir." "How great," I replied—to which he guffawed, "No, it's not, it's not interesting, it's shit and very boring but I'm doing it as a kind of exercise."

Why he wrote it or for whom we'll never really know. He was between projects, and maybe he *was* just having a go. He finished the book when he was fifty-seven, six years before his death, and we think that he was diagnosed as being HIV positive around this time, so maybe that inspired him to set down a record of his life for us, his daughters.

I am virtually certain that it was not intended for publication. The copy we found was badly typed, uncorrected, and full of omissions. I'm sure that, having written it, he never reread it, which was typical of him: he never looked back (even in anger); once something was done it was over, past, finished. On to the next . . .

Still, we thought it worth publishing: It is an entertaining, humorous, and very personal account of the people and places he loved, the films he made, and the things that were important to him. His recall of events is sometimes factually inaccurate and

5

frequently embellished; he always made stories funnier and wilder than they actually were. And why not? That was his *métier*. It is a generous book and a sad one too, as he talks of the plays and films he would like to direct and the things he'd like to do in the future.

He had six more years of brave and unselfpitying struggle after finishing this book. His last film, *Blue Sky* (still unreleased at the time of writing), is one of his very best, and he was working on a production of *The Cherry Orchard*, which was to have taken place in London, starring my mother, Vanessa Redgrave, when he died.

—NATASHA RICHARDSON

Acknowledgments

Many thanks are due to David Hockney, Bob Davenport, Neil Hartley, Joan Didion, Grizelda Grimond and Tracey Scoffield and Robert McCrum at Faber and Faber for their unfailing generosity, enthusiasm, hard work and support in pulling this together.

A proportion of the royalties earned on *The Long-Distance Runner* will be donated to charities dedicated to the fight against AIDS.

—NATASHA RICHARDSON

Contents

THE LONG-DISTANCE RUNNER

An Introduction

There are in my husband's and my house two photographs of Tony Richardson. In the earlier of the two, taken in what must have been 1981, he is riding a dolly on which is mounted a Panaflex camera, somewhere near El Paso, a man deliriously engaged by—besotted by, transformed by—the act of making a picture, in this instance a "big" picture, the kind of picture on which every day the camera rolls costs tens of thousands of dollars, the kind of picture on which the dailies get flown to the studio every night and everyone in the projection room tenses a little when the take numbers flash on the screen, a picture with a big crew and a bankable star, Jack Nicholson, *The Border*. The more recent photograph was taken on an exterior location in Spain during the late fall of 1989. What appears to be a master shot is in progress. We see the camera operator, the sound boom, the reflector. We see the actors, James Woods and Melanie Griffith. And, over in the far left of the frame, in jeans and tennis shoes and a red parka, we see the director, a man visibly less well than he seemed riding the dolly outside El Paso but just as deliriously engaged by—besotted by, transformed by—the act of making a picture, in this case a twenty-one-minute film for television, an adaptation of Ernest Hemingway's "Hills Like White Elephants" for HBO.

I never knew anyone who so loved to make things, or anyone who had such limited interest in what he had already made. What Tony loved was the sheer act of doing it: whether what he was making was a big picture or theater or twenty-one minutes for television, its particular nature or potential success or potential audience was to him irrelevant, of no interest, not in the least the

13

point. The purity of his enthusiam for making, say, an *As You Like It* to run for a few nights at a community theater in Long Beach, or an *Antony and Cleopatra* starring television actors at a theater in downtown Los Angeles, was total: the notion that these projects might have less intrinsic potential than the productions of the same plays he had done in London with Vanessa Redgrave remained alien to him. "Something absolutely magical happens at the end," I remember him promising about the downtown *Antony and Cleopatra*. He was talking not about his work but about *working*, about everyone making the moment together, actors and director and audience alike, all framed together in some larger proscenium. "Everything is magic, a dream," I remember him announcing when he called from Spain to ask for a minor adjustment (the script, which my husband and I had written, called for the principals to wade in a stream, but the available stream was too cold) on "Hills Like White Elephants." He was talking, again, not about his work but about working, about that suspended state of being in which the cold stream and the olive grove and the not entirely well man in the red parka could be composed and recomposed, controlled, remembered just that way.

"Magic" was what Tony always wanted, in life as in work, and, like most people who love what they do, he made no distinctions between the two. "I want it to be magic," he would say, whether he was planning a picture or an improvised theatrical at his house or a moonlight picnic on the beach: he wanted magic, and he made it, and in the interests of making it he would mortgage his house, put up his own completion bonds, start shooting on the eve of an actors' strike. When he was not making a picture or theater he would make the same kind of magic happen at home: a lunch or a dinner or a summer was for him raw footage, something to shoot and see how it printed. His house was a set, filled with flowers and birds and sunlight and children, with old loves and current loves, with every conceivable confrontational possibility; forests of Arden, Prospero's island, a director's conceit. "Come to France with me in July," I recall him saying one night at dinner, and when my husband and I said that we could not, he turned to our daughter, then fourteen, and announced that in that case she would come alone. She did. There seemed to be dozens of people in Tony's conceit that July, and by the time we arrived to pick up Quintana she was swimming topless in St.-Tropez, dancing all night, speaking French, had Roman Polanski's telephone number in Paris, and was being courted by two Italians under the misapprehension that she was on vacation from UCLA. "This has been absolutely magical," Tony said.

It was also in the interests of making this magic that Tony could be so famously dogmatic, contrary, relentlessly ready to strand himself on whatever limb seemed likely to draw lightning. Quite often, for example, I heard him speak emphatically and enthusiastically about the virtues of "colorizing" black-and-white motion pictures, in each case to someone who had just signed a letter or written an op-ed piece or obtained an injunction opposing colorization. "If they had had color, they would have shot color," he would say, emphasizing each syllable equally, the declarative enunciation that gave him what John Osborne once described as "the most imitated voice in his profession." *"That is just pretentious nonsense. Color is better."* On two occasions I heard him rise to a passionate defense of the tennis player John McEnroe, who had done, Tony declared, "the most glorious thing" by throwing down his racket in a match at Wimbledon; the case Tony made derived partly, of course, from his quite fundamental anarchism, his essential loathing of the English class system and attendant sporting rituals.

Yet it derived equally from a simple wish to provoke the listener, structure the evening, make the scene work. Tony thrived on the very moments most of us try to avoid. Social consensus was to him unthinkable, stifling, everything he had left behind. Raised voices were the stuff of theater, of freedom. I remember him calling on the morning after a dinner in Beverly Hills that had abruptly become a shambles when my husband and an old friend, Brian Moore, began shouting at each other. There had been eight at the table (six, after my husband walked out and I fled), including Tony, whose delight in the turn the dinner had taken seemed absolute: the fight was the unexpected "magic" of the evening, the quiet dinner among friends dissolving into peril, the dramatic possibility realized.

I thought of the first sheep I ever remember seeing—hundreds of them, and how our car drove suddenly into them on the back lot of the old Laemmle studio. They were unhappy about being in pictures, but the men in the car with us kept saying:
"Swell?"

"Is that what you wanted, Dick?"

"Isn't that swell?" And the man named Dick kept standing up in the car as if he were Cortez or Balboa, looking over that gray fleecy undulation.

—F. SCOTT FITZGERALD, *The Last Tycoon*

Tony died, of a neurological infection resulting from AIDS, at St. Vincent's Hospital in Los Angeles on the fourteenth of November, 1991. He had begun this book some years before, during one of the many periods when he was waiting for one or another script or element or piece of financing to fall into place so that he could once again stand up in the car as if he were Cortez or Balboa and look out over whatever it was he wanted to make. Most people who make pictures learn to endure these periods of enforced idleness, some better than others, and since Tony was one of the others, he tended during such periods to multiply whatever balls he had in the air, commission a new script, meet one last time with the moneyman in Chapter 11, undertake some particularly arduous excursion ("You just don't like to have fun," he said accusingly when I declined to consider a weekend trip that involved cholera shots), *improve the moment*. Writing this book, he said on the evening he first mentioned it, was "something to do," and then he did not mention it again. When we asked, some time later, he said that he had abandoned it. "It is worthless," I remember him saying. "Absolutely worthless." Whether he believed that the book was worthless, or that the act of writing it was worthless, or that looking back itself was worthless, I never knew.

Nor did I know, until the afternoon of the day he died, when someone who had typed for him gave his daughters this manuscript, that he had finished the book, and I am still not at all sure when he finished it. The book does not deal with the work he did during the seven years between *The Hotel New Hampshire* and the time he died, and he mentions in the closing pages that he is fifty-seven, which would seem to suggest that he wrote them six years before he died, yet there is about those closing pages a finality, an uncharacteristic sense of *adieu*. This was not a man who had much interest in looking back. Nor was this a man afflicted by despair; the only time I ever saw him wretched was when he perceived a sadness or pain or even a moment of fleeting uncertainty in one of his daughters. And yet he wrote:

> Snapshots of my three daughters look directly at me from a bulletin board as I'm writing. And as one of their gazes makes contact they seem to be asking the one question—what's ahead? In the theatre, just as there's a well-known superstition you can't ever quote or mention 'the Scottish play' *Macbeth* without bringing bad luck, there's also a superstition that you should never say the last word or the last couplet of a Restoration play until the first night. I'm finding this as hard to finish as to say that last word. I can say to Natasha and Joely and Katharine I love them very much, but I sense they want more.

Did he know for six years that he was dying? Or would he say that to speak of "dying" in that sense is sentimental nonsense, since we are all dying? "There isn't an answer," he wrote earlier in this book about learning something he had not known about someone he loved. "Just a kind of spooky sadness—angels passing over us, or like that moment in Act II of *The Cherry Orchard* when Madame Ranevsky hears a distant sound like the string of a violin snapping." I suppose there were not many weeks during those six years when we did not talk or have lunch or spend an evening together. We spent holidays together. His daughter Natasha was married in our house. I loved him. And yet I have no idea.

—JOAN DIDION

I am part of all that I have met;
Yet all experience is an arch wherethro'
Gleams that untravell'd world, whose margin fades
For ever and for ever when I move.

ALFRED LORD TENNYSON, Ulysses

I

Ghost Sonata

If you stood facing the block, our shop was the second from the right. There were six in all in the block. First was a little bank, with the entrance diagonally on the street corner; then us; then a bakery; then a kind of haberdashery with hats in the window; then a not very enticing or successful butcher's; and, on the far corner, a shop that seemed always empty or filled with junk and which had no specific identity. Behind you (still facing the block) was a lone fish-and-chips shop, with streets of stone houses sloping down-hill at right angles to the main road.

The block stood near the end of a shopping street on the main road from Bradford to Bingley, Keighley, and beyond. On our side was, immediately, an isolated grocery store with steps leading up to it, then some waste ground, then some smaller shops irregularly spaced; on the other side the shops stretched in a regular and un-broken facade. Down the center of the road were tramlines, with the wires and poles for the trolleys above. The road always clanged and creaked and whistled as the trams passed or stopped or shunted in their points. The noise was comforting and not obtrusive. Some time, I don't remember when—perhaps when I was about six—the trams were replaced by trolley buses and the old tramlines were ripped out. The new trolleys had thick rubber wheels and were much faster, and the constant rattle was replaced by a swift, slick hiss. The change felt momentous, like stepping into the space age.

Our block was higher and somehow a bit more impressive than the rest of the street. I suppose it was built a bit later, probably around 1910. Each shop was three storeys high, with a sloping attic on top and a cellar below. You could see the half-moons of the cellar windows behind the gratings on the level of the stone-flagged pavements, the flagstones interspaced with metal hatches through which deliveries for the shops were made. Our shop—the family shop— was a pharmacy, and the big traditional phials—pink and blue, with pointed glass stoppers—perched on a shelf above the window. Every week or so the window would be dressed and re-dressed, with the newest cosmetics or wines or patent medicines, or the season's novelties, but the apothecary's insignia never moved—a symbol grave and eternal.

Inside, the house was amazingly territorial; everyone had his own space and sphere, and we collided only at mealtimes or in the evenings, and not always then. The living room between the shop and the kitchen was mine—or at least I spent more time there than anywhere else or than anyone else did. But it was also a busy traffic way from the kitchen to the shop, with stairs leading down to the cellar, and another staircase behind a half-glassed door up to the floors above. The furniture was arranged for the traffic: a sideboard against one wall; a rolltop desk crammed with my father's business receipts, bills, and documents against another; paths of lineoleum in front of each. A three-piece "suite"—two armchairs and a sofa of dark fake leather—was placed on the vaguely Indian carpet in front of the fire (almost always alight). The double-leafed table, always covered, with a cloth whose colors and texture depended on the time of day, stood in front of the window, which looked on to the tiny stone backyard. There were three or four bookshelves with uniform editions of classics and encyclopedias and medical textbooks, and beside the table a low cupboard with cut-glass doors held cut-glass glassware. Later on, a tiny aquarium sat on top of the cupboard, housing a lonely green terrapin. The room was papered up to a foot or so below the ceiling with an anonymous beige wallpaper—that was at least a little less dark than the rest of the house.

The kitchen was my mother's territory, a place of constant drudg-

ery and hard work. When, occasionally, even today, you hear someone assert or nostalgically imply that those were "good old days,"
I wish them in that kitchen. Stoves and boilers had to be filled and
cleaned, pans scoured, floors and tabletops scrubbed, scuttles of
coke hauled up, mangles turned, washing hung and rehung (lucky
was the day when the line and pole outside could be used), plus
the incessant preparation for the next meal and the next and the
next—work day in, day out, without respite and without end. It
was finally as breaking, or almost, as the production line in a factory—and as inward-turning too, as was the case with my mother.
Because when you have that amount of work to do, and for that
many people—and people with different needs—it's probably eas-
iest just to grit your teeth and get on by yourself.

Of course I didn't know it at the time. Nor did Bob. Bob was
my closest companion after he arrived, which was when I was about
four or five. Bob was an Old English Bobtailed sheepdog. He was
wonderful—gentle, loyal, affectionate, infinitely patient. I don't
know how or why my parents ever chose him. From my mother's
viewpoint, although she loved him, he was the most impractical
dog. Every day when it was rainy or sleeting or just plain mucky,
Bob would come in with a trail of dirt from every paw. Buckets
had to be filled; each paw had to be washed and rinsed and dried.
And this procedure was repeated every time he went outside. His
fur picked up every bit of twig and burr and matted into thick hard
pads which then had to be combed and teased and clipped—day
in, day out. He endured it all, even when, as you hacked away at
a knot on his ear, it was excruciating, and though it was obviously
to him incomprehensible, because he would have been at least as
happy to be as tousled and matted and smelly as when he rolled
in a pit of manure. But, however often my mother must have wished
Bob out of her life, and our life, for me he was worth it all.

The shop was Father's territory. A counter with a glass showcase
on top faced the door. Running the length of the right wall were
high shelves which masked the sanctum where prescriptions were
meticulously prepared. Drugs were ground in pestles with mortars
of different sizes, carefully weighed on brass balances, and packaged
in little sheets of white paper. Ointments were scooped with a broad
flat knife into round cardboard boxes. Then everything was neatly
labeled with a description of the contents and instructions for the

dosage or application. My father's writing was tiny and indecipherable, but no one seemed to complain. Every label was lined and at the bottom read "C. A. RICHARDSON PHARMACY, 28 Bingley Road, Saltaire, Shipley, Yks." Round the walls of the store were mahogany drawers with wooden knobs and old gold glass-covered labels with a mixture of Latin names and some more recognizable ones—senna, linseed, etc. Above a wooden desktop where prescriptions were recorded was a tiny glass cupboard in which poisons were always kept locked. A big weighing machine with a round face stood by the door. Its use was free.

Below the shop were two cellars where packing cases were delivered and emptied. Straw and wrapping paper strewed the floor and, although there was a perpetual attempt to impose some order, everything seemed confused. The smells were antiseptic and sometimes, when ammonia was being poured from kegs into smaller bottles, very acrid. The back cellar was darker, with a coal store in one corner, the grating above giving a streak of light from the street, and the coal and coke dust spilling out into the corner of the room. Wooden packing cases were splintered with an axe into kindling for our many fires. There was always a pile of the sharp, thin wood ready—one of the few tasks I was later assigned was chopping the wood. (I didn't do it either well or with much enthusiasm.) In the back cellar were also racks for the wine bottles. Chemists' shops often doubled as liquor suppliers, perhaps because of some long-lost medical association. A license provided much of the profit of the business, though at the beginning we were licensed only for wine, not spirits. Wine meant sherry and port, and various sweet semi-alcoholic drinks like Wincarnis. There was no demand for the French or Italian wines we all drink today.

The cellars were part of my life, if slightly dreaded—the wood, the coal scuttles—and there was always activity there. Father usually had one or more assistants or an errand boy. The assistants wore long yellowish-brown linen coats, to distinguish them from the trained pharmacists, who wore a short white one. But we didn't have a second pharmacist until much, much later on: Father did all the dispensing himself. He wore a darkish blue or brown suit with a waistcoat, a stiff collar, and always a bow tie. I don't think I ever saw him, even up to his death, with a normal tie. The bow was a badge of office: a symbol of authority, dignity, and finally, proprietorship. And he never wore a white coat—it would have compromised his rank.

Although the shop was cool and its odor vaguely pleasant, although there was a kind of fascination in the drugs and mystery in their preparation, for me it was all alien. I never felt comfortable there. Later, very occasionally, I would be asked to wait at the counter, and every customer was then an embarrassment and a threat. I knew this was where I never wanted to be, never would be. Nor was there any pressure for me to be there. The other members of the family rarely visited the shop either; separation was the way of life.

Upstairs was a totally different world. The top floor had three bedrooms: for my parents and for my grandmother—my mother's mother—and my little bedroom, with a partly sloping roof and a small dormer window. On the first floor were a bathroom and two bedrooms (later to become a sitting room and a stockroom). With its murky wallpaper with vaguely jungly foliage, this whole floor seemed dark and oppressive—oppressive because it was dominated by illness of a very palpable kind. My father's mother, my paternal grandmother, Ra—the ultimate matriarch of the Richardson clan, owner of house and business and a semi-totemic mummy-goddess at whose altar the whole tribe seemed masochistically to sacrifice themselves—had her dwelling here.

Ra had advanced rheumatoid arthritis and was confined to a wheelchair or to bed. Nurses or companions or maiden aunts were always on hand in her umbra, in total subservience. Her room overlooked the street and the passing trams and trolleys. It seemed to be in semi-gloom—I can't remember one lamp or light-sconce, though there must have been many—and heavy dark velvet or serge drapes hung at the windows. The windows were screened by lace curtains through which the witchlike chorus of older women would constantly peer at the passersby and the traffic outside. At night the coven re-formed itself round the open fire and in its flickering quavered out old hymns—"Abide with me; fast falls the eventide . . ." I was often an attendant. Miss Havisham would have been a perfect participant. The atmosphere was spooky, stifling, and hieratic. Ghosts and table-tapping and séances should have been indulged in, but the imagination—and morality—of those present was too limited.

"Ra" as a name was then without connotations, but now its Egyptological resonance seems perfect for the immobility of the room. Time had halted. Nothing lay ahead but death, and the feeble gestures of the ossified woman becoming the mummified. And when death came it was a day of whispers and secrets, lowered voices, oblique hints. I was ushered away, maybe to school, too vulnerable to be exposed to what Henry James might have called "the unmentionable thing". But what replaced the obsessive demands of sickness was another kind of bleakness: a little-used room, a little lighter maybe, but as withering and drab as the new three-piece rose moquette suite that was substituted for the sickbed.

I was an only child. Apparently overweight or oversized at birth on June 5, 1928, I almost killed Mother in delivery. And then I almost died of some mysterious childhood disease. So I was brought up in a vague atmosphere of being delicate, and a bit guilty too. But my being "delicate" was the excuse for all the old ladies of the house to surround and cosset and pamper me, to instill cautions and warnings and guard me as far as possible from any contact with the outside world. A parental power vacuum left them able to sweep me into a world of skirts and inhibition.

Nanny—my maternal grandmother—was the one I was closest to at the beginning. The word "granny" had, it was explained, been split into "Nanny" and "Ra" to avoid confusion between the two resident grandmothers—if that had ever been likely. "Nanny" was a perfect and accurate description. She waited on me, dressed and fed me, and picked up after me. She took me for walks and, later—pleasure of pleasures—to the movies and to the theatre. The Alhambra Theatre, Bradford, was the grandest of the accessible theatres and had visiting movies, operas, musical extravaganzas, and, of course, its own special production—the yearly pantomine. I saw my first Shakespeare there—*A Midsummer Night's Dream*—and *Peter Pan* in the original production. Another of the shows we saw was *Around the World in Eighty Days*. This was wonderful to me, combining my growing love for the strange and exotic with my passion for animals and birds. I don't remember if there was any story or characters, but tableau after tableau of jungles and waterfalls and tropical sunsets—modeled after my favorite Tarzan-movie landscapes—followed one another in entrancing succession, with live jaguars and cheetahs, chimpanzees, and gibbons. One of the strongmen, surrounded by scantily leopard-clad Jane, was performing with a big python. He asked for volunteers from the audience to hold it. Instantly I ran down the aisle of the enormous red and gilt auditorium and took it. Nanny didn't flinch or comment, but when I returned to the seat beside her in the orchestra stalls (it was one of our secret snobberies that we had to sit in these, the most expensive seats; the dress circle was just acceptable, but the upper balconies and the "gods" were impermissible—infra dig), I could see her almost in tears with pride at my heroism. And there were real tears when, in a park, I picked forbidden flowers and she warned I would be arrested and locked away from her in some terrible prison. Even walking off the paths and on the grass seemed too daring for her.

Within the household, Nanny was very subtly patronized—or I thought so. She came from West Hartlepool in County Durham. My grandfather had been a shipbuilder, they said, but he had lost his money in some crash. So there was an air of shame hanging over her, as if it was somehow demeaning to be living with and off her daughter in her son-in-law's mother's house. And Mother was often short and sharp with her, ordering her about. But Nanny never argued or complained; she accepted everything with gratitude and tolerance. With her round figure, her round breasts, her round granny glasses, her round bun of hair, she was like a warm, pliable rubber ball. She was always accommodating, always making the arrangement work. Yet she had an inner loneliness, because she was never quite admitted or accepted into the inner circle of the Ra sanctum.

Perhaps this was because all my mother's other relatives (there were lots of cousins and cousins of cousins—I could never sort them out) were slightly, ever so slightly, grander than the resolutely "trade"—i.e., chemist—members of the Richardson clan. Nanny's mother's family, the Ingles, came more from the Northeast. They lived in Harrogate and Stockton and by the sea. They had tennis courts and Labrador retrievers and guns. They didn't live over shops; they went to offices to conduct their businesses (I never knew what). Some of them were musical, and they had the ease that the more affluent always have compared with those who must work round the clock and count every penny. We visited them on Sunday expeditions in our bull-nose Morris car, but not too often—as if that might be "taking advantage" or presuming too much. Later, when I was at school in Harrogate, I often visited one of the families—Uncle Douglas, Aunt Phyllis, and cousin Paul—for lunch. The food was a great relief from the horrors of school fare, and the visit itself was an escape from horror. Cousin Paul was a charmer, but some of the distance between us was evident—if not quite Oliver Twist, I was his very refined shadow. And I hated the way Uncle Doug beat his gun dogs—it was supposed to be necessary "to teach obedience," but they loved me more.

The Richardsons were something totally different. They came from Hadfield, near Glossop in Derbyshire, and unlike Nanny's side of the family, they were numerous. My Richardson grandfather was long dead, but, before his last business had failed, he had been the pharmacist patriarch and his children had all been brought up to follow in his footsteps—even though the women, of course, hadn't been expected to qualify for their licenses. There had been six of them in all. All had wonderful banal lower-middle-class Victorian names—there was no doubt of their allegiance to Queen and country. In order, they were John William Radford, Florence Ethel, Ada Mary, John Alfred Francis, Clarence Albert (Father), and Cecil Antonio. The Antonio was the one lapse in the nomenclature. The story of this was drilled into me from birth, because it was my name too.

This is it. An earlier Richardson, probably a great-granduncle, had been a wanderer and adventurer. Finally he had settled in Argentina. He was reasonably successful, with estates and slaves. Apparently, however, and whenever emancipation happened in nineteenth-century Argentina, there was one old slave who remained faithful. He was called Antonio, and afterward it was to be a family tradition that his name was to be perpetuated in the family as a token of gratitude. What happened to the two of them thereafter I don't know. I think a few dusty curios and relics remained in our attic until Mother, who had a mania for getting shot of rubbish, threw them out; and there was also a curious rug, mottled red and yellow and brown, with a queer rough bristling texture on one side—like a horse blanket but not quite—which was used on my bed. This haunted me in an odd, vague way. I didn't like it, but it gave me some kind of imaginative point of departure to lands far-off and unknown.

I still don't know whether to believe the story—only the sentimentality rings convincingly. Anyway, Cecil Antonio was the name of the youngest Richardson—who was also Father's favorite brother. They went to the First World War together—young recruits, and Cecil Antonio physically weak. Father tried to protect him as best as he could, but finally he was gassed in an attack somewhere on the Somme. His lungs were destroyed, and he died in Father's arms. So once again "Cecil Antonio" was vowed to perpetuity, and the names were given to me. I hated them. I couldn't understand why I was saddled with a Wop name. Mussolini didn't help, nor did "Oh, oh, Antonio, with his ice-cream cart" (which everyone in the family loved to croon at me), and in the Second World War it was worse. Even today I wince when legal papers come in. At home it was always "Tony." "Tony" I stuck to desperately, and I get very irritated when the helpful or formal amend it to "Anthony."

Going backward along the family lineup, Francis was the renegade. A very mild, hesitant personality, he broke the rules by not becoming a pharmacist and by leaving the North and moving to London, where he married my gypsylike Aunt Winnie. She had a cockney accent and was thought, by the family, to be slightly common. And Francis, who became some kind of engineer, was also not very successful financially, so he let the family down on that count too. Uncle Francis and Aunt Winnie had one son, Maurice. I had two first cousins, and he was the one I preferred. He was entirely obsessed with transport and read nothing but bus and train timetables. It was inexplicable (but later led to achievement and success).

Aunt Ada was the chatterbox of the family. Small, sharp-featured, beaked like a bird, with endless garrulity, cheerfulness, and energy, she drove most of the others mad by never letting them get a word in. The worst of her prattling was its detail. She would describe events and times with a precision that ground out whatever pathetic interest her stories or information might have had. Mother went icy whenever Aunt Ada arrived, raised her eyebrows, and made faces and an occasional rather cutting remark.

Aunt Ada had married another pharmacist, Uncle Lloyd Royle.

Their shop was in Middleton Junction, Manchester, and he and to a certain extent Aunt Ada spoke with a Lancashire accent. That differentiated them from the rest of us, who had Yorkshire or Derbyshire accents. But although Uncle Lloyd was perceived to be slightly beneath the Richardsons socially, his business, which was in a relentlessly grim Industrial Revolution district, was prosperous, which gave a smear of envy to Mother's malice over her sister-in-law. Aunt Ada was the first of the family to have a fur coat, and she lunched twice a week in the posher department stores of Manchester. Insinuations of "selfishness" of being "only interested in herself" were made. She seemed to be the businesswoman of the Royle pharmacy, interviewing traveling salesmen, ordering products, and dictating policy by sampling the latest offerings at the cosmetic departments of the Manchester stores. Mother was also jealous that Ada could talk professionally to Father: They would disappear into the shop and at mealtimes would jabber endlessly about the numbers of prescriptions dispensed and the kinds of drugs and goods in demand or obsolete. It was exactly like gossip about the latest fashions, and the *Pharmaceutical Journal*—a dry, khaki-looking magazine—was both their Bible and their *Vogue*.

The Royles had one son, Cecil. His age and size were impressive when I was small, and I cowardly used him as a sort of bodyguard to foray out into parts of our neighborhood where I would otherwise never have dared go, or even into the company of rough (i.e., working-class) boys. If there had been trouble, I doubt Cecil would have been very effective.

Anyway, Aunt Ada was generous and friendly and inexorably cheerful, and one of the more tolerable of the clan but, as Mother always summed up, "A little of Ada goes a very long way."

The most "selfish" of all the Richardsons, according to my mother, was the oldest—Uncle Radford. He was the most physically impressive—six feet, well built, with thick, distinguished-looking white hair which, as far as I know, he kept to the end of his life. He was married to Aunt Edna, a primary-school teacher with a very red, rather scaly face that looked as if it had been rubbed raw with sandpaper. I liked her—she had the kind of cozy condescension that comes easily to some teachers and which, if your teacher doesn't have it, seems encouraging and desirable. Uncle Radford and Aunt Edna were great walkers. They hiked, by themselves or in hiking clubs, up the hills and down the dales, and went for their holidays to natural walking places like the Black Forest in Germany. They wore tweeds (for a time he wore plus-fours) and scarves and woollen hats and mittens. They seemed devoted and withdrawn from the rest of the family. This self-centeredness was the core of Mother's indictment: Uncle Radford had shirked his duty, as oldest of the tribe, to carry on the family business and support his invalid mother; yet he, like all the others, clung to his share of the family inheritance while leaving my father as the only one who was willing to take on the burden and the responsibility. They cultivated their own businesses while father soldiered on, at a very minimal wage, and tried to make a success of what would finally be carved up among them. So Mother cast Father and herself as the family's martyrs—which in truth they were—and resented the others, and was bitter and bitchy.

I can't pretend I liked most of them. They used to descend on us for Christmas—almost all Christmases were held at our house (or sometimes Ada's), because Ra was there. They piled in; they crowded the house. There was a false intimacy forced on us. It made Christmas day the worst of the year for me: presents I didn't want; jokes and vulgarity I didn't understand or hated; kisses and embraces I suffered under. Why did they have to invade us? When would they go away? I wanted to retreat to the upstairs sickroom and the gloom of the firelight and the games of bezique and the twilight singing. All my mother's prejudices and squeamishness I absorbed and regurgitated, perhaps magnified. Nor did I like the motor visits we sometimes paid to Middleton Junction, where the Royles lived over the shop, or to Royton, near Oldham, where Uncle Radford lived, some miles from his shop in Rochdale. We were never invited to stay in Royton, nor to dinner—only to high tea (a distinction that Mother was only to happy to observe and comment on).

Father was oblivious or impervious to Mother's carpings. He was a good man—a good, good man—though I didn't realize it at the time. I was never close to him. Father—"Bert," as everyone called him—had wanted to break from the pharmaceutical mold and become a lawyer. He would have made a good one. But the First World War and the family disaster intervened, so he took on the whole burden, working as a wage-earner and as a dutiful son and determined husband and father. While Ra was still alive he earned a pittance, and the hours were infinite. Very few of the working people among whom we lived could afford a doctor, and there was no free medicine, so chemists became the poor man's doctor. They advised, consulted, attended—did everything short of being able to prescribe, which naturally they resented being forbidden, as they were so much closer to the people than the doctors.

Father's gentleness and patience were extraordinary. He had the most wonderful hands and skill in bandaging and plastering. He would look into eyes and throats. People came at all hours and on all days. The shop was supposed to open for only about an hour on Sundays, and this on a rota with the other chemists in the district—signs were hung on the window to direct people after shop hours to whoever was "on duty"—but I think we were the only ones who lived on the premises, so there was a continual line of people who would bang on the back door late at night or early in the morning. Father never turned them away, however boring or unnecessary the demand, however tired he was. He loved people. He related to them. They in turn related to him.

After Ra died and he was able to buy out the rest of the family, Father began to become commercially successful and to earn money for himself. He bought another store. He went into politics (Conservative). He was elected mayor. Twice he was offered the chance to stand for Parliament—and, at that time, in a Conservative constituency, he would have won easily—but, under pressure from Mother, and perhaps feeling it was too late, he refused. He wanted to do all the things he had denied himself earlier—to have a social life, to work for things he believed in, to play golf—but the early struggles had limited him. Perhaps he felt he'd imposed too much on Mother already.

Mother was naturally shy, anti-politics, and she damped his naturally gregarious nature so that his existence centered more on her; in the end they moved from Shipley, where his popularity lay, to Morecambe—to a seaside-resort suburban life which allowed her to possess him for herself and to compensate for the life of toil she felt she had been forced to lead. Occasionally, but not often, I would hear arguments—always about money. When I was in the cellar, "There's never been enough since I came to this house"; then, late in semiretirement, petty dreary bickering. I didn't feel any great separation, though. Father seemed always cheerful and upbeat at mealtimes, and on the family excursions every Sunday in the car, but he was choked from his real and natural self by Mother's neurosis. He died at 6:30 one morning, of a sudden heart attack as he woke up. I was living in the center of London, and the next-door neighbor called me. I took a slow bath, then drove over to their house—they were also living in London by this time. My mother took my hand. "The light of my life has gone out," she said. It was very corny, but true. I don't know whether Father would have said the same of her. I think he might.

I was never close to him, never appreciated him. Sacrifices, duty, are never very appealing. What he lacked was imagination, any understanding of what it was like to be a child. Yes, he was sweet to me as a baby. I remember how he would sing—just in tune, in a thin reedy voice—songs like "Oh, dem golden slippers"; how he would nurse and care for me when I was ill; how he would sometimes punish me, at Mother's urging, with a short dark cane that was kept on the ledge of a bookshelf. What he didn't do—what all the demands of the shop and the household didn't let him do—was be a real friend or father. I now have realized this. He sacrificed and slaved to earn money to send me to what he believed would be a good school. He didn't want his son to suffer the deprivations he had suffered, and he worked and deprived himself to prevent that. Occasionally he would make what he thought were the right, the necessary, gestures to compensate for the enclosed life that he saw I was leading—taking me to a soccer match or the golf links, and later to Rotarian luncheon, a Tuesday event. (He was a very earnest Rotarian—the motto "Service Before Self" was what he profoundly and passionately believed.) But such gestures were too sporadic. I belonged to the world of those dying grandmothers upstairs, so these excursions and occasions were scary and imposing and I dreaded and loathed them. He felt hurt and couldn't understand it.

Duty and morality aren't natural to children, but he couldn't understand that. He couldn't understand that I didn't appreciate the extent of his sacrifices, so there was resentment on both sides—exacerbated, later, when I was growing up and we were on totally different sides politically. He had worked to free me into a life he'd never had, but I was so unprepared for, so appalled and frightened by, the life he'd pushed me into that there was no meeting until the possibility of real contact and intimacy had gone. In *Luther*, John Osborne said, "fathers and sons always disappoint each other." In the end I didn't disappoint him, but in many ways it was too late.

Mother was a much less admirable character, but I loved her passionately and was always happy, as a child, to be with her, to go with her, to have her attention. She could do no wrong, though at times we fought bitterly. I remember hitting her savagely once and locking myself in the lavatory while she battered the door in. But it was her approval and solace I wanted. I loved her cooking. I loved watching her work. I loved her malice and her causticity. I don't know when the transition occurred from her being the active piston which kept the domestic engine pumping to her narrowing down, pressuring Father to give up everything he loved, reducing his and her sights to semiretirement, then retirement, giving up all friends and acquaintances, coming to London to live in a house I bought there so they could be near me—whom they rarely saw. She began to indulge real and imaginary ailments, and after Father died, retired first to an apartment, quarreling with every companion, then to one room, where she then refused to leave her bed, uninterested in her grandchildren, finally shutting down even the television set, wanting and waiting for death as the final enclosure. The decline was straight and continuous. Sad—and it led me to the final assessment of who my parents were, as distinct from what they meant to me: the reverse of what I thought or would have said.

I have left Florence Ethel—Aunt Ethel—till last because she was so important to me. She was almost as tall as some of her brothers— beanpolelike, with the longest of the Richardson beaks. She sometimes dressed in brighter clothes or skimpier outfits—"Mutton dressed as lamb," Mother would scoff. As an old maid, obviously unmarriageable, she was despised by most of the family, and even Father was often irritated by her. She was pushed around, ordered about, and gradually made to feel everyone's contempt. At the beginning she lived with us and was Ra's chief companion, hand-maiden, nurse, bedpan-emptier, bottlewasher. She was constantly under Mother's feet. But she adored and worshipped me, and I loved her. Then, even before Ra died, perhaps when I was about six or seven, she surprised everyone by suddenly marrying a rather dreary, dumpy widower, Ernest Bryant, who owned a cobbler's shop and a shoe-selling business. (Later this was sold and they became drapers.) They lived only a few hundred yards away—still on Bingley Road, but beyond the main street. It was a marriage of convenience, and plain from the start that Uncle Ernest held a very definite second place to me in Auntie Ethel's concerns and affections.

About this time, Nanny started or seemed to start to fade out of my life. Imperceptibly, we ceased to do as much together, especially after I went away to school. With all the other old ladies gone, there was much less to do in the house; and always self-effacing, Nanny hardly seemed to exist. Mother bullied her more and, as Nanny got older and frailer, eventually placed her in a nursing home. To me it seemed a terrible thing to do to her, though Mother produced a torrent of justifications and excuses—the work she had to do, the carrying of meals upstairs, etc. We used to visit her in the home—pitiful occasions, gradually made more bearable by the fact that Nanny ceased to recognize us. I couldn't bear to think about it. She didn't in fact die until I'd left Oxford and was living in my first rented room in London, on Praed Street, by Paddington Station. The room was in the flat of an acting couple— it was small, dark, smelly and noisy from the Underground passing. One day as I came in, the wife said, "Oh, your mother called to say that your grandmother has just passed away." "Damn," I said. The actress was shocked that I didn't show any other feeling. Somehow it had been used up a long time before.

Anyway, Auntie Ethel shifted into the place Nanny had occupied before: chief confidante and fan, provider of whatever was denied or forbidden at home. I couldn't have tropical-fish tanks: "Too much work," Mother would say. "You won't look after them." Auntie Ethel would step in. Gradually, with her grumpy complaisance, her house behind the shop was filled with them. Auntie Ethel hoarded her rations or any food that was scarce to give to me. Fresh orange juice was always squeezed, bars of chocolate were produced, cakes were baked and waiting for me to walk in the door—and not a crumb was to be touched by Ernest until I was there. She became my escort to the movies. We saw all the Saturday-afternoon serials every week: the Westerns (Tom Mix with his horse Tony was the favorite); the adventure movies—*The Charge of the Light Brigade*, *Stagecoach*, *Bengal Lancer*, *The Four Feathers*—the Sturges and Capra comedies—all the magic that stamped America forever as the most glamorous, exciting, desirable place in the world. It was a kind of love affair which supplied all the affection I never felt at home. When I was at school she wrote to me every few days, and once a week she sent a parcel of anything that was unobtainable in wartime conditions—she was obsessed by my health. I was skinnier than she was, and very highly strung and nervous. And, like all the others, she was desperately overprotective, instilling caution for every exploit.

When my parents moved from Shipley to Morecambe (Uncle Ernest had died by then), she moved too and bought a house near them so that on my school holidays she could have those glimpses of and moments with me which I'm afraid I was beginning to neglect as I grew up and which were the only times life was worthwhile for her. Mother continued to tolerate her with open contempt. Auntie Ethel died while I was at school, waking up one day, doing her laundry, putting everything away in neat order, making the bed, then lying down on it and dying—as if she wanted to make the least fuss and trouble for anyone. She didn't have much money. What she had she left to me, with a touching note that I was the only person in her whole life who'd treated her as a human being.

Auntie Ethel's story had an odd coda. In 1983 I was shooting *The Hotel New Hampshire* in Montreal. A letter arrived. It was from the wife of my cousin Maurice, who had followed his boyhood preoccupation with train and bus timetables by occupying management positions in various large bus companies. I perhaps met his wife once or twice while I was still in London, but I'd moved to California in 1974 and had lost whatever fragile connections I'd had with the family. The letter had an odd tone—almost aggressive. Just before the shooting there had been a royal visit to Hollywood and I'd sat between the Queen and Mrs. Reagan. The publicity had prompted my cousin-in-law to write, "Since you've joined the Establishment you probably won't want to know what happened to the Richardson family, but as I'm compiling a family tree I thought I'd give you the facts." These were pretty melancholy: illnesses, senility, deaths—even that of my other cousin, Cecil, who was only four or five years older than me. I think there was just one survivor. But at the end of the letter was a note that startled me: "Did you know that Florence Ethel had an illegitimate child— a girl—which was sent away for adoption?" I had never heard a whisper of it. Mother always had a taste for gossip and revelations, but she, Father, Aunt Ada, and Aunt Ethel herself had kept the secret absolute. Why had the child been sent away? Victorian morality? Keeping appearances up? Economic necessity? And why had my parents been so resolutely silent? Did they feel some guilt or shame over the affair? Did they suspect I would have disapproved of her action? I wrote to my cousin to ask for any more information, but there was none.

All the emotion that poor Auntie Ethel had wanted to give had been channeled to me. Would life have been any different had I not been cocooned by her devotion? There isn't an answer, just a kind of spooky sadness—angels passing over us, or like that moment in Act II of *The Cherry Orchard* when Madame Ranevsky hears a distant sound like the string of a violin snapping.

Anyway, those were the cast of my particular *Ghost Sonata*.

2

<hr/>

What Then I Was

The world outside was very different. The age-old rivalry of York-shire and Lancashire—the white rose and the red—had been re-fired by the development of the wool and cotton industries in the nineteenth century. The West Riding of Yorkshire was the center of the wool industry, and Bradford and Leeds were its capitals, the ubiquitous dark stone mill chimneys being the castles and keeps of new barons of immense wealth. Shipley, though still an independ-ent town, was virtually a suburb of Bradford. Saltaire was part of Shipley. It was, I think, the first of the model villages in whose name so many crimes have since been committed, conceived as a William Morris idea of the perfect environment. The great mill itself in design and decency was way ahead of its time, and spread around the demesne were streets of two-storeyed stone houses for its workers, cottages for the old and retired, a hospital, chapels, parks, spaces, memorials. And Saltaire did have a stone solidity, a spaciousness and a respect for human independence which contrast favorably with the jerry-built streets of true Industrial Revolution commercialism. It was a bastion of concern and patronage, laid out by the owner of the mill, Sir Titus Salt, who combined his name with that of the River Aire, which traversed the area, to name the village or project or whatever you like to call it.

With the recession of the 1930s, the decline of the wool industry was aggravated by the competition of imports from the empire, and then the Second World War brought development to a standstill—happily, many would say today. Shipley was in fact one of the first fingers of the urbanization whose hand would gradually grab away at the countryside surrounding Bradford and which today has squeezed the green hillsides into ocher and drab pink and gray suburbs, malls, and housing estates. But when I was growing up the country hadn't lost the battle. Walk half or a quarter of a mile and you could reach vast parks—Northcliffe Woods and Playing Fields, Airedale Park, Shipley Glen, Hurst Woods, Manningham Gardens. Real farms that looked like Constable paintings were in easy reach for Nanny and Bob and me on our daily walks. The footpaths of the River Aire seemed, with their lush plantains and foxgloves, like an Amazonian jungle. The canal, where the slow barges with their old, plodding Clydesdale horses are as rare now as a passing aeroplane was then, was choked with weeds, flags, water lilies—a reminder, like the railway tracks, though much more pleasant, of a previous century's bright idea that was already obsolete.

And, beyond that, all around were the moors in their rough and bracing glory—yellow with gorse bushes in the spring; purple with heather in autumn; sun, clouds, rain, snow changing them as often as the sea changes in a day. Baildon Moor, Ilkley Moor, Bingley Moor, and Haworth Moor, where the Brontës had sheltered in their parsonage and produced their great poems and novels. They were the testing ground, the moors, testing your manhood and growing-up by the distances you could gradually master, the weather you could endure in an exhilarating loneliness—your only companions sheep and grouse, curlews and lapwings, larks and plovers. From them came strength and independence and freedom.

The spirit of the moors is in the spirit of all true Yorkshiremen. That spirit is (or was) also remarkably free from what is the virus of the British—class. Not that we lived in a classless world—the petit-bourgeois pretensions and false gentility of the Richardsons were based on a lot of class snobbery. We were definitely not working class; we were isolated in our compound of minor taboos and assumed superiorities over the working world that surrounded us. It was on the altar of class that I was sacrificed to an awful school.

But in the larger context of the class system which was so clear and real and agonizing or haughtily taken for granted when I lived in the South, I realize that I was not really aware of it as I grew up. I was lucky, and I am still thankful. Money—"brass"—was what counted for those barons of Bradford. In that respect, in Yorkshire and Lancashire a whole society evolved where the basic values had much more in common with the values of America—those of the immigrant making his own way—than with the traditional values of much of England, where the social fabric is still, at bottom, feudal. All the outward symbols of England—royalty, the aristocracy, the upper-class rituals, ceremonies, and occasions—were acknowledged with a mocking, humorous tolerance; in comparison with a solid bank account or a towering mill chimney, they just didn't count. And there was a strength about the people who had got where they were through work and effort, not inheritance. They were survivors, with the patois of survivors (the Yorkshire dialect is almost a different language) and the pride and, above all, the humor.

Appreciation of these qualities came very much later. I lived in virtual isolation. "Nearly professional" was a distinction Mother prized above all others. And yet we were not at the time affluent enough to have real friends in the district. Because of Father's skill in the shop we had respect, but not intimacy. Even our relationship with our next-door neighbors—the bakers—was distant. Father would go to the club with the husband; Mother might occasionally go into Bradford on a shopping expedition with the wife; I very occasionally played with their son, Stanley, who was two or three years older than me. They were, I think, richer than we were, and that created an unspoken barrier. I was often in and out of the back door of the shop where the loaves and cakes were stored on greasy translucent paper on long, shallow wooden trays, and sometimes I even entered the bakery itself (which was across the back street from us and gradually extended), with its smells of baking bread and its fine mist of gray flour that covered everything. The only friend I had (or rather, was permitted) was a little girl—Joan, I think her name was—who lived in a cottage a few doors away. Even when I went to school contacts were not encouraged—we were definitely not working-class, and distance had to be maintained.

One of the ways the difference was maintained was in eating.

Certain things—tripe, blood sausages (black puddings), sweet-breads, rhubarb (which grew in the backyards of most cottages)—were definitely out. These proscriptions were as absolute as Nancy Mitford's "U" and "non-U" and I still follow many of them today—I don't understand why. Lace tablecloths, antimacassars on chairs, and linen napkins ("serviettes"—which would have appalled Miss M) were essentials. Mother did, however, bend over the question of fish and chips from the shop opposite for evening suppers. It must have been because it was something easy, something she didn't have to prepare. On the other hand I hated it, and always have. There was no romance for me in the newspaper-wrapped greasy chips, the fish in heavy batter sprinkled with salt and acrid-smelling vinegar from the shakers provided. I felt the same way about the store-bought sponge cakes Mother would indulge in: Even though they were just out of the oven, to me they were never a patch on Mother's own cakes, and I resented having to stoop to them.

I made only two friends in the district. One, Doreen Whitfield, belongs to a later part of this story; the other was a gardener for the local town council. "Mr. Baines"—Albert Baines—lived perhaps half a mile from us, so I think my friendship with him must have come later. He had a large hothouse of cacti, succulents, and rare plants. Under the dry shelves where the cacti were stacked were pools surrounded by moss and ferns where he kept frogs, toads, and fish. Among the plants, green lizards darted. In his gentleness Mr. Baines had tamed all these creatures so they came to him to be fed with the worms and insects he collected in tins during his regular work. The greenhouse spoke of the exotic and remote. It was warm inside, and totally unexpected among the drab gray houses. It was another world: Once inside you could imagine yourself anywhere and blot out the horrid reality of the streets and weather. I spent hours and hours there and brought contributions of frogs, salamanders, and lizards to help populate the mysterious clumps of rare foliage and nestle under the carefully arranged rocks. Although a working greenhouse, in which in his earlier days Mr. Baines had grown many prize cacti, it was also a completely insulated work of art. It was as if you had entered a canvas by Douanier Rousseau.

Mr. Baines could grow anything. He had the slow, careful movements of the born gardener. He was always dressed in tie, waistcoat, stiff collar, and tweed trousers, with heavy hobnailed boots. He seemed to belong to another century—straight out of the pages of early H. G. Wells. (Ra and her entourage also belonged to the nineteenth century, but a more nightmarish part—that of Edgar Allan Poe, perhaps.) After he retired, however, he became a sad figure. His sister, a sinister, witchlike creature, came to live with him for a time. They adopted a mongrel bitch—half Airedale—which, with her endless puppies, gradually took over the house. Mr. Baines abandoned his tie and his stiff collars, then finally his shirts, wandering pathetically around in a dirty thick woolen vest and stained trousers. He lived in one room, with a piece of discolored canvas over the bed on which the dogs stretched and stank all day. He still kept up the greenhouse and its collection of plants as best he could, but with enforced retirement his pride had been lost.

Keeping pets had always been an obsession—I don't quite know why. At home they were frowned on and more or less forbidden: too much work. After Bob, we had no other dogs, but after endless pleading I was finally allowed a single guinea pig and later a Dutch rabbit in hutches in the backyard. I surreptitiously smuggled the rabbit out one day and had it mated in a hut on a nearby allotment. I don't think I knew what was happening, but I paid sixpence as a stud fee to two aggressive fourteen-year-olds who jeered as the mating took place. Everyone was very surprised by a clutch of baby rabbits some weeks later. I affected total ignorance, and in the end immaculate conception seemed to be accepted in the backyard of 28 Bingley Road. Apart from these two, the only other pets I was allowed were various green and wall lizards, grass snakes, and tree frogs which were confined in different boxes in the gloomy cellars—the worst possible environment for them—and which always escaped or died. And the one lonely terrapin in its little aquarium in the living room. That, at least, didn't make work.

I don't know how this instinct to possess animals developed. Perhaps it was a wish to join in another world from which they came—rather as, earlier, I could contemplate for hours the little "Japanese gardens" made with living mosses and ferns, decorated with china pagodas, a pond made of a little mirror, and Japanese fishermen, maidens, and bridges, which we used to arrange in a shallow bowl. Or maybe there was some unconscious imitative wish to control and dominate their lives as my own was dominated by a gaggle of controlling and protective adults. I don't know. But the instinct has remained with me so that now, when I know a great deal better, I still get an orgasmic rush when I see a store or quarantine station full of a new shipment of soft-billed birds. As a boy, the obsession was total: animal toys, animal magazines, the *National Geographic, Zoo World*—these were the only things I wanted. In Shipley Glen there was a pathetic little zoo which I would revisit again and again in the hope of a new addition—a squirrel, a badger, anything, but preferably an animal I'd never seen before. There were also many traveling circuses, and I always pestered to be taken. There would be an argument—Bertram Mills, the biggie, was in a remote part of Bradford, off our normal trolley routes; the little circuses that came to Shipley were in an area thought unhealthy and slummy—but I usually succeeded in getting to them. One of the highlights was an act entitled "Is it an Okapi," in which a pony with half-painted striped flanks came into the ring and drew a sword from a scabbard strapped on to its side. And as a sideshow there was a flea circus, where the fleas wore tutus, carried paper umbrellas, pushed miniature balsa-wood barrels and were finally rewarded when the proprietor rolled up his shirtsleeve to expose a tattooed arm on which he placed the fleas, explaining that it was now time for their lunch.

Horses, of course, were still part of our everyday lives, and not just for the rag-and-bone men, junk merchants, and greengrocers with their pathetic starved nags; coal deliveries were still done by vans pulled by dray horses. Just behind our house, in the waste of allotments, kitchen gardens, and chicken runs which stretched up the hill behind us to the new housing estate and the hills beyond, was an old smithy. I was both fascinated and terrified by it. The smell of the burning hooves as the smith pared them, the clang of the shoes hammered straight on the anvil, the roar of the furnace where the metal was heated white hot and then battered into shape, the sparks flying and bouncing off the thick leather apron of the blacksmith—gigantic and terrifying as if he breathed the same fire and sparks as his furnace—the big horses being calmed and gentled: These formed a spectacle I was drawn to watch again and again—

Vulcan, the Middle Ages, the Industrial Revolution, the satanic mills all at the same time. But the number of horses dwindled; the blacksmith died or disappeared; the forge went cold.

By now I was going to school. School was private—"exclusive." Mr. Manning's "Private School" was about a mile away from our house in a street shaded by trees with, beside it, an apology for a playing field in the middle of an orchard of uncared-for apple trees. The school was housed in the two ground-floor rooms of Mr. Manning's old Victorian house. There were maybe twenty to thirty pupils divided into two forms on either side of the entrance hall. Equipment was nonexistent—just gnarled desks, blackboards, globes, and worn textbooks. For the beginners there were huge cardboard alphabet letters, broken at the edges; the letters in yellow, pink, and green were held up by little girls in Victorian smocks and boys in sailor suits. Instruction was mainly the three Rs plus geography and scripture, maybe history too. Mr. Manning was an impressive-looking, barrel-chested, white haired man with a wooden leg and a walking stick. The school was obviously his last attempt to eke out some kind of living, and I don't think he enjoyed it very much. It was a duty, like so much else in our rigorously moral world. And it probably worked—I did learn to read, to write, and, though I never learned math, to do basic arithmetic. But it was a place without joy. Nanny and I set out twice a day (for a very long time I wasn't allowed to walk there or back unaccompanied, even though the distance was so short)—we came home for lunch, then went back again. I don't remember ever hating it or ever liking it, except for one term or one year when Mr. Manning had some illness and a lady teacher took over. The atmosphere then became lively and pleasurable. We had nature walks (the only exercise with Mr. Manning was to be turned loose in the decrepit orchard for twenty minutes each day to play—as in *Great Expectations*—and there may have been footballs, and wickets, and cricket bats in summer, but I always avoided these). We had French, in which I became immediately proficient. It was a period of expansion and achievement. But then Mr. Manning returned, and we went back to the bleak and numbing routine.

There was one freckled, ginger-haired boy I got reasonably friendly with; that's all. Now the whole of Bradford is full of Indians and Pakistanis, but then the only Jewish family in the area was something of a phenomenon. I know I looked up to the oldest boy, Brian, who was much older and played cricket effectively. The younger—Alan, my own age—I didn't much like. Anyway, whatever friendships might have developed weren't encouraged—"too rough," "not refined," even though we were all definitely the children of the privileged; it would have meant a total loss of self-respect for my parents to have let me go to a normal state school rather than Mr. Manning's institution.

The only breaks in this stultifying routine were the summers. Every year we did exactly the same thing—we went to a bungalow on the sea at Seaton Carew, just outside West Hartlepool, where Mother came from. I don't know whether we owned it or rented it, but it was as if it belonged to us. It was a long, one-storey building; whitewashed plaster over rough stones, a simple lawn in front, with lavender bushes. The lawn sloped down to the road, and as soon as you crossed the road there was a paved promenade with steps leading down to the beach. At the back of the house was an overgrown, out-of-control garden with collapsed outhouses and an enormous laburnum tree in which I spent many hours. I spent hours in the next-door garden too. It was a total contrast, with beautiful flowers always in bloom—petunias, carnations, lupins, geraniums—and a white wicker teahouse. The lady of the house, Mrs. Lumley, was always in white, with a white picture hat. She seemed to adopt me during the holidays and had me to tea nearly every day. Her husband had been a tea planter in Malaysia, or something similarly colonial, and they played mah-jongg every evening. The house was full of dark, carved-teak furniture, Chinese screens and fans; it had two storeys and white shutters, and was in every way out of our class.

The beach was quite wonderful. It seemed to stretch endlessly, with golden sand that faded to gray as the tide receded for nearly a mile, trebling the area of beach. If the sun had been out, the returning tide was amazingly warm. There were lots of shrimps in the sea, which we would catch in triangular-shaped nets and bring back to boil pink for high tea, and further along there were rocks where you could find crab and even lobster. About a half a mile away was a small funfair with roundabouts, a Ferris wheel, dodgems, coconut shies, and various sideshows. My favorite was one where you bet on a number on the perimeter of a round table.

In the center was an enclosed box. When all the bets were in, the box was raised by a little pulley. Underneath was a milling group of white mice which started gradually to run to the outskirts. The winner was the number first reached by a mouse. The mice were then herded back and the game restarted. There were many groups of ponies, horses, and donkeys for hire, and I used to love watching them file along the road in front of the bungalow in the morning and return in the evenings after work. For years I was allowed only on the slowest, oldest donkey—it was white and also called Tony. Ponies were thought too dangerous. Swimming was absolutely out (there were some horror stories of Father going blue and nearly drowning in the English Channel), as was cycling. A gentle paddle was the most exercise allowable, and it was better to be static building a sandboat or castle.

My holidays were mostly spent with the grandparents and their companions—it was for their health we went to the sea breezes. Mother sometimes came for a week at a time, but usually she only drove over with my Father on Sundays. On those Sundays when he was not the rota pharmacist on duty in the district, they would arrive for lunch, and afterward we might go for an extra-long walk or crabbing in the rocks. Sometimes we visited a great-aunt and -uncle who lived in a tiny wooden cottage deluged in hollyhocks and lupins, behind which they kept and bred borzois—beautiful, but terrifyingly savage. Father and Mother always took two weeks holiday in the summer, when a locum came and took over the shop. They didn't spend the fortnight with us; they went to Italy or France, the Canaries or the Channel Islands, sometimes on a cruise—the equivalent of a package tour today. They returned with photos, little presents, mosaics, or curios. I suppose my own passion for travel was generated by hearing of their trips and adventures, the smattering of French or Italian they jokingly practiced, and maybe by a subconscious resentment at not being taken along. They were in France and got one of the last steamers back when the event occurred which was to mark the first real change in my life—the Second World War.

With the outbreak of the war I was sent away to boarding school. My previous eleven years had been calm, sheltered, placid, tepid. Now I was to be made "a man" and prepared for the real world.

Perhaps Father and Mother realized how debilitating and soft was the life I had known—too much behind ladies' skirts—but certainly they knew that if I was ever to succeed in the kinds of roles they might wish for me in life—diplomat, barrister, Foreign Office—it was essential that I be sent to one of those institutions from which the upper echelons of British society were almost exclusively recruited. This was the hard reality of the class system, which I never felt but which induced my parents to toil, skimp, sacrifice so that their son would have the opportunities they never had. I would be expected to emerge with a new accent and ease of manner, a flow of contacts, and as a champion athlete and sportsman. So the visits to prospective schools were made, the uniforms ordered, the linen purchased, the Cash's name-tapes—C. A. RICHARDSON 39 (I was already a number)—sewn on. The night before I left was the grimmest I'd ever experienced. A numb dread, a cold deep nausea, almost anesthetized me from the oncoming horror, But not for long.

Many people have written of the vileness and degradations of the British public-school system. My school was probably by no means the worst, but it is impossible to exaggerate the misery, the sordidness, the continual and recurring nastinesses of a sentence to a gulag from which there was no escape. The emotional and moral blackmail to which you would be submitted by your sacrificing parents if you did escape would be almost as bad as the place itself, so there was no alternative—at least that's how it seemed to me. As a child, there's no other world out there: you endure what's given as best you can, no matter what the bruising entailed.

My particular gulag was Ashville College, Harrogate—about twenty miles from home. It had a preparatory school—a halfway station to Siberia—about a mile from the main school, whose lone tower on the skyline of a hill was as ominous to me as the guard towers of any prison, and to which we prep-school boys had to walk in crocodile—two by two in caps and uniforms—twice on Sundays for school chapel. (The school was Methodist in denomination—an indication of its lowly ranking within the school system, as all the best schools were resolutely Anglican except for a few Catholic ones. Anglican was an option for us, but popery never.)

The preparatory school was a black, gloomy stone mansion. Elms and horse chestnuts engulfed it—to protect its horrid secrets—and their black leaves were already falling on the cold October day when Father and Mother deposited me and my heavy trunk. (School beginnings had been delayed that year because of the outbreak of war.) Father was cheerful, Mother breaking down; I was choked and frozen. It was a new world: bleak iron beds, rough sheets, battered wooden desks, gnarled wooden benches in hall, slop food, and a world of hostile savages. The humiliations began. We were herded into a dark and filthy form room. We were ordered to write an essay on "the most exciting day in our holidays." Nothing exciting had ever happened to me. I wrote about a pet mouse escaping, in despair and apologizing. "Quite well written," the master said, "but, as you say, not very exciting." I felt marked for life. I was dubbed "Dopey" (*Snow White* had been the summer hit in England) because I had big ears—I still have. Lining up in the corridors in the morning, we new boys had to walk the gauntlet of all the older inmates, who tripped and pushed us until I fell and gashed a hole in my chin, from a nail sticking up in the uneven wooden floor. The hole is still there.

At night it was freezingly cold. The weather had gone bad early. We new boys—about twelve of us in all—were all in one dorm together. We had only one blanket to each bed. For warmth we crawled in with each other. It was totally innocent, despite what many would think today. The boy I got in bed with had, I remember, been nicknamed "Whammy," because he farted a lot. Even with the extra warmth it was still glacial and unhappy. After two or three nights, suddenly, in the middle of the night, the lights were flicked on and the headmaster, a Mr. Hawkins, stormed in, shouting. He lined us all up and beat everyone—hard. I'd no idea why. Then we were ordered back to our own beds. It was days before I had the courage to ask Whammy what it had all been for. "Rubbing-up, I think," he replied. "Rubbing-up" was an even greater mystery to me; I never dared to ask what that meant. And at that moment began the process of almost complete isolation from the other boys in school.

This was exacerbated a few days later when one of the older boys, a natural bully, saw in me a natural victim and was roughing me up—probably in a not too serious way. Suddenly I turned and, by some wonderful fluke, managed to land one punch, which cut his lip open. He was completely shocked by my violence. And that one gesture earned me the right to be not liked, or at least to be left alone. So I assumed the role of loner which I was to keep for the next seven years. As for Mr. Hawkins, he was later that year arrested for buggering some wretched little boy in his control, but the scandal was all hushed up under stiff upper lips and overshadowed by the one distraction with which the war helped to relieve a little our wretched lot.

England and Germany were in the period of "the phony war." After the first flutterings of potential catastrophe, things had settled down, and apart from strict rationing, gas masks, and gas-mask drills, the war whose progress was piped to us every day on the BBC made little impact on our daily lives. With the retreat at Dunkirk, things changed drastically. Under Churchill, England began to go to war seriously, and "the Few" fought in the skies against the threatened invasion. In the North we were still untouched: there were no bombs, no alerts, no aeroplanes. But as England mobilized it was decided that the headquarters of the RAF should remove to the North and establish a command there in a relatively bomb-free zone. Every building of any size was needed. Schools were ideal. So the order was issued to requisition Gulag Ashville and devote it to a more immediate national necessity than the training of a potential office class of the future. A search began for where the school was to go. It settled on Bowness-on-Windermere, in the Lake District.

The Lake District is one of the most beautiful parts of England and, because of the inaccessibility of its lakes and mountains, is of very little use militarily (except in a last-ditch guerrilla situation). The land of the Lake poets—Wordsworth, Coleridge, Southey— it is rich in romantic and literary associations. At the time, all that was a bit too far ahead and fancy for me, but what was welcome was the change from the prospect of the barrack-like atmosphere of the forms, dorms, playing fields, and changing rooms of the main school, which I was destined for in my second year. Bowness offered a relatively humane environment—even if to reach it meant an agonizing train journey under the appalling conditions of the railways in wartime Britain, and hours of waiting in Carnforth Station (immortalized in David Lean's film *Brief Encounter*) to connect with the local branch line that ended at Windermere.

The physical layout of the Royal Windermere Hydro made it

impossible to impose Ashville's usual prison conditions. it was a spacious stone and stucco Edwardian building. Pretensions to being a spa had been a must for the period, so there were big Turkish baths with pipes and marble tiles and cubicles that, even with most of the boilers closed down, still emanated heat and relaxation and were converted into laundries or sickbays. Inset in some of the corridors were banquettes whose red-velvet–studded upholstery transported me into another world and time. The billiard table had gone: scoreboards were converted into blackboards; cue-holders held chalk and slate dusters. There were no vast dormitories where sleeping figures could be easily surveyed, but corridors off which rooms housed four or six beds each and down which the prefects padded at night, listening at doors to catch any whisper and beat the offender with a "house-shoe" (a kind of leather and elastic slipper). Control in the absolute was impossible: There were too many avenues of escape. There was no gymnasium, just one very distant football field, so sports and teamsmanship had to take a less prominent place. Improvisation brought a kind of humanization which the school authorities, however much they struggled against it, couldn't quite avoid. Regimentation was imposed as much as was practical—there was now a cadet corps whose thick itchy khaki uniforms and heavy black boots were a new nightmare. The food was much worse; there was still vigilance and spying; and every day started with an inspection of how you had made your bed by the headmaster's wife, a dumpy, squashed, malevolent woman in an incongruous chintz flowered dress, accompanied by an equally hideous snuffling Pekingese-like dog (she had the headmaster beat me once for "dumb insolence"—the way I looked at her when she regarded the sheets, which I was always incompetent in smoothing). But, despite the dreary routine, you could get away. You had only to climb up the hill behind the hotel and you were lost in the trees and rocks. The school was lost too—no dominating silhouette on the skyline, but the overwhelming mountains and hills and woods. Maybe it was just my age, but I've never before or since felt nature as such a living, breathing force. Outside, by myself, I was all throbbing Wordsworthian:

> For nature then . . .
> To me was all in all.—I cannot paint

What then I was. The sounding cataract
Haunted me like a passion: the tall rock,
The mountain, and the deep and gloomy wood,
Their colours and their forms, were then to me
An appetite; a feeling and a love, . . .

Whenever and as often as I could I disappeared, always by myself—climbing the mountains, wandering the lake shore, crossing on the creaking slow old ferry to the far side of the lake, and beyond the mountains as far as the hamlets of Near Sawrey or Far Sawrey (where Beatrix Potter wrote all her children's books and lived in a little thatched cottage with replicas of all her characters in the picture-book garden—which should have been horrific, but wasn't). Or if ever there was any transport, which there almost always wasn't—with strict petrol rationing, we were almost completely cut off—I went to Rydal Water, Grasmere, or Keswick, or to the awesome, forbidding gray scree of Wast Water. Curfew always hung over me, but the exhilaration of the terrain somehow stayed inside me and sustained me through the blankness of most of the days.

The education was dull and limited. Free expression, imagination, had never been heard of, and music there was none—except for private piano lessons given by a lady from Bowness town. I tried them for a while but, sitting in a cold corridor at an out-of-tune piano, I never got beyond barely learning how to read a score. (There were, of course, hymns and organs. I still can't hear an organ today with any pleasure.) Art was dry and academic—another visiting lady laid down perspective in pallid water colors—so I've never been able to draw. Mathematics beyond arithmetic I could never grasp. Geography was taught by Mr. Steggal, who looked like a dropsical version of Lewis Carroll's Gryphon and was the butt of staff and boys alike. History was taught by the headmaster, J. T. Lancaster himself, in his study, which, having a coal fire, was one of the few warm places in the building and therefore a bit pleasant. His habit of sucking on his pipe and then scratching the instep of his foot was the thing I remember most vividly, but I did absorb history easily. Latin was endlessly painful and pointless: I've never understood the "finest training for the mind" argument—it seemed to me as dead as it was. Funnily enough, Greek seemed or sounded much more beautiful and exciting to me (maybe I was thinking of all those plays), but there was no possibility of learning it—or Italian, Spanish, Russian, or even German, all of which I had at one time or another a passion for learning, only to be quickly frustrated. French was back to square one—the first form started at the beginning. I was already fluent, and the consequence of being forced to step back was that I totally lost my ability to speak (as distinct from read) it. Only English was reasonably well taught. The English master, C. N. Pleasance, was the most agreeable of the staff and was able to put some kind of feeling into his teaching. But modern poetry ended for us with the Georgians, and set books imposed too early spoiled them for me for years. *Moby Dick* gave me nightmares for months, and it was ten or twelve years before I could overcome the terrors Dickens inspired and discover the delights of our greatest novelist.

Then there was the endless boredom of religion. Besides scripture classes, there were prayers night and morning, grace before and after every meal, and two long and wearying services on Sunday. On Sunday morning we had the choice of going to the local Anglican church or the Methodist chapel, and each Sunday the school was divided into two crocodiles en route for their heavenly destinations. I used to alternate between one and the other. The Anglican service was prettier, with its incense and colored vestments, but the Methodists had more hell-raising sermons that varied the ritual a bit. You made your choice, but hated both. (I even got confirmed, but only because the rectory involved quite a long walk and time off classes and even tea and cakes and was lined with cases of butterflies and bird eggs; again it broke the routine a little.) The evening service was simply for the school itself and on the Methodist pattern.

After a while I found an escape from the Sunday monotony. Because of problems of wartime food supply and to demonstrate the right patriotic spirit, the school kept pigs to consume the waste food. They were looked after by the school gardener. Sunday was his day off, and labor was very hard to find in the wartime Lake District, so I volunteered to feed the pigs. This involved pulling a wheelbarrow with two garbage bins of slops and swill about a quarter of a mile along the road and into a little wood where the sties were located. You then had to empty the swill into the troughs and see as best you could that all the pigs got their fair share. It was heavy and tough work for me, as I was physically very weak, but heaven in comparison with the divine services. Of course I was supposed to clean up and come in to the service later, but I soon learned that if I made a few appearances I could often escape.

I think I got the pigsty job (not that there was a lot of competition) through the intervention of one of my two friends at school: Sarge, the school janitor and boilerman. He was a giant, with a wooden leg acquired in the First World War, cropped iron-gray hair, and arms like tree trunks from wielding the shovels of coke that fueled the boilers and ovens. All day he was in the furnace room at the back of the hotel, surrounded by mounds of coke and ashes, swaying in an old wooden rocker or stomping off to fill one furnace or another. Sarge never said much but he tolerated me, and for that I was very grateful. He kept chickens in an enclosed run in yet another of the outlying woods and I used to accompany him and, as he threw down the grain or stale bread, collect the eggs for him. I don't know who got to eat them, as during the whole war we had artificial eggs made from a particularly nasty yellow powder. Perhaps a few of them went to the sick bay, where my second and best friend was.

Nurse was always in a navy uniform with a stiff white nurse's cap. She was a stout, vigorous, anarchic Irishwoman—middle-aged. For her dispensary and her sitting room on the side, she had taken over two rooms in the most remote wing of the hotel—actually it was an adjacent house which at some stage had been joined to the main building by a passageway. Here she presided with hatred and scorn for all the rest of the staff in the school—and especially the headmaster's wife, about whom she relayed many vicious and bitchy stories. She guarded her independence and domain completely, refusing to eat with the school and making minimal appearances at major events, special days, parents' day, etc. I was her confidant, imbibing from her a growing resistance to all authority and an ability to mock it. As a reward, I was given the precious chits that would let me off the games and physical education that I loathed, and she would make me little delicacies besides.

So gradually I developed a tougher and tougher attitude to all the accepted values which I had always despised. I learned how to say no. They could put me on a football field, but they couldn't make me kick a ball. They could make me change into singlet and shorts, but I wouldn't go through their exercises with any will or effort. In the end, what could they do? Beat me? Throw me out? That for them would be an admission of defeat, so I was eventually granted a kind of tolerance and license, and was accepted—not with much grace—as the school non-teamplayer.

The other problem was that I was much cleverer than most of the others and in many subjects academically ahead of them. And in what I did shine I'd become a show-off. Debating was easy for me. I could win any contest, whether I was arguing one time as a true-blue Tory or next time as a deep-dyed Red. I ran all the school plays (and could persuade the other boys into joining me in these), manipulating the repertoire ruthlessly for whatever role I particularly wanted to play, even if it meant replacing someone else. One time we did *Henry IV*. In Part 1 I played Hotspur, but when it came to Part 2 I decided that Prince Hal was the only role and replaced the wretched boy I'd cast in Part 1. I directed and starred in all the shows. But none of this made me closer to any of the other boys—nor did it make me any more popular. I had for a while one friend, who became a stage designer, John Dinsdale. But I bullied and dominated him cruelly, and our friendship was soon over, though I became friends with him again later. Now I can't remember a face or a name of any of the other four hundred or so boys who must have passed through the school during those years. They were like faceless fog people through whom I wanted the sun to break.

Although I was intellectually overdeveloped, in many other ways I knew nothing, because I took no part in the normal rites of puberty or growing up. Looking back, I'm sure there was a great deal of sex going on at the school—as was usual in that environment—but I never saw or felt any of it. When there was talk of sex, I shut off. I was puritanical to the point of total bewilderment. I'd never masturbated, and I didn't know why sometimes, in the morning, I found my pajamas stained with some weird fluid. This seemed totally unbelievable ten years later, but as I had no one to talk to, and as there was no suggestion of any sex education, my mind blocked everything out and I remained ignorant—even until and for a time at Oxford.

I went off more and more on my own. I developed my own

hobbies and passions. One of these was an owl which someone had found fallen from a nest. I nursed and fed it, and taught it to fly. Tawny was his name. Finally I had only to call out and he would fly to my hand from wherever he was perched. I took him home in the summer vacation and finally gave him to some acquaintances of my parents who had a house on the verge of a private wood. With them, Tawny lived happily for twenty years. I repeated this with other birds and animals—hedgehogs, magpies, jays, ducks— always trying to escape further and further from school.

I became more and more incongruous. I was very tall but very weedy. I had a big personality but I just didn't fit in. I was finally promoted from monitor to prefect to senior prefect because the headmaster and other authorities just didn't know what to make of me. And I was disliked all the more for my prominence by the boys, who had just despised me before. The only thing they gained was that, being interested in advancement only as a means of getting more freedom for myself and goofing off as much as possible, I never tried to exercise any authority or leadership but left them alone even more. I think the school finally appointed a deputy head prefect who conscientiously performed all the necessary duties and played the game while Mad King Ludwig raged in his own way at the top.

All I was waiting for was to get out as soon as I could and into the world I'd chosen—and there was never any other choice— directing.

3

Flashes of Lightning

No one in my family—in its furthest reaches—had any connection with or, as far as I know, any aspirations toward show business (which is probably what attracted me to it). Along with my toy animals, my favorite toy was a Punch and Judy show. I'd spend hour on hour inventing scenarios for the three characters—Punch, Judy, and a monkey named Chimp. I performed the shows over and over again, changing and reinventing them for my captive audience of old ladies. But when I grew out of that there was nothing I could participate in—I could only be an obsessed audience myself.

I loved stories and being lost in them. That's why I adored the movies. But for them to ever be part of my life would at that moment have seemed like contemplating a trip to the moon and planets. Movies came from a mysterious place called Hollywood. If such a place existed, it was as unreal to me as the ocean is to tribesmen who've lived all their lives in the jungles and mountains of New Guinea.

Theatre was much more familiar and accessible. The shows on the pier, circuses, the local theatres—these were a constant. Always I was attracted by the story and the spectacle. I saw many of the famous comedians—Max Miller, Vic Oliver, Ethel and Doris Waters, Wee Georgie Wood, George Formby, Flanagan and Allen,

Frank Randle (the Lenny Bruce of northern comedy), Norman "Over the Wall" Evans. Many of my contemporaries have recorded how much they loved and enjoyed them. I never did. I simply didn't understand them. The basis of their jokes and schtick were sexual allusions, innuendoes, puns. I didn't get them, and if I asked Nanny she wasn't about to explain them. Mummy impressed on me that they were "suggestive," cheap and vulgar, so I suppose I finally blotted them out. Their routine always seemed painfully the same and they bored me. I preferred the musical comedy of the Brokers Men, the knockabout, the end of the Chaplin tradition (that's why I always hated the clowns in the circus—they were so bad at their gags). But what I loved were the adventures, the dangers (though I could never understand why the principal boy was played by a girl), and the transformation scenes when the forest or the caves became a palace, or terraced gardens, "magic casements, opening on the foam/Of perilous seas, in fairy lands forlorn."

What finally hooked me for ever was Shakespeare. I suppose I was seven or eight when I saw *A Midsummer Night's Dream* in a touring production, probably awful, with tattered realistic scenery. Life was never to be the same again after the experience. Although I have done it once—disastrously—and have seen it in every kind of production, it's still probably my favorite play. Everything I'd ever imagined came together, was clear and yet totally imaginative and satisfying. I understood every one of the characters, loved the story, was transported by magic, fantasy, and fairies, and totally identified with Puck. Wonderful as so many later productions have been—like my friend Peter Brook's, where everything was suggested and the play reilluminated—there's a big argument for any director remembering that a production of Shakespeare is always a first for someone in the audience—especially for children, for whom fairies will always be fairies. Much later on, on vacations in France, Vanessa Redgrave and I used to put on shows for our kids to act in when they were still young. Vanessa one summer decided to do the *Dream*. All the girls were delighted, imagining their costumes of gauze and leaves. But Vanessa had been reading the latest Polish wizard, Jan Kott, who decreed fairies to be malignant worms and insects, so she announced they were all to be dressed in potato sacks, their faces rubbed in earth. Instant rebellion and tears. We, the grown-ups, tried to save the situation by doing the

Mechanicals' plays, but the girls' pleasure was completely spoiled. Back with gauze wings and on points.

The conventional production I saw decided me: I wanted, decided, to be part of that totally riveting world. It was my road to Damascus. How I was going to get there I didn't know, but I knew I would. And one of the only mitigating circumstances of the sentence of boarding school was that, in its prospectus, drama was promised as a part of the curriculum.

The first play I appeared in was *Hereward the Wake*, when I was still in preparatory school. I think it was in one act, and it probably lasted twenty minutes. The set was some kind of medieval fortress behind the fence of which I had to pace slowly back and forth carrying an outsize pike. Nothing has ever seemed as momentous to me as that walk. Other boys crawled behind the cutout scenery and tried to trip me, but I was determined and desperate not to falter. It was as if all my life was being decided then and there. I probably did stumble a few times or revved up to a pace that was beyond that of the normal Saxon sentry, but I made it.

Due to the transition to Windermere and the general chaos the move caused, it was quite a time before we got round to doing drama again. During the interim I saw my second Shakespeare. It was a touring wartime production of *King John*, directed by Tyrone Guthrie, who, together with Peter Brook, was one of the great theatrical geniuses of my generation. Its cast wore stylized costumes and rug-wool wigs. I remember the Dauphin of France had blue hair. It seemed startlingly, blazingly modern. And Sybil Thorndike as Constance intoning "a grave unto a soul" seemed the spirit of mysterious tragedy. I went back to school and agitated. One big form room—I think it had been the original cards room—had a tiny stage at one end, which we used for school assembly. It was all I needed. Play followed play. I think the first was a stage version I wrote of the Bette Davis movie *The Private Lives of Elizabeth and Essex*. Then Philip King's *Without the Prince*, Gordon Daviot's *Richard of Bordeaux*, *Henry IV* (both parts), and *Twelfth Night*. All of them staged with the sole purpose of my indulging and promoting myself. Nothing was directed: it was thrown on to exploit the talents of an actor-manager—like most of the British classical theatre at the time.

Something else was happening to me, though, without my being aware of it: I was beginning to learn what serious theatre was about. This coincided with and was partly inspired by a new friendship at home, a friendship which became almost a love affair. Two doors from our shop was a grocery store, an old-fashioned grocery store with its mystical smells and aromas. The proprietors, Mr. and Mrs. Whitfield, had a daughter, Doreen. She had been sent to London and had trained as a classical dancer. She was a success. She had been taken into the Sadler's Wells Ballet—the top company, which evolved into the Royal Ballet. She had emerged from the corps and was beginning to get secondary roles, and seemed destined for stardom. Then polio struck her. Vaccines hadn't been developed then. She lost the use of one leg. She was forced into iron braces and a life of sitting in a wheelchair in the back of her parents' shop, unable to move without help. I was drawn to her by her plight and her acceptance of it—she never complained or pitied herself. Her attitude was so positive that I willed and fantasized that recovery would be possible. I was also drawn to her by the world to which she had belonged. I had never seen a ballet at that time. I think the first I saw was a boring version of *Swan Lake* by the Mona Inglesbey company, a well-known but inferior company of the time. I was baffled and, apart from a few moments in Act 2, it left me cold—but fascinated. I knew somehow that, if I could penetrate it, there was something wonderful there.

Anyway, Doreen was my first contact with the real world of the theatre. She enthralled me with her stories and with the seriousness of her vocation. We spent hours and hours discussing dance, plays, theatres. I began to buy books and magazines, to study photographs and theory, to learn about different companies and personalities, to learn that this was no world of simple mindless fantasy but an art that could express and encompass almost every aspect of life. I began to learn what a serious company was, and if there was ever an opportunity—and there were few, because of the war—I made every effort to get to see one. In Bradford there was the Civic Playhouse, run by a Tyrone Guthrie protégée from the Old Vic, which offered classic movies, good amateur productions—sometimes with guest professionals like Ernest Milton—and lectures by theatrical personalities like Michel Saint-Denis, who talked about staging in the round, Tyrone Guthrie himself, and the local literary lion, J. B. Priestley, who began his talk, "Like Paul of Tarsus, I come from no mean city."

But of course the theatre was London, where I'd never been. I pressured Mother and Father relentlessly: I had to go there. Finally they yielded. We went for three days, staying at the Strand Palace Hotel. This seemed the apex of luxury, and sitting in Lyons Corner House the peak of sophistication. The first thing I saw on the menu was whitebait. I'd never heard of them, so naturally they were what I ordered. I don't know whether I enjoyed them (I do now), but I wouldn't have shown it if I didn't. Theatre was still sporadic—I think it was 1943—but we went every night. I remember some vast adaptation of *War and Peace*—a gesture to Anglo-Russian solidarity—and J. B. Priestley's *They Came to a City*—a dream version of an imaginary future after the wars were over, staged on an almost bare stage. It seemed incredibly imaginative and avant-garde. After that, when I saw Donald Wolfit (the prototype of the actor-manager played by Albert Finney in *The Dresser*) with his touring company playing eight different Shakespeare plays in a week, I could see what was wrong. I remember one matinee of *The Merchant of Venice* when, as Wolfit took his bow in front of the main curtain, panting and exhausted (although he'd already been offstage for an act), the whole audience of schoolchildren booed him loudly and he strode furiously off, wrapping the purple velvet drapes with their gold fringes around him like his own personal mantle. Still, he did a wonderful service in making Shakespeare accessible when no one else did.

That was much later—when the European war was over. The RAF had abandoned the school, and Ashville College returned to reoccupy its buildings, still in something of a state of shell-shock. As I was now senior prefect, I had a study of my own. I shut myself in, cut myself off from all the school administration, and read obsessively. Everything—poetry, novels, plays. I became the compulsive reader I am today. I could race through anything, so that now if I don't have a new book with me or a classic I'm having to reread, I'm in a state of bad anxiety. (Aeroplanes are a terrible threat.) At night, unscrupulously exploiting "the insolence of office," I'd get a bus to Leeds to see whatever was playing at the

Grand and the movies. I suppose the authorities knew, but were glad to get rid of me.

It's hard to remember precisely when all these transitions happened or when particular events occurred because the overall misery of school blotted everything out, but the school productions had taught me something basic: Acting wasn't what I wanted to do. It wasn't just that I hadn't the talent—which was certainly true. I have the worst voice possible—dry, anti-erotic—and, growing up too quickly, I was stooped almost to being a hunchback and was uncoordinated, awkward, and very self-conscious. But these deficiencies might or might not have been overcome—with the help of elocution lessons, I'd already eradicated most of my Yorkshire accent except for one flat "a," which I still have (and which is an almost American sound). It was rather that acting was boring to me. I could never make that simple but gigantic leap of suspending myself and becoming an imagined character. It's the same as Keats's negative capability—identifying with a sparrow picking about on the gravel.

Acting is imagination at its finest. Acting is the ability to enter into and believe absolutely in the mind and blood of someone else. Technique, important as it is, comes after. Depending on the range and skill and resonance of the particular act, technique only repeats, replaces, supports, or fakes something that at one moment was a spontaneous and devastating act of imagination. And what distinguishes a star or a great actor or any kind of great performer is the ability to create such moments so revealingly that they startle us— the imagination is so surprising and the execution so forceful that the effect is instantaneously experienced and apprehended in a way that's unique and unparalleled. You come at writing slowly, by contemplation. You can take time with "Keep up your bright swords, for the dew will rust them," but Kean made people *feel* Shakespeare by flashes of lightning. I've experienced this once with Olivier, and I know that, once they have been recognized, an actor of great technique can reproduce such moments so that no one except those who've seen the real thing will ever be able to tell the reproduction from the truly felt. This is what great performing is about—even Wolfit was said to have planned his Lear as "thirteen great moments."

I knew that I never had this talent, nor even wanted it. By the time I'd got through the series of star-turns I'd put on for myself, acting had become desperately boring to me—as had much of any kind of public performing. My last role at school was Malvolio in *Twelfth Night*. It's an impossible part anyway, but I could find no excitement in the parade anymore. I could hardly get through it, but I wanted to be part of the theatre as much as ever. And from what I had read or observed I now knew that there was this mysterious figure called the director—a concept I'd never even heard of a few years before.

Things were beginning to get easier with the end of the European war, and a semblance of normality returned. There was some interschool festival. It included drama. We were asked to decide what to perform. I chose *Everyman*, the old morality play. This was a perfect choice, as it didn't expose the deficiencies of school acting but, in its simplicity, capitalized on them—and for the first time I thought only about the presentation. Our resources were almost nonexistent, but what there was I used—simple costumes, a few spotlights, a bare stage. While all the other plays in the festival were copies of what couldn't be achieved, we created theatre. We won the festival. I was written about in the press. But none of that was important: I knew what I was and would be for life.

School ended soon after that. I'd been up for both Oxford and Cambridge but both seemed problematic. Ashville was not renowned for academic distinction—no one, I think, had gone on to a major university before—and now, with the servicemen flooding back, competition was keen and places were at a premium. I had always—not just for romantic reasons (the "dreaming spires") wanted to go to Oxford. Oxford at that time was supposed to be arts; Cambridge science. The Cambridge entrance examinations came up first. I was ill in the days before the exams—suspected appendicitis. Father took time off and went with me. I was interviewed by King's. I felt nervous and out of place, found the interviewers very snobbish—for the first time I felt what class was really about. Perhaps I would never make it. I was turned down. The Oxford exams were two or three weeks later. I went up—I don't know whether Father came this time—and was interviewed by several colleges. I was still hopelessly nervous and self-conscious, and not sure of having done well in the tests. But the ending was happy: I'd not just been accepted, I'd won a bursary at Wadham College (the home, though I didn't know it then, of the outsiders and the eccentrics—two of my close friends to be, George Devine and Lindsay Anderson, had been there). I was a "scholar at Oxford," which meant that, instead of the short black jacket most of the students wore, I wore the more romantic and elegant gown. The original mark of the poor was now the sign of distinction.

I said good-bye for ever to Ashville without any regret on either side.

A curious period of waiting happened now. Although both the European and the Japanese wars were over, there was still conscription—for a period of a year or more. The university recommended that service in the forces be performed before going up: the more maturity, the more you would get out of the university experience was the argument. I was dreading conscription more than I had originally dreaded going away to school, convinced I couldn't survive the routine. It wasn't that I was afraid of danger (even if the war had still been alive): It was the physicality, the reduction of me as an individual to a battered equality, I couldn't face. But there was no way out that I could see. I was never a pacifist. War has always been endemic to men. Anyone who had grown up in the world of Adolf Hitler knew absolutely that war was justified and sometimes necessary. So conscientious objection wasn't an option, the kinds of evasions and lies that many employed, quite understandably, to escape the Vietnam war, for example, were just lies to me. So I steeled myself for martyrdom, for crucifixion.

The dreaded khaki OHMS envelope arrived after a month or two. I went for a medical in Leeds. I don't remember much about it: Deep nausea blocked it out. Finally I emerged from the physical, sick and shivering (I was anorexically skinny, and nervous in the extreme), to the interview, where you were streamed into whatever service seemed suited. A red-faced major looked me over. "Young man, what do you want to be in the defending army?" "Nothing." "You've got to be something." "A Shakespearean actor." "You won't find that in the army, young man. But the army has a lot it can teach you. . . ." With this all-encompassing threat, he dismissed me contemptuously. I hadn't been broken yet, but I knew the breaking would soon come. I imagined every possible scenario—having a complete nervous breakdown, shooting myself, and so on. They all had a similarly bleak ending.

I waited for weeks, stretching to months. My parents urged me to take fill-in jobs, maybe help in the shop. I was too paralyzed by the hell in store to be able to function or to think: I could only endure from day to day until the fatal OHMS summons arrived. As the weeks passed, there was another worry. I had my place at Oxford a year ahead. If I was delayed longer by service, that would mean I would have to wait another year—it wasn't possible then to enter midyear. There was nothing to do but put my head on the block. I wrote to the army asking it to get my entry over with—the sooner the better. Three weeks later the envelope arrived. Sick as can be, I opened it. I was c3, and the letter explained that this was a category that the government had no use for in peacetime. It was too good to be believed. But for my parents I think this was a shame comparable only to being a "conchie": There was to be no sharing in my celebration (more real than any Christmas) of the reprieve.

Now came the problem of how to fill in the year ahead before Oxford. There was a course in acting at the Civic Playhouse I would have liked to attend. My parents were adamantly opposed, and by now we were pretty much at loggerheads as I had what they considered disgraceful Leftist views as well as being openly unpatriotic and unfit (after all their sacrifices for my magnificent athletic schooling). As I already knew that acting was never to be my *métier* and as I didn't have any great belief in the quality of the Civic Playhouse, I didn't struggle much. If one had been raised in an American school, this was the moment one would have been dishwashing or waiting on tables or packing groceries—all of which would have been thought far too demeaning for Master Tony, despite his nasty Red tendencies. In fact a sinecure was found for me (Father was now mayor). Exchange programs had already started in the gush of postwar American aid. An American teacher was coming to one of the local junior schools. She needed an assistant, an interpreter to explain the system and the lingo. That was to be my job.

I think this young lady was the second real American I'd ever met. The first had been a distant GI cousin who visited once during the war and who seemed, in his GI uniform and his pockets stuffed full of candies and goods from the American military stores, the most mysterious and (with that voice of the movies) the most glamorous human being I'd ever met. The second was just as glamorous. She came from North Carolina, had a Scarlett O'Hara accent, and often wore a black and yellow felt bellboy suit with brass buttons. ET had arrived. I was in love for several sticky weeks. The only problem was her excessive demand for the kind of gallantry which may have been *de rigueur* in the Old South but was beyond the stamina of a neurotic Northern teenager. She was a big girl and I was finally floored when, at some dance in a local mansion—the kind of events which always embarrassed me because I was so maladroit—she demanded to be carried in my arms across the threshold. My infatuation ended with that particular humiliation. I think she left on the dickey-seat of some local hot rod.

But as a teacher she was superb. The school was in the roughest, toughest neighborhood of the town. The kids were the roughest, toughest lot. I felt as if I'd never lived when some hard, stubbly, undernourished boy would talk of a sibling having been fished, dead and green, out of the canal with the same equanimity that Mother would have talked of the kind of sandwiches she was cutting for afternoon tea. But Miss North Carolina achieved in the quietest simplest way the kind of discipline and receptivity that not even the hardest and most experienced masters could achieve. She touched those kids as no one had touched them before. In terms of making them listen, Southern courtesy and insistence on good manners won down the line—and proved to me the superiority of the American method of education (which, in comparison to British methods, is still true today). Her efficacy was such that it was clear she had no need for me to be around. The school was hopelessly understaffed, and I was soon drafted into teaching in my own right. I was hopelessly incompetent—observing a trained American for a few classes didn't make anything rub off on me, and I was probably overwhelmed by the reality of the kids themselves, so far from any world I'd ever been in. At best I could just hold them by reading some story or play. I hated it all, hated them, disappeared whenever I could, and finally just faded out. Teaching was another thing I would never be fit for—and still am not. Many people think directing and teaching are akin, and some practitioners have done both or have elements of the other's skills in them, but they in fact require totally different skills, techniques, and attitudes and, as they are essentially so different, even the moderately talented have been unable to be successful at both.

Directing (and the theatre) obsessed me. The only conceivable outlet was still the Bradford Civic Playhouse. By being around it, I had begun to meet a few of my contemporaries who had similar interests. The Playhouse was a stuffy organization with little welcome for newcomers. Its choice of plays was conventional—mainly three-set naturalistic *démodé* dramas, Galsworthy, James Bridie, Priestley, Rattigan, and various lesser-known dramatists of the 1920s and 1930s. Casting was almost always confined to members of the various committees that controlled the Playhouse and for whom the plays were chosen. And as for the idea of taking on a young director, well . . . It was a time when the serious theatre world was calling for "poetic" theatre. T. S. Eliot was writing; Shakespeare and other Elizabethan dramatists were being performed in London; Stratford had reopened. It was that kind of theatre we were dreaming of—theatre that was color, music, dance, poetry, more vivid and more potent than life. The Playhouse at best appeased our dream with a yearly Shakespeare, but, as by now the members of our group were already classed as upstarts, rebels, and renegades, we were to have no part in the making of these shows. There was only one solution. I decided: We had to make our own theatre—a theatre affirming the principles we believed in. We must form our own company. We did. We called ourselves "Young Theatre."

The only resources we had were the classics. We didn't know anything else, and we didn't know many of the classics—Chekhov we'd never seen or read, nor Strindberg. We knew the Elizabethans, the Restoration, the eighteenth century, maybe a few of the safer Ibsens, and Racine and Molière (but in no playable translations). We'd no money and no place to work, and only a few enthusiasts— but enough. The first play we chose was Milton's masque *Comus*. We found a local school hall with a tiny stage; we cajoled materials out of local mill owners (I remember some stained velvet remnants perfect for period costumes); we squeezed a few pounds here and there out of parents, relatives, friends. We printed a poster and a program. We organized the making of costumes with the same well-wishers, who thought we were all mad. Doreen organized the movements and dances. I directed. Somehow we built sets—John

Dinsdale, from Ashville, was the designer. The company wasn't without future talent: It included the dramatist Donald Howarth, who played the Attendant Spirit, and the director William Gaskill, another neighbor, who by a different route was due to go up to Oxford at the same time as I was. We rehearsed; we opened; we were noticed. What we thought we were doing presenting this seventeenth-century court entertainment to an audience who'd hardly seen a serious play, let alone heard verse spoken in public, I don't know. The director of the Civic Playhouse came and sniffed, "This was the kind of thing we put on in the servants' hall when I was young." But we survived; we made our scheduled number of performances, and as soon as we'd finished we began rehearsals for our next production—*Romeo and Juliet*, even though the stage wasn't high enough for a balcony of more than three feet. (I was, of course, directing.)

In the summer of 1946 a group of us, Doreen included, went up to Stratford for a week. We lived in a boardinghouse, all in the same room, eating nothing but seeing eight separate plays in the same week, including Peter Brook's first big production, *Love's Labour's Lost*, and Paul Scofield's Stratford debut, demonstrating his versatility as a performer. And somehow, because of what we'd done, we felt not intimidated but stimulated and spurred on. Young Theatre went on for a little while even after I'd gone on to better things at Oxford. There were, as in all groups, schisms and political battles, with Bill Gaskill fighting for control—to the disgust of my parents who, after their initial opposition, had become very proprietary because of our survival, if not success. Bill succeeded in doing a production of Fletcher's *The Faithful Shepherdess*, which hadn't been revived for three or four hundred years (and maybe not since), in which you could see all the groundwork for his later work in Restoration comedy. But by then I'd forsaken Young Theatre and immersed myself in Oxford.

4

As a Duck to Water

Just as it's impossible to write anything bad enough about English public schools, it's impossible to say anything good enough about Oxford. Keep the dreaming spires, sink the punts in the Isis—for the first time in one's life just to be young was very heaven. You went past the heavy wooden gates, met the porter at the lodge, were assigned some paneled dark rooms for two up an old staircase—a sitting room with two bedrooms attended by some ancient "scout" who waited on you, made the beds, attended to your wishes. You ate so many dinners a week in college, sitting on the benches in the dark paneled hall; graduated in Latin, wearing your scholar's gown, the only public-school–type dread was of being "sconced." This meant being challenged for some breach of etiquette and forced either to drink a huge silver sconce of beer (several pints) without drawing breath or paying up for drink for the whole of the rest of the college. I think it did happen to me once. I paid.

But it wasn't inside college that I prospered, it was in the context of the whole university. This was one of the big distinctions you soon learned. Many stayed inside a college setup—dining, common room, college activities—but others, like me, despised such parochialism and preferred to swim outside. Wadham was a college tolerant of eccentrics. The Warden, C. M. Bowra, was one of the most famous figures of the university. When I went up, in 1948, he was on sabbatical in America and I never got to know him. When he returned I was invited to one of his famous sherry parties. I saw nothing but a tubby, pretentious, snobbish, eunuchy-effeminate little man. I'm sure I was wrong. Anyway, I was by then established in university circles and I'm sure my dislike and suspicion were reciprocated. I never met him again. But my tutor, J. B. Bamborough, was something different. He was tall, in his thirties, I think, a bit dry and academic, but infinitely tolerant. "Work the first term, then enjoy yourself," he said. I did. I used to see him once a week, supposedly with an essay or whatever the curriculum required, but by then I was often so caught up in other activities that I didn't complete it or, if I did, it was the expression of some crazed literary enthusiasm of the moment which he winced at. But Bam never pressured me, just encouraged. He knew freedom was much more important.

Freedom was the most vital release Oxford gave (gives) anyone. Achievement wasn't the aim—unless you wanted to achieve, when you could achieve in the avenue you wanted. Forget all other pressures—family, country, love, honor. Find yourself. Find yourself by being without pressure. Spend the days drinking coffee in the cafés, lying in the grass, drinking late at night in your rooms. Find yourself with people doing the same as you, wherever you came from, with whom you chose and wanted. The choice was infinite. Though not in academia—that was confirmed. The courses then were few and set, and probably not much changed from the eighteenth century. PPE (politics, philosophy, economics) was the latest innovation, the most in touch with the world we were living in. There were no theatre or film courses: I had to choose from among the old standards. I took English, though my scholarship was in history. But the limited academic choice forced you to pursue your enthusiams in the clubs, which were intra-college and controlled by the undergraduates themselves. This meant that you were already challenging and competing with your peers on an equal level without control from authorities above. And the beauty of this competition was that it wasn't set up or forced: It was as instinctual as breathing, as natural to the inhalation as fresh air. At least that's how it seemed to me. Maybe to many there were other goals—athletic, academic, scientific, determined, institutionalized, or personal—but I never met anyone with these. The only real toilers were the ones who wanted to justify their inclusion in what they deemed the select by a degree of this or that class. And they were the dullards, the college proles—happy in their own self-confinement. The rest of us were in a great sea where we could splash about, exhaust ourselves if we wanted to, run occasional races, dive if not down to great reefs then at least into a sandy, glittering, underwater world—because, even if sometimes you didn't recognize it, you were still in the kiddy pool; you couldn't get out of your depth. But the kiddy pool was such an accurate simulacrum of the big world that, when you finally swam out through the paths in the barrier reefs, the colder, bigger ocean would never seem intimidating in the way it would have done if you hadn't been nurtured in the Oxford pond.

Probably the two most eye-catching of the various pools in the reef were the Union, the pool of the politicians, and the dramatic societies, the pool of the would-be entertainers. The dramatic pool, for which I headed straightaway, was also divided into two: the established Oxford University Dramatic Society (the OUDS), the presidency of which was the second most prestigious university post after the presidency of the Union, and the Oxford University Experimental Theatre Club (the ETC), which was both junior and in opposition to the OUDS and quite unlike its title—because at that time "experimental" meant very little—the home of more lightweight entertainment like musical revues. Each college (or most of them) also had its own dramatic society, which was a kind of preparation for the real "right stuff."

Theatre life in Oxford had been dominated by two influences. The OUDS, the established influence, had for two decades been the fief of the dean of Exeter College, Nevill Coghill, a charming, academically obsessed professor with a penchant for charming young protégés, the most famous of whom during the war had been Richard Burton. Coghill had also had some professional experience, and at one stage after the war John Gielgud, still the leading classical actor, had engaged the two dramatic gurus of Oxford and Cambridge—Coghill and George Rylands—to direct two of his West End "serious" seasons. Nevill Coghill still controlled the main choice and policy of the OUDS and had, I think, some kind of official veto because the society was still built into the fabric of university life. The other influence—almost a myth—was an individual: Kenneth Tynan—a myth more for style than for achievement.

The war had imposed on England grayness and anonymity: equality, sacrifice, rations, coupons, spartan living, no luxuries, no indulgence. This also held true in the universities. Once the centers of privilege, recklessness, nonconformity, the bright young things of the 1920s, the famous King and Country debate of the 1930s, the universities like everything else had knuckled under to the effort against Germany. After the war, the attitude of austerity persisted—even hardened. The majority of the students were older, had had service experience, and were now determined to start their lives, to earn their livings in a serious way, aware of the straitjacket possibilities that were all that postwar Britain had to offer. Frivolity was out; earning a degree, proving worthy of the privilege of study, was in. The first and most prominent figure to challenge this was Ken. Oscar Wilde was reborn. Flamboyant waistcoats, effeminacy, hints of sexual depravity, self-indulgence, effetism were his style. Just as later he was to try, less successfully, to be the figurehead of the sexual revolution in *Oh! Calcutta!*, by his life-style, his dress, his writing and his theatre productions he relaunched personality in a khaki world. He was, as someone or other said, his own lost work of art, and that persona he created and flaunted in his Oxford years was something that haunted him for the rest of his life and which, unfortunately, he was never able to live up to in any of his later endeavors.

Ken was about to go down as I came up in 1948—I think I overlapped with him for one term, as I did with others like Lindsay Anderson and Gavin Lambert, whom I didn't get to know until much later—but his myth was palpable, and his reputation within university circles was gigantic. I was not very tempted by the style, though a bit of me—the actor in me—was still seduced by the outrageousness, which led to my determination to score a first in the Union in the course of some debate, by firing blanks from a revolver as the climax to my argument. I was, however, stimulated and challenged by the reputation of Ken's dramatic productions (the latest a First Quarto *Hamlet*), which were outside the OUDS, and I was determined both to challenge their innovatory reputation and to contest both the OUDS and the ETC themselves. I immediately joined both societies. The secretary of the OUDS, a golden boy called Anthony Richardson, immediately called on my rooms with an ultimatum to change my name, as I could never hope to achieve anything in the shadow of his position. I defiantly refused with "We'll see."

It took some time. My first production was on the college level— *King John*. I'd become obsessed with German expressionism and with stage lighting, with a heavy dose of balletic study. The play had been an enthusiasm ever since the wartime Tyrone Guthrie production. The only remarkable thing about my production was the number of lighting arcs, which had never been rivaled before or probably since. There wasn't much equipment, but every speech or so spotlights were switched on or dimmed, or colors appeared or changed, supposedly to reflect dramatic mood or character development. If nothing else, it established my reputation as a master of the switchboard. I followed this with another production of *Romeo and Juliet*, which went on a semi-university tour during the summer vacation and was played near home in the town hall at Ilkley. The production gave me a new notoriety as a talent spotter. I'd seen some girl in the Cadena café, pronounced, "There's my Juliet," went over and persuaded her, and three months later she was on the balcony at Ilkley. I'm not sure if it was true, but it was part of my myth-building, and by the autumn I was already elected president of the ETC.

The ETC had been always the poor sister of the two societies. The OUDS productions were staged annually at the Oxford Playhouse, a professional repertory theatre with not a bad standard (among the productions I saw there were a very good *Three Sisters* and a *Heartbreak House*). The ETC (even under Ken Tynan) had been forced to confine itself to other locales, without professional resources. I was determined to rectify this and prove that anything the OUDS did we could do better. I don't know how we got the money to rent the theatre but we did, and at the end of the second term I staged *Peer Gynt* at the Playhouse.

A girlfriend told me much later that at the first get-together of the cast I announced, "I see ropes—nothing but ropes." I don't remember it like that, but ropes there were, and a lot of them. I decided to employ all the theories of experimental theatre for the production: of Meyerhold and Reinhart, of the Denishawn school and Martha Graham—none of whose work I'd ever seen. The set consisted of a series of ramps and rostra that, to keep shapes constantly changing, were easily movable by a cast dressed in a loose balletic uniform of Norwegian green, with minor decorations and props to indicate place or character or rank—and of course the ropes, which could be the bars of the madhouse, the rigging of a ship, palms in the desert, or the slimy twistings of the Troll grotto (the huge cast included the director John Schlesinger as the Troll King). It was supposedly ensemble acting, like the later Living Theatre. At that time nothing like it had been seen before, certainly not at a university. It was a big success, and my position was assured.

I'd already become the theatre critic for *Isis*, the university magazine. I was now elected president of the OUDS (and promptly organized a vote which eliminated the last traces of the don's power) and I retained, unprecedentedly, the presidency of the ETC for a second year. This was quite unfair, since as you went up in the world, you were supposed to renounce your earlier positions for the next generation. But, like many a politician, I managed to turn my declaration that I would let the ETC position go into an election speech (there were no speeches, just a secret ballot) which ensured re-election. So by the end of my second year I was in secure control of both the university societies and could more or less dictate what I wanted to happen in either for the next year.

By now I was on a total high of power, success, excitement. Like most, this high had a downside—in my case, such a degree of nervous tension and hyperactivity that I could literally pass out with excitement (on one occasion on the steps of the Sheldonian, when I was tended by a great friend, Shirley Catlin—later Williams—with whom I was half in love). Besides all the other excitements and friendships, and besides the theatrical activity, I'd at last been able to begin one of the other passions of my life. At the end of my first year, after the production of *Romeo and Juliet*, I'd gone abroad for the first time, with two old friends from Young Theatre, Roger Suddards and John Dinsdale.

Travel at that time was slow, difficult, and laborious—especially when you had virtually no money and much parental opposition. I was determined to start to see Europe, to see the paintings and buildings I had stared at and studied in books. We went to Italy for three amazing weeks. Roger and John had gone ahead; I followed by train. The journey took two days, with long waits. First came a rainy Channel crossing; then a long dreary evening trek through northern France, down through Alsace-Lorraine—dark and black as a Gericault nightmare, the train crowded with dark black faces like miners and miners' families, but friendly, sharing a sausage and bread in incomprehensible dialects and accents—then numb and jogging into a standing sleep in the tunnels of the Alps; and finally morning bursting as we came down into the glorious summer slopes of Italy, into warmth and olives and vines. Then heat and weariness again, and a bewildering change of trains in the clanging Milan terminal where a contemptuous urchin selling ice robbed me of my only lire (whose value I couldn't figure out); the crowds again, and more heat and dust and standing; then dusk. Finally, at midnight, a taxi's confused driver got us lost in the old back streets of Rome, where an old man in a nightdress and skullcap poured water out of jugs over us—something straight out of an opera. At last I sank in flat-out exhaustion into the *pensione* bed in the room I was sharing with Roger and John, and the landlady's curses at being roused and having to provide for the driver the lire I didn't have died in my ears. But all travel hardships are almost as good, later on, as the arrival.

Having hardly any money, we had to find somewhere else to stay. We took a little room behind a *latteria* next to the Pantheon, down a dust-filled, crumbling corridor sprinkled with tattered chickens and mangy cats. Food was no more than peaches—which were wonderful—and fresh bread. But what did it matter? There was the Sistine Chapel, the Vatican Museum, the Forum, the Pincio, the Coliseum, St. Peter's, and the loud crowded streets and the music of the people. After two weeks came Florence's Duomo, more firbidding after the light and sun and dust of Rome, but with the Uffizi and Santa Maria Maggiore, the Botticellis, the Mantegnas, the Masaccios, the Fra Angelicos, the still-ruined bridges and ramparts of the Arno, and the hills with their cypresses and monasteries surrounding the city. That trip made me know that forever, whenever possible, I'd "sail beyond the sunset, and the baths/Of all the western stars" and explore all the wonders I could.

The next opportunity was at the end of my second year. It had the best and most thrilling of prospects—a trip to the U.S.A. with a university production of *King Lear*, which I was to do. It all went wrong. The group had all the best actors in Oxford, including Shirley and Peter Parker, a postgraduate who was later to become the head of British Railways and who had been Ken Tynan's Hamlet. What they hadn't got was a director. I had no vision of *Lear*, and I have never before or since been able to do anything good unless I knew what I wanted. The only incentive was the trip to the magic U.S.A. I was in the middle of an abortive, infatuated love affair with a girl, Angela, who wasn't on the tour. I was burned out with the strain, highs, and turmoil of the last eighteen months. I withdrew. *Lear* disappeared into undistinguished oblivion. Summer vacation was upon me, without plan or purpose. Luckily, as president, I'd organized another theatre tour—the old regime's production of *A Midsummer Night's Dream* with my protégé Bill Gaskill's version of *The Knight of the Burning Pestle*. This was loosely inspired by Marcel Carné's film *Les Enfants du Paradis*—one of my great passions. Bill, realizing that, from the heights, I was suddenly in the lonely depths, and having my girlfriend in the company, suggested I come along to speak the prologue and act as a vague mime character based on Jean-Louis Barrault's Deburau in the movie. We were to go to Germany, still in the throes of non-recovery.

First stop Berlin. The devastation was spectacular. Devastation extending devastation. The old baroque zoo with its art-nouveau wirework twisting into and out of recovering trees; the vast deserted Unter den Linden; and the pillared facade which was all that remained of the Reichstag, already transformed into a new theatricality, great blood-red banners with gold hammers and sickles filling the space from top to bottom between the columns to announce a new tyranny as assertive and almost as malevolent as the old: Stalin's new empire confidently proclaiming itself in all its young pride and confidence—as dramatic a statement of conquest as any in history. Then on to Bonn and Cologne, where, still in a state of nervous hypertension, I collapsed on stage and was rushed in an ambulance—Angela, I think, by my side—to some military hospital in the middle of the night. There was, of course, nothing wrong except strain and late-adolescent pangs, and I was released almost immediately but forbidden to go on with the tour (which was almost at its end anyway). Then via Munich (for the pictures), Nuremburg (shades of Hitler), and a gray musicless Salzburg I went to Vienna, where I was to rendevous with Angela—an endless train journey through enclosed mountainous valleys with fir trees whose dullness was as monotonous as the gum trees of Australia were later to be. Except for the Brueghels in the museum, I remember Vienna only by night. Like Berlin it was divided into Four Power zones, but somehow in this dark city the controls seemed to be more intrusive, and everything seemed impossible, with barriers everywhere. The affair had fizzled out. I had developed, or rather confirmed, a revulsion for most if not all things Germanic, and I left for Italy. Although I've since been back many times—mainly to see magnificent theatre—I've never been comfortable in Germany, and I don't think I ever will be.

There are places you've imagined beforehand which turn out to be a disappointment or to be different, unexpected, in some odd, dislocating way—though some are a delight because you expected them to be disappointing. Only one place has been exactly as I imagined, only better than I could have ever imagined—Venice. Again on arrival by night (I think all the places I've ever been to I either arrived or remember arriving to at night). A gondola; dark mysterious ripples; shadows of shuttered magic palaces; lamps gleaming, disappearing. A dreamscape, but dreams tied to the reality of San Marco, the Rialto, Santa Margherita, the Accademia, the Palazzo Ducale and the pictures—the Bellinis, the Tintorettos, the Titians. No place ever has been created with such visual gluttony, such ravishing magic, as Venice. For most of the time I was alone, though I had planned a rendezvous with another Oxford friend. We were both in the city, both leaving notes for the other poste restante, but neither thinking of asking for the notes left for us. It didn't matter—I was breathing and gulping and absorbing this wonderful place in the same kind of love affair I was to have later with New York. In both cases, the place was sufficient. For one of the few times in my life, I didn't need any human companion—the look, the feel, the movement of the water and the sweet rotting smell were all.

Eventually my friend (Bill Driver) and I did meet just as our money was running out. We set out on the journey home, stopping briefly to meet other friends in Florence and for me to immerse myself again in the Uffizi, then onward, with one long moneyless day wandering round Paris, between connections, where I saw for the first time that great city which I love almost as much as (and often more than) New York.

The third and last undergraduate year in Oxford is a quieting-down time, a time of consolidation. It wasn't that finals were up ahead—I didn't much care about them, as I knew a degree would never matter for me, and anyway I was arrogant enough to believe I could wing through the exams. The most important thing was my OUDS production, which would get some sort of national attention (or at least, as in so many student situations, one imagined that) and which could, I thought, be decisive careerwise. It was my second production in the Playhouse and resources were more substantial than for *Peer Gynt*. I chose to do Webster's *The Duchess of Malfi*.

Webster, obsessed with death, was my current passion: his sputtering poetry, his theatricality, his horrors, his atmosphere—Rembrandt and horror movie combined. Visual inspiration was a key to all classical production at the time, and I wanted to be in the mainstream. The costumes and sets were based on Grünewald and Cranach, calling for an elaboration of execution which finally was beyond what our finances could provide—just as the roles, which require a fantastic degree of physical and vocal skill, are beyond amateur actors. The problem too with Webster is that, unlike Shakespeare, although the theatricality seems amazing, the inspiration is primarily literary (like Keats's being in love with wonderful phrases) and the dramatic underpinnings are weak and haphazard. Webster is theatre seen not by lighting but by a guttering candle, with all the splendor of that kind of chiaroscuro but with only glimpses of humanity (the problem for me with horror movies). And, in *The Duchess*, the central complex character, Bosola ("That we cannot be suffer'd to do good when we have a mind to it!"), has none of the vivid and potent language, the poetic force, of the suffering duchess and the crazy brothers, the lycanthropic duke and the cardinal. So, in the end, in the theatre the experience has none of the plain human satisfaction that Shakespeare gives you. But we didn't come off too badly—especially on the visual side— and the play, in which I crammed every bit of baroque invention— hounds, dwarfs, and macaws—was respectfully reviewed. The BBC offered me a contract as a trainee director.

We were to go on tour to France during the Easter vacation—the last before our exams. We visited Bordeaux, Tours, and Paris. In the provinces we played huge theatres where I made an introductory speech in French so extravagant and hyperbolic—"*Nos coeurs tiq-toquent ensemble*"—that everyone thought I was drunk. We stayed with provincial families, where we were naturally uncomfortable with each other, and on our side—certainly on mine—very bad-mannered. I was the leader of the tour, but another ex-student, Simon, knew French well and had been appointed manager. The finances of the student exchange were chaotic, and our money much less than we imagined. When we arrived in Paris, the company was put in some vast gray warehouse with treble-tiered bunk beds and blankets so filthy and decrepit that we rebelled and refused to perform. I think the hostel had housed German POWs and had never been cleaned or fumigated since. The French minister of education—stuffy but sympathetic—agreed to advance the funds allocated to the enterprise for us so we could find housing for the troupe. Simon rushed about Paris, but all we could afford was on the Left Bank—daytime bordellos in which tired actors could sleep from midnight till ten but then had to vacate their rooms until after the performance. Anyway, they were a big improvement.

The minister himself had a tiny one-floor apartment in a back street on the Left Bank, in a house which had once belonged to Talleyrand and had battered blue plaster sphinxes on either side of the front semi-courtyard. He offered Simon and me cots in the corridor of his house. We were grateful to accept, as they were one cut above the flea-ridden hotels. Then, by some bureaucratic fluke, just as the company was leaving after the final performances (which had gone surprisingly well), the remainder of the promised funds was handed to us. Shamelessly, we decided to stay on—the two of us—to enjoy ourselves. Even better, the minister had a young attractive wife and a two-year-old child. The minister had to tour a lot, and, as soon as he left, his wife summoned the maid to whisk the child off to her home in the suburbs while Madame departed for a lover in Geneva, handing us the keys of the apartment and giving us *carte blanche* to exchange our camp-beds for the comfort of her own room. We spent ten glorious days in Paris, living it up on the funds left to us, and departing, in a great hurry, only when we learned that the minister was heading back in a jealous rage, having heard that we were both sharing the favors of his wife. I don't know whether Madame managed to make it home before he did, or how the marriage turned out: We were back across the Channel, and I was reading for my final term.

Central as the theatre life was, Oxford opened up many other aspects of life and friendship. I had looked at politics—some of the politicians who were up when I was were Jeremy Thorpe, Shirley Williams, William Rees-Mogg, and Peter Parker, and Harold Wilson was lecturing as a new college don. I had dipped into journalism—Alan Brien, Robert Robinson, Anthony Curtis, and Godfrey Smith were among colleagues. But some of my greatest friendships came from other worlds. These were varied and many.

There was, for instance, an Australian postgraduate—Peter X— who was doing research on water shrews, which he nurtured in elaborate aquariums and fed with fat earthworms. He gave me lots of sexual advice: Always wear clean underwear before the first time; an orgasm was a flight of barbed-wire sparrows through the hasp of your dick. He and his girlfriend lived in a room in Blenheim Palace. The Marlborough family had retreated or been confined by wartime requisitioning to one small wing. The rest had been emptied. The room where Winston Churchill had been born was used for coal and coke storage. It was fascinating to wander down the long, damp, deserted corridors. Every room was empty except for the pictures. It was amazing to drift into a bare-floorboarded room and see a grime-encrusted frame and realize that under the dust was a Watteau or a Boucher.

But the biggest group of non-theatre friends came from the liberal-left scientific fringe—Shirley Catlin, the Mitchisons, Francis Huxley. Francis, also a postgraduate, was the mirror image of his uncle Aldous rather than his father, Julian, whom later I met often at his lovely Georgian house in Hampstead, littered with artifacts from all over the primitive world. Francis was a gentle, charming humorist with a fascinating anthropological career in the Brazilian jungles ahead.

There were only two of the vast family of the Mitchisons left at Oxford. Valentine was a great friend of Shirley's—funny, independent, slightly sardonic—and I was a bit in love with her, but as an alternate to Shirley—like salt and pepper. It was her younger brother, Avrion (I think the name was Greek for "tomorrow"), who became my closest friend. He was big-boned and gentle, with an enormous head and a slight stammer, a large body and an inherent diffidence of manner. I didn't know quite what drew us together—except difference. But I was much more comfortable with him than with anyone else at Oxford. We spent long evenings talking—discussing poetry, philosophy. One night, walking by the Isis, we were talking about swimming, which I'd never learned. Avrion described how easy it was. I had such total trust in him that I immediately plunged in, got out into the middle of the river, and sank. Mud and water filled my throat. I was drowning—in panic—nothing I could do. Avrion hauled me out. It was probably a great mistake.

Avrion and Valentine's parents were the writer Naomi Mitchison—a kind, gypsy-looking woman and a writer of eccentric talent, wavering between mythic novels and children's books—and her husband G.R.M., a QC and later a member of Harold Wilson's first Labour government. They were Scottish and had a family house, Carradale, near Campbeltown on the Mull of Kintyre opposite the island of Arran. Because of the Gulf Stream, this peninsula, which stretches south almost level with Glasgow, has a climate like the west of Ireland—extremely mild with hot, muggy, cloudy summers cooled by the breezes. Their house was a huge Victorian mansion—a bit of a joke, with antlered stags carved in stone over the doorways. Behind stretched vast heather-covered moors full of deer and grouse, hares and partridges; streams full of trout and salmon; big kitchen gardens with peaches and nectarines espaliered against the walls; fruit bushes under netting; cow pastures and hayfields stretching down to the beach of Kilbrannan Sound a half mile beyond the house.

Of all the Mitchisons' many individual creations, Carradale was one of their most important. In summer they kept a kind of open house for their friends and their children. It was there I learned the pleasure of country-house living. The mix of people was extraordinary: intellectuals, literary figures, politicians, students, relatives. There was every kind of activity: shooting (it was here I first learned to shoot, and disgraced myself completely when the only stag of the day moved in front of me—"my shot"—but I couldn't bear to shoot and lowered my rifle, and so was cursed for the rest of the day), fishing, haymaking, swimming, picking fruit, parlor

games, discussions, debates, dances, Scottish reels. But the most
wonderful thing about the Mitchison atmosphere was that there
was never any compulsion, or any feeling of compulsion. Running
a house in the south of France now, I know how demanding and
incessant are the problems of keeping a large group of people housed
and fed and happy. Naomi never made you aware of the immense
behind-the-scenes labor—it seemed an idyll, effortless and continual as the long northern days and the never-setting suns. If you
were obviously hopeless at physical taks (as I was), or probably just
plain selfish and spoiled, you were never made to feel it. It was a
kind of magical liberty hall, as nurturing in its way and as civilized
as Oxford was in another. It was the best thing Britain could offer.
It has stayed with me forever, inspired what later I tried to do in
France, and if ever Naomi—who is, I think, still alive—or any
other member of the family reads this, I want them to accept so
much that I have been able to do since as my living thank-you letter
to them. I never went back to Oxford after I left, but I went back
again and again to Carradale. The Mitchisons were always welcoming, were all-permitting. Campbeltown was a second home, and
Oxford's and the Mitchison's aura were one.

With all the good things in life, you know you have to let go,
and when. Much as I loved Oxford, I knew I wanted to go on.
Oxford had made me ready; I didn't want to cling. The last term
was a natural winding-down, culminating in Finals. I was rather
disappointed in the result—a third—as I was expected to do brilliantly, with weaknesses only in more academic studies like Anglo-
Saxon, in which I had no interest. Oddly enough I did well in
them and not in all my strengths, but university politics also entered
into the examining. Anyway, it didn't matter: I wanted to be on
the road. London was ahead. After spending the summer of 1951
in Scotland, I rented my first squalid room in London, opposite
Paddington Station. I was, really, on my own for the first time.

5

On the Road

Television in the early 1950s, although supposedly more advanced in the UK than anywhere in the world, was very much the despised poor relation of the sound-radio corporation. Visual images were somehow vulgar, like comic strips in the back pages of newspapers. The BBC course on which I'd been promised a place was, I think, the first of its kind. No one knew what to do or when, and the course was postponed and postponed until you doubted it would ever be reality. In the meantime I had nothing except for a subsistence allowance my parents gave me—their generosity overcoming their deep misgivings. I knocked at all the available theatrical doors without success, and spent the time at movies, at theatres (whenever I could get free tickets), or seeing friends from Oxford. It was pretty bleak. I did one production of a thriller at a repertory theatre on the fringe of London, but whatever ripples I'd made at Oxford had now died away and the only thing to do was to wait for the BBC.

The course finally came through in the spring. It was for six months. It was hopeless. There were a few weeks of theory—at a level which a first-week film student today would despise—then, in preparation for being integrated into this horrifically benevolent institution, you were attached as an assistant to one established television director after another, and given tasks like shooting inserts—a flag being raised, a sign on a doorway—for which no resources were provided, so the result could only be ludicrous. Outside the UK, many have a very erroneous view of what the BBC is and was. Because of its supposedly independent character, it is often seen almost as "the Fourth Estate" itself—especially in America, where there is also a typical self-abasement at its "quality." In reality the BBC has always been an out-front-and-proud-of-it bastion of mediocrity, and its pensioners—an aggressively complacent and philistine bureaucracy; the lowest common multiple of talent and intelligence; a world of the self-congratulating, the would-bes—whether they're journalists or politicians or interviewers or directors who think they're the ace. Attending the meetings of the Drama Department was to me totally disillusioning—none of the directors ever saw a movie or a play, but they talked about their own middlebrow productions as if they were discussing the Festival of Ephesus, though they were, of course, more interested in whether a particular rehearsal had adequate lavatories or catering facilities. I knew straightaway the BBC wasn't for me. So did the BBC. And the work! At the end of the course you were allowed to do a thirty-minute show. I think I did the *Apollo of Bellac* by Giraudoux, with Denholm Elliott and Natasha Parry. It was thought to be a bit fancy. As far as the Drama Department was concerned, I was a renegade and as such unemployable.

Something much more powerful had happened during the course, however: I had, for the first time, fallen seriously in love. Among the twenty members of the course—none of whom I can remember—was a twenty-seven-year-old girl, Perdita "Ming" Craig, with a fantastic smile, wonderful legs, short hair, and rather smart, stiff organdy skirts or suits. She was swift and sharp and had the same capacity for seeing through the pretensions of the people around us that I had. Within ten days we were never apart. We exchanged everything; we spent all our time together. Her mother, Dona—a clever, sexual, sympathetic lady—had been widowed and was now married to Christopher Salmon, a wonderful-looking and very charming man who belonged to a different age. He was the younger son of an aristocratic family, born to have income and not to work, a *démodé* belletrist and *bon vivant*. They didn't have much money. They lived on the fringes of the BBC (the posh, the sound, side), but they were very friendly. Ming (I never knew where the nickname came from and for some reason never asked) and I soon became engaged. After the course, we went to Carradale for a kind of pre-honeymoon in the summer. She was welcomed as openly as I was. Then on our return Ming fell ill. It was soon clear that the illness was serious. Leukemia was diagnosed. She was advised to go to a clinic in Zurich. Dona moved there to be with her, and I joined them for several weeks in a depressing, snow-drizzly Swiss winter. Ming kept up her humor and her energy in a marvelous way, but it was hopeless. She died early in the New Year.

It was a low, low time. I was bitter and broken about Ming. I had no money and virtually no prospects. The Salmons were supportive and comforting, and most of the meals I ate were with them. One of their friends in the BBC was Mary Adams, the head of the Talks Department (the BBC was rigorously compartmentalized, and any kind of crossover was frowned on). She was a charming and intelligent woman who was respected (and naturally denigrated) as one of the more independent spirits who had somehow managed to operate within the system. Mary tried to help me. She gave me little assignments. There isn't much you can do with a static camera on one speaker, but it paid the rent. Then gradually she slipped in a few narrated short stories, with bits of sets and maybe occasionally a camera on—*grand luxe*—a crane, and actors, and I started to do a bit more. Then came a series conceived by J. B. Priestley that was the first real crossover between the Talks and Drama departments. "Jolly Jack" Priestley, from my hometown, had made a great reputation as a national broadcaster during the Second World War, being (certainly in his opinion) a rallier of opinion second only to Churchill himself. This series was conceived as his exploration of television. (There was a lot of talk about what the art of television really was. I've never been able to see it as more than film with reduced resources, aimed for a specific audience.) The idea was to take a few actors and, against skeletal decors, perform short dramatic pieces, skits, monologues, etc. For instance, you might get the same sitcom scene performed *à la Rashomon*, from the points of view of the four different characters. None of it was any great shakes, but in the TV context of the day it was different—even refreshing. And it reestablished me—grudgingly—within BBC circles.

There was also a period of infatuation among all the participants, including Jack himself. As a consequence, he asked me to direct the actors of the series in his next play, a realistic Northern comedy, *Mr. Kettle and Mrs. Moon*. It was to be my first West End commercial production and, though I didn't think much of the play, I was grateful to Jack for the opportunity. I was a disaster. The play was an average commercial comedy that required from a director a command and understanding of a kind of artificial skill and technique that I didn't even have an inkling of. I could wire clouds across the stage, create groupings and spectacle, but how did you move people from chair to chair or across a room when in truth there didn't seem to be any reason—characterwise—why they should move or where they should be? I'd never thought about those resources of drinks and cigarettes and naturalistic business that were second nature to the actors themselves. That kind of invention was both alien and pointless to me—I couldn't function like that, and such suggestions as I had were banal and pathetic. The actors, from thinking me this brilliant TV wizard, soon lost all confidence in me. I didn't know how to handle or listen to an author in the theatre, I was incompetent and arrogant and, after the opening out of town, I was quite rightly fired and Jack took over. But I was allowed to keep my .25 percent royalty and even, which I didn't want, my billing. I was treated by everyone in the gentlest and most generous way. Jack spruced the production up with a lot of inventive stage business (I'd mistakenly tried to be faithful), and the play later had a respectable commercial run of a few months at the end of 1955.

I went back to the BBC and started working again on minor play assignments, one of which was to change my whole life. It was an adaptation of a Chekhov short story, *The Actor's End*. The story itself is very slight. A down-at-heel provincial company is presenting some historical drama, elevating the "character" man, the "heavy," to a role beyond his usual scope. He is ill as he's making up (most of the story takes place in his dressing room). The characters act and speculate on his condition—drink, stagefright, inability to learn his lines. They force him on stage. At the end he falls dead in his boyar costume, unnoticed.

I offered the central role in the anecdote to George Devine. The casting decision was based on the only time I'd seen him act, when

I was still at school—he had been Mr. Antrobus at the Leeds Grand in a production by Laurence Olivier of Thornton Wilder's *The Skin of Our Teeth*, starring Vivien Leigh—but I knew, of course, much of the detail of his already distinguished career. He'd been in and around all the good classical revivals of the 1930s, been in the Gielgud and Old Vic companies, and, together with Michel Saint-Denis (his mentor) and Glen Byram Shaw (his buddy), had formed the triumvirate which ran the Old Vic school. This was based on the prewar London Theatre Studio, which Saint-Denis, himself the pupil (and nephew) of Jacques Copeau, had founded in London, and which was once the intellectual rage of the theatre elite. Then there was a period when the triumvirate ran the Old Vic in preparation for a National Theatre, only to be ignominiously fired on the whim of Tyrone Guthrie. George was married to Sophie Harris, part of the famous designer team of Motley.

He accepted the role. I don't know whether some subconscious calculation—to ally myself with the mainstream of the British theatre to which I was a complete outsider—underlay the decision. Whatever, it was one of the best—no, *the* best—I ever made. Among the many extraordinary qualities of George's personality were his openness to new personalities and a total unconcern for his own seniority (if the word wasn't loathsome, you'd say humility), his giving response to the new, his ability to see through arrogance and stupidity to what might be worth protecting and developing. He would have made a great farmer in the best and widest sense of the word. He was like Dr. Dorn in *The Seagull* (a role he was to play much later for me) when Dorn speaks of Konstantin's play: "There was something in it that excited me." From the first moment, we "clicked" perfectly.

He had everything to teach me: his awareness and knowledge of theatre as a craft, as a business, as an organization, and his experience as a physical practitioner. He knew everything about the physical realization of a play and the way to relate to the craftsmen who could create the results. What had I to offer? Only, perhaps, some sense and smell of a new generation, unarrived and unproven. I came, too, at a moment in George's life when he was groping for something new, though I doubt he could have articulated what. It's not unfair to say that Michel Saint-Denis had defined and framed George's then vision of the theatre. It was a vision basically of form, stretching from Gordon Craig through French intellectuality with dreams of Russian glory into British romantic literature. George sensed it wasn't enough, though probably he never admitted its limitations to himself—loyalty was a total fabric with George, and he remained in awe of and passionate about Michel to the end of his life. But he knew he couldn't go on trying to revive what hadn't worked. He wanted another theatre, a new theatre—he didn't know what. I wanted a new theatre too, and I didn't know quite what and I didn't know how. George did know how.

After the show, which went well, we talked and talked for hours. We began to outline a plan for a new theatre in all its details. The practicalities all came from George. But we had no material. We were both beginning—and this was another great bond between us—to see the limits of the aspirations of the "poetic" theatre that had a brief vogue at the end of the Second World War. Just as Michel and George had been drawn to a physical theatre, before the war there had been the Group Theatre, a semi-amateur organization which had presented the Auden-Isherwood plays and T. S. Eliot's *Sweeney Agonistes*. After the war this flame was fanned by Eliot's later experiments (with a certain number of followers, the most prominent of whom was Ronald Duncan, who had a future role in this story). Eliot is, of course, one of the leading figures of twentieth-century literature, having created great works which changed our imaginative landscape. He was drawn to theatre, but he realized instinctively that the literary tradition of theatre, based on copies of the Elizabethans, from the *Cenci* through Tennyson to the *Dynasts*, was going nowhere. But in tackling this, he boxed himself in. He tried to accommodate himself to the British commercial tradition of the time—the tradition Arthur Miller called "a theatre hermetically sealed from life" (and Miller should have added "linguistically" too). By creating his "commercial" comedies, jacked up with a ludicrous shot of metaphysics (or Christianity, depending on which side you're on), Eliot castrated himself and encouraged a theatre as sterile as Shelley had done. I don't suppose George and I knew all this at the time, but we felt it and discussed. We drew up our repertory for our new theatre—it was almost entirely based on foreign writers: French, German, American—and it was here I was most complementary to George, because I had begun to read many foreign dramatists, most of whom were unknown in England at the time. Wartime also brings its constraints of publishing and knowledge.

Through our discussions, our scheme became reality *as* a scheme. We had a blueprint on paper. We visited theatres, many of which were still damaged by bombs, and discussed potential sites. Then there was the question of money. This was long before the days of foundations, funding, subsidies; but I had a friend. In the 1930s, when women were almost *personae non gratae*, it had been the custom to employ professional actresses to play the female roles in amateur productions to give the production extra lustre. The war had stopped this practice, but there were some ladies who hovered around the shows and took part when required. I had become very friendly with the most famous of these, a dotty theatrical lady whose husband controlled a large fortune based, I think, on chemicals. She aspired to be a kind of patroness, with a salon, and she had a house with a beautiful garden in Addison Road, Holland Park, almost opposite a more modest house in which George and Sophie rented a floor. I had kept up my friendship with her. She was kind to me, and encouraging. When I told her about my idea for a new theatre, she was at first very supportive and enthusiastic. She could lay her hands on the necessary finance and, with the knowledge of her potential backing, George and I refined our scheme.

The theatre we settled on was the Royal Court, in Sloane Square. This was a small theatre of five hundred seats but wonderfully placed; out of the West End, between the smartness of Knightsbridge and the supposed bohemia of Chelsea. It was the theatre of Bernard Shaw and Harley Granville-Barker, who, as a director, singlehandedly revived Shakespeare and became a formidable dramatist. This was exactly the tradition we wanted to revive. The theatre had been bomb-damaged and, without structural support, was allowed to open only in limited club circumstances, though these building requirements were being attended to. The theatre was the propriety of Alfred Esdaile—an amiable Cockney rogue who today would be erecting shopping malls and supermarkets. We discussed the deal and came to an agreement. Detailed as our scheme was, we knew we weren't ready, so we planned to put a commercial revue in first. If successful, this would help to fund the theatre.

During the months all this planning had been progressing, I had completely abandoned television and given myself up to the cause.

I had been keeping in close touch with our patroness, but George had other professional commitments and a living to earn, and she had never met him. Now all was to be finalized, and a meeting of the three of us took place. It was fatal. Elaine took one look at George and it was over. Maybe it was as simple as a lady who could fantasize about controlling some inexperienced know-nothing of twentysomething realizing that there would be next to no role for her around such a consumate professional. She withdrew, and the whole balloon collapsed. The final irony was that the show we had chosen to keep the Court warm—Laurier Lister's *Airs on a Shoestring*, which opened in April 1953—was such a success that with the arrangements we'd made we could have funded our whole first season without a penny from our patroness.

It was a bitter time—we had been so sure, and now we had nothing. George had lots of Shakespearean and operatic offers. I had let all my TV contacts lapse and had more or less exhausted all my money. Avrion Mitchison came to the rescue. He had been away for a year, doing research in India as a Commonwealth Fund fellow. One of the conditions for the fellows was that they should spend several months of their fellowship getting to know America during the summer vacation. Avrion's grant gave him enough to purchase an old Ford. He suggested I join him for a three- or four-month trip. It was just what I wanted. I bought a ticket on a student charter—from London to New York by the cheap route took twenty-four hours then, with stops in Ireland, Iceland, and Canada—and after paying for the ticket I had $100 left.

I had been in some wonderful cities. I had lived, as you do live when you're growing up, in places and among people I knew, liked, didn't like; but until I got to New York I never realized that in some deep, alienated way I'd never felt totally comfortable. Coming to New York—where I knew no one, had one or two introductions at most—I felt for the first time totally at home, totally belonging. I spent the first night in some cruddy fifth-rate—and costly—hotel off Times Square. Next day I moved to some other cruddy—but cheaper—hotel off Washington Square. I had a week to spend there before joining Avrion in Bloomington, Indiana. There was a classic New York heat wave with humidity to match. I drifted in a haze of total rapture. I think I called on one contact—who was, if I remember, Alfred Barr, of the Museum of Modern Art—and I saw

some theatre—certainly *The Crucible;* maybe something else. Otherwise I just drifted, drifted, drifted—overwhelmed, dazzled,
happy as I'd never been before. It was all like a good dream that
you could move in and out of at will: A fantastic reverie, independent of sleeping, eating, sightseeing, gallery-going, in which
the inner and outer corresponded and blurred so that both place
and time dissolved into buildings that were dreamscapes and neigh-
borhoods and their people who were as solid as the rocks on which
Manhattan is not built but moored. There have been moments of
higher drama in my life, but I don't remember any week of such
sustained intensity.

After a week I had to leave for Bloomington. In Avrion's bare
college apartment the evening I arrived, we ordered pizza—a huge
pizza, the first I'd ever eaten. Next day we set out. We had a third
companion—a friend of Avrion's from college. He was rather
strange, somewhat chip-on-the-shoulder, slightly deformed (a
twisted leg), and a Marxist. He made heavily socially loaded litho-
graphs. As I took against him, I never imagined he could be any
good, and I was surprised much later to find two of his prints in
a corridor at the Museum of Modern Art. He embodied the kind
of superior moral-reproval high ground that many extreme leftists,
or imagined leftists, claim for their own. He did, however, drive
(which I didn't—so I was purely a passenger on the trip), and he
spoke Spanish. As we intended to go into Mexico, then practically
a *terra incognita*, this would be useful. (I'd had an obsession about
Mexico ever since I'd seen Eisenstein's movie *Que Viva Mexico.*)

From Bloomington we drove southwest across the farm belt to
Oklahoma—endless flat green landscapes of wheat and corn—then
headed south for Texas, through hundreds of miles of scrub and
mesquite where the new cities of Houston and Dallas rose from
the desert like gleaming dishwashers unpacked from their wrap-
pings. We sweltered for the night alongside bums in a twenty-five-
cent flophouse, then moved on across the border through the squalor
and picaresqueness of Laredo, then on through endless unrelieved
desert and cactus to broken-down Monterrey, where, still not reading Spanish, even if there were any warning signs (which there
probably weren't), we crashed into a sidewise broken-down bus and
were stranded for several days. We took a side trip to Tampico, a
tropical oil port on the Gulf where, in the palm-shaded plaza, girls

and boys of seven to ten were for sexual sale at ten cents. Then on to the hard, mountainous, and yet tropical trail to Mexico City.

Travel in Mexico was very difficult at that time. There were no main highways. The roads were appalling and tourists rare. Often we would go through villages where a car would be stoned by all the inhabitants. On the other hand, on our way to Tampico, in the middle of a pitch-black tropical night, we had a flat and drove off onto what we thought was a grass verge to fix it, only to sink up to our axles in a green swamp, Indians materialized from nowhere, within minutes produced a Jeep, hauled us out of the slime, and, with great courtesy, refused the little gifts and money we offered them.

In Mexico City we saw the beginning of the excavation of the pyramids, watched the hummingbirds in Desierto de Los Leones, deposited our companion in the artists' colony where he was hoping to thrive, and admired the Orozcos, the Riveras, and the Tamayos. We then passed on to the pretty tiled roofs of Cuernavaca before turning west to return through Guadalajara, where we slept on and off in a brothel, and Morelia, in front of whose pink plateresque cathedral we tried to eat in one café (also a whorehouse), where rats the size of cats frolicked across our feet. Then back to what we now called home. Exciting, visually extraordinary, as the Mexican part of our trip had been, there had also been a permanent sense of strain—almost of danger—and when we crossed back to the USA at El Paso (which later I was to know so well) we checked into some decrepit motel, took our first shower for a long, long, time, and collapsed into a twenty-four-hour sleep.

From El Paso we drove north past the White Sands to Albuquerque. Hazards and dangers weren't just on the Mexican side of the border: With our dry British voices and Oxford manners, we'd been something of a joke or a cause for suspicion all along the road in the cheap cafés and hotels we'd lived in. At Albuquerque we had our first encounter with that least attractive member of the American subspecies, the redneck. We were just about to leave the broken-down motel on the outskirts of the city when the door was thrown open and two tough cops barged in—the first shouting, "Where's the money?" As neither of us had any idea what they were talking about, we became confused, further confirming our guilt. Finally the accusation emerged: We had stolen money from another group in the hotel. The night before we had eaten in the greasy spoon attached to the establishment. There had been a group of four other people there. At the end of the meal we both found that, having just arrived, we'd left our wallets in our room and had no money to pay the bill. I went back to the room, got our money, paid, and went off to bed. I was during this trip back to the room that I had allegedly found the money the other group had supposedly dropped by mistake near the door of the café, pocketed it, and departed. As always in such cases, we retreated into grand and defensive Britishness, but no way was insisting on seeing a non-existent British consul going to get us out of our trouble: The cops would accept no word of defense, assured us we faced several nights in jail and a good beating-up on top, and got very rough indeed. They were now emptying our luggage and hauling it about the room, overturning mattresses, and so on. It was ugly, and we were pretty frightened.

In the course of their search, one of them came on our papers, among which were various letters of introduction with official-looking letterheads—some even from Washington. He stopped, puzzled. "Who'd you steal these from?" When we said they were ours, they were sufficient to make them a bit uneasy and unsure. The threats abated. They consulted together and, taking all our papers and car keys with them, and with a strict admonition not to leave the room, they zoomed away in their cop car. Half an hour later they returned, grinning. The money had been found in a local gas station. "We thought you were a couple of bums. Didn't realize you were people like these" (whatever "these" were). They handed us our keys and papers back, wished us a good time in New Mexico, departed. We, as they say in the movies, hightailed it out of the state and on, via the Grand Canyon, to Los Angeles.

At last I was in the capital of my dreams, though I remember very little about it. We stayed with some friends or relatives of Av's above or near Hollywood, perhaps in the Silverlake district. We visited Hollywood, maybe a studio once—I had a few introductions. The thing I remember most was meeting my greatest idol, Luis Buñuel, who was in Hollywood to dub the Spanish version of his film *Robinson Crusoe*. He screened it for me and, back in England, I reviewed it for *Sight and Sound*—ecstatically. Years later I met him again, never expecting him to remember our first meeting. But he brought it up: "You were such a skinny kid—and now—

you are a man." We met Francis Huxley's uncle Aldous, and through him had the first meeting with someone who was later to become one of my greatest friends—Christopher Isherwood. But I was much too shy to pursue many of our introductions. We just drove aroung, marveling at the luxury and beauty of the houses in Beverly Hills, the crumbling coastline of Santa Monica, and the derelict charm of Venice. The only other thing I can remember was the indignation of our hosts (perhaps they were lawyers) about some castration sentence on a sex offender—common practice throughout many states, but already thought barbaric in California.

We stayed almost two weeks in LA—which was very welcome after a different bed night after night during weeks spent on the road. Then we made our way up the coast, admiring all the marvels of Big Sur and Carmel, to San Francisco. This was the only bust of our whole trip (and has been ever since for me, no matter how hard and in how many different circumstances I've tried to love it). Splendid as the harbor is, and the great bridges, San Francisco has always seemed to me a dreary provincial town pretending to be a great capital—its light and its most typical indigenous architecture reminding me of a British seaside town. If it had ever had days of glory, they'd long gone, and the people we met seemed colorless and snobbish.

We planned to go further north—more into redwood country—but time was running out on us. Money already had, and that was one of the thrills of Reno. I was probably down to my last twenty dollars, and Av, who had been funding most of the trip, had almost nothing. For me, gambling is fun only when you're risking everything you've got—if you lose, no bed and no hamburger. Otherwise it has always seemed pointless, because the risk is only money. Luckily we were lucky—not in a big way, but we made a few extra dollars for the trip back. We headed slightly north, through Salt Lake and Idaho, so that, crossing the Rockies, we could hit Yellowstone—see the moose, the buffalo, and the grizzlies—then down through the Badlands and the Dakotas to Minneapolis, and then on to Illinois, arriving at night in Chicago, where, on cue, we saw a shooting and a car with broken windows gun away into the dark. Then, from Chicago, the dull and dreary stretch back to New York.

Our Kerouacean marathon was at last over. We were totally broke, totally exhausted, but full of a splendor of images and an exhilaration at the great expanse of a country whose scale of land-scape, so accepted by Americans, is so amazing and alien to Europeans. (Look at any European film today and, whatever the screen size, you'll see exactly what I mean.) I couldn't bear the thought of going back. I wanted to stay and become part of this country forever, but I had no idea what to do, and I hadn't the resource-fulness I think is bred into Americans. Av, who had already used up all his year's money—a large portion of which I'd absorbed—was terrified by the idea that somehow I'd become his responsibility and that he would have a homeless, visaless, unemployable waif on his hands. I also knew that I had other things to do in England. So, sadly, I used my return air ticket and left—desperate to return, but with no idea how or when.

If movies have so far seemed to play a small part in the story, it isn't that they weren't a constant passion: Rather, the cinema was like Hamlet to Ophelia—a prince, out of my star. The British have never been a race of moviemakers, moviegoers, or movie buffs. After the few makers of any note—the early Hitchcock, the David Lean of *Brief Encounter* and *Great Expectations*, Carol Reed, Alexander Mackendrick (of the Ealing comedies)—where do you look? But, beyond the smallest of its productive contribution, the attitude of British society was to denigrate. Movies were popular and therefore inconsiderable; American-dominated and therefore vulgar. Above all, they were never to be taken seriously (Graham Greene's brief period as a critic in the 1930s was the exception and little known about): They were to be dismissed as something childish and cheap, to be thrown away like wrapping paper after a present has been opened.

At school, movies were forbidden—except for a dutiful tracking to *Henry V* at a special school matinee. (Apart from the usual snob-bery, there was also the faint idea that picture houses were sources of unnamed diseases and infections.) Gradually, though, I began to realize that there was another cinema: the cinema of the silents, of the Russians—Eisenstein, Pudovkin, and Donskoi—of Chaplin and Griffith, Langdon and Keaton, of the German expressionists, of René Clair and Renoir and Vigo and, of course, Buñuel. Then there were movies like *The Grapes of Wrath* and the comedies of Preston Sturges, and the terrific impact of the postwar Italians—of *Shoeshine* and *Bicycle Thief* and *Open City*—which seemed to make life more real and more vivid than anything one imagined. All these crept up on me without my knowing exactly how: It was like emerging from a house whose windows and rooms have long been boarded up and air and places and people being revealed outside. It didn't seem like art—it was life itself.

At about the same time, a group of people was doing some hard thinking and writing about the cinema. Most of them came from Oxford; most of them were there just before me. They were centered about an Oxford magazine, *Sequence*. Leaders of the group were Lindsay Anderson and Gavin Lambert (later to be joined by Karel Reisz from Cambridge). A similar kind of work but maybe more loony, and with too much moral metaphysics by André Bazin, was being done in France. It's no exaggeration to say that the *Sequence* group changed the whole way of feeling and thinking about film in England—at any rate for a few inspiring years, before the British sank once again into complacency and philistinism.

As distinct from Bazin, who focused on the philosophical implications of technique (he too regenerated a whole generation of filmmakers—the *nouvelle vague* of the 1950s), Lindsay and Gavin concentrated on the poetic and humanist life of movies, a central tradition which I think today is pathetically ignored by most of the film schools—nonexistent then, but everywhere today—who think that the technique of shock in a horror movie is more important than cultivation of a sense of a filmmaker's own vision and feeling of life, the creation of characters and of stories based on character. Lindsay reassessed Ford, stressing the poet rather than the commercial filmmaker. Gavin revealed the anarchy and brilliance of Preston Sturges. They looked at the roots of cinema, at *L'Âge d'or* and *Zéro de conduite*. They discovered the British past and the contemporary documentarist Humphrey Jennings (of *A Diary for Timothy*). They ripped aside the falseness of the conventions and acting of studio productions and went back to the life basis of great cinema, peeling the varnish off masterpieces of the past and questioning (often too much) the motives and gloss of current productions. All this is now history, but then it was vibrant, alive, and as crucial and positive in its way as Roger Fry's advocacy of Cézanne, because the motive behind their writing was the only one that ever gives criticism any value—to ignite the possibility of the new by communicating what was true and exciting in what has already been accomplished.

I met them all after I'd moved to London, and gradually I became part of the group. *Sequence* had become *Sight and Sound*, and we all wrote for it. I was never much good at it, but all our writing was important not so much in itself but as an indication of what we hoped to achieve. There was a big difference between the two worlds of the theatre and the movies. In theatre you worked within the structures that already existed, even if you rejected their establishment context; in the movies, as far as we were concerned, you worked as you liked. The dialectic of cinema was more intense, the passions more divisive, the morality more keen, and often puritanical and often finicky (as would later be true of the young theatre writers). In theatre circles you swapped anecdotes; in the movie world you fought about what you liked and attacked the falseness of the current product. It was intellectual in the best sense, passionate, idiosyncratic, and crazy.

We all wanted to make movies, but there were no avenues, no resources. We were all outsiders and poor: ridiculous to everyone within the industry, and totally pathetic to British society as a whole. Eventually, by different means—by begging, borrowing, and stealing film and equipment—we began to find tiny opportunities. Lindsay made a series of industrial films, then another more ambitious Jennings-type documentary, *O Dreamland*. An Italian protégée of his, Lorenza Mazzetti, made a charming poetic anecdote, *Together*. Karel Reisz and I teamed up to make a twenty-minute film of a north-London traditional jazz club, *Momma Don't Allow*.

The film was shot over a period of weeks during the hours the club operated, with Walter Lassally, the first of the pioneer cameramen, doing everything technical. John Fletcher recorded the sound. Karel and I were very different personalities. I veered from wanting to expand or hint at dramatic situations involving individuals outside the group to using ideas of montage as abstract as a music video. (Alone of the group, I was a keen Eisenstein fan.) Karel had a much calmer and more straightforward approach, respecting the musicians' wanting to record their achievement without letting an imposed aesthetic get in the way. It's a line he has continued, with insufficient credit. His latest movie, *Sweet Dreams*, shows the same attitude. He is a remarkable talent and has an infinite charm. A Czech Jewish immigrant, by the time he was ten he had become so integrated into British life, not kicking against the pricks, that he was more at home there, more at ease on both the actual and the emotional cricket field, than I would ever be. In this too he was very different from the quirky, magisterial Scotsman Lindsay and the fanciful, elliptical Gavin.

The film, which lost £100, didn't work out too badly, but it was hard to know what to do with it. Among his many talents, Lindsay has always been a sublime and sometimes pugnacious publicist. He decided to put all our films together and eventually got them shown as a series under the title "Free Cinema" at the National Film Theatre in February 1956. He wrote a statement of belief which we all signed and to a large extent subscribed to. Many people (academics and film critics) have tried to inflate this into a manifesto—a rallying call to action and achievement. It read:

> As film-makers we believe that
> No film can be too personal.
> The image speaks. Sound amplifies and comments. Size is irrelevant.
> Perfection is not an aim.
> An attitude means a style. A style means an attitude.

To be honest, it wasn't at the time much more than a publicity blurb, but some of it still seems pretty valid—and nothing more so than "Perfection is not an aim" (a dig inspired by commercial production of the school later typified by *Lawrence of Arabia* and *Dr. Zhivago*).

In my scanty film education, I think I'd been lucky. I was still out of my star; the movies I loved had a contact with life which studio productions, American or British, never achieved. The cult of 1930s and 1940s studio Hollywood is something I've never understood or admired. Sure, they had to get out a lot of product, and sometimes something good slipped through the net or there were gleams of what might have been a directorial talent. But the golden years of Hollywood never produced movies of the quality that the silents or the Europeans of the same period achieved. Individually, a great, great star like Garbo might achieve her own evanescence, but she could never transcend the level of her scripts, *mises en scène*, and co-actors. As for the mass of studio players who have become kitsch cult figures, they have always seemed to me to be more or less talented members of a museum stock company. Once movies retreated from the open air and the winds behind the still doors of sound studios, life waited outside. The studio kinds of set, direction, lighting, playing are as remote to me as kabuki. That's why westerns are in many ways the liveliest of all Hollywood. Compare the Ford of *The Informer* with the Ford of *Stagecoach*—the puny empires of Goldwyn and Louis B. Mayer, of Zanuck and Selznick, dissolve with one shot of Monument Valley and leave not a trace behind. (They are alive only in the old posters and the rhetoric of a few French critics, and maybe some new Hollywood ones.)

In the 1940s Buñuel, desperate for a job, was working at the Museum of Modern Art. When it was discovered that he had made *L'Âge d'or*, he was fired. Today the museum recognizes it as one of the greatest masterpieces of its collection.

Apart from *Momma Don't Allow*, nothing much seemed to be happening to me—creatively. I saw George all the time. He and Sophie had moved to a new house, on the Mall by Hammersmith Bridge. At the top of the eighteenth-century house was a modern apartment—designed by the modernist architect Maxwell Fry. It was a long, low studio room divided by screens, with a flat roof and other features rather like a ship. George asked me if I'd like to rent. I loved the space, the air, the sight of the river, but I still hadn't much money. However, I met an American who, working for the Ford Foundation, had to be partly in England. George Goetschius seemed to be the perfect roommate, and ended up as personal guru for everyone he met.

I went on working in television, getting bigger and more prominent dramatic shows. The best of these was an *Othello* for which I cast Gordon Heath, a black American folksinger. Although he had already played the role in a minor stage production, it was thought to be revolutionary at the time to give a black such a spotlight. I, on the other hand, have never understood how, when there are so few roles written specifically for black actors, any white actor dare play it. Othellos played by white actors have always seemed travesties to me—and none more so then the acclaimed effeminate coon-singer of Laurence Olivier's. But, although all this work was better than doing nothing, I was dreaming of other things. How they happened is another story, with another mixture of personalities.

6

Debut at the Court

The regime of the English Stage Company at the Royal Court Theatre (the two names are synonymous) was born in the ashes of the old literary verse theatre. T. S. Eliot had gone on to other things, but one of his most ardent disciples, Ronald Duncan, had tried to follow his earlier precepts. (I myself had a bit of contact with Eliot over some abortive reading of one of his works at a cellar theatre.) In 1945 Duncan had had a *succès d'estime* with *This Way to the Tomb!* at the Mercury Theatre, the original London home of Eliot's *Murder in the Cathedral.* He hadn't achieved anything else. Burned by the experience and disillusioned, he decided to activate theatre in Devon, where he lived. He allied himself with a group that included Benjamin Britten and the painter John Piper. It was the old dream of integrating all the arts. Duncan hoped that, like Auden with Stravinsky, he would be the Britten librettist, and he did write the libretto for *The Rape of Lucretia.* Beyond that he enlisted George Harewood, a member of the royal family, as a member of his board. (For a royal to espouse an artistic cause was almost as revolutionary as storming the Winter Palace, but George Harewood, mainly an opera devotee, has been one of the people who have radically changed the way the British establishment feels about the arts, and he has made innumerable contributions to British life.)

But the enterprise's efforts, though worthy and ambitious, were still in a backwater: Duncan realized that what was needed was more exposure and, above all, more financial backing.

Enter another character. Oscar Lewenstein and his wife were members of the Communist Party. (She, I suspect, was the more fanatical. She was also a dedicated potter, and a founder of *Ceramic Review*.) They had worked as labor organizers in Glasgow, linked with so-called workers' theatre. Oscar loved the theatre and, after the Northern movements he'd been involved with had fizzled out, came to London to earn his living in various kinds of theatrical management. I had met him a few years before when I tried to pick up the pieces of some projected London season Gavin Lambert had been involved in. One of the plays was Henri Montherlant's *The Town Where the Child Is King (La Ville dont le prince est un enfant)*— probably his best play. I went to see Oscar, who was running the Embassy Theatre in Hampstead, in the hope of staging it there. He told me he was so horrified by homosexuality, with which the play dealt, that he could never soil himself by having anything to do with anything which touched on the subject. After that Oscar had moved to the Court—then still a club—and became the manager for Alfred Esdaile. During his tenure there he distinguished himself with a presentation of *The Threepenny Opera*—the first time Brecht had been produced in England, I think. Oscar had met Ronald Duncan when he had taken one of Joan Littlewood's Theatre Workshop productions to Devon, and Duncan had invited him to join his board.

Enter now one of the most improbable characters in this story, something of a rogue elephant/black sheep of the Marks & Spencer family—his second wife, Elaine, being the daughter of Michael Marks, an eminently respectable Jewish pillar of the Establishment. Exactly who involved Neville Blond remains obscure—his only creative credit was a history of the rubber proofed clothing industry. Why he became involved is even more obscure—perhaps the family encouraged him as a distraction from its business. But involved he became, and as chairman, with the stipulation that Duncan's group must have a London showcase and, like any other store, a responsible manager. In this he showed remarkable insight. The group then cast about for a home and settled on the derelict Kingsway

Theatre, whose lease, like that of the Royal Court, was owned by Alfred Esdaile.

Duncan's group now had London premises, but they also needed someone with greater theatrical experience to run the company. Through his association with the Royal Court, Oscar Lewenstein knew about George's and my earlier scheme for the theatre, and he suggested George. George agreed to join them, on condition that I was also taken on, and the creation of the English Stage Company was announced.

Difficulties arose in renovating the Kingsway, and Esdaile offered the Royal Court as an alternative. George recommended accepting the offer, despite the repairs that the Court too would require, and so the marriage between the English Stage Company and the Royal Court Theatre came about.

All this happened not long after I'd come back from America, when I wasn't much established in television, and from being a principal in the initial scheme I was now an outsider. I was also regarded by some of George's circle as a fairly malevolent influence. But George stuck to his guns and invited me aboard.

We started work in earnest. The theatre was now strengthened architecturally. A permanent surround for the first season (dictated by a mixture of conviction and necessity) was in production with the Motleys. We couldn't get the rights to *Waiting for Godot*, but we did acquire Arthur Miller's *The Crucible*, and, against our real feelings but as the pound of flesh, we had to pay Ronald Duncan for the rights to two plays on the Don Juan theme, neither of which George and I liked. But at that point we had nothing else. I was looking at the work of every British writer of note. Angus Wilson had written a play for the first time, but it was promised to the Bristol Old Vic. I'd read a novel, *Cards of Identity*, by a brilliant comic satirist, Nigel Dennis, which I believed had dramatic possibilities, but we had no new British plays, which we had determined were the real point of our existence. It was the same weakness we'd had before. We drew up our credo. We took some ads and got as much free press coverage as we could. A few days later the first typescripts came in. Dipping into number five, George came up the stairs to my apartment. "They're all awful," he said, "but I think this one might have something. Look at it." I opened the script. It was *Look Back in Anger* by John Osborne. I started to read it. By the time I was through the first act I knew, whatever the battles to come, we'd win the war.

George read the play immediately afterward and responded as enthusiastically as I did—though we both knew the kind of opposition it would meet and the commercial risk it might be. John—then quite unknown—was living not far away, in Chiswick, on a barge in Cubitt's Yacht Basin. A meeting was set up, but the tidal river cut the boat off and George was forced to row himself out to the rickety barge. He returned fascinated but a little puzzled. I think he had hoped for someone more naively forthcoming but had sensed a hint of the truculence that was already there. No touching of the cap from that quarter.

I met John soon after. He was sharing the barge with Anthony Creighton, a bit-part actor with whom he'd been in repertory and with whom he had written *Epitaph for George Dillon*. They were living on the dole, in near penury. The barge was the cheapest accommodation they could find. It was narrow and smelly (from the stench of cabbages—they were both vegetarians at the time), and its gloom was relieved only by posters of Marlon Brando in the *Wild One* and *Julius Caesar* and other American muscled movie stars. All this made for instant speculation that they were homosexual lovers. This was never true—quite the opposite—but John was prepared to accept the care and attention that Anthony lavished on him, clucking and fussing like some mother hen with a large unpredictable chick whose beak was already sharp enough to stab. Despite his poverty, John had a real style—almost dandyism. Tall and lean, with crinkled, wavy hair, full lips and a broad face, with deep-set, almost Slavic eyes, he was sensual and fragile. We gradually became friends, but it was a long time before his guard and his mistrusts were overcome.

George and I both tried to get him to improve the play with rewrites, and John even tried—he was hungry for the production—but we soon learned that rewriting wasn't among John's formidable talents. What came out was what you got, and it was up to you to make the best of it. John had already written at least three other plays, a blank-verse tragedy, an American thriller with a McCarthyite setting, and *Epitaph* (which many thought for a long time to be his best play, as his own voice was muted and some of Anthony's sentiment was up front, though some scenes were pure Osborne and powerful). The season was quite a way off, and the Osborne-Creighton ménage continued unchanged during this period of my getting acquainted with them. I helped a bit, as I was doing more and more television and, if nothing else, could fit them in as extras, but the wolf was always at the door.

The work was mounting. We had not only to prepare a season but also to recruit staff, organize workshops, and prepare production facilities. At all of this George was superb. He had an innate respect for craftsmen of all kinds, a total understanding of their jobs (and an ability to do most of them). As we had so little money (we scratched around for grants and subsidies, but those were lean years when that kind of thinking wasn't familiar), they had to work for pittances, but work they did—slavishly, devotedly—all entirely due to George's leadership.

Among the recruits was someone who was to be hugely important in all our lives, and especially in George's. Jocelyn Herbert had been a member and an aficionado of the prewar London Theatre Studio. She was the daughter of (later Sir Alan) A. P. Herbert and his wife, Gwendolen. A. P. Herbert was a famous writer of musicals, children's books, and journalism from the 1920s on—and then a lively, eccentric MP representing one of the university constituencies (a sixteenth-century electoral anomaly). Jocelyn had married young, to a successful London lawyer, Anthony Lousada. She had had four children. During the war she devoted herself to cinema, but the pull of the theatre was always there and as the children were now in their teens, she became our scene-painter. There was another pull—George and she had always been attracted to each other. Until now they hadn't allowed themselves to fall in love— they were both too respectful of their other commitments—but the Royal Court brought them together and the inevitable happened, however guilty in some ways they felt. It was to be the relationship of both their lives, and one of the few that you could call miraculous.

Jocelyn lived near us at the time, in a comfortable house with Renoirs and Monets on the wall—all of which she gave up for George. I became friends with her during this period, and was more than half in love with her too. The Herberts also had a house in between, and at the far end of Chiswick Mall were the Redgraves. (My first sight of Vanessa was of a beanpole seventeen-year-old at a Christmas Eve midnight carol singing.) It was quite a district.

My own role was dealing with the scripts, with which we were now deluged. I covered at least a hundred a week. Quick reader that I am, I nevertheless had to evolve a method. This is it—it works about 99 percent of the time. Read the first page, the last page, and any page at random in the middle. That will tell you the quality of the writing—whether the script's worth reading at all. That's the first sorting out. Of those that survive you read the first act, rejecting as necessary, and so on. This method helps you quickly dispatch tragedies in rhyming couplets, melodramas from the 1890s, musical operettas from the 1920s, and suchlike, which all the world and your neighbor have had secreted in their back drawer for years. (Unfortunately it doesn't work in the same way with movie scripts, because even if they are badly written, they might have a fascinating story that would be worth considering.) There were quite a lot of unfortunate experiments from established writers, long ago rejected by commercial managements, that were unloaded on us. They required special diplomacy in rejections: George had to handle those! On top of these were the scripts of the board, and the scripts of the friends of the board.

George had no automatic authority: The board had to approve everything (no nonsense then about artistic direction). We were learning political realities. Ronald Duncan was already casting a malevolent eye on *Look Back*, but was mollified when George,—ever self-sacrificing—assured him he would direct his Don Juan plays himself. On top of the plays we'd already collected, we'd also acquired the right to Brecht's *The Good Woman of Setzuan*. Peggy Ashcroft—an old friend of George's, and one of the most generous and supportive figures in the initial struggles of every developing theatre—instantly agreed to do a play for us, but she wasn't free until the autumn, so *Good Woman* had to wait until then. But this gave her a seat on the board and us one secure and passionate ally.

We had decided to present our first season of plays in repertory. Repertory was, in fact, the first article of faith in all serious theatre at the time. It was one of the parts of our "statement" that George was most grafted to. It involved forming a company, most of whose members would perform in a majority of our five plays. This was an area in which George and I collaborated closely. Some members were easy to agree on; over the rest, we came, as they say, from different places. George tended to favor graduates of the Old Vic school, who I thought were lacking in personality and better in masks and mime than in creating contemporary characters. I preferred stronger personalities, even if a bit amateurish and deficient in technique and experience. I know George thought some of my choices, like Mary Ure, commercially motivated. Funnily enough, our biggest quarrel was over an Old Vic student whom I wanted to employ and George didn't—Joan Plowright. I thought she was perfect for Mary Warren in *The Crucible* and Miss Tray in *Cards of Identity*. She came back to audition and read several times. Finally George said, "Michael said Joan can never play queens." "I thought we were starting a theatre where we didn't want queens," I replied. Generous and understanding as always, George yielded. Joan became part of our company, along with Michael Gwynn, Rosalie Crutchley, Rachel Kempson, Kenneth Haigh, Mary Ure, Alan Bates, John Osborne, John Welsh, Sheila Ballantine, Christopher Fettes, and others. Special single appearances were to be made by Gwen Ffrangçon-Davies, Joan Greenwood, and Keith Michell. As most of the younger members of the company were unknown at the time, it wasn't a bad roster.

Meanwhile we launched a publicity campaign to try to get help with our season. As usual with anything new, the theatre journalists were superior and grudging. Both George and I wooed and lunched all the main critics, according to age and seniority. Ken Tynan, then with the *Observer*, was the flashiest and most fashionable of them all. We had our lunch. He was very sniffy. When I ran down our list of plays and got to *Look Back in Anger*, he sniffed, "That'll never do. It's just like *Cage Me a Peacock*. [This was a third-rate musical then running in the West End.] Tell the author to change it." Although he did write a rave review for the play when he saw it, Ken, like most of the other critics, never helped us in any way whatsoever. That he did was one of the many myths surrounding the Court: When the bandwagon was rolling, Ken above all tried to claim he had helped start it, but it wasn't true. We were trying to promote new work, even if it wasn't completely successful: "The right to fail" was our rallying cry. But few critics have ever been interested in investing in the future, only reflecting or condemning the immediate result. Ken's first article of faith—built into all British critics, and a big difference from the basic philosophy of American critics—was to entertain your readers at all costs. Grab them and damn the practitioners.

Our first production, Angus Wilson's *The Mulberry Bush*, was a compromise choice. It had been done at Bristol, but it was a new play by an important British writer—exactly the kind of writer we wanted to bring into the theatre. After the initial production, Angus had reworked it. George did a lovely and sensitive production, bringing all his humor and humanity to it, and Gwen Ffrangçon-Davies headed the cast—as a gesture to George. It wasn't particularly exciting, and by the time the play opened on April 2, 1956, we secretly knew Angus wasn't quite the English Chekhov we had hoped for, but it was okay. *The Crucible*, our second show, opening a week later, is a thrilling, noble piece of theatre. I had desperately wanted to direct it, but I was thought to be too untried and I acted as George's assistant—a role in which I contributed nothing. The production was solid but a bit passionless—I don't think George was ever really comfortable with American theatre. Again, it was either a draw or a scrape through on points. Next was *Look Back*— my first show.

Rehearsals were terse and a bit glum. I hadn't got a lot of personal confidence—only confidence in the play. Jimmy Porter was played by Kenneth Haigh, a gifted but self-indulgent star *manqué* whose moods and pouting shed a gloom that I wasn't experienced enough to dispel. But Mary Ure, Alan Bates, and Helena Hughes—an Irish actress playing Helena—were great. The play opened on May 8. The audience response was good, but the next day's notices were almost universally disastrous:

Look Back in Anger . . . sets up a wailing wall for the latest post-war generation of the under-thirties. It aims at being a despairing cry but achieves only the stature of a self-pitying snivel.
Milton Shulman, Evening Standard

Its total gesture is altogether inadequate . . . The piece consists largely of angry tirades.
The Times

Like one of Strindberg's women-haters, he [Jimmy Porter] ends in a kind of frenzied preaching in an empty conventicle . . . Numbness sets in.
Philip Hope-Wallace, Manchester Guardian

John and I sat in the little coffee shop adjoining the theatre and opposite the Sloane Square tube station, frozen in depression, with little belief in our futures. Then came the Sundays—the key British notices. Both Harold Hobson in the *Sunday Times* and Ken Tynan in the *Observer* gave it out-and-out raves. They helped the business, but they didn't have the instantaneous effect that notices have on Broadway. In England, *Look Back* was never a commercial success (another myth that needs dispelling): it didn't ever sell out at the Court. Some six months later we were going to do a three-week revival at the Lyric, Hammersmith—a theatre less prominent than the Court. I did a TV version of Act 2 that created enough interest to sell out those three weeks. On later revivals we did okay but not sensational business. No West End theatre would accept us, and no commercial management wanted to take us on even as partners. But what the two notices did was something more important: They made us the theatre of the moment, the place where it was happening, take it or leave it, love it or hate it. Ken Tynan wrote, "I doubt if I could love anyone who did not wish to see *Look Back in Anger*." So the theatre people came, sheeplike. And then, though most of them didn't like what they saw, they slunk back and took another look, thinking maybe this was what they'd better be part of. That, over a year, was to have many consequences. Binkie Beaumont, the most astute commercial manager of the time, summed it all up: "If you can take the trouble, that young man [J. O.] is going to make a lot of money. But I can't be bothered."

So often in the theatre, the advance calculations you make turn out to be disastrous. Though *Look Back* was our favorite, George and I had thought it our worst bet, so it was to be protected by opening our next show—*Don Juan* and *The Death of Satan*—a week later. George had done a wonderful production—delicate, inventive, imaginative. He had used (in accordance with our manifesto) the talented painter John Minton for his designer. John was something of a precursor of David Hockney, and he did a magnificent job. But nothing anyone could do could save the plays: They were total flops, and had to be taken off in a week or two (the one time the repertory idea protected us). Ronald Duncan quite unfairly blamed George and never forgave him. Even John Minton was destroyed by the experience. During the production, he'd fallen in love with Kevin Maybury, an Australian carpenter.

This led to growing unhappiness, and the next year he killed himself.

The fifth and last production was *Cards of Identity*. I directed. It was my idea to commission an adaptation of the brilliantly funny novel. If the gods were just and if ever any writer should have been a dramatist it was Nigel Dennis. The gods gave him the gift of wonderfully speakable, funny dialogue, brilliant conceptions, dazzlingly dramatic ideas for scenes—imagination that could cut loose and crazy. What the gods, alas, withheld was the ability to create characters whose development could take them beyond a facetious cartoon level. All this wasn't quite so evident at the time. The novel itself had been inspired by Ben Johnson's *The Alchemist*, which gave it a good core of a plot. If it did seem to peter out, well, maybe staging would fix it. And, along the way, what riches! In the novel, as well as the central *Alchemist* intrigue, there is a club where members read papers on their change of identities—eccentric British medievalist to Communist to whisky priest, etc. In the dramatization, these papers became stand-up comic monologues of fantastic brilliance. George's performance as Father Golden Orfe, the priest, was unbelievably brilliant too. The first act consists of the Jonsonian rogues taking over a deserted country house; these scenes were extraordinary too. It was one of those shows that everyone loved doing and whose audience laughed and enjoyed itself more than at many a more successful evening. The problem was that the high of the comedy was so high that it made the petering out of the characters in the last act all the more disappointing—in all his plays, Nigel was unable to come up with some intellectual coup that might have dazzled enough to cover up the lack of emotional reality. (I think finally he despised the theatre.) But it was fun. The reviews caught that, and the response was such that the score card showed a win on points.

George and I drew up our *bilan* of the first season. No out-and-out hits, but only one disaster. Three wins or draws on points, and another creating more and more reverberations—even worldwide. A theatre already recognized as like nothing anyone had seen in England for decades—a venue already attracting the attention of every new creative spirit. And even some sense of a different kind of actor—more physical, less dependent on the traditional skills of

verbal inflection, timing, and twirling cloaks, and without a so-
called gentleman's accent.

On the debit side, the idea of repertory had been dented. It is
too expensive, when you have no funds, to pay actors when they
are not performing. Also, a modern repertoire often required very
different kinds of skills—for example, to handle the difference between the Angus Wilson and the Nigel Dennis. And probably there
was an apprehension that a new author, with perhaps not a totally
successful work but one well worth presenting, would be the first
to claim martyrdom and blame failure on the repertory ideal. On
my part there was disillusion with our scenic ideals—the permanent
surround. And our resources were depleted; we needed to make
some money. In fact our jury was still out—both the public and,
more dangerously, the board. Onward . . .

7

Another Season

The first season at the Court had almost been an end in itself. Now we were faced with feeding an ongoing institution, with very little money—we had pathetically small subsidies from the Arts Council, Chelsea Borough Council, the neighboring Peter Jones department store, and the council members' initial investment—and with the constant strain that keeping a theatre open demands. What were the plays to do, and how long could we keep each one going? Six weeks was an ideal (it was also about as long as it was fair to ask actors to work at salaries well below their commercial value, and even below what most of the other subsidized theatres paid). But we knew that many plays couldn't support six weeks, and we tried to make as realistic a guess as we could. Then there were many scripts which were not strong enough in themselves but whose authors had exactly the promise we wanted to confirm and encourage by seeing their plays performed. "The right to fail" remained our rallying cry, and we solved the problem of the weaker scripts by inaugurating a series of "productions without decor" which we performed for a club membership on one or two Sunday nights. And we had great luck. On the heels of John Osborne emerged the talents of Arnold Wesker, John Arden, N. F. Simpson,

Ann Jellicoe, and Michael Hastings, and an original play was promised by Nigel Dennis.

We badly needed other directors too. Originally George and I had to do everything between us, and George, despite his gifts, didn't, I think, really like directing—he was more of an *homme du théâtre* in the French sense. I brought in William Gaskill from the Shipley Young Theatre and Lindsay Anderson from *Sight and Sound*. John Osborne introduced me to John Dexter from his old days in the Derby Rep, and later I found Anthony Page in New York. We still had a hard battle with the press, and our political problems with the board.

Our second season was to open with *The Good Woman of Setzuan* on October 31, 1956. There is no question that one example of seamless theatre, where writing, direction, decor, costumes, playing were totally integrated (the ideal of every theatre worker), was the Berliner Ensemble. There were, you may say, various reasons for this: They were dealing with the work of only one dramatist, and they had all the resources of a state behind them—limitless rehearsals, limitless money, a company untempted by other career possibilities. Nevertheless, to all of us who witnessed the range and brilliance of their shows, the achievement seemed monumental, and to witness those productions was indispensable for any serious theatre practioner. The echoes of them—especially in design and staging in England, in opera, and, to some extent, in America—have reverberated ever since. Salute! Then the reservations.

Brecht is one of the two great revolutionary dramatists of the mid-century—the other being Beckett. Revolutionary artists create an air of unease and awkwardness about them. No one quite knows how to approach them—especially when theory, as in the case of Brecht, or mysticism, as in the case of Beckett, intervenes. But plays, like children, have a life of their own, and if their creators try to control their development, they risk sooner or later producing the sterility of the D'Oyly Carte versions of Gilbert and Sullivan, the frozen production of *Peter Pan* or the Moscow Art's Chekhovs. It is even worse when a theatre has a swarm of proselytizers who believe, like Jesuits, not only that theirs is the only right way, but that Brecht's genius as a writer didn't exist outside of and without their theatre. This is what happened with the Berliner Ensemble.

They sent their gurus, their stars, their designers, their musicians scurrying over the world as relentlessly as Laura Ashley milked the V & A of its fabric designs.

With his natural humility, his lack of ego, George was a perfect prey for this nonsense. The set for *The Good Woman* was by Teo Otto, an Ensemble designer, the music by Paul Dassau, and the great Helene Weigel herself paid an advisory visit. All George's humor and theatricality disappeared as this drab, hopeless copy of an Ensemble production appeared. The play itself is difficult—moments of lyricism alternating with sardonic comedy, intellectual rigor combined with a frame of fable. (I've only seen a successful production once—by Andrei Serban at La Mama, in New York. He used a pile of giant spillikins to form the decor.) Peggy Ashcroft was too romantic and personal an actress to be at home in the role of Shen Te, which alternates between woman and man. It's a role that would suit Vanessa—you have to be able to step swiftly and with perfect definition from one side of a personality to another. The rest of the cast varied widely, from eccentric camp to fake macho. A remnant of the original company remained—notably Miss Plowright and Mr. Osborne, giggling on the floor together as they pretended to be starving Chinese peasants. Luckily Peggy's following protected us financially, and we were proud to have attempted to do Brecht.

One of George's greatest talents as a director was his work with period comedy. Part of our original policy was to revive lesser-known classics, and we needed a success. I thought Wycherley's *The Country Wife* was perfect for Joan: It's a surefire audience success if you have the right Mrs. Pinchwife and the right director. (I'd done a production myself earlier at Stratford East: I hadn't and wasn't.) I finally persuaded George. He did it beautifully, in a black and white setting. Joan was delicious, and the production, which opened a couple of weeks before Christmas, was our first commercial hit, transferring later to the West End. It even had a further life—Laurence Harvey, who played Homer and was adequate but no more, got it transferred to Broadway the following November. Julie Harris, a wonderful actress, replaced Joan in New York, but she wasn't at all right for Restoration comedy and, with its linchpin and key to its success removed, the production limped along for only a few weeks.

Of the various plays I directed at the time, my favorite by far was Carson McCullers's *The Member of the Wedding*, in February 1957. (I'd now been cast as doing all the American plays.) In fact I think I loved *Member* as I've loved no other play ever. Geraldine McEwan played Frankie, and Bertice Reading played Berenice Sadie Brown—the role originally created by Ethel Waters. As we had a forestage bringing the actors very close to the audience, I'd insisted on having a contact lens made to meet Miss McCullers's description of Berenice's one blue and one brown eye. Contact lenses were just coming in, and the cost of the lens was just about equal to the cost of the rest of our budget for scenery and costumes. Bertice lost it at the dress rehearsal. Even if we'd had the money, it was too late to get another made, so her eyes ended up the same color. No one from the fourth row back could have told the difference anyway.

Our second season also had a new play by John Osborne. There is a great myth in the theatre that playwrights write plays for actors. It's not true, although at some time in the course of creating a play they may, of course, get an idea for casting a role, and the chosen actor or actress is then only too pleased to claim to have "inspirated" the finished work. John had started writing *The Entertainer* early in 1956—before *Look Back* had even been premiered. With its music-hall setting, it came out of his childhood and his greatest passions. He'd nearly finished Act 1 when Arthur Miller, one of the strongest supporters of the Court, brought Laurence Olivier to see *Look Back*. Olivier didn't like what he saw.

For more than a decade before 1956, Laurence Olivier—"Larry"—was the undisputed king of the British theatre. He had eclipsed all his earlier rivals; he was an international star in movies as well as in theatre; he was an acclaimed director; he had his own theatre, the St. James, and a powerful producing company. And his consort, albeit an uneasy one, was the stunning Vivien Leigh—easily one of the most beautiful women ever. Together they presided over Notley Abbey, a big country retreat where they could indulge in entertaining with the kind of grandeur and snobbery to which all British actors of the time aspired.

Under the surface it was another story. At heart Larry was what the French call a *cabotin*. The term is difficult to translate—not exactly a ham: a performer, a vulgarian, someone who lives and dies for acting. The grand seigneur was one of the roles he played, but at heart it was foreign to him. And at heart too he knew—or perhaps he didn't know at the time—that his attempt to transform Vivien into a great classical actress was a failure. Vivien was a great star. She loved being a star. But acting as such she didn't really enjoy—although, under Larry's tutelage, she performed with great professionalism and an immaculate manner. She was also a manic-depressive, a condition that was worsened and intensified by Larry's pressure on her to be what she couldn't be. She had already had some mild outbreaks and public affairs, but her charm was such that she could always flick her elegant, fascinating whip and Larry would return, her slave. But he was restless, and part of him knew that his work—as in his Festival of Britain season, when he performed the two Cleopatras (Shaw's and Shakespeare's) with Vivien—had reached an artistic stalemate.

It was in this mood that he had come to see *Look Back*. Although he had not liked it, the whiff of something new and exciting had stayed with him, instinctive showman that he is, and he came back—I think encouraged by George's old friend and partner Glen Byam Shaw, then the director of the Shakespeare Memorial Theatre. On the second visit Olivier met John. Maybe he met me as well. Anyway, from his great height, he suggested John should write something for him. George told him of the half-finished *Entertainer*. Larry became passionately eager to see it. He was finally shown one of two acts. The character of Archie Rice, which tapped into aspects of Larry's personality that he'd never used, immediately obsessed him. He accepted the play before it was even finished. He accepted me as a director, and for the Court to have the king join us on our terms was a great triumph.

However, politically, inside the Court, the reaction was different. George's and my choice of plays and policy was still subject to approval by our peculiar and disparate board. When we presented what we thought of as our great coup, the response was unbelievable. The majority of the board, including our supposed ally Oscar Lewenstein, voted against having Olivier in the theatre and against doing the play. The event which would not only confirm our achievement but was potentially our most lucrative success was rejected. George Harewood went to work. He explained to Neville Blond—who didn't understand anything of the jealousies, envies, and resentments so typical of British theatre and of British life generally—what was being rejected. Neville knocked heads together, threatened to withdraw his support, and finally enough of the truculent board—there were to the end several holdouts—were cowed into reversing their vote.

Larry was another problem. In the second act it became clear that Archie's pathetic wife, Phoebe, was a wonderful role. Larry, with the zeal of a convert, wanted it for Vivien. He was determined she should play something for which she was hopefully unsuited—not least because of her looks. These, he explained to John and me in the elegant drawing room of the suite in the Hotel Connaught where they were living while their new home was being decorated, would be no problem: Vivien would play Phoebe in a rubber mask, with appropriate warts and wrinkles. It took several meetings—and probably Vivien's innate sense of self-preservation—before the idea was dropped.

Rehearsals were something else. The cast included Brenda de Banzie, George Relph, Richard Pasco, and Dorothy Tutin, with whom Larry had had an affair during Peter Brook's 1953 movie *The Beggar's Opera* and who was still in love with him. It was my first direction of a major star. If I had had any nervousness, I needn't have: Larry, once he began to work, was a total joy. His understanding of Archie was so complete that he could make anything work. He infected everyone with his enthusiasm. At last, after all the regal years, he'd cast off his mantle, been let out of school, and he capered and preened as the hoofer he really was.

With one exception. At the end of Act 2, Archie—broken, drunk, beaten down—remembers as his one glimpse of glory a black blues singer with whom he had worked in a vaudeville bill, and he pathetically imitates her act before collapsing totally. The singer was John's conception of Bessie Smith. Larry didn't know anything of Bessie Smith, claimed he couldn't understand the moment, and evaded it in rehearsals. Act 1 also ends, for Archie, in a kind of collapse. He is talking late at night to his daughter Jean, whom he has just rediscovered. He is keeping up his usual jokes, obscenities, patter, but underneath his thoughts are with his son, sent to Suez in 1956. Suddenly the emotion boils up. He breaks down in tears, revealing his own vulnerability and bringing Jean, for the first time, to an understanding of her father. It was understated, quiet—you could call it Chekhovian. Larry played it beautifully and loved it. He wanted to end Act 2 with a similar effect. Apart from this being obviously repetitious, however, Act 2 called for something much more extreme, more openly theatrical, more original. But like some great athlete saving himself before a major event, Larry ducked the moment, stopped before the leap, excused himself, apologized.

By now the rest of his performance was in shape, including his tap dances, songs, hoofing. His grasp of the character was complete, but we still had no Act 2 curtain. We got to the last run-through before the dress rehearsal and technical. This is often when you see a play at its finest—its essence untrammeled by sets and costumes. Before the run-through, I tackled Larry once more about Act 2. He started to talk about Act 1 again. "It's no good, Larry." He stopped. "All right," he said, "describe exactly what you want me to do and I'll try to do it at the run-through. Exactly!" It's not the way I liked to work as a director, but there was no other choice. I roughed out an idea—stagger over to the proscenium, try to sing a blues phrase, fail, slide down the proscenium, then stagger over to a ladder at center stage, collapse, and the curtain to fall. "Okay," he said.

The run-through was going well. In Act 2 George Relph, who played Billie Rice, Archie's father, was sitting next to me. George had been associated with Larry often throughout his career. He was a great gentleman, almost Edwardian in manner, and a wonderfully subtle actor. Act 2 was coming to an end. Larry started lurching toward the proscenium, and extraordinary sounds poured out of him, seeming to come from his gut—strange wailing notes cutting through sobs and gasps perfectly evoking the singer whom he had never heard, and yet keeping it within the hopelessness and shabbiness of Archie's own existence. It was devastating. If performance art ever touches greatness, this was it. George looked at me. "It was just like that when he discovered his great cry as he blinds himself offstage in *Oedipus*, and his 'God for Harry, England and Saint *Geoooorge*' in *Henry V*. That's why he's a genius." No one else spoke for minutes—nor did Larry. He knew he'd made it: The flag had been planted on Everest. It was the most thrilling single moment I've ever had in the theatre.

But it wasn't quite as simple as that. The next time he would

get a run at the play was after the technicals, at the first dress
rehearsal, with an audience and Vivien. Larry was very nervous.
At the end of Act 1 Vivien went around to his dressing room, full
of excitement and praise. Act 2 came; Larry played the end okay,
but not as fully as before. Again Vivien went round. The dressing
room was full of people. "You disgust me," she said. "You see
Brenda de Banzie's going to get all the notices with her cake scene,
so you try to steal them back again with your cheap King Lear
tricks." She swept out. It was a knockout punch. The next two
days he couldn't play the moment: He walked through it, but he
knew he was walking through it. On the day of the first night,
April 10, 1957, he said, "You've got to help me. Send everyone
away and give me a count." "What do you mean?" "A count."
"Larry, you're being silly." "No, I mean it—five—eight—whatever
you like. How long at the pros and then how long back before the
fade and the curtain. Then I've got something specific to hang on
to." So I did: It was planned as precisely as if it had been chore-
ography with a musical beat. It worked. Larry once told me afterward that, in all the times he played *The Entertainer*, after the initial
run-through he only twice played this moment fully. But Larry's
technique is so prodigious (and his genius in discovering the moment) that it fooled—fooled is too pejorative: it astounded—most
of the audience most of the time. Much later, when we were about
to start filming the play, Larry said to me, "Darling heart, let me
give you a tip about directing a movie. Time every page and every
scene before we start. Write it down on your script. Then, when
we're rehearsing or shooting, tell us, 'Darlings, you've got to take
four or six seconds off this.' Otherwise it'll be our timing, not
yours." I may not have said, "I don't work like that, Larry," but I
knew that in our approach we were planets apart.

The notices were ecstatic, and Archie Rice became one of Larry's
definitive performances, when, with more than a great actor's skill
in creating a character, he transcended himself and, as with Henry
V, became the embodiment of a national mood. *Henry V* had been
made during the last great moment of heroism for the British:
Archie was the future, the decline, the sourness, the ashes of old
glory, where Britain was heading. And it was this ability to transcend himself, vouchsafed to fine performers whatever their sphere
of greatness, that set Larry above all his peers.

But beside Larry the lad, the charmer, the humble member of the company, was another side. Act 3 of the play opened with a blues song, sung by Frank, Archie Rice's second son. It was an indication of post-Suez blues and depression. There were also, from the younger members of the family, a number of lines, mild in themselves—"a gloved hand waving from a golden coach"—which were thought by some to be subversive or unpatriotic. Two days after the opening we had a pre-performance meeting to check on various details. Out of the blue, Larry launched an attack. "What about the cuts?" "What cuts?" "That terrible song—I can feel the audience dying—not your fault, dear boy [this to Richard Pasco, who sang the song]—and all that anti-Queen shit. The audience freezes. It's disloyal. You and John have had your notices, now we've got to do the fucking thing and they're getting in the way." It was the first time Larry and I had had any real open difference, and his vitriol shocked and hurt me. I replied, probably a bit pompously, that we hadn't founded the Court to sacrifice authors on the altars of stars, even one as great as Larry, nor did we exist to try to change a writer's political commitment. So the clash ended for the moment. But when we were going to revive the play commercially (its initial run at the Court was six weeks), Larry made it a part of his contract that these cuts were imposed. They didn't make that much difference to the play, but Larry felt he'd bravely defended the Queen.

The play went on from glory to glory. It played six months at the Palace in London, and a further six months on Broadway—a total sell-out. New York managements had fought to get it. I had been wined, dined, taken to the most fashionable first nights, and threatened with never being able to work again in New York if I didn't push the production the right way. We stayed with David Merrick, who had stuck his neck out by taking *Look Back* for production in New York later that year, and after it opened on Broadway in February 1958 he had a field day by cooking up minor feuds with Larry about matters as trivial as repainting a dressing room before the run ended (fighting has always been one of David's great pleasures).

Among the other productions in our second season were Nigel Dennis's new play, the *Making of Moo*, in June 1957, which George, John Osborne, and Joan Plowright played in. It was an amusing

enough idea—the founding of a new religion in a colonial setting—
but it remained just that: an idea, an extended skit that, composed
today, would be better played on *Saturday Night Live*. The dialogue
again had great style and elegance, and it brought George and Nigel
closer together. In fact, Nigel and later Samuel Beckett were the
only writers with whom George felt at home. I'd wanted George
to direct the play, but he preferred to perform in it.

Earlier, in May, Ionesco's *The Chairs* was the intellectual play.
Joan and George acted together with great success, and the climax—
the stage filled with chairs for a lecture with a nonexistent audience—was phenomenal theatre. Joan and I did the show again in
New York, with Eli Wallach, early in 1958, and then later that year
we re-revived it in London. Underneath all the surface brilliance
of the Romanian playwright there is a brooding poetic sadness that
gives his plays a resonance that Nigel, alas, never achieved.

In the summer of 1957 there was to be a big youth festival in
Moscow. Owing mainly, I think, to the promotion of Oscar Lewenstein, we were invited to present *Look Back* at the Moscow Arts
Theatre. The designer, Alan Tagg, couldn't come with us, so Margaret "Percy" Harris, of Motley, came to supervise the reproduction
of our set in the Arts Theatre's workshops. She and I, accompanied
by John and Oscar, went ahead to prepare. It led to a series of
clashes.

We imagined, or Oscar imagined, that we were being invited as
Honored Artists; however, we were dumped in a summer camp
outside the city—half tent city, half abandoned institutional buildings with shared bathrooms and camp food. Although we were
supposed to have cars allocated to us, it was exceedingly difficult
to get transport into the city for our work at the theatre. Even
worse, being non-Communists, we were ostracized by the main
British delegation, of which neither they nor we considered ourselves part. I even interrupted some parade ceremony by storming
up to the leader of the British Red delegation and threatening that
if we didn't have a car immediately we would cancel the upcoming
performances and announce that he was to blame. The tactic
worked. Meanwhile, as only a Party member could, Oscar dragged
us to meeting after meeting with the Russian authorities in Moscow
to complain about our treatment. They received us with absolute

disdain. Oscar's sense of injustice became so violent that we couldn't spend a moment without listening to his invective about bathroom conditions. I had been long reconciled to them and, being an inveterate traveler, suggested that we put up with what we couldn't change and enjoy Moscow while we could.

But, as often with inefficient bureaucracy, something had gone into the pipeline and one day, after our protests had stopped, long black limousines swept us away from the camp and the British Reds, and we were installed in huge, hideous suites in a vast old hotel, now the newest tourist center, called the Stalinskaya. The company arrived the next day.

John and Oscar had to return to London, so, once the performances were on, Percy and I spent our evenings in Moscow alone. It was extraordinary—half *Alice in Wonderland*, half Kafka. The hotel had a huge restaurant—marble-floored, pillared, with a ten-piece string orchestra and a Tolstoyan giant of a doorman, with a three-foot-long beard and a great topcoat with gold buttons, who bowed to you as you entered. The menu was the biggest and most tantalizing I've ever seen; printed in five or six languages, it was as thick as a volume of the *Encyclopaedia Britannica*. It listed delicacies like Siberian ptarmigan and Azerbaijanian sturgeon, Arctic chamois and Caucasian lobsters. But whatever you ordered you always got the same thing—some watery cabbage soup and an unidentifiable breaded cutlet. It also took hours to order. Tiring of the orchestra, who repeated endlessly such international repertoire as *The Blue Danube*, to get any service we used to have to pick up the plates on the table and literally smash them on the marble floor. The maitre d' never protested at our behavior—they got on with the service.

But we were luckier than the company. The canteen at the Moscow Arts closed early, and all you could get was a bit of salty red caviar on dry bread. There were no restaurants, and in the Stalinskaya there was only a miniscule kitchen for room service for the whole enormous establishment. This was on my floor, so the company piled into my suite and conducted hourly raids on the kitchen, demanding food and drink. All there was was eggs and sausages, tea, or beer. On alternate nights an ancient slobberchops maid was on duty who, left over from an ancient regime, spoke a little French, which made communication a bit easier. Even so, they never got anything until three or four in the morning. Once, the company having long drifted back to their own rooms, I was woken up at half past nine with eggs for twelve ordered at eleven o'clock the night before.

Theatre tickets (for Percy and me) were the same hazardous problem. You never knew what you'd get. Once, when we succeeded in getting standing-room places, during the first act I spotted that the central principal loge in the first tier was empty. In the intermission we marched up to it, waved imperiously at the babushkaed attendant, and shouted in English. She unlocked the box. We went in and had the chairman's seats in the resplendent theatre. Just after Act 2 had begun, the door again opened and a whole African delegation in wonderful glistening robes trooped in. We remained in our seats in front of them and we were never questioned.

Our own performances were a wild success. It was thrilling for us to be performing in the Moscow Arts and to see that famous curtain with the seagull embroidered on it open for our play. The staff were superb: Not only did they reproduce our set beautifully, but they learned the show—which, though seemingly simple, had many light and sound cues and a lot of property changes—in a single rehearsal, and all without either side speaking a word of the other's language. People fought for tickets outside. I don't quite know why: The play must have been incomprehensible to most of the audience—and inaudible too, as those who did pretend to speak English kept up a running commentary that drowned out all the sounds coming from the stage.

Our relationship with our interpreters was fascinating, making one aware what a gulf of values lay between our two cultures. They would take us on tours of the city. We would always want to stop at the old wooden cottages, which, with golden sunflowers outside, seemed straight out of Gogol and Tolstoy. These were all naturally scheduled to be obliterated. As we raved about their charm, our interpreters took it to be gleeful cataloging of the backwardness of Russia; when they showed us hideous concrete blocks of new workers' flats, our lack of enthusiasm was a willful denigration of Soviet accomplishment. Our favorite place was Gorky Park, where we could see people walking, playing, and relaxing naturally—this was our capitalist taste for frivolity. There was a little Czech pavilion there which sold beans and frankfurters (restaurants for tourists were nonexistent at the time), and we insisted on going back again and again. One day the attendant was very clearly a gay queen, covered with rings and jewels. Our interpreter that day was a very serious young man. We tried to find out what he thought of the bartender. We skirted the subject. "Isn't he bizarre?" "He seems a bit effeminate." Finally Miriam, our secretary, came out with, "Is he a homosexual?" Our interpreter went blood red. He stammered, "In our country we do not talk of these things . . . but we may *suspect*." Our own moment of real triumph was with our other interpreter, a bossy twenty-four-year-old girl who was particularly censorious of us. On the day of our departure she suddenly appeared with lipstick (that unspeakable vice) and even a dab of rouge. It wasn't going to boost Revlon in Moscow, but we had scored at least that for our side and we burst into tears as we hugged each other good-bye and wished each other *mir i druzhba*.

Apart from George, John, and Jocelyn, Mary Ure and Joan Plowright had been my closest friends inside the original company. I'd forced both of them in, and I worked with them continually. I'd first seen Mary in Peter Brook's 1955 production of *Hamlet*. In her harsh, strident mad scenes, she was the first Ophelia who seemed really deranged and therefore believable. She was very beautiful, with thick blond hair and sensual lips and body. She looked the perfect romantic actress, but there was a toughness, a Scottishness, a lack of musicality, that didn't quite match up to her image. I had always been attracted to her but was never confident enough to pursue her. She was a strong performer who easily slid into a note of harshness, and she was a "star" who, like Vivien, I don't think deep, deep down really felt comfortable with acting. She liked the excitement of it, could deal with crude raw emotion, looked a dream, but I think she was carried more by the surface than by the center. George always thought she was a bit of an amateur; I thought it was something more complex—perhaps a kind of Presbyterian disapproval of performance itself.

Soon after the opening of *Look Back* she hooked up with John. They were married in July 1957. Again, I never felt she loved John or knew who he really was: It was the excitement of having caged the original "angry young man" (a journalistic label we all detested). She was loyal, passionate, and fun. She had a great sense of style. She laughed a lot, yet she hadn't much humor.

*   *   *

The next stop of the *Look Back* progress was America. David Merrick, then at the beginning of his ascent on being Mr. Broadway, had negotiated bringing it over intact. (At the time, American Equity was wonderfully generous and welcoming to British performers; it was only later, when British Equity refused any kind of reciprocity, that the situation became more and more grudging and difficult and the Americans were forced to retaliate.) The rehearsals—short, as the original cast had been reassembled—were rather funny. The atmosphere was slightly like the morning after a party where everyone knew they'd behaved badly the night before and so were now on their most proper behavior.

We moved to New York, into the Lyceum. We didn't have many hopes for the play. We did a couple of previews; then, on October 1, the first night. There wasn't much response, and the applause was tepid. Nobody came around or said anything. We were taken to Sardi's, seated at a table, offered one drink each. Food was clearly not to be asked for. We all felt as though we were carrying some unnameable, unspeakable social disease. David looked more and more anxious and on edge. We heard murmurs like, "Four pairs of orchestra for the first two paras." We'd no idea what this meant—the press agent was negotiating with typesetters for an advance on the notices. Then the first paragraph of *The New York Times* came through. Menus were produced. We were invited to order. We were a hit.

Of the many things around which Manhattan revolves, theatre is one of the most important. And to have success there for the first time is like no success you will ever have again: The whole town celebrates with you. Success is palpable and instant, with none of the backbiting and grudgery you always find in the UK. Everyone you meet knows you're a success—even people you don't know know you and love you.

How the show would hold up was another question. A few nights after, John and I dropped into the Lyceum. Kenneth Haigh was not only not performing but was totally inaudible and cutting some of the most brilliant monologues in John's play. I called the cast on stage for notes. As I attacked Ken, his only response was to gesture toward Mary and Alan. "Why do you always pick on me? Why don't you blame *them*?" They were giving impeccable performances against a hole in the center. "Why were you cutting those speeches?" "I couldn't reach them tonight. Do you want me to give the audience *lies*?" "The answer is yes—I want 'To be or not to be,' whether the Hamlet feels it or not."

David Merrick was a master promoter. Within weeks he hired a girl—a feminist before her time and, as such, supposedly outraged by Jimmy Porter's attitudes to women—to climb onto the stage during a performance and belt Ken Haigh in the face. It was all conveniently timed for the next day's headlines—and a subsequent controversy as to whether the gesture had been plotted or was spontaneous. David wouldn't admit it at the time even to us, but with stunts like these he established the play for a year on Broadway and afterward a year's tour.

8

A Little Touch of Harry

A new character enters the story. Canadian by citizenship, he came from managing Continental circuses and spoke at least French very well. During the Second World War he had been attached to the Supply Depot of the Royal Canadian Air Force and had, it was alleged, been involved in various scams, including smuggling juke-boxes—then impossible to get—inside crates of Red Cross bandages for sale in Europe. He had managed to escape the rap and was now based in New York, supposedly working in theatre and film. It was in New York that George and John met Harry Saltzman.

George and John had been enjoying that first wild, sweet fling of success, which is wilder and sweeter in New York than in any-place else in the world. George was now rehearsing *The Country Wife;* John was enjoying the fruits of *Look Back.* They were being lionized, feted, courted, but of all their suitors none was so assid-uous as Harry. I'd gone back to London to man the boat, and letters and phone calls began to arrive depicting this mystery mogul, this Maecenas who was showing them the town: Thelonious Monk at the Five-Spot, Birdland, the Apollo—Wednesday amateur nights at the Apollo being the caviar of the feast. Then there were hints and propositions for some kind of business relationship. This, ac-cording to George, would provide the steady income the Court needed. We would be protected, assured, safe. When they returned they were full of enthusiasm for the plans—and for Harry, who'd given them such a wonderful time. I was to return to New York to continue working on the details of the scheme.

I think Harry picked me up at the airport in a limo, or he may have sent a limo and I met him just afterward. He had a perfect mogul's figure—stocky, tubby—crinkly gray hair, and the face of an eager, coarse cherub. He bubbled with plans, and he had great charm. He was a splendid raconteur. By his generosity in big and in small things—he always loved to give—he radiated affluence. He was living in a vast apartment in Alwyn Court, at Seventh and Fifty-eighth. It was dark and dingy, with dark green walls and shag carpets, and looked as if it had seen neither daylight nor cleaning. There was an old Latino crone who baked in some hidden kitchen. But Harry had let several of the kids from our shows stay there—including Mary and, I think, Bob Stephens, who was in *Country Wife*—and now I moved in. It was all great fun, especially since you never knew who'd walk in next—all the world had keys, and often you'd be woken, at any hour of the day or night, by a couple walking in and the guy sheepishly mumbling, "Sorry, I didn't know this was occupied."

What Harry was able to exude in abundance was potential. You always knew he would somehow, somewhere, discover the magic carpet that would transport you to riches. His schemes veered wildly. He'd come back from Paris and have sat on the plane next to someone with whom he was going to market penicillin; or he'd arrive laden in London with special products you could get only at the American military stores. One of the denizens of the Alwyn Court apartment told a story of being woken by Harry at four one morning and ordered to get a map of greater New York. "What the hell for, Harry?" "Do you want to make big money or not?" So dutifully he trots out. When he produces the map, Harry lays it out on the floor and draws a great ring around all the communities within easy commuting distance of Manhattan. Harry: "Now, what do all these guys want? Want most?" "How the hell do I know, Harry?" "Blue Chip stamps." "Blue Chip stamps?" "So we'll give 'em Blue Chip stamps for theatre tickets. We'll control Broadway. We'll buy the theatres. No one else'll get a show on without our Blue Chip stamps!" And the fantasy began, and Harry's energy could carry you along with it. Never mind if it was digestive biscuits tomorrow; sooner or later you knew Harry would hit the jackpot—as he did, finally, with the James Bond movies.

What we didn't know was that Harry hadn't a bean. He was—though the word wasn't in vogue then—a hustler, but a sublime hustler. And I don't mean the word pejoratively. The more I worked on the Royal Court partnership, the less there seemed to be any substance or subsidy in it—inexplicably, of course, for we were all very naive. More and more it just seemed like creating a company which got a free option on any of the Court shows—something we had neither the wish, the right, nor the authority to do. Eventually the scheme dwindled to creating another company—to do shows in the USA—but with no greater involvement than any other company and no money. So it all fizzled out, and George himself, although he still liked Harry and was often charmed by him, realized he'd been led up the garden path. But out of all these negotiations, and out of the contact with Harry, I'd sensed another possibility: to push Harry's energies into an area which he claimed to have knowledge of (I'm now not sure that he did)—making a movie of *Look Back*.

I had wanted to film *Look Back* from the first, but the prospects were negative. The British industry was smug, very closed, and very opposed to new directors. After the success of the play, especially in New York, there had been a certain amount of sniffing around the film rights. Dirk Bogarde, then a popular British star, had supposedly been interested. But it was clear that any production by an established British studio would emasculate the play; and from the studios' point of view emasculating *Look Back* seemed more of a problem then they originally thought. John, loyally, stuck with me in every way he could. Finally we got Richard Burton (the pre-Elizabethan Burton) interested in Jimmy Porter, and Harry persuaded Warner Brothers to finance the movie. To do it, we formed a company. We called it "Woodfall." John and Mary Ure had rented a little house on Woodfall Street, Chelsea. As we hadn't a name, we just looked out the window, saw the sign, and christened our enterprise.

Harry moved to London. He rented a house in the fashionable part of Chelsea—Lowdnes Cottage. This belonged to the composer William Walton and had, oddly enough, previously been rented to

Larry and Vivien Leigh. Harry immediately installed a mini-empire. Secretaries, chauffeurs, multilingual cooks arrived from wherever; international hookers rotated in the guest rooms. I moved in too. Harry was always very solicitous, even down to the thermos of cocktail which he had prepared for my drive in a limo to each day's shooting. We gave parties and dinners. Hollywood stars like Kirk Douglas and Burt Lancaster, producers like Charley Feldman, were often guests. It was a heady, crazy world. We never questioned it—how it happened; who paid—Harry was totally in charge of the business side. Anyway, it was all part of the magic of movies, and all our friends were sharing it. It was great fun. Harry created a wonderful atmosphere, and I—and John too—enjoyed every minute of it.

The filming itself, in the autumn of 1958, went well and smoothly. My main collaborators were the experienced cameraman Oswald Morris and an extraordinary art director, Ralph Brinton—a former naval commander—with whom I was to work again and again. Ozzie is an extraordinary craftsman of cinema—very painstaking, very thorough, and very dedicated. He took me in hand, taught me an enormous amount, and kept me constantly up to scratch. The director-cameraman relationship is probably the most crucial in any production, and I was extremely lucky to be able to work with someone as meticulous as he was: It was like being brought to the state of the art at the time—all in eight weeks.

John reworked the play a little, adding a few extra characters—notably Ma Tanner, played by that great, great actress, Edith Evans—and letting us see Jimmy's market stall. The end was played in an atmospheric railway station (an homage to *Brief Encounter* and *Quai des brumes*), but the core of it remained as it should have done—a filmed play. But I was already chafing at the bit to do something freer and more liberated than something created for the theatre. Once material and characters have been poured into that mold, it's very difficult to free them for re-creation in another medium. I never look at my old movies—once done, they're over; the faults can't be changed, the achievements are what they are, so there has never seemed any point to me—but I'm sure *Look Back* remains in the category of that hybrid, the filmed play. I've always thought it one of my greatest weaknesses as a director that I loved writing too much and respected it too much.

John and I took a cut of the movie out to Hollywood (another of the perks Harry arranged) to show it to Jack Warner. He was completely gaga—pretended he'd seen it but probably hadn't. Afterward Harry whisked us to Las Vegas. We were comped at some hotel and comped also with one gargantuan hooker between the two of us (Harry disappearing with someone much more attractive). Each tried to unload the poor girl on the other till, not succeeding, we made a quick escape together when she momentarily disappeared into the ladies room. It was all part of Harry's magic carpet.

The reception of *Look Back* was respectable, but not overwhelming. For an "art-house" film it was quite expensive, and it was a long time recouping the investment in it. John got a little money for the rights, I think, but neither of us got more than a pittance for the script and direction. Still, we'd had all our high living at Lowdnes Cottage, which what might have been our fees had obviously funded.

Back at the Court, in May 1958, we staged a fascinating play by a West Indian, Barry Reckord. Clumsy in its construction, *Flesh to a Tiger* had at moments a passion of language which was extraordinary, especially in its evocation of the brutalities of slavery. It was a first, and a first too for the principal actress, Cleo Laine, who later married the jazz-band leader Johnny Dankworth and went on to a brilliant singing career. At the time there were very few trained or talented black actors in England, and the cast I assembled had a wild variety of accents, ranging from Trinidad to Brooklyn. When we were rehearsing or improvising—especially improvising—there was a life and spontaneity in their performances which, maddeningly, I was never able to recreate on stage. The play itself intimidated the cast and they became stiff, awkward, and, with a few exceptions, amateurish, but the attempt to make it work was wonderfully worthwhile.

During the first two years at the Court I hadn't done any classics, though they were still a great love. I was thrilled, then, when Glen Byam Shaw, part of the original Old Vic triumvirate with Michel Saint-Denis and George, and now director of the Shakespeare Memorial Theatre, asked me to do a play there in 1958. Unlike the lugubrious Saint-Denis, Glen was a great charmer, with a crazy, almost lecherous passion and a wild, gleeful humor. I adored him and loved working for him, as did everyone around him.

The play was to be *Pericles*. One of the late plays, it's not often performed. Some scholars have even questioned whether it's all by Shakespeare. I think they're wrong. It was written when Shakespeare himself had fallen out of fashion and the theatres had moved indoors, where, in a court atmosphere, emphasis was on scenery and effects—the great days of Inigo Jones. On one level it's a comic-strip adventure fable (almost a *Raiders of the Lost Ark* or *Romancing the Stone*) but underlying this are all the great themes of the "late" plays—wanderings and loss, innocence and reconciliation, music and the sea—and they're what transforms cartoon to poetry. In the 1958 season, headed by Dorothy Tutin and Michael Redgrave, it was planned as a showcase for the younger members of the company—and for a new director.

I had been working with the designer Loudon Sainthill, a gentle Australian with an exotic and luxuriant talent. We planned to do the play on a kind of ship, whose elements—bridges, decks, forecastle, holds—could be instantly transformed into the myriad settings the play needs while Pericles wanders in exile and in search of his lost daughter. It worked wonderfully, the play was a great success—the hit of the season—and the whole experience was a great pleasure, marred only by a bit of jealousy on Michael Redgrave's part when, envious of the lesser players' success in "his" season, he tried to destroy their confidence in Loudon's costumes.

In the play there is a narrator—Gower, based on the poet John Gower, Chaucer's contemporary—who speaks in a sort of Chaucerese: short rhyming couplets sprinkled with Middle English vocabulary. This was clearly a parody on Shakespeare's part of some contemporary success now disappeared, and I hit on the idea of having Gower's lines set to music (by the splendid, now almost forgotten and underrated Roberto Gerhard) and sung. In the course of trying to cast Gower, I suddenly thought of Paul Robeson. Robeson had been ostracized, maligned, and discriminated against for years, and it seemed a wonderful opportunity to make restitution for some of the suffering he'd endured, and a wonderful role for him to make a comeback in. Glen, with his innate sense of show biz, became very enthusiastic. Paul and I met for lunch—at the Algonquin (even this seemed almost a revolutionary gesture at the time). He was tempted but not totally, and finally he couldn't make it. The role was played by Edric Connor, a West Indian, and was very successful.

But the offer had tempted Paul enough to make him decide to come to Stratford next year, as Othello. (I think up till then he'd thought his whole acting career to be over.) The 1959 season was the eightieth anniversary of the opening of the first Shakespeare Memorial Theatre, and had big guns in every show—Laughton, Olivier, Edith Evans, and so on. *Othello* was to be the opening production. Mary Ure was Desdemona, Albert Finney Cassio, Zoe Caldwell Bianca, and Ian Holm, Peter Woodthorpe, and Angela Baddeley were in supporting roles. Understudying Mary and in the crowd was Vanessa Redgrave. In the Cyprus scene, she set a record for getting back and forth across the stage with pots and baskets on her head—twice as many as anyone else. As Iago I cast Sam Wanamaker, who then lived and worked in London. By choosing an American, I thought Paul's accent would blend more easily into the ensemble. Loudon Sainthill again was the designer. We had decided to take a traditional approach but very elaborate, with costumes inspired by Titian, and with the pace of an American musical.

Rehearsals were fascinating—Paul was Othello, but, alas, the years and his persecutions had left their mark and he no longer had the energy and technique he once had. When he made his first entrance and when he told his entrancing story to the dupe and the Venetian senate, he was perfection. Zoe Caldwell, I'm told, when working on another production, described his presence as so sensual you could actually smell the sun glowing from him. But when it came to the great rages and explosions of jealousy, he could not totally rise to them. (I have never seen an Othello who could.) The love and sympathy the audience radiated toward him sustained him, but the staying power just wasn't there. He was also surprised to learn for the first time what the words meant. Paul told me that the director of his first *Othello*, Margaret Webster, told him only one thing: "Be a black panther and stalk." For the first time he heard the words dissected and discussed; when we improvised scenes and speeches to make sure that everything was understood, it was infinitely touching to see him struggling with a technique that he'd never encountered before but to which he gave himself with the generosity and the humility of a great and extraordinary artist. The actors loved him.

The production, though a success with audiences, was mauled savagely by the critics when it opened in April. What we thought of as traditional—even the set was structured basically as an Elizabethan stage—was called revolutionary and vulgar. The anti-Americanism always latent with many so-called Europeans boiled up and, as Paul was sacrosanct, was directed mainly against Sam ("cowboy," "Hollywood," etc.), who in fact was giving a fine and striking performance. But Loudon and I made one very bad mistake. We'd placed Desdemona's bedroom on the upper of the stage; then, knowing that the scenes there need to bring the actors as close to the audience as possible, we had cantilevered it out. It gave anyone sitting near in the stalls a dangerous, vertiginous feeling. At the time you had only four weeks' rehearsals and two or three dress rehearsals, so there was no question of rectifying it. Despite that, and despite the violence of the reception, *Othello* was a production I was proud of, and the "cinematic" values—the pageantry, the pace, the frenzy of the brawls and duels—were ones I think the play needs. And I was very, very proud and privileged to have been able to work with Paul.

I also remember some dinner where I had a long argument about nuclear power with Vanessa—who had been the greatest of enthusiasts about the production—but our relationship had no other overtones at the time.

Soon after *Othello*, a farcical chance, and a lot of alcohol, brought the next change in Mary Ure's life. I was directing another play I adore, Tennessee Williams's *Orpheus Descending*. It was the British premiere and starred the Italian actress Isa Miranda as Lady Torrance. She had immense talent, and a capacity for work like the toughest horse. At her best she was extraordinary: Peggy Ashcroft told me she thought Isa's performance one of the greatest she'd ever seen, and Tennessee, at a preview (the film *The Fugitive Kind*, based on *Orpheus Descending*, was about to begin shooting with Anna Magnani and Marlon Brando), said, "Magnani can't be better, only different." The next night, the opening, the story was different: "How could you employ a rank amateur to ruin my beautful play?"

Isa was a kind of masochist: She got some sort of kick out of abusing herself physically. In the last act of the play, Lady Torrance is shot and has to die spectacularly draped round an iron circular staircase. One night during the run, Isa threw herself head downward over the staircase and might easily have been killed had not the actor playing Valentine (Gary Cockrell) rushed and broken her fall. Anyway, during the final preview, in her big scene with Valentine, Isa fell badly but immediately picked herself up and finished in splendid form. The next day her leg had swollen alarmingly. From any sensible point of view the performance should have been canceled and the opening postponed, but at that time postponements were unthinkable and, besides, Isa had such courage and determination that I let the show go on. A doctor had been called and what Isa (and the doctor) didn't tell me was that he shot her full of morphine to kill the pain so she could make the show. The result was appalling: She played the first act at half speed and slurring her not all that comprehensible English.

Orpheus Descending is a fascinating mixup. A marvelous first act has some of the most extraordinary poetry Tennessee ever produced. Then the play meanders for a while into fairly corny melodrama in Act 2, only to recover with the extraordinary arias of the ending. The British critics were quite wonderful: Almost to a man they wrote about a sluggish and turgid first act followed by a blaze into life and theatricality in Act 2. The drugs had worn off by Act 2, and Isa was able to perform with her natural vitality.

But to come back to Mary. The role of Carol Cutrere, the southern renegade, was played by Diane Cilento, the daughter of a rather grand northern Australia family. I had known Diane for several years. We'd first worked together in 1954, in an early, almost-amateur Sunday-night production of Middleton's *The Changeling*. With her long, mermaid-blond hair, her sea-blue eyes, her long, lithe body, her electricity and sexuality, Diane would have been a great movie star. She'd been under contract to some of the British film companies but, with their inability to see what they'd got and their lack of imagination, they'd tried to fit her into their own stereotypes—self-sacrificing nurses or jolly barmaids—to all of which her exotic temperament was completely foreign. Perhaps had she gone to America her whole career would have been different. But there was also a quirky, metaphysical side. She dabbled in Gurdjieffism and worshipped at the feet of the then-fashionable movement guru Yat Malmgren. As an exercise teacher Yat was extraordinary (he helped me a lot), but unfortunately he elevated his physical principles into a dogmatic structure for creativity which even as gifted and funny a movie director as Alexander Mackendrick accepted. Diane's instinctual talent looked after her in the end, but she often talked the jargon.

Like many others, I was made about Diane and had been in love with her on and off for years. I had a date with her after one of the dress rehearsals or previews of *Orpheus*. To my fury, Robert Shaw turned up at the end of the show, also with a date with Diane. (Robert was an old acquaintance from Stratford days, when I'd been an assistant and he was a junior member of the company.) We had a nasty confrontation—as near as I've ever come to physical blows—then we separated. I had a few more notes to give. Diane had disappeared—obviously with Robert. Feeling very sorry for myself, I walked out of the theatre and into the next-door pub. There was Robert, looking equally black and equally convinced that the lady had gone off with me. We both realized in a flash what had happened and started to laugh. At closing time, after a few drinks, there was only one thing to do: We would go together to Diane's and confront her. When we arrived there, we could hear through the door that she was entertaining someone else! We banged on the door, we roared insults, and made ourselves as embarrassing as we could.

It was quite late and, as usual, everywhere in London had closed down. We went back to my apartment, where I had about half a bottle of vodka (those days were still far from affluent), to drink what we had and to have one of the all-night daft soul- and career-searching conversations that you have at that age. When first light was breaking over Hammersmith Bridge, our energies were still up and our alcohol supplies nonexistent. We tried to think of who of our friends might be better stocked. I thought of John and Mary, so we drove round and, in the early summer morning (it was about 5 A.M.), banged them awake. John was furious and truculent, but it was just the kind of escapade that excited Mary. Within minutes the champagne corks were popping, and suddenly I realized what inadvertently I had done by bringing Robert. Within days Mary and he were seeing each other. She soon left John, and finally she settled down and married Robert. Somehow we all stayed friends.

Later, in 1961, I even did a production with the two of them—

Middleton's *The Changeling*. Middleton is one of the greatest of the Jacobean dramatists—though not critically recognized as such, because his language is sparser, less romantic, less poetic than that of the "fine-phrase" dramatists who have always been admired by the English academic establishment. T. S. Eliot did something to rehabilitate him, certainly in relation to *The Changeling*, but even he did not give enough credit to the daring and brilliance of Middleton's theatrical technique and his approach to middle-class conflicts and characters. In fact, if you examine Middleton's work as a whole, there's nothing like it in literature until Balzac and the nineteenth-century French novelists. With its theme of paying the price for action committed—in this case, murder—*The Changeling* was astonishingly contemporary. De Flores's famous line, "Y'are the deed's creature," could have been a slogan for the existentialists, and Middleton's linking of crime and physical ugliness with sexual excitement anticipated Genet by three centuries. I'd done an abortive production earlier, but it hadn't been staged professionally within memory. Jocelyn Herbert and I took Goya as our inspiration, and the whole play worked beautifully.

George and I had a policy of trying to put on potential hits to protect what we often knew at the onset had to be "iffy" at best—though of course it never quite worked out as we imagined. One of these money-makers, more or less, was *Look After Lulu*—Noël Coward's adaptation of Feydeau's *Occupe-toi d'Amélie*. Ever since Larry's success in *The Entertainer*, Vivien's competitiveness had made her want to play at the Court. It seemed an ideal vehicle for her, and George and I were both great lovers of Feydeau (who hadn't been performed in England for years). It was my turn to do the "commercial" show, though in terms of temperament and background George was much better equipped to do it. But he felt he was needed to play in it—which he was, and did. The rehearsals were sad. Vivien—great star though she was—hated acting. Playing a scene, losing herself, gave her no pleasure. She never knew inside when she'd done anything well, so she was in a state of perpetual anxiety: "Was it all right? Is it okay?" Of course her manners were exemplary, and in a way that was the problem. Larry had trained her so well that if as a director you said, "Vivien, stand on your head for the next line," she would have done it without question. In her *fin de siècle* dresses she looked a miracle, of course, but there was no joy and none of the fierce obsessive reality which is the key to all playing of Feydeau. When it opened, in July 1959, Noël's adaptation was violently attacked by the critics as being too witty, too much in his own style—I still think unfairly, as Noël followed Feydeau with precision and faithfulness—but the production was enough of a success to transfer for a while to the New Theatre, though it was never the money-gusher we'd hoped for.

In fact the only fun of the production was Noël himself. This great man of the theatre appeared from time to time—always helpful, always expert, always a delight. Except with Vivien. They fought cat and dog. After a few drinks, the evenings would always end with Noël screaming, "Thank God you and Larry had a miscarriage. Any child of yours would be a monster three times over." Even I thought their friendship must have been broken, but always next day they were as devoted and fond as ever. On the first night in Newcastle (where we were trying the production out) Vivien was talking to me about the mechanics of the bed cover which plays a crucial role in the second act. Noël stormed in, heard the end of the conversation, and shouted in front of a crowd of people, "When you learn to play my play better, then you can have opinions about the scenery," and, wagging his finger at her—a gesture for which he was famous—"A diligent *amateur!*" Exit.

9

Bread and Honey

It may seem odd to give *Requiem for a Nun* special attention, but it caused repercussions that were so odd and sometimes bizarre that I have to. William Faulkner had written *Requiem* as a dramatized novel. It was the sequel to *Sanctuary*, which he had called a "potboiler," though I believe this to be a much richer and more powerful work than the sanctified, cleaned-up, metaphysical *Requiem*, with its white ambivalence about the treatment of the blacks in the South. The actress Ruth Ford—later married to Zachary Scott, the movie actor—had been one of his loves or had had an affair with Faulkner, and he'd done a dramatization of the dramatization for the stage, giving Ruth the stage rights.

The only actual production of the play had been in France, in French. It had been a great success. For some reason the character of Temple Drake had become a symbol of occupied France—"Je suis sale, je suis sale, je suis pute"—and it had been taken up as only the French intellectuals can take up a metaphor. Probably it sounded better in French, but they reveled in Temple's masochistic confessional. By chance I met Ruth and Zachary at Harry's Bar in Venice. We got on. They talked about the play and suggested we might present it at the Court.

In truth neither George nor I cared greatly for *Requiem:* It was too high-minded, too sententious, too humorless. But it was by a great writer, it was a world premiere, and we were short of material. Ruth and Zach had stipulated in the deal that either George or I must direct. George claimed he'd no understanding of the material whatsoever, so I was drafted. And it had a very effective role for my old friend Bertice Reading. Percy Harris of Motley did an effective set, and the play was very easy to stage, the second central act being more or less a monologue. It opened in November 1957. We didn't expect much more than at best a respectable failure, so the reception surprised us: The notices were more or less raves—especially for Ruth. "With her scream she stopped the traffic in Sloane Square," wrote one critic. So we did sell-out business while it played at the Court, but we knew it had no legs beyond that for a transfer, and we had no offer from an outside management.

The Scotts were naturally anxious to exploit their triumph and were chafing to get on with it. It was then that we thought of our neglected theatre company with Harry Saltzman, "Woodfall America." It seemed logical to present the play in the place where it belonged. We made a partnership with an American management, and the production with the Scotts, Bertice, and the Motley set was planned to open in Boston en route for the Golden in New York.

Nothing went as smoothly as in England. Ruth had a bad case of pre-Broadway jitters. She took against the actor, Scott McKay, who'd been cast as her husband at the Scotts' suggestion, and who had been a friend of theirs. She demanded he be fired; reams of notes appeared night and morning under my bedroom door and his at the Ritz-Carlton; she made all kinds of allegations professional and personal. Actually he was an improvement on the British casting, but the Scotts would have none of him, and since the only real problem was their anxiety, there was nothing to be done. The play opened in New York in January 1959, to chilly reviews—at best respectful of Faulkner; Ruth was no novelty to the Broadway critics as she had been to those in London. It was rather the reception we'd expected in England, and the show closed after a few performances. Yet somehow—certainly as far as I was concerned—an aura of a *succès d'estime* hung over my contribution and over the play.

*   *   *

Though the film of *Look Back* did eventually recover its investment, the time it took to do so didn't make the financing of Woodfall's next project, *The Entertainer*, any easier, in addition to which Larry was sliding toward becoming what today would be called unbankable. Harry rushed about with much less result this time, despite the overwhelming success of the play. One of his obsessions was that the brewers of Bass, which is prominently featured in the play as Archie Rice's staple diet, would fund the film in return for publicity. (This was long before any stars deigned to participate in advertising campaigns, and for Sir Laurence in particular this would have been unspeakably infra dig.) Finally Harry did succeed in piecing enough finance together, mainly from British sources. (At the time you reckoned that a British film would be made with 70 percent British money and 30 percent from the USA and the rest of the world; later it was 50–50; later 30 percent British and 70 percent US. Now you'd be very lucky to get 5 or 10 percent British money for any production.) But even after this he still persisted in his Bass mania. One day when we were rehearsing on an empty stage at Shepperton Studios, stagehands wheeled in behind the group of actors a twenty-foot cutout of some bottles of Bass which Harry had surreptitiously had constructed, hoping, by sneaking a shot of bottle and famous knight, to convince the beer company to invest. How he imagined that this construction would go unnoticed is unimaginable. The knight was not amused!

The Entertainer was much more difficult to translate to screen than *Look Back*—or rather it had to change its nature much more radically. In Archie's monologues and sometimes in his theatre routines he was both a third-rate entertainer and a metaphor for a world and an England disappearing. In one phrase, John (underscored by Larry's skill) could suggest resonances beyond the immediate context of the vaudeville sketch. Yet the bedrock of the play is the reality of felt and observed characters. This is something that many of John's followers have not understood: They've created the metaphors but left out the reality—and a pretty thin and sour dish we've been left with. But in the movie, that aspect of the play disappears completely. Film is a totally realistic medium and Archie Rice can only be a failed vaudevillian; our only entry to him is through understanding his own vulnerability and squalor so deeply that we can empathize with the individual without extending the character to thoughts about society. The detail of the performance was what had to count, not the leaps to beyond. I was also trying to free myself more and more from the confines of the theatre, and with its alternation of digs and the theatre, the failed world of show biz, *The Entertainer* lent itself more naturally to "opening up" than *Look Back*, where much of the violence and emotion of the characters comes from the feeling of their being caged in one attic.

As our basic location I'd chosen Morecamb, where my parents now lived. The setting was perfect—a failed popular resort with decaying piers and crumbling theatres, the second-class sister to the livelier, more raucous, still-popular Blackpool. In both of them I'd spent dreary, horrifying wartime holidays with my parents, hating the concrete pavements, the mean boardinghouses, the vulgarity of the restaurants and shows. Now I could understand them better and could use feelings that came from way back in childhood to help the film.

Larry couldn't understand my insistence on location shooting, on natural sound, on responding to the light and shadows: The only scenes he was really happy in were those we shot in the studio. But he was very loyal and accommodating, and he cooperated in every way despite great fatigue through having to commute (in an ambulance) from Stratford-upon-Avon, where he was playing Coriolanus. It confirmed me for ever in the opinion that, except in special cases—a subject like a musical, for example, or a scene with special technical problems—studios were anathema: Their artificial conditions produced artificiality in acting and image (which for me has been the greatest criticism of all the American studio films of the 1930s and 1940s, for which I have never had and will never have either admiration or reverence), and that I would never be happy shooting except in the open air or inside real locations. So, although I couldn't have articulated it, never having been introspective, *The Entertainer* was a key moment in my development, because all the ideas and convictions I was to work with afterward were crystallized in its making. I began to sense how great a jump would be involved when my great mentor and friend Ozzie Morris thought I was becoming too careless and irresponsible: I didn't insist on take after take; I didn't care about minor imperfections. I thought I was becoming free. Ozzie, ever the technician, thought

I was becoming spoiled and sloppy. From the Free Cinema manifesto, "Perfection is not an aim" came back to me. Life was more important. That's what two great technical perfectionists, Larry and Ozzie (a good vaudeville double bill), taught me.

My parents were, of course, delighted to have me working so near home, to come on the set, to meet the stars. But we also had three strippers, whose presence and behavior scandalized the locals—especially when, to get reactions for the extras' shots, I sent one of them (she was ecstatic) onstage naked to perform. My mother commented, "Oh, Tony, it's so lovely to have Sir Laurence here. But, oh, those girls—they do let you down!"

In the film of *The Entertainer*, the part of Jean, Archie's daughter, was played by Joan Plowright, who had also played the part during the later stage revivals. Though a fellow member of the original English Stage Company, Joan was quite the opposite of Mary Ure. She was a born actress, with a wonderful ear, great humor, a marvelous sense of comic timing, a sensuality that was more material than emotional, and a slyness and deviousness that were as foreign to Mary as Joan's grubbiness was to Mary's chic. Joan loved acting, and she had a sense of truth in character that made Mary in comparison look like an action painter throwing the raw pigments violently at the canvas. And Joan had a sense of what she wanted and where she was going. Attractive when animated, she had no glamour or beauty, and had been made to feel that all her life. When she came to the Court, she was married to a young actor, but the marriage was already disintegrating. Larry claims in his autobiography that he fell in love with her during *The Country Wife*, where, with her sloe eyes and Nell Gwyn wig, Joan looked her loveliest, but it was during the period of *The Entertainer* that they drifted together. For Larry, Joan was the epitome of the new world of theatre he had opted for; for Joan, Larry was the epitome of all she'd never had.

I remember when she first told me of the relationship (which, of course, to insiders was already common knowledge). Joan and I had been taking lessons to brush up our French in preparation for a winter holiday in Morocco, early in 1960. As I picked her up in the basement where she lived, she said she couldn't make the lesson, then burst into tears. I asked her why. She said she knew I'd disapprove but she was in love with Larry and was going to marry him. She couldn't have been more wrong about my disapproving: Although I was critical of aspects of Larry, at the time I believed him a great friend and I was delighted that Joan and he had found happiness together and that the nightmare of the later part of his relationship with Vivien would finally be dispelled. I was happy for both of them, and later, when the news broke in the press, they hid away in my Hammersmith apartment.

Incidentally, our Moroccan holiday was a total and nearly fatal disaster. We were all very tired with our activities, still had little money, and needed a rest, and naively we imagined Morocco would provide that. The party included Joan, my roommate George Goetschius, and Jock Addison (the composer who'd written the music for *The Entertainer*) and his wife. The weather was horrible—cold, rainy, forbidding. Morocco had not long been independent; the French had departed with a callous shrug. Conditions and food were bleak. Tangier was miserable. En route to Marrakech, to Churchill's favorite hotel, the Mamounia, I caught a fever and was in bed for several days while the others tramped the souks in mud and rain. Finally I recovered sufficiently to make the journey across the Atlas to Agadir. We hired a car. It was uninsurable. We soon found out why—it broke down twice. But worse than the car was the road. It was unpaved and most of it had crumbled down the mountain, which was littered with ominous wrecks. In many places it was single-track, passable only when you drove right against the shoulder of the mountain. Thick fog came down, and we had to take turns walking ahead to keep the wheels on the broken track. When, in the middle of the night, we arrived at the concrete blockhouse of a tourist hotel, there was nothing to eat or drink. The young manager—a dyspeptic Swiss—and his pregnant wife were in despair at the desertion of the French and the tourists. There was a bit of sun, but the winds were cold. After three grim days I said, "Let's face it, we're hating this. Let's chuck it, go to Paris for the weekend—blow all our money and have some fun." Everyone agreed. We changed our reservations and left. That night was the Agadir earthquake. Everyone in our hotel died.

The fortunes of Woodfall did not run smoothly. As with the Court, the concept of Woodfall had not been just to showcase John's and my talents but to use what clout we developed to create opportunities for others to create their own movies (as Francis Ford Coppola and Steven Spielberg were to do in America). But so far we had had little success. Neither *Look Back* nor *The Entertainer* was the kind of financial success that could overcome the usual cooking of books by distributors and exhibitors.

Our immediate project was for Karel Reisz to film Alan Sillitoe's novel *Saturday Night and Sunday Morning*. I had also plans to buy the rights to Shelagh Delaney's *A Taste of Honey*—again a play, but without the tight structure and the heightened rhetoric of John's work. The play had originally been staged by Joan Littlewood at the Theatre Royal, Stratford East, in 1958. There, with her Theatre Workshop company, she had done much fascinating work—some classical, but most notably Brendan Behan's *The Quare Fellow* and *The Hostage*. The latter fulfilled perfectly Joan's policy of mixing working-class drama with pub vitality and vaudeville songs. For me, her technique had worked less well on *A Taste of Honey*, where it made the play seem coarse and forcedly jolly. Joan's heyday in the theatre was splendid, but what is the East End's loss has been the Rothschilds' gain, and the working-class revolutionary has ended happily in, if not the arms, then the cellars of Baron Philippe.

As usual, money was our problem. Backing was hard to find. We didn't have enough to keep the Lowdnes Cottage establishment running, and Harry rushed from one impossible scheme to another. Deals of more and more dubious kinds were being proposed. I was growing up and, under Harry's tutelage, had begun to understand how the business side of films worked. I became more and more appalled by our financial state. Harry wouldn't admit to the reality, however. A certain amount of bluff is very much part of all show business, but when you're bluffing your own partners you're in bad trouble. We didn't mind knowing the worst, John and I said: We accepted that we were in the same boat. We'd had the good; we could take the bad. It was no use—up blew some new fantasy or some transaction about which we knew nothing. There was intrigue with or against Karel. Harry became more and more unhappy with the way *Saturday Night* was shaping up, and most of the other ideas he attached himself to were projects neither John nor I could believe in.

I don't remember exactly what triggered our breakup. I'd managed to get an option on *A Taste of Honey*, and at one moment Harry did a deal to sell it behind my back to Charley Feldman. I sent off angry cables, denying his authority to consummate the sale. Maybe it was that, or maybe it was just our total artistic incompatibility. The showdown came. We voted Harry out of the company. I took over the total production of *Saturday Night*, leaving him a credit only and as much as we could possibly afford to give him. The Lowdnes Cottage establishment was closed. The staff were all given the choice of staying with the company or going with Harry. As Harry used to bully and harangue them, I thought that, being the good guy, I would win the popularity contest hands down. Not at all. They all voted for Harry—except one, a reckless Polish chauffeur, Jan Niemcynowicz. He became my friend, driver, nanny, valet, bodyguard, babysitter, watchdog, whipping boy for the rest of his life.

After the split, *Saturday Night* settled down and, under Karel, ran easily. It turned out a huge success, but that was down the line. Meantime we had no money and no prospects for *A Taste of Honey*.

A telephone call from Paris. Darryl Zanuck had bought the movie rights to *Requiem for a Nun*. He was interested in me directing it. Would I go meet him in Paris? My real motive was either financing for *A Taste of Honey* or at least money to secure the rights completely. Zanuck did express interest in *A Taste of Honey*, read it, and offered to do it—"Anyway ya like, young fella—only one condition: a happy ending." "It has a happy ending—Jo is happy waiting for her baby to be born." (The father in the play is a black sailor.) "That's the point—the baby's gotta die, and Mother and girl go off to a better life." I said no, thank you. *Requiem* was different.

It was my first up-close encounter with a real Hollywood mogul. Darryl lived at the time in a suite at the Plaza Athénée—waited on by, amongst others, an old friend of Harry Salzman's, John Shepridge, an ex-agent producer who was dispatched every so often to walk Darryl's miniature schnauzer around the block (John and I called him "the most expensive dog-walker in the business") while Darryl waited nervously and despondently for a phone call from Juliette Greco. Darryl claimed to have seen *The Entertainer*. He and his son, Richard, whose second production *Requiem* was to be, wanted a fresh look. The film was to be an amalgamation of *Sanctuary* (which I loved) and *Requiem* (which I didn't). I was immediately free but, after a series of meetings, we agreed that I would work on a script in England and then leave for Hollywood to start production. I was very excited to be working in the capital of the movies, especially on my own terms—location shooting in Mississippi, my own casting and script. I asked the novelist Doris Lessing, to whom I was close at the time, to work with me. Darryl commissioned her, and together we produced what was probably quite an effective adaptation, mainly of *Sanctuary*. Armed with this, I set off for my first Hollywood assignment.

Reality was diametrically opposite from promises. First of all, the script was a totally futile exercise (and a waste of money): I arrived to find that a famous Hollywood screenwriter, James Poe, had been contracted for the project. Work with him was bitter and acrimonious. "You only like that scene because it's written by Faulkner," he'd scream when I suggested we'd incorporate this incident or that. Or again, "You're only hired because Mr. Zanuck thinks you'll make more money for him than anyone else. [How wrong he was.] That's why I'm hired too—we're all whores at heart." Most of the time he incarcerated himself in an office without a phone above a gas station in Brentwood, where his secretary procured girls for him. Lip service to my ideals of location shooting was reluctantly paid by the studio's agreeing to a scouting trip to Mississippi organized by Wyatt Cooper (later Gloria Vanderbilt's fourth husband). Everything proceeded from negatives—avoiding the worst. Wyatt had only been hired at my insistence to escape the horror of the fashionable Southern adviser Marguerite Lamkin, who later became a London doyenne.

The trip to Mississippi was fascinating. This was before the civil-rights movement, and it was probably not much changed from the Civil War. In Oxford, where Faulkner had been brought up, we stayed in the grandest hotel. All the way down the bedroom corridor there were still saloon swing doors, opening at top and bottom, to provide ventilation for the humidity and heat. Next to my bed was a rectangular wooden box hinged to the floor. Not able to imagine why this sinister object was there, I forced it open. Inside was a coil of thick rope, nailed at one end to the floor—the fire escape. The state was dry (though the only state revenue was from a tax for selling liquor) except for Natchez, on the river, where you could get a glass of sweet sherry with your gumbo, served by genteel

Southern ladies in Civil War dresses in the beautiful antebellum homes—all before tourist exploitation.

The most fascinating—and horrifying—two nights were spent with a relative of Wyatt's in a little town. He was the sheriff: a quintessential redneck who took us into the jail and paraded his niggers with every detail of their misdeeds and personalities as if they were tame zoo animals. He and his cronies—spurred on by the challenge of someone they thought of as having a critical personality—reveled in descriptions of beating blacks "until their butts couldn't get into their jeans," stomping their faces with boots—always ending with, yes, "Nigger, don't let the sun rise on you in this town." It was like a deliberate obscene challenge to any kind of human judgment you might dare to bring: I think probably you'd find the same attitudes in South Africa. Yet this same brute had a pathetic yellow-looking wife, stricken with polio, whom he had to wait on hand and foot, feed, take to the bathroom, wash and clean after every excretion. It was a relief to leave and arrive at the fake gaudiness of New Orleans. Returning to the hermetic studio bungalows of Hollywood was like visiting another world: Telephone calls and agents replaced nightsticks and work boots and the arid, hot poverty of Mississippi.

It was becoming clearer and clearer to me that what the Zanucks wanted was not *Sanctuary* but some kind of sanitized *Requiem*, and every day became simply a battle not to succumb to the worst compromise. Dickie Zanuck had no confidence of his own and he used to wait trembling for the four o'clock call from Poppa, when orders and abuse were barked down the phone. The film had also been planned to push Lee Remick (then under contract to Fox, and the star of Elia Kazan's movies *A Face in the Crowd* and *Wild River*) into absolute stardom—and sex symbolism. Brad Dillman was to play her husband, and the role of degenerate Popeye (now sanitized to Candyman in the script) was supposedly to go to Laurence Harvey. I'd never been an admirer of Larry's—least of all, being the local boy, for his performance in *Room at the Top*, which was unauthentic to the point of absurdity—but Darryl wanted him and we ran and reran his movies. The alternative "hot" offbeat Fox choice was Yves Montand. I'd loved Yves's work in *Le Salaire de la Peur*, and between the two I was for him. The decision would be made and confirmed, then next day I would go into the office,

Dickie Zanuck would have had a meeting with some agent, and the insane discussion of the two actors would be repeated again.

Every day it became clearer this was to be a routine on-the-lot studio movie. Why had they hired me? There were many more skillful studio directors. But it was the old nonsense—still alive today as ever—that you hire someone to give you something different, fresher, whatever, and then take away all the tools and personnel that make it possible for him to do the very thing you wanted him for. There's only one rule in movies: You get what you pay for. Imagination can sometimes add a little, but it can't make up for poor working conditions any more than a carpenter can make a deal table look like mahogany.

Battles with the studio were at all levels in every department. The first scene we had to shoot was set in a whorehouse. There was the madam, a group of whores—some of whom had the odd line—and extras. None of the lines had yet been assigned. The studio assistant director was an ex-marine veteran twice my age and size. The whole crew was watching to see how this incomprehensible limey would perform. I started to rehearse the scene. "Try taking this line," I said to one of the girls. A voice as if on Pendleton parade ground boomed from behind, "Oh, no she won't, buddy." What hadn't been explained to me was that some of the girls in the group had been hired as actresses and therefore could speak a line, others as extras, who would have to be paid a few extra dollars if given anything to say. I knew the moment was crucial, and for once I felt calm. I turned slowly around, looked up at my sergeant-supervisor. "Oh, yes she will, buddy. And [pointing to the stage door] if you ever speak to me like that again you'll walk out of that door." One down, but many more to go.

Casting for bit parts was difficult, as I didn't know many actors in California. The casting department liked to feed me only one choice at a time—theirs, and usually, one suspected, in return for other favors—and usually so late that if he or she didn't seem right it was difficult to find a substitute. I rebelled and demanded to interview at least ten for every role. In two days' time we were doing a college ball with about ten small roles. At 8:30 the next morning the studio doors rolled open and the assistant casting director marched in with a hundred young men behind him. "You asked for ten, you got 'em. Now pick 'em." I asked him to apologize to the group for being kept waiting and to tell them that I would interview them all but, with shooting going on, it would take time. And I told him that he, the casting man, should wait with them to the end.

The art department was one of the worst of all. The art director, who had worked on some of the great Fox and MGM musicals, was a hero to me from the days of *Sequence* and *Sight and Sound*. I looked forward to working with him. But he had become a studio bureaucrat whose only interest was in keeping his department's budget as low as possible, even though by doing so he put up the film's overall budget by thousands of dollars. For instance, one of our main sets was a corridor with two interconnecting bedrooms. The set arrived with each room built with two fixed walls and sharing two extra floating walls, instead of having two floating walls for each. As the two rooms were dressed and decorated differently, this meant (as well as making some shots impossible) that each time you moved from one room to the other the floating walls had to be repainted and repapered—a process which took hours, while the crew for the whole film waited around. I refused to shoot until the extra flats—a few hundred dollars' worth of lumber—were made. But saving Fox money didn't make you a hero; it made you difficult.

There was also an in-house studio censor who viewed the dailies and ruled on cleavages, underclothes, behavior before any footage was presented to the real censors. "Bumps and grinds" were strictly out. Orders for reshooting were screamed imperiously, and as for the famous corn-cob . . . The simple truth was that under the then conditions (rather like the customs and practices committees that rule network TV today) it was idiotic to have even considered making *Sanctuary*. Now it might make a great movie, but at that time all that was vital had to be removed from the story.

Nothing was right (least of all the director). Lee—a lovely cool actress—tried hard, but she belonged in fresh northern climates, not in the heat and sultriness of a Southern brothel. Yves was then at the height of his affair with Marilyn Monroe. She telephoned hourly—a fact Yves loved to announce to every grip and stagehand. "Tell her to wait. Poor girl. But what can I do? I am French." Of all the male stars I've known, he was probably the most vain. He had this extraordinary craggy face, but for a Hollywood movie he wanted to be photographed on only one profile, and he spent his time trying to maneuver his positions to persuade me to put the camera on what he thought of as his good side. It wasn't long before everyone lost all belief in the product.

After it was over, I did a cut of the movie and was then quickly dispatched. I didn't work on the finishing or with the composer or the mixing. I have never seen it. Sometime much later, after the success of *Tom Jones*, some journalists from *Life* researching the Fox vaults found my original cut and almost talked the studio into releasing it. Finally Fox decided against. They were right: It would have been shame-making.

Life outside the studio was something else. I rented a house on Montana Street in Westwood. It belonged to Eva Gabor and was furnished entirely in ivory and gold, mainly from TV talk shows. There was a pool and a yard in which Japanese gardeners appeared periodically and dumped down trees or a lawn in an attempt to make a garden. There was a black maid who came at about ten at night and stayed until three. She hated all other blacks, and whenever a black friend of mine was there she would turn off all the lights, TV, music in whatever room they were. She also read everyone's letters and sold information to Louella Parsons and Hedda Hopper.

A Cadillac went with the house. Power brakes had just come in. I nearly had two very bad accidents. I had the brakes fixed. The same night they went again as I pulled out from being parked on one of the steeper Hollywood Hills. I sideswiped a car parked in front, went through a lamppost, fusing all the lights in the immediate area with an electrical explosion, and crashed down the hill, through the kitchen wall of a house, and into piles of crates of liquor for a party the next day. I was okay (I luckily hadn't had anything much to drink), but the Cadillac was totaled. Everyone was charming; the two ladies whose house I'd hit found out I was a director and asked me for a job, the cops told me not to worry and drove me home, and the insurance took care of the rest. I never heard any more about it. Mary Ure, who was staying with me at the time, made me a strong cup of tea and half an hour later I started to shake uncontrollably with shock.

The house had three or four bedrooms, and in that summer of 1960 it became, as Christopher Isherwood said, the setting for a Feydeau farce. Friends and friends of friends packed in. There were parties every weekend, and escapades and adventures and frivolity. Mary had come to LA to play in Giraudoux's *Duel of Angels* with Vivien Leigh, who was constantly in and out with her new lover, Jack Merivale, and the play's director, Robert Helpmann. Christopher had taken Mary and me to a wild, half-gay bar on the beach at Santa Monica—there were broken-down shacks of bars on the beach then, pre-hippie, where musclemen danced the Madison with butch ladies and painted queens cavorted with pythons. Mary foolishly told Vivien, and Vivien was determined to go. After their Saturday show at the Huntington Hartford, we set out all together. Jack Merivale took one look at the types strewing the place, said, "I want no part of this, no part of this at all," and sulked in their Rolls. On Saturday the bars closed earlier and the forbidding ladies in the alley entrance wouldn't let us go in. The Madison was at its height, the crowd elbow-to-elbow, sweat-to-sweat, and the arrival of Scarlett O'Hara, which would have entranced them, passed unnoticed. Vivien wasn't going to be missed, so she climbed onto the bar and started pouring beer (the only drink served) over the half-naked dancers. But it still didn't work—they only thought her some half-deranged drugster. And the evening had a sad consequence. Reports of Vivien's presence got into one of the gossip columns, and the cops, saying the fire precautions were inadequate for the prominence of the persons now frequenting the beach, closed the bars and destroyed the buildings.

Joan Plowright (of whom Mary was very jealous) was due in on the heels of the others as the Giraudoux play moved to San Francisco. David Merrick had bought the stage rights of *A Taste of Honey*. He'd wanted me to direct it in Los Angeles, before moving to Broadway, and I'd suggested casting Joan. Angela Lansbury had been contracted to play the mother. David was adamant that he needed the play to open at the beginning of the Broadway season, but this meant a direct conflict with *Sanctuary*. The sensible thing would have been to let someone else do the play, but so far I'd only been able to raise about a third of the money to film it. I knew if the play flopped it would make funding the movie much more difficult—if not impossible—so I decided to rehearse the play and film *Sanctuary* at the same time. It was the kind of mad decision that you can make at thirty but will never have the energy to repeat—and it was helped, of course, by my disenchantment with *Sanctuary*. George agreed to come over for three or four weeks to be my assistant. In return, I brought over Jocelyn and two of her children so they at least could have the holiday the production had deflected. At weekends George and the family drove up the coast. We worked like this. I would shoot *Sanctuary* until six, then rehearse *A Taste of Honey* from seven to midnight; Saturday and Sunday I rehearsed all day. Part of the time I was shooting nights, so then I rehearsed a normal day and only slept while setups were being lit. It was a killing schedule and, as there were so many people in the house and so much noise, I rented another apartment in Westwood to try to sleep on Saturday and Sunday nights. By then I was so tired that even that was impossible. We rehearsed onstage at the Royce Hall in UCLA, and with a small jazz combo we improvised and invented the song, "A Taste of Honey," which became an international hit. I forgot—dumbo—to claim part of the royalties.

We were to open in the old Biltmore Theatre off Pershing Square, still in its beautiful old state (long before it was "cleaned up" and all its life destroyed), with palm trees and benches and secret walks, pushers and hustlers, whores and winos. The dress rehearsals were especially difficult as the theatre wasn't well equipped and Oliver Smith's set had been miscalculated so that some of the sight-lines and measurements were practically impossible. John had joined Mary, before her play moved on to San Francisco, and after the first act we went for a drink in the adjoining bar. Knowing Mary's antagonism to Joan, and her feelings of being excluded, I asked her advice about some details of makeup (in which she was very expert). In the course of this, Mary managed to insult Joan, who burst into tears. John called Mary a bitch; Mary screamed, rushed out of the bar, and disappeared into Pershing Square, into the downtown LA night, John in pursuit. Much later I had to take Joan out, still distraught—"Why *does* she hate me so much?"—and comfort her. Back home John and Mary had returned, drunk and quarreling. Joan went to bed. Some time later I saw a pink shadow throw itself into the pool and disappear: Mary, naked, was trying to drown herself. John had given up, and I was forced to plunge in and haul her out. Joan, awakened by the commotion, came out and proceeded to gang up with Mary, the two of them attacking John and me and then disappearing together. We cracked the fourth bottle of champagne as dawn broke, but we were both too tired and hungover to drink a glass. A typical night on Montana Street.

The play opened to good notices and business, and I was polishing it when I wasn't shooting—it was to go on a short tour until the end of the movie. All was well until David Merrick showed up for the last preview. I'd put in a few changes after Friday's performance and was coming to see them on the Saturday evening. David wanted to have dinner between shows, but I was much too tired and said I'd meet him later. When I arrived, he attacked me violently for not turning up when first invited. We got into a shouting match and he fired me. He appointed the stage manager as director and flew off to Las Vegas. Next day a rehearsal had been called—the last before the tour. All the actors refused to appear. David was forced to withdraw his action, but I was now determined to play the game and I refused to be reinstated without a full personal apology. David waited for his revenge until after the first night on Broadway. The notices were good, and it was clear we were set for a year's run. Next morning, without consulting me, David cut half of Oliver's scenery and reduced the band to two. He also refused to pay me a cent of royalties—until I took him to court. This was normal Merrick in-fighting.

That was more or less the end of my first long working stay in America. Much as I loved all the surroundings, it was time to return. There was a lot of work to do both at the theatre and with Woodfall, so I closed up Montana Street and went home.

10

O Wonderful, Wonderful, and Most Wonderful Wonderful!

Saturday Night and Sunday Morning had opened. The notices were excellent. So was business. We had a three-picture deal with Albert Finney and were full of projects. The success of Karel's film, plus the Broadway *A Taste of Honey*, enabled us to get financing to film the play, and I reassembled all the key people from my old team. Walter Lassally, who had photographed *Momma Don't Allow* for Karel and me, joined as cinematographer. He was an important figure in England, being the first of our lighting cameramen (as distinct, for example, from what was happening in France with the *nouvelle vague*) to be able to work in what was becoming known as the Free Cinema style—a minimum of equipment, real locations, and a natural, unmade-up look. A young, adventurous crew was headed by a remarkable, sensitive operator, Desmond Davis. (The roll of the operator in a unit is one of the key differences between the European and the American systems. In England, the lighting cameraman controls the overall look and style, lights the set and the actors, and watches the printing and the quality, but the operator works directly with the director in laying out the details of the shot—the composition, the movements of the dolly, the laying of tracks. In the USA, the director of photography is God and does everything. American operators are usually nonentities—order takers—whereas the British breed are lively personalities, usually with great humor. Americophile as I am, in this I think the British system is best.) Ralph Brinton, tireless in his late sixties, scoured the back streets, the canals, the smokestacks, the docks of Salford—where Shelagh Delaney, who had collaborated on the script, had come from—for locations. An old paint store that was part of the Royal Court workshop was adapted for one of the apartments, and even Blackpool, that childhood hell, was transformed for a beach weekend. Dora Bryan, a warm Lancashire comedienne, played Helen, and Murray Melvin, with his extraordinary face like an Egyptian hieroglyph, was to re-create his original role as Geoffrey.

But there was no Jo. All the actresses who had played it in the theatre were far too old for film. We started an immense search. It was very thorough: first photos, then interviews, then readings or improvisation, and finally a full-scale film test. I saw well over two thousand girls. I'd short-listed the best and still felt unconvinced. Out of nowhere, a young girl called Rita Tushingham turned up from Liverpool, with her mother. She wasn't very prepossessing. The only experience she'd had was being the hind legs of a donkey in a local pantomime. More out of kindness than interest, I let her read, then improvise. For improvisation she had an immediate talent, but she was too fierce, too spiky, too hard-edged for what I was looking for. I said no. Then came the tests. I rehearsed each of the final six girls with a different boy. Still that little hedgehog from Liverpool haunted me in some way, so, at the last minute, I decided to send for her for the tests. She didn't have a rehearsal and was rushed through at the end of a long day. How right I had been initially—she was hopeless! Next day came the dailies—with a group of workers, backers, etc. We were short of projection time. I was already disappointed with what we'd got. "It's hardly worth running the last girl—she's so hopeless." Five seconds later a close-up of Rita with her all-speaking eyes was on the screen, and the search was over.

Casting, the key to all film reality, is always a mysterious business—at any rate, for me. Sometimes you have to look forever. Yet for my next project, *The Loneliness of the Long Distance Runner*, the central role of the boy who refuses to conform and deliberately throws the race he's destined to win, was filled when I met Tom Courtenay at a party. He was just out of drama school, and had

had one job—Konstantin in *The Seagull*, I think (*The Seagull*'s always been my good-luck symbol), which I hadn't seen. But, meeting him, I offered him the part on the spot and never thought of anyone else.

Once Rita had been found, everything went wonderfully—a lovefest with both crew and actors—and I felt free and happy making a film for the first time without constraints of any kind. It was an experience without problems. Jock Addison wrote a lyrical score, and even the British critics relaxed a little in their attitude. Rita won an award at Cannes, and the American reception and business was even better. *Saturday Night* too was collecting all kinds of awards and recognition. It seemed as if Woodfall had made a breakthrough.

Loneliness followed with practically the same team and same spirit. I love making all films, but *Loneliness*, like *A Taste of Honey*, was one of the great pleasures to make. (I was soon to learn that the joy of doing a film has nothing to do with its success or even necessarily its achievement.) And in between the two films something happened to make me even happier.

But first, in the summer of 1961, came *Luther*, John's new historical play. Albert Finney, in the title part, was stretched to the full, and it was to be our most successful collaboration. He gave himself to the bowel-bound, sex-obsessed German revolutionary with a passion that for me he has never achieved before or since. The architecture of his performance, from shivering epileptic novice to the resigned middle-aged sensualist, was monumental. And in the fury of the great sermons—"Shells for shells, empty things for empty men"—his voice had tones of a natural electricity and a harsh clarion ring that he has, alas, subdued in his later assumption of a well-produced National Theatre voice—almost Donald Wolfitian in volume but devoid of the nerve and rawness he had in so many of his earlier performances. *Luther* was one of those extraordinary moments of hardhat-type theatre where the crew—John and I, Jocelyn as designer, Jock as Gregorian chant–master, Albert and George in the cast, and other old friends like Peter Bull and John Moffatt—were united in drilling and hammering the blocks of theatrical masonry together. And wherever we played—Nottingham, the Paris International Theatre Festival, the Court, the West End, Broadway—the play worked.

*   *   *

During all this period I hadn't much time for personal life: The activity was too intense and too consuming. I was still living in the apartment in Hammersmith, still sharing it with George Goetschius, my American roommate. It had become increasingly difficult to live in such close contact—much as I loved and still do love living in a crowd. Also, during a long stint in India for the Ford Foundation, George had contracted a very bad case of hepatitis—almost dying of the disease. Although he seemed to recover medically, psychologically I don't think he ever did. The guru who'd been such a strength, friend, and adviser began a slow unconscious process of withdrawing from life and was forced to give up much of the work he'd done before. I had no idea how hard the disease had struck, and sharing became more and more of a strain.

I went to the theatre to see the Royal Shakespeare Company at the Aldwych. Being away in America, I hadn't been in contact. Glen Byam Shaw had left and the regime had changed. I had heard of Vanessa's great success at Stratford, but I didn't expect to be overly impressed. The play was *As You Like It*. It had never been a favorite of mine (and didn't become so until much later, when I did a production at the Long Beach Terrace Theatre and learned what a deeply moving, funny, human play it is), although the production, by Michael Elliott, couldn't have been better. And at the center was this great golden flame—so light, so fluid, so involving. The miracle had happened: The positive, determined girl had become a woman of radiance, warmth, life, fun. Entrancing. I was in love. I went round to see her. I made a date for a few days later.

Vanessa was then the toast of London and had many would-be boyfriends. One of them was Bernard Levin, then a famous drama critic. By chance, a night or two later we ended up in the same restaurant, Vanessa with Bernard. I sent a note round by the maitre d'. Vanessa has always been very near-sighted and it never occurred to me she hadn't brought her spectacles. She handed the note to Bernard to read to her. It ended with "and tell Mr. L. to go fuck himself." She didn't get any more invitations from Bernard but, in fairness, his rave notices continued.

Luckily, during *Sanctuary* I'd bought my first car, one of the classic Thunderbirds. It was brilliant red. I'd had it shipped to London. It was unique there. And what I might not have been able to do, the T-bird did. Every night it was waiting outside the Aldwych Theatre, and within a very short time Vanessa and I were living together. I moved out of Hammersmith, Vanessa moved out of her flat, and we lived in a series of rented apartments, the first of which was loaned us by John Osborne, who now had begun his romance with and subsequent marriage to the writer Penelope Gilliatt (I'd introduced them with some of the same half-involvement I'd had with Mary before her relationship with John). There were by now so many professional friendship ties between us that there was great excitement among all the Devine clan and Rachel, Vanessa's mother, with whom I'd worked very happily several times. It was difficult to see as much of each other as we wanted, with theatre commitments and commuting to film locations, but this probably added an excitement: Every reunion was a celebration, and our various refrigerators never had anything in them but champagne and (I'm told) the occasional tin of caviar.

Neither of us believed in marriage. And sometimes I think we might have gone on forever had we not decided to get married. However much you reject an institution, it exerts its own discipline. Suddenly you begin to take each other for granted in a way that you never do when the door is always open. But we were very much in love, and we both wanted children strongly. It would be more comfortable for their sake if we had a legal union. (Even this is dubious to me now, but I've never yet discussed it with my third daughter, Katharine, who was born out of marriage.) We were married in April 1962. To avoid all publicity I arranged for the registrar at the Hammersmith Town Hall to open early, and our only witnesses (we had told them that morning) were George and Jocelyn and my chauffeur, Jan. Vanessa insisted on having a drink of champagne with her family in our rented mews flat; I didn't tell my parents until afterward—which hurt them. By noon we were on a plane for a five-day honeymoon in Corfu and Greece. (Vanessa was still playing in repertory at the RSC.)

Corfu, with its transparent seas and swimming and lobsters and solitude, was blissful. But we decided we had to see the Parthenon and Delphi too. I hired a car with a lady driver for the long drive to Delphi. The lady pursued us relentlessly through the ruins, with me trying to explain that we wanted to be alone. Then, returning in the dark, Vanessa asked her to recite some Greek poetry. Vanessa immediately went to sleep on my shoulder, but the chauffeuress, excited at last, gave me a nonstop lecture on the various styles of Greek pottery—the red and the black—all the way back to Athens.

On the Saturday—too soon—we had to return to London, where Vanessa had two performances of *As You Like It*. We got to Athens airport at 6:30, long before the plane was due to depart. There was already pandemonium at the airport (not for the first or last time there!) and it was clear that the plane was totally overbooked and the passengers were in a murderous mood. Conscientious as we were, it was inconceivable to Vanessa that she might miss two performances (those times!). I finally went to one of the managers of Hellenic Airlines and told him that my wife had to play a royal command performance that afternoon and that if she didn't arrive it would create a diplomatic scandal between Britain and Greece. Reluctantly he agreed to bump two passengers. The plane had just arrived from Karachi, and some disheveled and middle-aged couple from Kansas were told that they would have to wait for the next flight, due to some technical fault. I pointed out the transaction going on to Vanessa (who knew nothing of my threats to the manager). Impulsively, she rushed over to the couple, embraced them, and thanked them for sacrificing themselves to her art. Had they not been so dog-tired and bemused, the RSC might not have had a Rosalind that afternoon.

We went house hunting. We finally settled on 30 St. Peter's Square in Hammersmith—the house I think I have loved most in my life. This square of late-Georgian houses had been built by the grateful nation for the officers victorious over Napoleon at Waterloo, their victory being symbolized by stucco eagles on the porticos of many of the buildings. What attracted me was the garden. It was created by a famous designer and was one of the most celebrated small gardens in England. It combined a large lily pool and statue with an extraordinary variety of trees, evergreen and deciduous shrubs, perennials and bulbs, so that at no season of the year were there not blooms and color. And its only upkeep was pruning and clearing the leaves. It was as perfect an organization of planting in gardens as I've ever seen. The house too, which had three floors, plus a big, light basement for the dining room and kitchen, was just what we wanted. I installed aviaries in the garden and a sun room and an extensive indoor tropical bird room in what had been the garage. I had toward the end built a bird room in the apartment in Hammersmith, and the birds were still there, looked after by a gentle old lady called Miss Anns. Miss Anns's toucans, soft-billed birds, followed us to St. Peter's Square. Vanessa's Yorkshire terrier, Marvellous—supposedly named after my most-used adjective in rehearsal—was already installed and was joined by a whippet (my favorite kind of dog).

I recruited a cook, a cleaning lady, and, later, nannies. Jan was always around, though I think he basically disapproved of my ever getting married. "Downstairs" was a continual swirl of competing personalities, but we loved the house and were very happy there. It was always full of people—friends, parents (I'd bought a house for them nearby, and they moved to London), co-workers, neighbors, staff. There was a large drawing room the length of the house, with big, high windows overlooking the square and the garden. It was white and bright with lots of light color. Vanessa sometimes muttered that I spent more time with friends and with work than with her, but these were never complaints. Natasha, our elder daughter, was born on May 11, 1963. It seemed all very good.

11

Tom Jones

As far as movies were concerned, I was looking for a change of pace. I was thinking about various projects when suddenly I thought of *Tom Jones*—Fielding's great sprawling love-of-life comic odyssey with its wild range of characters and its unstoppable narrative. It had never really been filmed before, because of its sexuality and irony, and probably because it's so long and movie people haven't got a great ability to read. The title role was ideal for Albert, now a hot young star. It would give me a chance to use color, and color film was becoming much faster and more sensitive. There had been a lot of prejudice against color, which I, to my shame, had shared—we had all thought it to be too crude and brash. There had been a lot of talk about "taste"—again, today, to my shame. In fact this snobbery still exists, and many people, inspired by their passion, still imagine that there is something intrinsically subtler, better, more artistic about black-and-white. Even after *Tom Jones* I did three more films in black-and-white (and one of them was as well photographed as it is possible for black-and-white to be), but I now wish they—and all my earlier movies—had been in color. Many people think this heretical; to me it is just natural. We see in color. What started with inadequate technology—which, like all inadequacies, can produce its own beauties—becomes, when used today,

158

an imposed aesthetic. It always seems to draw some life off the screen.

Anyway, we started on a vast series of tests and research. Jocelyn Herbert was to design the film. It was her first major movie assignment, and we had determined to make the English countryside look as if it was unchanged from the eighteenth century and the people as real as today. I'd invited Ozzie Morris to photograph the film, thinking I needed his expertise, but after a few discussions when there were too many art books consulted and too much aesthetics talked we realized that our philosophies were even farther apart than before (and also, the only foreseeable budget couldn't accommodate his requirements), so soon Walter Lassally took over. It was a sad parting with an old mentor and friend.

John had never read *Tom Jones*. When I gave it to him, he loved it as I knew he would. I asked him to write the script. This was only half a good idea. John, like many serious writers, loves movies, wants to be part of them, and likes the money (not that at that time he was getting much) and the glamour, but he has never understood the process of rewriting. He resents it. He regards a script once finished as the script of the play, with the director being responsible for staging the author's vision in the most effective way he can. But in movies the director's is the final sensibility: Every choice, every decision, has to be filtered through him, and he converts them all into images the way a writer converts his experience into words. (This doesn't mean that the writer isn't vital to the project, however—the substitution of director for writer was one of the excesses of the so-called *auteur* theory at its height.)

The script of *Tom Jones* was as near as John and I got to collaborating successfully on film (as distinct from when I was making films of his stage works, which were halfway houses). It worked like this. I took the book and did a breakdown of the main events, characters, and even scenes I thought usable. One of the most difficult parts of this was elimination, as the characters and the twists of the plot are so astonishingly prolific. John took this and produced a screenplay. Into this screenplay—especially in some of the descriptive passages—he got his own passion for the book and the force and enjoyment and vitality that it creates. This was helpful to everyone, because it gave a glimpse of what the finished film was aiming for. But a lot of the details of the narrative were missing—

as well as the precision necessary for production. He did grudgingly produce one set of rewrites, which were more like pastiche Congreve than anything to do with movie narrative, and then he left me to do the rest. Many in the crew—especially the most professional, like Ralph Brinton—complained a lot about many of the inadequacies of the script. I was under siege with all the preparations, and I resented the fact that John wasn't going to be more of an understanding or active partner. At a time when I wanted to be free for other things, I was having to rewrite and rewrite—a task that continued during the shooting. The script John published is, I think, the final continuity script of the film: It wasn't what we started with. Anyway, our partnership worked—even if, as in an uneasy marriage, there were a lot of spoken and unspoken criticisms on both sides. And I knew as far as John was concerned I could never change the nature of the beast.

Financially we were really under siege. The money the other Woodfall films had brought in was still comparatively small, and we had already plowed it straight back into the coming projects. We had a loyal group of workers who were either on salary or to whom I felt committed. But with the additional preliminary expenses of a period film—we were already making costumes and wigs, constructing props, buying and training our own horses— we were, moneywise, at bottom. We had a tentative deal with British Lion and Columbia (which had been involved in *Loneliness*), but they had fixed a budget plucked, as so many company figures are, from the air. Our own budget was minimal, £500,000. But horses and costumes cost money, and, however we tried, we all knew we couldn't make the Columbia figure. It got ludicrous. I flew to Cannes, where all the top brass were ensconced at the Carlton, was given champagne, handshakes, encouragement; but back in London their representatives wouldn't move. I would add a new piece of casting, say Diane Cilento. She would cost £1,500 in all. Fine, they'd say—but you pay. Word got back on the grapevine that their executive knew we were overcommitted to the point of bankruptcy and therefore we would be forced to undertake the movie at the numbers they imposed.

One of the strictest policies we maintained at Woodfall was that we'd never cheat or lie about budget. There are very few reasons why any film should ever go over budget. You can shoot in any weather, you can insure against most catastrophes: The only thing you can't cover for is the sudden bad behavior of a star. The only two things that can really make a film go over are the dictates and temperament of a director or of a lighting cameraman. Not that you don't know the requirements of these to begin with, more or less: It's clear you wouldn't make the calculations exactly the same for a script directed by Godard or by David Lean. But unfortunately studios and financiers have always regarded artists as whimsical, impractical, devious ignoramuses, and have consequently imposed their own budgets—made by so-called experts and accountants who've never been encouraged to meet with the filmmakers—which encourage the filmmakers to lie and cheat, to accept figures and schedules they know to be wrong in order to get the film made. (We used to have the same arguments with "financial wizards" at the Royal Court too.) We believed, and I still believe, that the best approach is to treat the director and the production company as adults and, as such, financially responsible: To ask directors and producers to make their own budgets and to guarantee completion with their own fees and investments. In other words, you give them the choices you would give to a construction company that had contracted to build a house or a piece of furniture. The principle works. On any project Woodfall has done and been in control of, we have never gone over budget in any significant way, whereas our people have gone over like everyone else when they have tried to work on other projects and not had control. There's no incentive not to go over in those circumstances, and companies should realize that the kind of double-talk they practice removes the very protection they would get if they trusted the people they employed. But often, as in the case of *Tom Jones*, budgets which should be simple, open, and practical become pawns in games of muscle and power. "Show me where to cut," I'd say. "Show me where we're over." "You'll find out," was always the answer.

We were getting near our projected shooting date and we had no more money even for the continuing work. Suddenly a fairy godmother arrived. My agent, Cecil Tennant, a splendid, lofty former Guards officer who was also the head of Laurence Olivier Productions, said, "There's a new chap in town who might be able to help." The new chap was David V. Picker, the recently appointed production head of United Artists and one of the best executives ever to head any motion picture company. We met, got on. David read the script overnight, approved the budget, and made the deal next day. The Columbia group now protested with all the hypocrisy that only blackmailers and bullies can summon—we knew they would have always made the deal; we were betraying them; etc. It was a relief to be set and to be working with human beings like David, his London representative Bud Ornstein, and the rest of the UA team under the brilliant Arthur Krim.

Problems weren't over, though. Albie didn't like the role. He'd felt frustrated by his recent stage work, and he wanted to "act." Tom Jones was too "passive," too "reactive" a character. He realized he was obliged to do it under our options, but he was truculent and unhappy. He did, however, want to "learn about film business." John and I then offered to tear up all our options and make him an equal partner with ourselves: He could be an associate producer and participate in all the problems. He accepted this enthusiastically, but he never fulfilled the producing part of the bargain; he never tried to understand the problems and pressures of the production. He complained, sulked, and created scenes, and only fitfully during the ten weeks we were shooting during the summer and autumn of 1962 did he display the kind of buoyancy of temperament that his characterization so effectively portrayed on screen.

Tom Jones wasn't, then, a "happy" or cohesive production in the way that *A Taste of Honey* and *Loneliness* had been. There were many wonderful compensations—the English countryside in summer, heavy with the scents of grass seeds, dog roses and cow parsley, a green richness that seems to last longer than anywhere else. There were the great houses we used: one with a lake gorged with water lilies and yellow flags; another (Cranborne) majestic and elegant with a labyrinth of garden succeeding garden, glimmering with white and yellow roses. And the smaller houses, still unrestored and neglected, and populated with strange eccentrics—a vast, overgrown seventeenth-century manor house, with windows rotting and ceilings falling, inhabited by an old crone whom I met one day gathering twigs for her stove, dressed in a witch's hat and cloak, a straight-line descendant of the Plantagenets; or Nettlecombe (then a girl's school, which we converted for various sets), whose owner imagined he was a bird, lived in a tree and descended once a day on all fours to pick off the grass crumbs deposited by the butler from a silver platter.

The son of Nettlecombe's owner was an artist who camped out in the derelict stables. One night during shooting, he decided he wanted to visit his ancestors buried in the crypt under the family chapel in the grounds. During rainy weather their coffins floated and could be heard during services bobbing against the stone floor of the church, he said. We went there with strong prop men who could pierce the frail bricks that blocked the entrance shaft of the crypt, but when we finally broke through there was nothing but slime and mold and maybe a dozen twentieth-century lead coffins whose lids he gleefully ripped open with a chisel. Instead of the expected gorgeous relics of armor and helmets contemporaries of Sir Francis Drake and Sir Walter Raleigh, there was nothing but a few wet bones and oily skulls. This particular episode caused quite a local scandal. The parson's son, a boy of about eight, entered into the spirit of the occasion, went into his father's robing room, borrowed his surplice, and capered around as a ghost during the exploration. Everything was carefully sealed up again, but, come Sunday, when the parson donned his surplice he found it covered with finger and fist marks of red Devon clay. The truth came out. The proprietor's son was unrepentant: He claimed he had as much right to visit his ancestors as the parson had to harangue his congregation and, anyway, the parson held office only at the pleasure of the lord of the manor.

The eccentricities didn't extend just to the locals. The cast included Wilfred Lawson, a great actor (he was far and away the best ever Captain in Strindberg's *The Father*) whose greatness was destroyed by alcoholism but who retained a zest and humor and wickedness, and Hugh Griffith, unique, original, and Welsh. At the beginning of the shooting, when we were staying in the sedate little seaside resort of Weymouth, they had already caused horror by hanging some barmaid upside down out of a window. Wilfred, who played Black George, the gamekeeper, had only a few days with us, but Hugh was with us for the whole shoot, although he had to commute to London, and often assistants would be phoning frantically to his home to try to find him, then frantically rescheduling, only to discover him passed out in a fold full of sheep, his Rolls crashed in a ditch. Part drunk, part amateur, wholly child,

Hugh lived the part of Squire Western in real life. When you see him turn the horse like a corkscrew after he's charged the steps of the Allworthy house, you're not seeing something planned or rehearsed—he quite literally twisted the animal's head so much that it reared, turned, and fell back on top of him. All the crew thought the weight of the horse would have split him open and killed him (if there was a frame more of the shot used in the film you would have seen assistants rushing in), but he was so drunk that the relaxation produced by the alcohol cushioned him completely. Another day he somehow got hold of a shotgun and started trying to pot the crew as they were trailing home to sleep, and before he was overpowered he discharged a barrel into the roof of my T-bird. He and Edith Evans, who played Miss Western, were an extraordinary contrast. She couldn't stand him, but, being the great actress she was, she could understand how effective his personality was and always tried to make things work. Edith would arrive for rehearsal word-perfect, always on time, meticulously made up and costumed; Hugh would shamble in late, lurching, mumbling. Occasionally in exasperation she would give him a good swat with her parasol.

Hugh could, however, be almost lethal. One night Edith was resting in a coach. Hugh, seeing the driver leave his seat for a moment, lashed at the horses with a riding crop, trying to make them bolt. The six horses with Edith and the coach took off, but luckily they were still in the confines of a big stable yard and were calmed and held before there was a real tragedy. Giving a whip to Hugh was like putting a child on a toboggan at Christmas. I warned him; the cast warned him; Albie, who had to be pursued by Hugh while wearing nothing but a thin linen nightshirt, warned him most of all. Lots of the crew and the cameramen were flicked and lashed until I got the prop man to wire the end of the whip to the stock so that it could be flourished but was relatively safe.

The sequence with Albie took two nights to shoot. The second night the prop men repeated the operation. I saw Hugh playing with the whip, muttering Celtic runes to himself. When the camera was turning, I saw he'd unpicked the wiring and, predictably, the whip came down *crack* on Albie's back, cutting a long red weal. Albie stopped, turned, said, "I can't abide to be whipped, Squire," and hit Hugh full in the face, cutting his lip open. Then they both marched off the set, swearing they would never work with each other again. It took me a couple of hours to persuade them back. From any other actor it would have been impossible, but somehow from Hugh it was the wickedness of a bad child daring to be naughty. It was without professionally calculated malice, just pure Welsh devilment—the old medieval devil's tricks; Puck with the milkmaids in the farmyard. Of course, I hadn't been on the worst of the receiving end, and I valued his input as the character so much, but I've seen professional actors (and actresses) cause less damage but hurt more because of their coldness and bitchiness. Hugh had finally a purity of spirit about him.

Years later I had a macabre experience with Hugh. I was making *Joseph Andrews*. There was a tiny role of a squire at a hunt, and it seemed a good idea to make the part into Squire Western. I hadn't seen Hugh in years, but I knew he worked from time to time so I thought it couldn't be too much of a risk to use him. When he arrived it was appalling—a disintegrating wreck of a man, hardly able to walk on the set, his voice and health gone, trembling, pathetic. Replacement was impossible: We were miles from London, with a big crowd of extras, a full hunt, a pack of hounds. I asked for Hugh to be made up—we had his original wig, costume, and stills for his *Tom Jones* makeup to be matched. When he came back on the set it was exactly as if you'd run the years backward—forget the great party at the end of Proust, you were back on the walks at Combray. But I knew what was behind the facade. The prop man stood by, and before each take we fed Hugh a spoonful of brandy. It had to be measured exactly: Too much would have put him to sleep, but without it he had not a flicker of energy. Keeping him sitting in a chair, during take after take, we'd get one usable line in this take, one look in another, until we got enough to piece together some sort of just passable sequence. It was the last time I ever saw him.

Making movies teaches you about a lot of things you'd never normally know about, things that cause problems you have to solve —like a hunt. It seems easy on the surface: You just hire a pack of hounds, recruit the horsemen, dress them up, and turn on the cameras. It's never quite like that. First of all, in the eighteenth century they mainly hunted deer; today it's fox. Also, the hounds are trained to follow the scent and trail of their quarry, which might not go where you want or can make your camera go. There are drag-hounds, trained to follow a pre-laid trail, but they will only follow that same bit of trail once or, if you're very lucky, twice—after that it's stale or the dogs are bored. And then the hunting fraternity is very defensive. Very early on they decided—on some kind of animal instinct—that we were against blood sports, so they wouldn't cooperate. We decided, therefore, that we had to buy our own hounds, drag-hounds, so we could set the route and train them. But buying hounds isn't an easy thing, because either they're some-one's adored pet or they're practically about to be destroyed. Even-tually we did assemble a pack of about twenty or thirty of the most motley, broken-down old curs imaginable. Some of the local fox-hounds owners weren't quite as antagonistic as others and we used their animals for closer shots; our group was used for the longer runs with a drag trail. Then, as the climax, I wanted a shot of the hounds tearing into a deer. We already had permission to cull venison from an overstocked herd. For several weeks we fed "our" hounds nothing but venison, so they would have the taste. Before you hunt, the dogs are kept hungry so they'll be keen. We followed the formula. And all was prepared, with a newly killed deer for them to devour. But, the night before, some of the local hunting associations, getting wind of our shot, had broken into our kennels and stuffed our hounds with meat. When we came to shoot, our dogs were too bloated to do more than sniff at the carcass and back away. Three days later we had to repeat the operation with the deer stuffed with expensive beef liver. We only just managed to get a viable image then.

These kind of problems recurred and recurred. For instance, the eating scene. John and I had planned this—food transforming to lust—from the first draft of the script. Details had been left to be worked out in the doing. Eventually when the scene loomed up it was discussed with the prop men, who were responsible for the preparation of the food, and with Joyce Redman and Albie, who had to perform the ordeal. We worked out the menu—starting with oysters (one of which turned out to be bad and left Joyce sick for days afterward). We'd planned more or less everything, including a piece of business with the wishbone of a chicken. But when the actors started to disembowel the chicken we discovered that, being a battery chicken, its bones were so gelatinous as to be practically nonexistent. Panic; then the prop men had to construct a fake wishbone out of matchsticks before the scene could be performed. From beginning to end, with buckets strategically placed beside Albie and Joyce, it took about three hours to shoot the whole sequence, but the physical effect on the two of them lasted for days.

Throughout the shooting we all felt we were fighting the smallness of our resources, our shortness of time. There were, of course, occasional moments of exhilaration—when, inspired by a sudden shower, Albie and Susannah York plunged unexpectedly into a pond, or when they danced spontaneously in a sunlit rose garden—but these were the exceptions. Jocelyn was working tirelessly, trying to perfect everything from the tint and texture of paneling to the detail of every extra, but even her energy was limited. George, who played quite beautifully the thankless role of Squire Allworthy, was often with us, providing quiet moral and spiritual support. And there were moments of off-screen emotion and harmony. Vanessa visited when she could—once disguised as a boy extra, leading me to shout at Peter Yates, the first assistant, "Tell that fucking idiot to lose himself at the back." There was a great car chase down the steep one-way Dorset lanes when a to-be-famous lady writer started, to my embarrassment, to perform fellatio on me: Her husband was in the car behind, and I had to keep ahead, out of his headlights, while facing a certain crash if any vehicle came the opposite way. We had a memorable dinner at which we played the "wishes" game—who you would most like to be. People's fantasies ranged from astronauts to Diane de Poitiers to Sherpa Tensing, but Edith capped everyone by announcing, "I'd just like to be me—only even more marvelous. Anything else would be an insult to my parents."

And we all lived in extraordinary places and houses. My first was a broken-down castle with an attached pig farm—one of the first in England to practice the scientific raising of pigs, so that with a controlled diet the exact weight of each piglet could be calculated from birth to slaughter. The last house was a sad eighteenth-century pile in Wiltshire, with a dining room hung with rotting military banners and at one end a lectern with a family Bible full of the deaths of unnamed infants, perishing from whooping cough or fever from the 1780s to the 1810s. Portraits on the walls showed tortured-looking eighteenth-century children whose groans and cries seemed forever recorded in the creaks and sighs of the wainscoting at night so that, for the first and only time in my life, I believed completely in a place being haunted. I even invited the set dresser, Josie MacAvin—a dedicated, almost nunlike Irish Roman Catholic—to move in to exorcise the evil. Her prayers didn't seem to help. The house was in a narrow slit of a valley where the skies were always gray and sullen, and the newts in the basin of a long-defunct fountain turned black and malevolent.

The last part of *Tom Jones* was shot in London. It was an anticlimax. The strain of the rest of the shooting was telling on all of us, and we were more and more conscious of all we hadn't achieved, all we had skimped, all we hadn't been able to do. The sustaining presence of the country, the earth, the weather, the landscape, had gone: We were just cobbling the last bits together as best we could and realizing how impoverished and threadbare our efforts were in so many ways. This sense of disappointment, that we were so far away from what we'd started out so bravely hoping to achieve, overhung all the editing process. The editor was Anthony Gibbs; I'd worked with him before, and we worked well together, but somehow this time I hadn't got all the material I wanted, yet we had to get it together and make it work. Jock Addison helped enormously with his score, and the wicked, witty Irish actor Micheal MacLiammoir narrated a commmentary I concocted from John's original and from the book. But I was still very disappointed. I think we all were.

The prognosis was not good. The head of British distribution for United Artists saw the finished cut. He pronounced disaster: The film would be lucky if it made £40,000 worldwide. (At about the same time, Bud Ornstein, the head of British UA production, told the same gentleman that he'd just signed the Beatles for their first film. The distributor replied, "But who's going to star?") The notices arrived and I remember coming down in a robe early in the morning and starting to read them. *The Times* said, "There is nothing in this film that could give any member of the audience one moment of enjoyment." Vanessa came in with mugs of coffee. She looked at me. "It's the usual story," I said. We were inured to it.

But then, just like in the finale of *The Threepenny Opera*, the Queen's messenger rode in and Macheath, on the scaffold, was given his reprieve. Lines were forming round the London Pavilion. Rock and roll had just broken through in England with the first impact of the Beatles. The sixties were starting to swing, and *Tom Jones* became part of the "revolution." The movie went on to success after success beyond our financial dreams. The budget had been met, and the film generated its own publicity, so, measured by the ratio of profit to investment, it was comparable to some of the biggest hits of all time. Success is, of course, a very agreeable thing to have to deal with. John and I gave much of our proceeds away, in percentages to the creative participants, which seemed only fair. But it meant we could launch into a lot of new projects for Woodfall, including Desmond Davis's first film, *Girl with Green Eyes*, with Rita Tushingham and Lynn Redgrave.

Tom Jones won prizes and finally Oscars. I didn't go to the awards, not to strike an attitude but because I had never understood their importance in the eyes of the industry, and they were never important to me. But there was something more than that: I felt the movie to be incomplete and botched in much of its execution. I am not knocking that kind of success—everyone should have it—but whenever someone gushes to me about *Tom Jones*, I always cringe a little inside.

12

Natural Affection

Even before the editing of *Tom Jones* was over, I returned to the theatre. The enterprise wouldn't be worth writing about if it wasn't one of the most bewildering and inexplicable that I was ever involved in. The play, by David Turner, was *Semi-Detached*—a free contemporary update of Molière's *Le Bourgeois Gentilhomme*. It had premiered in Coventry with Leonard Rossiter in the leading role, and had had great critical success. The rights had been bought for commercial production by Oscar Lewenstein, who, after a stint at the Royal Court and in the commercial theatre, was to join Woodfall as a film producer. He got Larry [Olivier] to agree to play in it, and both of them begged me to direct.

It wasn't the kind of play that I liked, but, after an eternity in the eighteenth century, I wanted to return to now. It would be a great pleasure to work with Larry again, the rehearsals were to be quick, a commercial success was guaranteed by Larry's presence, and I needed the money (this was before there was any glimpse of the *Tom Jones* windfall). It seemed to me a very logical vehicle for Larry. It was about a car salesman, the reverse of Willie Loman: someone who wanted to be up-market and up-class; posher in speech; nattier in dress. There were echoes of the fake, the show-off side of Archie Rice, and there were marketing speeches to fuel the kind of fireworks in which Larry could so brilliantly excel. Larry was preparing for the opening of the National Theatre; he needed some quick money. It all seemed so very clear and easy.

Except for one thing: Larry himself. Somewhere—on the train to Brighton, I think—he'd seen some sad character (he called him Chekhovian, but I now think he was probably Larry's idea of how Willie Loman should be played) with a dirty old raincoat and a Birmingham accent who was the image he had of the role. The play is set in Birmingham, but the Birmingham accent happens to be the ugliest of all the British provincial accents and the whole point of the character that Larry played was that he wanted to dissociate himself from his milieu. As soon as we discussed the play, I outlined to Larry what I believed it to be about. After an initial dispute, he seemed to agree. His rehearsal manners were always perfect, but he was secretly determined—he spent his time out of rehearsal perfecting the abominable accent. The play, in a one-set suburban home, staged itself easily. But, in contrast to *The Entertainer*, Larry started missing rehearsals, pleading fatigue with his National Theatre labors and the problem of learning his lines. Then, when he did rehearse, he would beg me with all his amazing charm to leave him be until he made himself word-perfect—then he would adjust anything, etc., etc. It was quite clear from the outset that he was killing all the humor in the play and destroying both the character as conceived and any success we could have. It was like watching someone commit suicide blindly—and all for a commercial comedy. Finally I relied on the audiences—his natural showmanship would recover itself once he faced their reaction. Not at all. We opened out of town. It was funereal. The comments of his departing fans were like one-line obituaries. "He's aged, poor thing." "Didn't he once play Henry V?" "Oh, no, he couldn't have. . . ."

It wasn't just me that Larry fought: Cecil Tennant, his manager, came up with Joan (she and Larry were now married)—we all told him the same thing. At the end of the first week in Edinburgh I finally got rid of the rumpled old mackintosh, took him on a shopping expedition, dressed him in a blazer and gray slacks, and with the new costume he put out a little of his old energy. The play immediately warmed up and the laughs started to come. But even this encouragement didn't goad Larry on: Brummagem kept trying to come back.

The play opened in London in December 1962, to not-good notices (including Larry's). For the first time in a long while there were empty seats in a theatre with Larry's name on the billboard. It still is inexplicable, and, without either of us admitting it, it killed our relationship. We never worked together again, and we never professed friendship until much later, in Los Angeles, when I met Larry and Joan's charming and talented eldest son, Richard, on a tennis court.

I hadn't worked in America since *Sanctuary*. I was now traveling extensively in Europe—to Italy, to Greece, and most often to the south of France—but New York was my Mecca. I would find any excuse to visit, even if only for a weekend. I needed its rush, its excitement, its high like a drug. What I wanted more than anything was to do an original American play—the equivalent of what the Court did in England. I wanted to prove myself an American. For a long time I had longed to do a musical. Many projects came up, but somehow I never felt enough belief in any of them. And the American musical theatre seemed to be running to its end, with the world of rock and roll taking over. *Gypsy* was for me the last great Broadway score. Then Oliver Smith—the designer of *A Taste of Honey*, who'd become a good friend—came up with a proposition. He jointly with Roger Stevens had bought the rights to an unperformed play by William Inge—*Natural Affection*. Roger was apparently not so keen on the play but was very keen on Kim Stanley, with whom it was rumored he had had an affair and whom he had presented in London in *Cat on a Hot Tin Roof*. (She was superb.) Oliver and I were both avid fans of Kim. She read the play but was ambivalent about it, so we journeyed out to her old stone-flagged farmhouse in Connecticut (like a sprawling version of a Cotswold cottage). Kim and I hit it off in a flash and I talked her out of her objections. The show was set.

Until now I had only worked with one great actress—Edith Evans—but in limited roles and in her declining years. Since then I've been lucky enough to work with several—each with her own particular qualities. What they all shared—despite their ambitions, their egos, their vanities, all those things which make and are even indispensable to being a "star"—was an absolute immersion of themselves in the work they were performing and the reality they were creating. Once they understood something, it was a total commitment. Vanessa with her emotional flow and understanding; Peggy with her authority; Edith alternating between the highest style and the humblest humanity; Jeanne Moreau with her precision, elegance, understanding of film and how it works; Kate Hepburn with her feistiness and humor—they were all unique and extraordinary. And then there was Kim. Searching for an image to describe her overwhelming talent, I can only come up with a bag lady. But her bag was life itself. Never, before or since, have I worked with someone of such variety and impact. Kim was at the height of her power, the queen of the Actors' Studio and of "Method" acting.

The Method has been talked about, written about, discussed, distorted, abused, and traduced to death. As a path and training, it proceeded in its own way, but the goal it sought—absolute human reality on stage and screen—was exactly what all good acting has always been about. If you had put Edith and Kim on the same stage and in the same play there would have been a difference in accents, but in their access to the portrayal of life on stage they would have been equal. All those technical necessities of any important actress—sense of stage, perfection of direction, awareness of rhythms of both character and text, grace, ease, fluency: all those things which Method actors, immersed in their own internal conflicts and emotions, were supposedly deficient in—Kim had them all. Directing Kim was as if you'd been given a piano and suddenly found you could play as well as Glenn Gould. She was like Larry at his best, only more so. And her range of understanding of human and physical experience was endless. She could play the same scene over and over again in a totally fresh way, yet always respecting the others onstage with her, reacting to and building on and up to everyone else's reactions and contributions, and never distorting the pacing or truth of the play. "Infinite variety" is totally applicable to Kim.

We opened the play in Washington. Vanessa came out to stay with me. She was equally in awe and admiring of Kim's prodigious gifts. The cast included Harry Guardino, Tom Bosley, and a slightly catatonic young actor, Gregory Rozakis, whose presence

was effective but whose impulses were so nonreactive that sometimes Kim would clap her hands in his face to get even a blink. It
was the only thing she failed in. I have never worked on anything
before or since where rehearsals were such a sustained joy—all
because of Kim.

William Inge was a strange, rather sad man—always conscious
of being in the public eye, the poor third of the triumvirate of
Williams, Miller, and Inge. His talent was quite different from that
of any other writer I've known. Most writers take you into their
world—the *vieux carrés*, Vladimir and Estragon's crossroads, Jimmy
Porter's rented apartment—and into the minds and feelings of their
characters, so you emerge from the theatre feeling expanded by
having been into some corner of experience where you've not been
before. Bill Inge does the opposite: He shows you your world—
the recognizable—and your pleasure comes from your recognition
of dialogue (his ear was impeccable—almost extrasensory) and situation. He was—and I don't mean this as a put-down—a sitcom
writer of genius, or near-genius. Just how recognizable, how accurate, his language was took us all by surprise. We opened at the
National Theater in Washington. The laughs and applause started
from the first lines—"Whadya want for breakfast?" "French
toast"—after Kim had dragged herself out of bed, pulled on a robe,
and stared out at the cold early morning. The audience adored the
play. Never in my experience have I ever done a show with such
immediate and extensive reaction. But the audience was running
the show: All the serious (and sentimental) subtext was being lost
in the welcome. Even with all Kim's stage command, it took us
four days to get the play in balance and let the other facet speak.

Natural Affection was not a good play. The plot concerned a
delinquent boy returning, after a stay in prison, to his mother—a
shallow woman who had little place for him in her life and whom
he therefore found rejecting. In response to this rejection he kills,
arbitrarily, a hooker living on another floor of their apartment
house. This was based on a true case from, I think, Kansas, where
Bill came from. It was a much more serious theme than he'd ever
tackled before and, once he'd taken it up, Bill lost courage, admitted
he was frightened of it, thought he probably should never have
started it, and took refuge therefore in the scenes of the mother's
relationship with her new lover and with the neighbors at a drunken

party—all of which he depicted accurately but which were pe-
ripheral to the situation of the boy himself. When the murder came,
it seemed arbitrary, unmotivated. The critics called it a deliberate
attempt to shock, thought Bill was trying to be too serious—that
he should have confined himself, oh so tidily, to his cozy familiar
territory of heartland American types and behaviors. The real problem with the play was the opposite: It wasn't serious enough—Bill
had pulled his hand off the material as if he'd touched an electric
hot plate.

When we started rehearsals there were two, maybe three, drafts
of the play. I begged Bill to choose among them. He wouldn't. We
had to piece together what we found most effective in rehearsals.
During run-throughs and during the run in Washington (he attended every performance), I would ask for notes, question him
about this or that. He would never give any opinion, pro or con:
He just went along—amiable, sad, sweet. He ate a lot of desserts,
especially pink custard and Jell-O. I heard from him once a day
regularly, on one subject only. "Tony, I know you're worried about
Gregory and thinking about replacing him." "What do you think,
Bill?" "Oh, I don't know, but I have a young friend here, an actor
[or non-actor] who I think you might find very suitable. As a favor
to me, would you please let him read for you?" So every day, after
rehearsal, I would read a new "young friend." Gregory wasn't
replaced.

Actually, Gregory provided one of the most bizarre moments of
the production. He told me he had a friend and that the friend was
obsessed with "big cats." He arrived for the opening in Washington,
with a leopard. Because of the animal, they had had to stay in a
hotel in the black part of town—Washington was still virtually
segregated. With my passion for animals, I couldn't wait to see the
leopard, and between rehearsals I went with Gregory to his hotel.
The room was large, white-tiled, with two iron cots. The door to
the adjacent bathroom had a handwritten sign to the maid: "Do
not clean. Cat inside." They opened the door and out bounded a
lithe, beautiful, eighteen-month-old leopard which stalked around
the room with fantastic grace. But to be in such close quarters with
it was scary, especially as the animal would suddenly spring against
a wall, do a back-flip upward, bouncing against the ceiling, and
land on them, or you—on your shoulder or leg—facing the direc-

tion it had started in. Neither its teeth or claws had been filed. Once it stretched its claws against my jeans and ripped them open for three feet. Much as I admired its beauty, I felt relieved to emerge with my two big ears still flapping. On the first night at the traditional party at the Variety Club, Gregory's friend told me he was three hundred years before his time because his mission in life was to domesticate the big cats, who will live with us then like alley cats and mutts do today.

The history of *Natural Affection* was even more curious. Roger Stevens had given me one piece of initial advice, which was to "clean up the play." There were, I think, two pisses and a son-of-a-bitch or so in it (about four years before linguistic permissiveness broke with *Hair*). When Roger had presented *Cat on a Hot Tin Roof* in London, he had forbidden his wife and daughter to see it as that too was a "dirty" play. I only wish I could have dirtied *Natural Affection* up. When we went to New York in January 1963, Roger either removed or threatened to remove his name from the marquee, saying it hurt him with the Democratic Party (he was a big fundraiser), and with the Kennedys in particular. Though the New York critics slated Bill Inge, the audience reaction and the ticket sales were as enthusiastic as ever. But Roger, whether his name was up there or not, was the controlling producer, and he decided that whatever happened, he would close the show after six weeks—when we had to move to another theatre. So, despite sell-out business, that was the end of the "dirty" play.

The lure of New York was becoming more and more potent. The New York production of *Luther* was on the way, and through *Luther* I was to meet one of my major collaborators for the future: Neil Hartley. We had in fact met during the Boston tryout of *The Entertainer*, in 1958, and had not got on. Neil had just begun work as David Merrick's production manager. There was some dispute with our stage manager. I, always casting myself in the role of defender of the weak and "oppressed," supported our stage manager and thought Neil a front-office bully. I was wrong; Neil was right— the man had been very inefficient. With the passing of the years Neil had grown in confidence and power. From the mountains of North Carolina, he had New England WASP good looks with Southern good manners and gentleness, and an extraordinary sensitivity to people. He was also technically knowledgeable and thorough beyond belief. I got to know him again first through organizing the American production of *Luther*, then through setting up my next two projects in America: *The Resistible Rise of Arturo Ui* and *The Milk Train Doesn't Stop Here Anymore*. I marveled at the efficiency with which auditions were held, design and technical problems were solved, lighting and technical rehearsals were arranged. While always loyal to David, Neil's ultimate commitment was to the work and to the workers. He knew how to wait out the storms of David's temperament and how to diplomatically outmaneuver the crass interference of David's money-men so that in the end we always got what was right for each show. It was an amazing performance.

I contrasted it in my mind with all the people working back at Woodfall. Personally they were all charming—"jolly good chaps," in the British tradition—but I felt that after success, and especially after *Tom Jones*, they had become complacent and were drifting back to the lazy ways of the traditional British movie people, subtly pushing me toward the kind of conformity that deep down they yearned for. I had for a time wanted a shake-up. Neil seemed the perfect answer. At the time he knew nothing about making movies, but I was about to do *The Loved One* in California. He could come as an observer, and I knew he would soon grasp the problems of movie production as surely he did those of the theatre. I suggested he join us. Always an Anglophile (perhaps his one defect), he accepted. And we have been partners ever since—during the good and the bad. Always prepared, efficient, caring, supportive, loyal to me even when I know he has had the greatest inner doubts and reservations, he has been amazing.

I had long wanted to do a Brecht play. David owned the rights to *The Resistible Rise of Arturo Ui*—Brecht's comic-strip parallel to the rise of Hitler, told in terms of 1920s Chicago gangsters—in the effective translation (partly in rhyming couplets) by George Tabori. He offered it to me. I was very excited: I wanted to be free of the shadow of the Berliner Ensemble and to start again—to work on a Brecht play as if Brecht the director had never existed. To do *Arturo Ui* in America with Americans seemed ideal. To start with I asked Rouben Ter-Arutunian, a remarkable and pure artist whose elegant work for George Balanchine (to me, far and away the greatest choreographer alive) I had long admired, to design the show. We took all the George Grosz designs and decided to stage the play as if Grosz had painted a cross between carnival façades and vaudeville backdrops. One of the amazing things about David Merrick, who could be so vicious about trifles, was the scale of his risk-taking once he decided to plunge. Into this violently politically slanted anti-Nazi piece—"The bitch that bore him is in heat again"—was poured money equivalent to the budget of the biggest musicals. Even the extras' trenchcoats were executed by Karinska.

Christopher Plummer played Arturo. Christopher is a brilliant, incisive character actor, and he excelled himself. With Neil's help we searched out the hoods and gangsters from 1940s Hollywood movies: Elisha Cook, Jr., and Lionel Stander (a wonderful comedy eccentric, given his first opportunity to return to Broadway after years of blacklisting in Hollywood and New York by the Un-American Activities Committee), Madeleine Sherwood, James Coco, and Michael Constantine were all in the huge cast. It was a fantastic roster.

We opened to ecstatic previews, with lengthy standing ovations every night. Even today I meet people who describe it as one of their great nights in the theatre. A few months ago a local critic here in California told me it had changed his life, making him decide to work in the theatre ever afterward. David was very pleased, thought he had a sure hit, and then started the kind of cat-and-mouse game with the critics for which he was famous. (He had once found local citizens with exactly the same names as all the critics, paid them to give one of his shows rave quotes, and printed these in a full-page *New York Times* ad.) He switched the date of the opening. No one knew what the logic was behind this—it wouldn't have made any difference. The notices were respectful but tepid—there was still a fear of supporting any Brecht production that didn't have the stamp of Iron Curtain respectability (and preferably stayed behind the curtain). In a fit of pique and disappointment, David ordered the show closed within a week. Despite the enthusiasm of the audiences, he wouldn't nurse it, wouldn't give it a chance. Everyone in the show and connected with it rallied. They believed in it. A group of other investors was found, and another theatre. The show would go on. But on Friday November 22, 1963, Lee Harvey Oswald's bullet put an end to everything.

In the grief surrounding the tragedy of President Kennedy's assassination, a Broadway show didn't seem very important.

At the time I was in rehearsal for Tennessee Williams's *The Milk Train Doesn't Stop Here Anymore*. The history of this ludicrous—at times farcical—debacle is, perhaps, more entertaining than the achievement. They play had originally been done at Spoleto, then had failed in an earlier Broadway production. Tennessee had rewritten it and desperately wanted a second chance. David Merrick's reputation as a producer was based on his musicals and his British imports; he used to complain bitterly that top American playwrights and their agents didn't give him a chance to do their work. In presenting *Milk Train*, David saw an opportunity to corner Tennessee's future product. When asked to direct it I was very ambivalent. I had been away from England and Vanessa and Natasha for a long time; on the other hand, I adored Tennessee's work. Although *Milk Train* wasn't top Tennessee, it had fascinating writing and scenes. He had reshaped it and given it a kabuki framework, with two "Stage Assistants" who commented on the action and acted as stagehands—an elegant stylistic device that I liked very much. I loved doing a new play, especially an American play. I was flattered to be asked, and already thought of becoming a hero by creating success out of failure. Vanity and arrogance won out over family ties—I agreed, stipulating only that, whatever happened to the play, I had contractual rights to spend a week with Vanessa and Tasha at Christmas.

As leads, Tennessee wanted a young actor he'd seen play in one of his plays out of town (he had understudied Ken Haigh toward the end of *Look Back* and I wasn't too keen on him) and as Mrs. Goforth, Tallulah Bankhead. He claimed he had written the play for her. Implausible as it may seem, I hardly knew who she was— a name from the 1920s, the bright young things' years. I must have seen *Lifeboat* when it first came out, but I didn't remember it or her. I'd never felt comfortable in the world of "camp," so I didn't know that side of her. Neil did. In, I think, his first professional job he'd toured the South with her in *Private Lives*. His stories were hilarious. David would go along with anything Tennessee wanted. So the four—I think the four—of us went to visit the shrine: an airless apartment overstuffed with self-portraits and mementoes.

I saw exactly what Tennessee meant. In appearance and personality, Tallulah was the thing itself: the heavy-lidded, drooping ruins of a proud and striking beauty, with a growl of a voice, worn low by alcohol and cigarettes chain-smoked until she had burnt the flesh of her fingers down from the scarlet-lacquered nails to, quite literally, the bone. She was perfectly charming but, as I remember, didn't show much of her celebrated wit or outrageousness. Burnt-out cinders and ashes were the images—together with a slightly malevolent suspicion about us and the project, but neither energy nor vitality. I doubted she could do it. Tennessee was reassuring. I had, I thought, better ideas and, going to Hollywood for talks on *The Loved One*, I was going to try to realize them.

I suppose I must have written more than one fan letter, but not many—and only one that I remember. In my early days in London, just after I'd moved into my Hammersmith apartment, I saw a production of Shaw's *The Millionairess* which had one of the most effective and affecting performances I've ever seen: not just for its electric energy, the daring of its comic timing, the shamelessness of its gags—like a double entrance-exit-entrance (milked by the lady in subsequent productions)—but for a complete final switch to all-out lump-in-the-throat emotion. I can still hear, see, feel it all. I wrote my fan letter, ending with an invitation to afternoon tea (shades of Oxford). Of course I never imagined that it would be accepted. When it was, I hardly had the money to buy the cakes and sandwiches. Anyway, into my life that afternoon walked Katharine Hepburn, I suppose because of her quirky sense of adventure or maybe her pity for what she saw as my naïveté. I don't remember a moment of it; I was too overwhelmed and embarrassed. What she could have thought I can barely imagine—knowing Kate now, she must have been bored stiff and regretted every minute with my gaucheness, but she was very polite, had tea, said thank you politely, and disappeared. Since then I knew she had been living in virtual seclusion and retirement, looking after Spencer Tracy. I had heard talk of her from time to time through mutual friends—the Selznicks, Vivien, Simone Signoret, George Cukor, etc.—and I once saw her in long shot striding into a Beverly Hills cinema. She was my idea for Mrs. Goforth, with Tony Perkins to play Chris, the angel of death. I got the play to Kate without much hope of even an answer. Next day my phone rang. Kate. She asked if I'd be there for the next hour. She'd be right over. Characteristically, she arrived by some unknown subterranean staircase through the kitchens. She'd brought the script back. She'd liked it but couldn't do it for reasons she knew I knew. She meant Spencer, of course, but didn't elaborate. She'd come, she said (this was after *Tom Jones* and Oscar time), to see if I really was the one and the same boy she'd had tea with in Hammersmith. She said a few nice things, then disappeared by her secret route. It was typical Kate.

Tony Perkins didn't bite either, but through him or his agent I met Tab Hunter at the Polo Lounge. I'd always thought of him as a bit of a joke, but he did have the perfect golden beach-boy looks for Tennessee's fated charmer, and I was struck by the depth and warmth of his voice. I asked him to read. He was inexperienced and wooden, but again I was cocksure—I could get it out of him; I'd surprise the world by the way I could make Tab act. There was still the problem of Mrs. Goforth. I'd had other ideas, but they weren't good. It was either Tallulah or not do it. I ran *Lifeboat*. She wasn't any livelier in that than when we had met, but then the whole movie was to me (like all Hitchcock's post-1930s work) stiff, contrived, lifeless.

One of the persistent myths of the American theatre is Laurette Taylor's comeback performance in the first night of *The Glass Menagerie* in 1945. Marvelous as I'm sure it was, it has led to many disastrous decisions. Naturally Tennessee was one of the myth's most fervent believers. It would be the same with Tallulah: After her long hibernation, the creator of Regina in *The Little Foxes* and Sabina in *The Skin of Our Teeth* would emerge reborn and the *Glass Menagerie* triumph would be repeated. It wasn't to be.

Rehearsals—though they couldn't really be called that—were torture. It isn't pleasant to write as meanly as this, but Tallulah was the most unpleasant person I've ever worked with—or let's blame her senility and decay. After a few days I knew what we were all in for. On the way to rehearsal I'd have a frantic inner dialogue: "I've got to find a way to like her, to like something—even to feel sorry for her, feel pity, feel compassion." And every day she would hobble in, sit down at the worktable center stage, and proceed for an agonizing half hour to go through the squalid daily ritual of taking out makeup, smearing her gums with grease (she couldn't speak without it), and slashing her lips with thick lipstick until she was sitting in a circle of used Kleenex with her burnt-out hands awash with grease and pigment. Then, like a hideous old vulture on a carrion heap, she'd look around for which of the understudies or assistants had the cleanest, newest shirt or sweater, beckon, "Come here, darling," and wipe her hands clean on their fresh clothes. Why they put up with it I never knew, nor why even senior members of the cast would go with her to run lines while she sat on the lavatory, defecating in front of them. One of our two Stage Assistants was the black actor Bobby Hooks. She loved to humiliate him when there was a hotel problem. In Baltimore, where we were to open, below the Mason-Dixon line, she'd remark, "Don't worry, darling—I'll say you're my chauffeur." Tab and she hated each other instantly. Some hanger-on had questioned her about Tab's sexual tastes. She replied, "How do I know, darling? He never sucked me." But when she deliberately repeated this within Tab's earshot it wasn't so funny.

Directing her was totally impossible. "Loud or soft—how do you want it?" she asked me—and there wasn't any other choice. Tallulah was simply past it. She couldn't remember, she couldn't perform. Only Ruth Ford (of *Requiem*), whom I'd cast as the Witch of Capri, brought out a little, purely competitive, energy. In Scene 3 they had to play a dinner scene, either side of a table. The comedy of the scene and the lines is dependent on deft timing by the Stage Assistants in serving of the courses. Before Tallulah and Ruth went on, they'd say to each other, "Fifty-fifty, dear." Then each of them would try to subtly move her chair so she could upstage the other. One night they edged themselves against the upstage wall of the house, making it impossible for the Assistants to serve the meal.

One moment I remember above all. It was a typical Broadway rehearsal—the bare stage, the one rehearsal lampbulb, the director's wooden stool isolated at center. For once Tallulah was vaguely stumbling through the scene. Then from the wings came a very quiet low wailing that sounded like what I imagine the Irish mean by "keening." It was Ruth. There was an iron spiral staircase in the stage corner, and I thought she might have bumped her head on it, but there were plenty of people around her so I didn't see any reason to stop. In fact her distress seemed to be inspiring Tallulah. Then the stage manager, a very correct jacket-and-tie type, tiptoed gravely over. He whispered, "Mr. Richardson, I have to inform you that President Kennedy has just been assassinated." I don't know what I felt. I remembered that brave day (I was in Los Angeles) when President Kennedy had been nominated at the Biltmore (so eloquently described by Norman Mailer in probably the greatest political reportage of our time), and I felt strangely alienated. I suddenly felt European. What was I doing here in this empty Broadway theatre while this specter from the past was mumbling through Tennessee's lines? Here I was, captain of this particular group. What should I do? What gesture should be made? Two minutes' silence, like the memorial-day tribute that at school we paid to the dead of two world wars? I waited until Tallulah had finished the scene, then announced to the two actresses rehearsing (the other was Marian Seldes), "Kevin has just told me that President Kennedy has been assassinated." There was a moment of shock, then Tallulah dragged herself out of her chair. "So that's what that bitch has been wailing about," she screamed. "My daddy was a senaatorrr!" She rushed forward toward the edge of the stage, flung herself on her knees and began to howl. Ruth rushed from the corner and flung herself on her knees too, and the two outdid each other in a caterwaul of grief. In the middle of this, Tennessee arrived, pulling at his little silver pocket-flask of vodka, half in tears, half hysterically giggling, and murmured to me, "There, Tony, I told you—she [Tallulah] should have had a frontal lobotomy."

There was no way *Milk Train* should have opened in Baltimore, or anywhere else. Tallulah didn't have the stamina to do it. I begged David to scrap the show. But Tennessee was inexorable. The opening night was shameful—the prompter worked more than the cast. The only reactions came from the shrunken army of Tallulah's camp followers when she forced a caricatured upward inflection or panickedly improvised a few "Darlings." Rouben had done probably the loveliest set I've ever worked on, a kind of stylized Japanese house, isolated against a constantly changing sky. It was ravishing. We'd taken Tennessee's concept seriously. He loved it at first; now he hated it. Rouben was a villain and I, by returning to England for Christmas, was a rat. With the evidence of each audience, I saw that there was nothing to be worked on or saved. Again I begged to close. No—the Laurette Taylor myth was too strong. Broadway would be a different story—"it" would happen. It wasn't and didn't. We closed after two performances.

I Liked Your Play
Exceedingly

For a long time, George Devine and I had been debating the question of "popular theatre." We weren't alone: Elsewhere in Europe, Brecht, Roger Planchon and Giorgio Strehler were talking about forming permanent associations and companies which might penetrate to a wider audience than even the Court had envisaged. To a certain extent all our big recent successes had pointed to our being able to do this. But at home, desite much improvement in conditions, autonomy from the board, and some subsidies (inadequate), we were still back at square one. We had never attracted an audience that would stick faithfully with us in our "promising" failures, our encouragement of new talent, as well as our successes. We recognized, *au fond*, that we were a competing management like any other. Part of the answer seemed to be to find another home where we could stage larger-scale works with a bigger company while the Court would house "chamber" plays, experiments, and tryouts. Many have done this since—Joe Papp at the Public Theater, the RSC, the National, etc.—but at that time no one was doing it. We were trying to find another type of building, away from the West End theatre, and we looked at old music halls and deserted factories. (Had we known of its existence earlier, the Roundhouse at Camden Town would have been ideal.) We never succeeded, though both

George and I knew it was the way we must go if we weren't to stagnate.

Binkie Beaumont, the adroit, charming master impresario of the West End, proposed as it were a way station toward the ideal: that we take a West End theatre, the Queen's—a lovely theatre, with many associations for George and Peggy—and present an initial season of three plays there. All three plays were to star Vanessa and be directed by me. We agreed. Our opening choice was *The Seagull*; the second was to be Brecht's half-drama, half-oratorio *Saint Joan of the Stockyards*; and the third, we hoped, a still not finished play by Michael Hastings.

The Seagull was one of the rare and happy experiences when everything fell naturally and harmoniously together. Besides Vanessa, Peggy Ashcroft was to play Arkadina, Peter Finch Trigorin, George played Dorn, and Peter McEnery Konstantin. Rachel Kempson and Mark Dignam were also in the cast. Jocelyn designed the set and costumes. Most of us had worked together before, had old friendships, associations, family connections, and all of us were united in our adoration of this passionate, funny, poetic play. With its treatment of art and artist, new forms, struggling actors and writers, it was a fitting culmination to all that the years of the Court had been about.

George gave the performance of his life—the definitive performance of Dorn, the country doctor who scents and responds to the new in art without being able quite to express why, and who is alone in being able to see through the debacle of Konstantin's play in Act 1 to the young man's hopes and intentions. Peggy I found surprisingly difficult in rehearsal, especially in the notoriously difficult, ludicrous, monstrous, pathetic confrontation with Trigorin in Act 3. She would fight me, say she couldn't do it that way or this way, would be stubborn for hours, and then would suddenly do a complete reversal, break through, and play the scene extraordinarily. Even recently, people have described to me various bits of business—the way, for example, she put on her hat once she had recognized Trigorin: each hatpin going in triumphantly, one after the other—business I'd totally fogotten we'd created and which I'm sure all came from her. In fact I've always thought Peggy—the really, truly Good Woman of British theatre—to be at her best when playing characters one finds unsympathetic. Her Hedda Gabler, in its grasp, architecture, surprises, passion, was for me the best I'm sure I'll ever see. Peter Finch—a beautiful, understated, and, in the theatre, undervalued actor—was a perfect contrast to Peggy. Vanessa, wonderful in her grace and youthful romanticism in the first acts of the play, struggled with the fiendish last act— bringing on the battered, grubby, haunted provincial actress and fighting the passion and near madness of her still painful love for Trigorin—and most nights she conquered. Chekhov has always been my favorite author to direct. Without killing the comedy of the characters, I soaked the play in atmosphere and sounds, and it all seemed to work:

> 'I think we ought at least to consider the possibility that the girl's story could be true'; *'Je l'ai tuée avec une hache'*; 'Konstantin Gavrilovich has killed himself.' These—approximately—are the last words of three celebrated entertainments: Tennessee William's *Suddenly Last Summer;* the Compagnie des Quinze's *Crime and Punishment;* and Checkhov's *The Seagull,* which the English Stage Company presented at the Queen's Theatre last week.
>
> They have something in common, an air of finality; they are a summing up, a verdict, a closing of the account. When they are spoken, something has finished: A conclusion has been reached, the last stroke of the pattern has been drawn. That is why they give a feeling of such extraordinary fulfilment: The untidiness of life has been removed, and in its place we see a whole and perfect accomplishment.
>
> I have never felt this so strongly at any previous production of *The Seagull.* After the doctor's dreadful declaration, Arkadina the actress, the novelist Trigorin, the old landowner Sorin, their friends and their dependents will go on living, flirting, recalling past triumphs, regretting lost opportunities, writing new books. But on Thursday George Devine spoke the words with such accurate timing, the curtain came down so perfectly on cue that one realised with an almost physical shock that anything that might happen to them afterwards was of no importance. What mattered was not themselves but their relationship to each other; and this relationship had been brought to a supreme point of significance, and then broken.
>
> Here, as in the acceptance of the girl's terrible story of the boys on the seashore, and of Raskolnikov's reconciliation with surrender, we have one entire and perfect chrysolite. Nothing we could give would suffice to buy it. It is beyond price.
>
> It is of course intensely theatrical. *The Seagull* is a well-made play

if ever there was one. Nothing is wasted in it. The incomprehensible speeches in the first act are used again in the fourth with an irresistible impact. Melodramatic symbols are fitted exactly into the frame of naturalism. What is too fragile to be spoken is sung—and in French, too. Chekhov was always conscious of the importance of nature: To him the chopping down of a tree was as significant as the fall of an empire. But in *The Seagull* he is positively pantheistic; the god is everywhere and in everything. What is too deep and moving to be expressed by any human voice is said in the moan of gulls, the cry of crickets, the striking of a note on the piano.

In directing the play Tony Richardson does not shrink from the challenge of all this. He emphasises Chekhov's incredible suspended silences with sounds—a voice singing in the gathering darkness of a summer evening across a misty lake, a chord of distant music—that would draw the soul out of a weaver.

Harold Hobson, *Sunday Times*, March 15, 1964

In fact the spirit of the cast was as in no other play I've ever done. In the last act, when the elders leave for their supper while Konstantin and Nina have their final confrontation, quite spontaneously the actors got Jocelyn to build them a tiny room offstage where, bringing their own drinks and delicacies, they played the offstage supper (and provided the perfect aural background). They also formed a club to dine together after the show at least twice a week. Jocelyn and I would join them. It was a real lovefest at the Queen's Theatre.

Nearly thirty years earlier, Peggy had played Nina in another famous production. Then Arkadina in mine. Then about twenty years down the line Vanessa played Arkadina, with Natasha, our daughter, playing Nina. I had seen Tasha playing Shakespeare in Regent's Park a year before. Then only a year out of drama school, she was promising but still a student. Coming back, I found a star— a fully fledged actress with that same quality of being able to communicate emotion and let emotion flow through her fully and directly that her mother has. And, being younger than Vanessa, as Nina she even had certain advantages—the younger Chekhov's characters are played, the better. Chekhov understood the heartbreak of the young better than any other writer. And I remember I never totally understood Irina in *Three Sisters* until I saw Marianne Faithfull play her in 1967. Performance is the key to everything in Chekhov. Everything is there, even in the tiniest role, if it's brought out by the right casting. Otherwise parts of the play disappear like a ship under water: You don't even realize they exist, but then next time, done right, they emerge like the treasure hoard of a sunken ship—dripping, gleaming, revelatory.

The success of *The Seagull* seemed the best of auguries for our future. In fact, looking back, it was the summing-up of the past. George and the Court (of which, because of other commitments, I became less and less a part) went on to do other formidable work—George's Old Vic production of Beckett's *Play;* John's *Inadmissible Evidence, A Patriot for Me,* and *A Sense of Detachment* at the Court. But in a way *The Seagull* was the end, in that it was the last time we—George, Jocelyn, Peggy and I—were together. Maybe somehow subconsciously we all realized that and it gave the show an elegiac quality that underlies Chekhov as it underlies life. For all the absurdities, foibles, jealousies, the emotions of his people are finally the sense of Hopkins' poem:

> Margaret, are you grieving
> Over Goldengrove unleaving?

And when, at the end of the play, George announced, "Konstantin Gavrilovich has shot himself," in retrospect he was perhaps anticipating the end of the Court.

In a way, our next show—*Saint Joan*—was to prove it. The only Court elements were Jocelyn, Vanessa, and myself. *Saint Joan* is one of Brecht's greatest works. It's a free adaptation of *Major Barbara* (Brecht got her confused with Saint Joan), Sinclair Lewis, and *Das Kapital,* absorbed and digested by his own genius to produce a masterpiece of theatricality. It tells the story of a Salvation Army girl who tries to enlist the help of the capitalist boss J. Pierpont Mauler in her fight for faith in the stockyards of Chicago. In her struggle with the material reality, she learns what poverty is really like, succumbs to cold and hunger, and, at that moment, is taken up by the very capitalist forces that have destroyed her. As she then struggles more and more pathetically to denounce the God she once believed in, she is drowned out by a great cantata—the forces of religion and money combining—and becomes a saint. The play requires a huge cast of trained singers as well as the group of leading actors, and is consequently not performed as often as it should be.

It was a part Vanessa was born to play. She alone could find the coolness and comedy combined with passionate inner strength. Mauler was to be played by Lionel Stander. Vanessa and he hit it off perfectly—as did Michel Medwin, who played Sullivan Slift, his sidekick. Jock Addison had written original music and was superbly in charge of the choral training. Everything seemed set fair when rehearsals started during the run of *The Seagull*. Then, after a week or two, Vanessa began to be tired and ill. We thought at first it was just the strain of the two gigantic roles; then we realized she was pregnant. There were screams of rage from the commercial side of the management: "When's the abortion?" There was no question of that, though I supposed it could be said we had been irresponsible, in that the whole season had been built around us. Anyway, there was nothing to be done if Vanessa was to finish *The Seagull* and not endanger the baby: She had to leave.

We should, of course, have canceled the show, but the tradition of "The show must go on" was still uppermost, there was a considerable investment at stake, and we decided to continue. Siobhan McKenna, the Irish actress, who had played Saint Joan in Dublin, agreed to take over. It was a generous and heroic gesture, but, because of the shortness of time, she had to play it in a different translation from ours, and her thoroughly emotional style of acting (she had made a great success of playing Shaw's Saint Joan) didn't fit the Brechtian requirements. Only a good Irish Catholic could have passionately recited, "Therefore anyone down there who says there is a God when none can be seen, a God who can be invisible and yet help them, should have his head knocked on the pavement until he croaks."

Jocelyn had stripped the Queen's Theatre to its bare walls and had mounted a magnificent collage of blowups of photos of Chicago slaughterhouses, stockyards, and the money exchange, against which the play would take place. Jock had coached the singers to a high vocal standard, but there was still the problem of their acting. In the play they have to double for and be distinguishable as groups of money merchants, auctioneers, stockmen, etc. However vocally impressive they could be, they had no stage presence at all, and whatever I tried in the way of stimulating their acting abilities had absolutely no effect. They were also more trouble than a handful of great stars. Some of them had been among our plainsong singers in *Luther*, where we had similar troubles—there they balked at wearing what they called heavy cloaks and costumes, even in a scene when they didn't have to sing. In *Saint Joan* they were a disaster, and dashed our last hope that somehow, without an adequate principal performance, the production would be carried by its choral and group effects. In despair, at our final run-through Jocelyn and I decided there was only one solution—to put the whole crowd in masks and half-masks. Which we did. Jocelyn recruited the whole final-year sculpture class at the Royal College of Art. She and they stayed up two nights, at the end of which eighty masks had been produced. And on the masks went, despite the howls of protest. So visually the effect of *Saint Joan* was, I thought, unique and extraordinary, and the sound too.

But it was to no avail—when it opened, in June 1964, the critics ripped the show apart. In a way it was a repeat of *Arturo Ui*. there was a group of Berliner Ensemble devotees who thought any production that wasn't a slavish copy of the Ensemble style was diluting the faith; and there were others—the majority—who thought that to present Brecht on a commercial scale in a West End or Broadway theatre was somehow a subversive act. They often tolerated or patronized Brecht in small, regional, sometimes inadequate productions, but bring in the big guns and you were committing an act of profanity. Brecht the artist then didn't exist—staging one of his plays was a political act, desecrating the halls of commerce, as provocative as if a top KGB operative had penetrated a dinner party at the White House or Buckingham Palace. Commercial catastrophe though *Saint Joan* was (I think it closed in two weeks), it was nevertheless something I was very proud of.

The real problem of the Royal Court was the problem of a successful revolution. (The astonishing fact is that the Royal Court has been the home of two revolutions—ours and that of the Shaw-Granville-Barker period in 1904–7.) Where did it go from here? Both George and I saw and acknowledged the limitations of the Court. We had been the ram that had breached the walls of sterility, but the life and energies we'd released couldn't be contained by us—they were to flood out and fertilize the plains. Larry would raid the Court's most skilled directors for the about-to-be-launched National Theatre; Edward Albee, whose short plays we had presented, preferred to give *Who's Afraid of Virginia Woolf?* to a commercial management; Harold Pinter, whose plays we'd also done, had escaped elsewhere. (This was, in fact, my one regret at the Court. I hadn't been there when his double-bill of *The Dumb-Waiter* and *The Room* was put on in March 1960, nor had I known him when he worked in a minor capacity at the theatre. I flattered myself that had I been there we would have recognized his major talent more completely and formed a relationship that would have developed similar to our relationship with John Osborne. Who knows? It may just have been self-delusion.) What the Court had done was what it had set out to do: To make the whole of the British theatre open to new dramatists and new plays. It did that without becoming rich or protected enough by the revenues they could generate.

The history of the British theatre—the National, the Royal Shakespeare, and the fringe theatre—had been a history of competition for the new. In that competition the Court always had to be a loser because it couldn't offer anything like the resources that, later on, for example, the National would be able to do. The future had been determined by our tenure in Sloane Square. Where previously there had been two marginally supported classical companies and a floating number of commercial managements with different tastes, audiences, and policies, there would now be several state-supported institutions. The Court would become just one of them—a very minor, limited one: limited by the size of its house and by the impossibility of securing major new work. Then the other institutions would be both giant commercial conglomerates (the commercial aspects coming mainly from the natural ambition of directors) and insidious bureaucracies which would disguise some of their reach by cosmetic power-splitting arrangements—by having different auditoria, regimes, and directorates. In fact if you want a meeting of classic East and West philosophies and policies, you will find it today most plainly and most blatantly at the National Theatre. The commercial theatre in London, apart from musicals, and apart from the determined efforts of a few daring gamblers like Michael White and Michael Codron, has been killed by the Court and the theatre delivered over to institutions.

Institutions have their place, but in my book they don't have much to do with living art. (Preservation and conservation are different matters.) They also exact a dreadful toll. To maintain an institution—which is what the Court had become—before there was the state support which there is today (though most of the present incumbents of theatrical office would probably and rightly dispute that it is adequate) was the most killing job in the world, and the effects were telling on George. He was becoming martyred to what he had created and what it wasn't in his nature to abandon. Beyond that, we didn't want to face the fact that the Court had become irrelevant. We debated this often and at length, though I was inhibited both by my fondness and respect for him and by knowing that my own future was elsewhere. What we lacked, finally, was a policy for the future. What we talked about were either repetitions of the dramatists we'd already presented or the kind of my-values-are-better-than-yours splitting-hair snobbery that leads you nowhere.

Looking back, if you could play the game of what would have been the best of all possible worlds, you would have to say that the solution would have been for George, who had pioneered the revolution, to have run the National Theatre when it came into being, because only he would have had the foresight to make it a much freer and more flexible organization—where the sources of power might truly have been put back into the hands of different artists. This wasn't to be. The Court exacted its own loyalties even when they were already sadly academic. The fight went on, but out of duty, not vision. Duty finally kills. After our attempt at the Queen's season, the Court withdrew into what it has become ever since— a minor liberal institution with good intentions. That's why Konstantin shot himself.

Tony Richardson's parents, Bert and Elsie, on their wedding day, December 27, 1921, at West Hartlepool

Ra, Tony Richardson's paternal grandmother, in the garden of the Richardson home

Elsie Richardson with Bob, and (*below*) Aunt Ethel with a pet cat, in the garden of 28 Bingley Road

Tony Richardson at about seventeen

A young Tony Richardson with his mother, Elsie, during a family picnic on the
moors outside their hometown of Shipley

Uncle Cecil Antonio, Tony
Richardson's namesake

Tony Richardson's production of *The Country Wife* for the Theatre Royal, Stratford East, in 1955. The cast included Nigel Davenport (*second from the left*) as Mr. Horner.

Tony Richardson and John Osborne at the Royal Court during rehearsals for
Look Back in Anger, 1956

Alan Tagg's original set for *Look Back in Anger*

Mary Ure as Alison, Alan Bates as Cliff, Helen Hughes as Helena, and
Kenneth Haigh as Jimmy Porter in *Look Back in Anger*

Richard Burton as Jimmy Porter and Gary Redmond as Cliff, with Tony
Richardson, on the film set of *Look Back in Anger*, 1959

Sir Laurence Olivier as Archie
Rice in Richardson's produc-
tion of John Osborne's *The
Entertainer*, Royal Court
Theatre, 1957

Tony Richardson with Sir Laurence Olivier on location in Bradford for *The Entertainer,* 1960

George Devine as the Old Man and Joan Plowright as the Old Woman in
Ionesco's *The Chairs*, Royal Court Theatre, 1957

Paul Robeson as Othello at Stratford, 1959

Vivien Leigh, George Devine, and Anthony Quayle in Noël
Coward's *Look After Lulu*, 1959

Rachel Roberts and Albert Finney in *Saturday Night and Sunday
Morning*, produced by Tony Richardson and directed by Karel
Reisz, 1960

Rita Tushingham with Tony Richardson on location for *A Taste of Honey*, 1961

Albert Finney as Luther at the Theatre Royal, Nottingham, 1961

Tony Richardson in 1960

Tony Richardson with George
Devine in 1960 at Syon Lodge

Tom Courtenay in *The Loneliness of the Long Distance Runner*

Tony Richardson on location for *The Loneliness of the Long Distance Runner,* 1962

Tom Courtenay with James Bolam in *The Loneliness of the Long Distance Runner*

Albert Finney and Susannah York in *Tom Jones*, adapted by John Osborne and directed by Tony Richardson, 1963

Tony Richardson on the set of *Tom Jones*

Tony Richardson directing Hugh Griffith as Squire Western and Albert
Finney on location for *Tom Jones*

Sir Michael Redgrave as Hamlet, with his wife, Rachel Kempson, and his daughter, Vanessa, in 1950

Corin Redgrave

Vanessa Redgrave

Tony Richardson and
Vanessa Redgrave with
their first child, Natasha,
in 1963

Tony Richardson

Tony Richardson with George Devine on the set of *The Seagull* at the Queen's Theatre, 1964. The cast included Peggy Ashcroft, Vanessa Redgrave, Rachel Kempson, Peter Finch, and Peter McEnery.

Peggy Ashcroft as Arkadina in *The Seagull*

Members of the cast of *The Loved One*, 1965: *(left to right)* Robert Morse, Robert Morley, Jonathan Winters, Rod Steiger, Roddy McDowall, Sir John Gielgud; *(in foreground)* Anjanette Comer

Sir John Gielgud and David Hemmings in *The Charge of the Light Brigade*

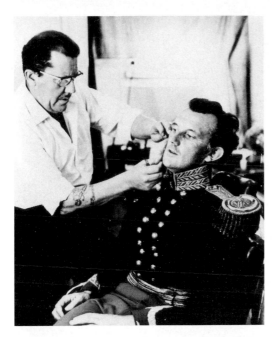

Tony Richardson being made
up for a walk-on part in *The
Charge of the Light Brigade*

Tony Richardson with his
daughter Natasha on the set of
The Charge of the Light Brigade

Vanessa Redgrave with daughters Joely and Natasha on the set of *The Charge of the Light Brigade*

Jeanne Moreau with Tony Richardson

Nicol Williamson as Hamlet in Tony Richardson's film adaptation of his
Roundhouse production, 1969

Mick Jagger as Ned Kelly,
the Australian bandit, 1970

Vanessa Redgrave as
Polly Peachum in Tony
Richardson's production
of Brecht's *The Threepenny
Opera* at the Prince of
Wales Theatre, 1972

Grizelda Grimond with her daughter, Katharine, in France in 1974

Peter Firth as Joseph
Andrews, 1977

Tony Richardson

Above: Tony Richardson with Harvey Keitel on the set of *The Border*, 1982

Below: Members of the cast of *The Hotel New Hampshire*, 1984, including Jodie Foster, Beau Bridges, Natassja Kinski, and Rob Lowe

Above: Tony Richardson in Rwanda

Below: Tony Richardson with HM the Queen and Nancy Reagan during the
Royal Tour of California in 1990

Tony Richardson's daughters
(*from top*), Natasha, Joely, and
Katharine

14

The Loved One

The genesis of *The Loved One* was like this. During the last days of the *Tom Jones* shoot in the dilapidated old Londonderry house (now the Inn on the Park) which we were using as a kind of studio, two Americans came to see me. One of them was Haskell Wexler, whose work, mainly documentaries, I had seen or knew of—he was spoken of as the American Walter Lassally. The other, who looked like a young East Coast college teacher, was exceptionally sympathetic and witty—John Calley. They had acquired the rights to Evelyn Waugh's book and proposed to produce it under the banner of the company John worked for—Filmways, whose boss was Marty Ransohoff. I had heard of plans to film the book intermittently throughout the years—once the film was purported to be being directed by my hero, Buñuel—but none of the plans had come to anything. I knew the novella well, and loved it—as I did all Waugh's *oeuvre*. This elegant satire of Forest Lawn and its denizens was to me a perfectly realized work. What could film add to it? Who was I to tinker with perfection? I passed, more or less, but we agreed to keep in touch.

Now there was a new spirit of humor abroad in America. It corresponded closely to my own. I'd been again and again, often with John Osborne, to performances by Mort Sahl and, most im-

portant, Lenny Bruce, whom I followed, a total fan, from his me-
teoric, inspired, improvisatory flights of genius to the sadness of
his ramblingly obsessive decline. There was a new book out too—
The American Way of Death by Jessica Mitford, whose autobiographical *Hons and Rebels* I loved and always believed could make a wonderful movie. Then there were the beat writers—Kerouac, whom
I knew slightly, and newer comic writers like Terry Southern. Then
I thought of how I could use some of my own experiences during
Sanctuary and how, instead of thinking of the book as pickled in the
perfection of its own 1940s aspic, instead of just trying to recreate
what was on the page, one could think of what Waugh himself
might find to react to in contemporary Los Angeles, then use the
book as a springboard to take off from.

This "updating" got me into trouble and caused a lot of offense
to Evelyn Waugh himself. During the preparation, I gave an interview to *The New York Times*. I talked about bringing *The Loved
One* into contemporary reality, and the journalist—Peter Bart, now
a producer—made it seem (I think unintentionally) that I'd suggested the book was out of date and musty. I consoled myself with
thinking Waugh would never see the article. I was wrong: A stream
of hurt and angry cables bombarded MGM. But even if the moguls
there had heard of him, what was the author of *A Handful of
Dust*, *Scoop*, *Vile Bodies*, *Brideshead Revisited*, and *Black Mischief* when
weighed against a hot young Oscar-pulling director? The controversy was even revived three years later, before the opening of the
film in England, by one of the more scurrilous columnists. This
time I wrote to Waugh, apologizing—a "should never talk to the
press" kind of thing—and expressing my full and deep admiration
of him. I got a postcard back. I wish now I'd kept it, but I've always
been a compulsive non-hoarder. He listed all the woes that had
fallen on him because of film plans. Besides me, these included that
he had only just escaped being directed by "a Mexican." The postcard ended, "and I hope the film will never be shown in Taunton."
As far as I know, it hasn't been.

I talked to Christopher Isherwood. He was keen to work on the
project and to work with Terry Southern, and so, with lots of
laughter along the way, we progressed toward a script and a commitment. My *Tom Jones* prestige was such that there was nothing I
couldn't have and no one who didn't want to climb aboard the train.

The two leads were Robert Morse—making his debut in movies, but renowned for his brilliant performance in the Broadway musical *How to Succeed in Business Without Really Trying*—and Anjanette Comer, also a virtual newcomer. All the rest were to be stars appearing in cameos. They included Jonathan Winters, Rod Steiger, Jayne Mansfield, Ruth Gordon, Liberace, Robert Morley, Paul Williams (later a composer), Roddy McDowall, a huge, fat piano-bar–player, Ayllene Gibbons, Dana Andrews, Milton Berle, James Coburn, Tab Hunter—and John Gielgud. One of the best personal things to come out of the experience was my relationship with John. He is, quite simply, the nicest, most human actor I've every worked with, and, together with Jack Nicholson, the most intelligent. John adores the theatre, theatre gossip, actors, actresses—he is steeped in them—but he equally adores books, poetry, music, films, travel. What he likes delights him, and he can delight you with his delight. And what he loathes he can amuse you with. He is a constant responder, a constant enjoyer. That is what has kept him so perpetually young, and perhaps is why he has outlasted so many of his great contemporaries who have fallen by the wayside. To work with him for the first time (he based his performance on Cecil Beaton) was pure joy, as it always is.

Most of the actors entered the film with the same sense of fun and pleasure. An exception was Robert Morley, who became a boorish prima donna. Terry Southern had written a very funny scene, an appearance by Morley in drag at a leather-bikers' bar which was meant to be the key to the secret life of his character. Once he'd been shot in another scene and therefore knew he couldn't be replaced, Morley refused to perform this, saying it would upset his children. Liberace, on the other hand, loved his role as the casket salesman so much that he wanted more. We had the idea of introducing him into an orgy scene. The Air Force top brass was being paid off for a space contract by a big party at Forest Lawn. At the end of this, the caskets were to be opened and beautiful stippers were to step out. A young good-looking colonel was to open his casket, and inside was to be Liberace. I told Leigh (Liberace's nickname). Pleased as he was to be in another moment, I could see he was anxious. Finally he came to me. "Tony, I've been thinking about your idea. You see, I have a reponsibility to my public, and they might be worried. But I know just how to fix it.

When that young man opens the casket, I'll give a wink [this was Liberace's trademark]. Then my public will know I'm all right!"

In any production there are always one or two problems which become obsessive for all the people involved. The ways of solving them are discussed, proposed, and experimented on more than all the rest of the production. On *The Loved One* we had two such problems—how to "do" the corpses, and how to achieve the moving statues in the climactic scene between Amy and the Dreamer. The concept of this was based on the original founder of Forest Lawn, who, it is alleged, had a huge collection of pornography—much of it mechanical: a saint's robe suddenly opening to reveal an erect penis, or a nun performing fellatio—that kind of thing. As the Dreamer tries to seduce Amy, he presses a button and the statues in the chapel take up erotic poses. Models, back projection—all kinds of ideas came up. Using live dancers became the favorite, and the whole scene became so self-important that even Balanchine was proposed to choreograph the moment. Even more astonishing, he agreed—if schedules could be worked out. Which they couldn't be, so Tony Charmoli stepped in instead and twenty or so dancers were recruited and, to look like real marble, covered in a special body makeup inches thick, which took hours to apply.

The scene took two or three days to shoot, and as the dancing was behind the action and was therefore out of focus I didn't pay much attention to it—until the last day, when I wanted to do cuts of the statues themselves. Then I suddenly saw how appallingly feeble their actions were. Tony wasn't around for some reason, so I started directing the dancers. They looked horrified when I said the action wasn't suggestive. I asked the boy of one couple to put his hand on the girl's breasts. He said it was un-American. I asked a couple of girls to kiss each other. They said it would make their moms cry. Finally I said to another couple, "Try doing a fucking movement." At which moment they all burst into tears, their tears making deep red rivulets, ruining their makeup. One of them shouted I'd made a beautiful thing ugly. They ran off the set and were sympathetically joined by the makeup department, all of whom, far from minding the ravage of their work, joined in a protest against this porn-minded pinko who was trying to slander the American Way of Life. Tony Charmoli arrived in the midst of the disaster, realized what had happened, and wagged a finger at me:

"Oh dear! If only, instead of talking like that, you'd said, 'Darlings, just do a *plié* facing each other.' "

Un-Americanism came up in another way. I was rehearsing a scene with Robert Morse. It was one of those occasions—luckily, increasingly rare for me—when you realize how far from home you are; that no amount of residence can replace being brought up in an American high school. The set was a small room almost filled by a casket covered with the Stars and Stripes and supposedly occupied by a dead astronaut. Bobby was, I think, supposed to be trying to find a hiding place where there wasn't one, and to convey a moment of panic and desperation. After two or three rehearsals he still hadn't come up with anything at all expressive. "What do you suggest?" I went on the set, watched by the whole crew. "I don't know. I might rush in [I started to indicate], look around, maybe [I picked up the flag, threw it on the ground] consider hiding here." As I did this, I felt from behind a chill as sudden and palpable as if a five-ton load of ice had been delivered. The first assistant, Kurt Neumann—very efficient and loyal, a friend—came up and whispered, "I know you love to provoke us, but you've gone too far this time." "What have I done?" I had no idea. What I had done, of course, was to hurl the Stars and Stripes to the ground. To a European, accustomed to doing anything with the Union Jack or the *Tricolore*, the act was meaningless. To the Americans it was worse than urinating on the high altar during Mass.

The dead-bodies problem had a grisly, macabre aspect. Again, every kind of solution to creating the corpses we needed had been touted. The only answer seemed to be to photograph a real corpse in identical conditions to a madeup actor, a wax dummy, and whatever other possible alternatives we had, for comparison purposes. "Decca" Mitford, who also helped on the script, has brilliantly described the practices and the power the funeral industry and lobby have in California. Among the many self-protective regulations is a law that unembalmed bodies are not to be seen by any but blood relations. How, then, were we to get a fresh corpse? John Calley struck a deal with a key mortician at a famous California hospital. A crew was put on standby. It was the kind of covert operation that Woodfall had been used to. When the call came that the stiff was there, the crew arrived in a huge MGM truck and tramped through the crowded hospital lobby with wig stands, cameras, and tripods and lamps—proclaiming their "profession" to any observer.

Once inside the tiny steel-lined autopsy room, the atmosphere was tense and merry. The mortician alternated between cracking jokes and sanctimonies—"I don't allow any butt-clutching" and, "After all, we've all got mothers"—with protests about the iniquities of funeral homes exploiting "baby jobs." Finally a trolley was wheeled in and the corpse was lifted onto the autopsy table. The sheet was pulled back, revealing a heavyset Jewish man in, probably, his mid-sixties, so newly deceased that the peculiar anonymity of death had not yet taken over. Once photographed, he was quickly wheeled back to the refrigerator and the nausea level dropped dramatically. An elderly extra, suitably grayed-up, was shot in the same conditions, and maybe a mannequin. We were joshing about, making jokes.

At floor level was a low door—not four feet high. It was a curious piece of construction, and I asked the mortician what it was. Smirking mysteriously, he asked me if I'd like to go in and look. He unlocked the door and ducked inside. I followed. Inside was a huge white-tiled vault. It was filled with rack after rack from which, as in a clothes store, were hanging hundreds of plastic bags, the size of aeroplane carry-on suit-bags. Moisture had condensed inside many of them, so they were slighty frosted. Inside each bag was a body. Each was on a kind of coathanger with two spikes from which they were hung—each spike piercing an earlobe (apprently one of the toughest parts of the human body). They were bodies donated to science—some of them mutilated by their manner of death, others dismembered from teaching and research. With some it was just about possible to recognize their age or sex, but all sense of individuality or life had disappeared. It was an obscene and devastating reminder of what we must all come to, and the stuff nightmares are made of. We wandered later through the student laboratory, where the mortician tried to lighten the tone by juggling with hands, feet, and penises—there were bins full of them—but it took me a while to gear back to Evelyn Waugh's and Terry's funeral fancies.

Because of the mixture of different personalities who were coming in for a few days' work, it often seemed that we were making twenty movies instead of one. Timewise it seemed like that too.

I've always worked best, and prefer, working fast. I was used to the fast, responsive rhythm of our Woodfall crews. For the first time since *Sanctuary*, I had no control of the production setup. Marty Ransohoff, one strand of hair carefully rearranged over his bald head, charged stockily in from time to time like a wild red bull in the proverbial china shop. John Calley, however, was good at distracting Marty with one deft flick of his muleta. John would then put the sword in by regaling all of us with Marty stories and Marty encounters until it was difficult to know which was the real Marty and which was John's comic creation.

The producer was always on the set because he was also the cameraman. He was also the owner of all the enormous amount of lighting and camera equipment, which he leased back to his own production (I've since learned that many other Hollywood cameramen do this, and it often leads to conflicts). To me, the relation between director and cameraman is the key relationship on any film set. If it isn't a real marriage made in heaven, it may just work tolerably (or sometimes), but it always affects the work itself. Haskell Wexler is a very nice man. His heart is, as they say, in the right place, but his head is often so tortuously screwed up that it leads him to do the opposite of what, starting out, he meant to. He's the kind of liberal who, in that particular presidential election, would end up voting for Goldwater instead of Johnson because it would force the nation to "confront" its realities or priorities or some such nonsense.

I had asked Haskell to photograph *The Loved One* because he subscribed to the ideals of the new-wave cameraman in Europe. All his work to date had been along those lines. Now was his chance to prove how well those methods worked in a fullblown, big-budget, big-studio situation. Haskell did the opposite: He wanted to demonstrate that he could do a big-studio film in a studio way. We were shooting on real locations, but we had more lamps and equipment in tiny spaces than you'd have on the galleries of two big studio stages. It was impossible to turn, move, or breathe, and the pace was *really* funereal. We were lucky to get two or three setups a day. I argued, ordered, fought. A stone wall. Once, in a rage, I ordered Haskell off and lit a whole set myself. Using reflectors, white cards, and bounce light, I lit with a tenth of the equipment, and a tenth of the time taken. I showed it to Haskell. "Oh, that's what you meant. I can do that too." He did—for one day. Then we were back to the jungle of cables and light stands and rigging.

I had invited Rouben Ter-Arutunian to design the production. He did it brilliantly, though his perfectionist aims and his some-times abrasive ways of achieving them occasionally alienated his helpers. We had envisaged everything in high-contrast black and white. Haskell still subscribed to the absurd myth (nurtured by many old-fashioned and incompetent cameramen) that you couldn't photograph pure black and white. Clothing next to the skin—shirts, blouses, etc.—had to be dipped in tea to give it a beige look. To come out black, paneling had to be brown. It was all rubbish, and their eyes should have told them so. We had converted the former mansion of the mining prospector turned oil tycoon Edward L. Doheny into the headquarters of Forest Lawn. Rouben had painted it a shiny glossy black. When we got to the set to shoot it, it was a muddy brown—Haskell had been in the night before and ordered a crew of painters, all on overnight overtime, to repaint it. I reor-dered it black, so there was no shooting that day. And that was how the production was run.

There were other problems too. I had rented a big sprawling house in Brentwood for Vanessa and Tasha, with a tiny beach house—like a bad Danish bus terminal—for weekends. We installed ourselves, with a cook, cleaners, assistants, and Jan, my driver. Neil, I think, stayed, and there were lots of guests, masseurs, and swimming coaches. Vanessa was heavily pregnant at the time—late 1964—and feeling down and unattractive, but she was living in a swirling crowd of meetings, interviews, parties. No one knew much of her already spectacular stage career: She was very much Mrs. Richardson—in the background, and often on her own. It wasn't so bad during the preparation period. She even made one hilarious expedition with Terry to Forest Lawn, which had, of course, im-posed an edict of total non-cooperation with the film. Terry needed some more research for a scene, so he made an appointment for him and his young British wife (just arrived and unused to the customs of the country) to see the managers there to discuss with them how to handle her mother, who was dying of some incurable disease and whom his wife wished to be transported there when dead so she could be near the remains. Each time he hinted at this,

Vanessa burst into floods of tears and Terry comforted her with a, "Now, my dear, we must bear up. Be a soldier." It was, Terry claimed, one of Vanessa's finest performances. Anyway, it meant that the Forest Lawn authorities called assiduously with messages of sympathy, suggestions, and inquiries to know if the dear lady had passed away and could be flown out.

But once we got to shooting, it got much worse for Vanessa. She has never been any good at making intimate friendships, and she's never been any good with servants—not helped by my insistence that I control household arrangements. I was away from the house all day and often stayed out late or arrived back with a crowd from the set to spend the evening rehashing the past day or planning the next. I know there are some directors who can shut off their work at the end of the day and find refreshment and strength by retreating into private life. I—and I know I'm not alone in this—am the opposite. The set is an environment I love so completely that I want, need, to stay in its atmosphere as long as I can, or to be with people I've worked the day with. For me it's an essential coming-down after the high of shooting—in the same way that performers after a show have to go out to restaurants, clubs, or bars to let the adrenaline subside again. The movie is your marriage, and there's no place for wife or mistress outside. During previous movies Vanessa had been working herself, so things had been easier. Now she was alone, she didn't drive, and, though she did her best, and did understand what I was doing, it was very hard for her. And I was neglectful and careless of her feelings.

Weekends were a bit better—especially in the winter, when we usually went to Palm Springs. Someone on the crew had found a marvelously spacious old motel on the edge of town. It used to be the haunt of Garbo and Chaplin, but it had long fallen on evil days and lost its liquor license and restaurant. Its only tenants now were servants working the more fashionable hotels. The Spanish bungalows were big and comfortable, though, so on Fridays we'd load the cars with goodies—pies and dishes, salads and desserts cooked by our Tennessee (Williams) Southern cook—and set off with Tasha and Jan for the weekend. But I always invited a crowd along (and others came). We spent time riding, swimming, lunching, playing cards. Vanessa still saw little of me, and she was heavy and uncomfortable. It was an awful time for her, made worse by the seeming endlessness of the schedule. In the end she went back to England.

I was getting restless too. Extraordinary as the past months had been, I felt at the same time that there was some excitement, some stimulation, missing. Although there were months of editing ahead, and even further down the line there was a big plan to do a new and truthful version of the Charge of the Light Brigade, I wanted a new project and where the action was, as far as movies were concerned, was in France, where a few years earlier the *nouvelle vague* had broken with all its vitality, force, and freshness. Truffaut and Godard had not only created wonderful movies: They, like the first writers at the Court, had cleared the fields for a hundred flowers to bloom—directors, actors and actresses, writers, composers, cameramen. As it had been for writers in the 1920s and 1930s, suddenly France seemed the place to be.

But meanwhile, among a lot of proposed ideas and projects I'd found only one that really intrigued me. It was to do a movie of Carson McCullers's *Reflection in a Golden Eye*. I had been asked to do it by a Hollywood producer who owned the rights. I loved the book, loved Carson. I agreed. I suggested Christopher to do a screenplay, which was commissioned, and which he did. Ironically, when the film was finally done (by John Huston) it was by and large with the cast I wanted. I asked Marlon Brando to play the major. He was interested, but then got scared of the homosexual aspect of the character. For the wife, the producer wanted Elizabeth Taylor; but, good casting as Elizabeth was, I had doubts about her acting; for the totally liberated sexual woman I wanted the queen of the *nouvelle vague*, Jeanne Moreau. (In changing the role to a Frenchwoman, I was subconsciously influenced by the extraordinary depth and effectiveness of Simone Signoret's performance—also transposed in nationality—in *Room at the Top*.) Anyway, there were disagreements and arguments, and even if I'd accepted Elizabeth she would only do it with Montgomery Clift. Clift was an actor I admired completely (who couldn't?) but, having met him and known him a little, I knew there was no way he could get through a film. (In any case, the character needed a harder, tougher façade.) In the end I withdrew—sadly, because I love the subject so much. Another project had come up which would lead to France.

It was time to go home, though it was to turn out not to be home for much longer.

Woodfall was active. We had just signed a seven-picture deal with United Artists which gave us virtual *carte blanche*, so the future seemed secure. I hadn't been happy with the editors I worked with on *The Loved One* (one of them, Hal Ashby, went on to make a good career as a director) and I wanted to transfer the film back to London, where I could work with Tony Gibbs. Neil was coming back to England to settle in and reorganize Woodfall.

In January 1965 Vanessa and I had our second daughter, Joely Kim. Originally we were going to call her Kim, after our love and admiration for Kim Stanley. But, when the exquisite blue-eyed baby was born, Vanessa felt that Kim alone sounded too harsh for this vulnerable little creature. During my long stay in LA we had an extraordinary swimming teacher, Jan, who taught babies—and Tasha in particular—to swim practically from birth. Vanessa became very friendly with her during her lonely hours, and appreciative of her skills. Jan had a daughter whom she called Joely. We thought, "What a pretty sound" (actually it was a Californian mispronunciation of the French *jolie*), so Joely we made it and Joely it stuck. Later Vanessa, so impressed with Jan's methods, invited and paid her to come to England. By her own efforts and using her own money, Vanessa had built a properly designed heated swimming pool for the girls and boys of a local Hammersmith school where, under Jan's guidance, they could learn to swim. It was entirely Vanessa's idea, and she fulfilled it unhelped. Jan taught there for maybe two years, until some stupid bureaucratic or minor regulation barred her from continuing. It's something little known about, as Vanessa has never been interested in self-publicity, but I'm happy to record this remarkable and generous achievement by my remarkable and generous ex-wife. It's odd that one of the fruits of *The Loved One* should be a London swimming pool.

15

Mademoiselle Moreau

One day during *The Loved One*, Oscar Lewenstein phoned me. He had found or been offered an original film script by Jean Genet which he thought I would love. I did. How Genet came to write this directly as a film script is still obscure. Apart from his short film *Chant d'Amour*—a story very simply made, amazingly intense, and poetic, a story of love in prison between two young men—I didn't know he'd ever thought about film. *Mademoiselle* is on the surface a story about a schoolmistress who commits acts of destruction and violence, but its real themes are sexual awakening and the violence and fantasy erupting from sexual frustration, isolation, and loneliness. It is set deep in the French countryside and is very much based on autobiographical boyhood experiences. I wanted to do it at once. It was a perfect role for Jeanne Moreau. I called her, told her the story. She accepted without even reading the scenario.

The other major role is an itinerant woodcutter. I sent the script to Marlon Brando. He responded immediately, liking and under-standing it as much I did. He talked passionately of the physicality, of the sex-and-summer feeling of the forests in which it had to be shot. Everything seemed to be set. Then another commitment in-terfered and suddenly there was talk of couldn't we postpone, shoot in winter on a Hollywood sound stage—after all, they're so expert at making snow. And so that dream pairing vanished. The role was finally played by the Italian actor Ettore Manni.

There were certain parts of the scenario which I felt needed more work. The logical choice was to try to get Genet himself to do this, though it didn't seem likely that he would. Then, to our surprise, his British agent said he'd like to do the work and—even more surprising—that he was living in England. A deal was struck. Genet insisted that we pay his whole fee for the rewrite in advance, otherwise we were implying we didn't trust his word "as a gentleman." It's not usual for these arrangements, but we agreed. So Oscar Lewenstein and I journeyed out to see him where he was holed up in a little hotel in Norwich. Jean Genet had been going through a very bad time. For several years previously he had been in love with a young Arab circus acrobat, whom he had celebrated in his *Les Paravents*—his relationship was apparently half-lover, half–mentor/coach/father. He had pushed his friend to work harder, try for more, take greater and greater risks, until the boy fell during a circus trick and was killed. Riddled with guilt, Genet stopped writing for a while, became ill, had a series of accidents in which bones were broken as if he had wanted to smash up his own body in penance for what he felt he had been responsible for. He had subsequently become involved with a young married racing-car driver who had business in Norfolk, and he was now nursing another broken ankle in Norwich.

When we arrived, the local desk clerk was very puzzled when we asked for Monsieur Genet. Finally, "Oh, you mean Monsieur Jeanette." He took us up to an attic bedroom. Jean Genet was lying in bed. His pale face and cropped white hair looked frail—the skull of an ex-flyweight had metamorphosed into that of a classic French schoolteacher. The racing driver appeared briefly, seeming nice, attentive, and affectionate. We were very happy, as we felt a new BMW or Porsche or whatever for him was probably the reason Genet was willing to give us his services. I had already done a long extensive scouting trip through France—extending into parts still untouched for decades and which I never knew existed. I talked about Jeanne (as she was a well-known actress, he disapproved) and showed him photos of some of the places we were considering. Looking at a closeup of some walls, Genet remarked, "With stones like these, why do you want a face like that?"—meaning Jeanne.

He had also had some elaborate theory that the movie should be shot in Japan, with Japanese actors, to "alienate" the story from its natural setting, in the Brechtian manner. Despite all this, we got on and he agreed he would come to London to work on the scenario as soon as he was well enough.

We installed him in a room at the Hilton, just up the block from our offices on Curzon Street. Every day, punctiliously, Genet would appear at eleven and work until one. We would discuss a section of the script, criticize it, and decide what needed to be done. Next day he would reappear on the dot, with those pages reworked—sometimes but not always following what we had outlined or I had suggested, but with any divergences always being for the better. We then discussed his reworked pages and continued with the next segment. Ostensibly he was working for me, but I felt as if I was in a formal pedagogic relationship—the student with his professor. We were never intimate, we never gossiped or socialized, but the work was excellent. The writer-director relationship is always a tricky one at best, and usually it is either covertly or openly hostile. Not with Genet. Then I made my great mistake. On the Friday, at the end of the week's work, I said, "You know, Jean, I've never worked with anyone who worked so easily and so professionally." He smiled and bowed, with a "Merci, Monsieur Tony." Monday came—no Genet. We telephoned the hotel. He'd checked out. We telephoned Norwich. They had no information. Neither had his agent. But when I explained what had happened, she (who knew Jean very well) said, "Oh, if only you'd said how hopeless he was, how casual, how irresponsible, how dishonest taking money for work of the quality he was producing." I never saw Genet again.

I'd seen and admired Jeanne Moreau many times: on stage in Félicien Marceau's *L'Oeuf* with Marie Bell, and in the 1956 Paris production of *Cat on a Hot Tin Roof* directed by Peter Brook; on screen in Peter's film of Marguerite Duras's *Moderato cantabile*, in Louis Malle's *L'Ascenseur pour l'échafaud* and *Les Amants* and, supremely, in Truffaut's *Jules et Jim*, in which she and the film in their truth and humor, sadness and effrontery, seemed to epitomize the spirit of the *nouvelle vague*. By now we'd met and talked, and I was already in love with her.

What no one knows until they have worked with Jeanne is the completeness and accuracy of her professionalism. When Jeanne goes on a set, she not only knows her own character and the requirements of the scene, she also knows, and appreciates, the contribution of every technician on the set. She treats them all like artists, and naturally they respond like artists. She has a gift of instant, non-patronizing intimacy that can make everyone feel a part of the process and proud to be a colleague of this consummate actress who treats them with absolute equality. I've seen Jeanne do this over and over—not just on set, but in stores, in kitchens, in restaurants, with the old and with children—and always I marveled at her ease and her directness. On a set too, without any intellectualizing, she can sense any kind of a technical problem (no "Why don't *they* [the technicians] make it work?"—the cry of movie amateurs) and solve it! Movie acting demands a combination of absolute truth in thought together with an understanding of the technical demands of the lens. Playing a screen, cheating an eyeline, or keeping eyes open during a kiss can be the difference between real expressiveness or a dull image.

Having searched throughout France, we had finally chosen as our location a tiny village, little more than a hamlet, Le Rat, in the Corrèze. The Corrèze is one of the poorest, most remote provinces of France. It has magnificent pine forests, but the soil is sandy and marshy and supports only minimal agriculture. The population is sparse, and its ways are those of the traditional peasant. It was ideal for the story, and we moved in, finding such accommodation as we could in a region where there were no hotels or fine houses. For Jeanne we rented the principal house in the one bigger village, Tarnac. I had a nineteenth-century hunting lodge buried in the woods a mile away. As usual every room was packed.

The crew was mainly French, but with some heads of departments being English. The cameraman was David Watkin. It was our first time working together, though Woodfall had been able to give David his first opportunity to photograph a feature, Richard Lester's *The Knack*. He had been ostracized by the established industry for years; not being willing to submit himself to its normal training, by working on documentaries and commercials he had been able to acquire a knowledge of technical processes, a daringness of experiment, a freedom of thinking which had been bred out of even the most experienced feature cameramen. *The Knack* had been shot mainly against walls painted brilliant white (anathema to the experienced). It looked wonderful. And although *Mademoiselle* was shot in black and white (now anathema to me), it looks stunning.

After discussing the almost classical treatment of the subject, we decided together that we would use a fixed-frame camera. We had engaged the most skilled French operator of the day—Philippe Brun. He had worked with Alain Resnais on *Last Year at Marienbad*. Not surprisingly, when he heard our approach, in which he had no chance to use his considerable skills, he was appalled. He argued, eloquently, that he could just do a little movement, an ease which would be so unobtrusive as to be invisible. When I first decide on a style, especially one so rigid as this, I'm sometimes tentative. Maybe Philippe was right. I went along with him. One the first day's work, Philippe eased his camera. Luckily I was prudent enough to do one take without any movement. There was no comparison—"breaking the frame" with movement of people in and out of it produced a totally different emotional effect, and the so-called unobtrusive eases were as enormous in impact as if they'd been shot with a long lens from a helicopter. I immediately made the same decision about sound—there would be no music, just heightened natural sounds.

However well we seemed to be working, I knew the collaboration between the French, with their natural chauvinism, and the English bosses had potentials for conflict. It wasn't long in coming. Ironically enough it blew up the first day after I'd given, on July 14, Bastille Day, an *entente cordiale* party for the whole crew at the hunting lodge. Vanessa, who was visiting, had made and lined the driveway with effigies of figures of the Revolution—Charlotte Corday stabbing Marat in his bath, Danton at the guillotine, that kind of thing. The food, cooked by a retired cordon bleu chef, was wonderful, and the wine never stopped flowing. Drunk in the sun, everyone pledged eternal friendship. Next night (we were shooting nights) the crew was on strike and no Frenchman would speak to an Englishman. This is why.

Very early on in the shooting we started having focus trouble. Everything was checked. David, who had taken the French crew on trust, diagnosed that the focus puller (his name was Vava) was incompetent. He wanted to replace him. I foresaw exactly the eventual repercussions and begged David to explore every other possibility. Equipment was tested, the labs were questioned, everything was rechecked, but the problem continued. Doubt was over: The man was inadequate, so I supported his firing. We then worked out a typically French deal. Vava was to be replaced with a letter recommending his excellence, and without any slur, plus *twice* his normal salary for the length of the movie. Vava himself was happy, as deep down he acknowledged his own inadequacy. We had a new focus puller (French) and honor was satisfied all round. There was to be only one formality; a ratification of the deal by the French crew. At the meal break at 1:30 in the morning in the meadow by the river where we were shooting there was to be a quick vote, then back to work. The English excused themselves and were having a drink when suddenly there were angry shouts and fists waved in the air. *A bas les anglais!* A strike was declared.

Until that moment I'd always imagined myself on the other side of the barricades; suddenly I was in the role of the wicked capitalist boss. My assistant, Christian de Chalonge—exceptionally intelligent, sharp, and efficient (later I was able to get his first movie as a director financed)—refused to look me in the eyes as he left the meeting. Work stopped. It was a complete stalemate. Yet David was indisputably right, and I couldn't go back in my support. Eventually the French heads of each department agreed to meet me and me alone. Now, as I've explained earlier, I used to speak French well, but then I let it lapse. In preparation for the shoot, I'd taken some lessons and brushed it up. On the first day of shooting, to my mortificaiton, when I was totally concentrating on how to make the movie, I found that with the extra effort of speaking another language I literally couldn't get out a *oui* or a *non*. Happily that had passed and my French had come back and matured. Now I—who hated any public speaking—had to address all the department heads in French. Bulky and hostile, they sat in the little primary schoolroom of Le Rat, on the old scarred wooden desks. I explained exactly what had happened. To my surprise, at the end I got a round of applause and a unanimous vote to resume work. There was only one other condition: I must now repeat—in the same words—what I'd said to them to all the other members of the French crew. But whatever eloquence I'd achieved had come entirely from nerves, and when the repeat performance came I couldn't find a word. Still, work recommenced. From then on the whole shoot was magical.

Not that there weren't other glitches. Jeanne had fallen seriously ill, and on the evening of the same July 14, Neil and I walked to the village where Jeanne was staying. To our horror, we found a huge crowd of tourists and village people standing outside the gates of the house, banging saucepans and pots and screaming for Jeanne—hardly the best cure for our invalid desperately in need of rest and sleep. We hurled ourselves into the crowd, shouting for them to disperse, to discover in the center one of our own assistants acting as cheerleader and organizer. This girl was a young student whom I'd taken on as a favor to Vanessa. She was one of those infuriating would-be helpfuls whose only talent was the infallible knack of always being in the wrong place at the wrong time, popping up with some inept and well-intentioned suggestion just when you're deepest in concentration—the type you want to strangle.

Taking up and then just as quickly dropping such impossible strays (who for a brief moment became best friends) was one of Vanessa's traits. Early on, when John and I had been renting a house for holidays in France, Vanessa invited along her "best school friend," just married to a Guards officer. They arrived direct from Balmoral, where they had been guests of the Queen. One dinner convinced Vanessa how far apart they'd grown, but we were stuck with them for two weeks. We were completely lost as to how to amuse them (the only thing the lady liked was denouncing me, which, as all the other guests were friends of mine, was hardly well received). Finally, one night in desperation we hit on the idea of changing sex for dinner. Dressed in his wife's Balmoral ballgown, it was the only time the Guards officer really relaxed. During *Mademoiselle*, Vanessa deposited in the house a family of nuclear disarmers and promptly disappeared. They were waited on all day by our cook, but in the evening, when members of the cast and crew came back tired from the long day's work for dinner, the husband would spend the whole time denouncing the frivolity of us capitalist filmmakers, unused as we were to the way the rest of the world had to toil! Finally I refused to let them stay any longer but, as it was their vacation, offered to put them up in a little hotel twenty miles away. There they proceeded to denounce the wicked ways of the French country bourgeoisie. They managed to smash up the hotel dining room—"Why should you be attached to property?"—and the management had them out and back on the road to England within a couple of days.

But something much more serious—especially for Vanessa—was happening: I had fallen in love with Jeanne (as did practically everyone connected with the film). It had started long before, subconsciously, but the closeness and pleasure of working—especially in summer in the wild and deserted countryside—brought us closer and closer. Almost from the first days of shooting we knew what was going to happen. Vanessa knew it too, and was desperately unhappy. Once we had married (which we had sworn never to do before we decided to have children), strains had begun to emerge in our relationship, though we were devoted to each other (and still are in different ways) and to Tasha and Joely. But I had never met a woman like Jeanne before—sophisticated, skilled, mature, lighting up and taking over everywhere she went. It was as if I'd never grown up before, but my feeling led me to rush into what was to be a complete disaster, in which I was to wreck the very relationship for which I sacrificed a film.

I have made many mistakes and wrong decisions; at other times I have failed to achieve what I set out to do; but only once have I subordinated my work to emotions outside it. The principle of "It's only the thing you don't do that you regret" has been something I have always believed in, so I can't quite say I regret what happened, but I almost do, because had I not rushed into this project so unprepared and so determined to meet a deadline the result might have been very different.

The Sailor from Gibraltar (*Le Marin de Gibraltar*) was based on a novel by Marguerite Duras, one of the most important of the new writers in France. I had had a slight resistance to her work as being a bit humorless, but *Sailor* was different. It was Jeanne's favorite book, she was dying to play the role, and, in our first meeting— long before *Mademoiselle*—she suggested it to me. I read it, loved the idea, and bought the rights.

The story is this. A youngish man, lower-middle-class, working in a dreary office job, takes a holiday in Europe with his girlfriend, an eager and indefatigable tourist with whom he's becoming as bored as he is with his job. He breaks with her and drifts off by himself. He meets and falls for a rich European woman with a beautiful yacht. The woman has been in love with a sailor, a half-criminal pursued by police everywhere. She spends her life searching for him. She accepts the Englishman, makes love, and he becomes her companion in the quest for the sailor, knowing that once she discovers him their own relationship will be over. They keep hearing hints and clues as to where the sailor is. They follow the trail from Italy to Greece, to Egypt, to Ethiopia, and finally to the jungle. The sailor is always one step ahead, and the final question is whether he exists or whether he is just a kind of talisman to keep the woman and the young man together. I still love the idea.

The script needed a lot of work as the book is full of highfalutin French metaphysics, but I was so enamored of the idea that I was sure I could make it work. I asked David Mercer (who later wrote for Alan Resnais) to work with me on it. We got off to a shaky start and he came out to Le Rat to work with me. The big mistake we made was to lock ourselves into dates: All the subsequent farces, dramas, and messes sprang from that. From the begnning, early that year—1965—we had conceived of shooting *Mademoiselle* and *Sailor* almost back-to-back. I was bursting with energy and arrogance and I was sure I could pull it off. I couldn't bear to be separated from Jeanne, and was convinced the only way to make us "work" was to sustain the relationship without the long break her going off and making another film would have meant (it was a time when she was deluged with offers). Both films were to be prepared, and then once *Mademoiselle* was in the can the crew was to be shifted into high gear on *Sailor*, with editing on both films waiting until the following year. There were also some real production problems of a boat's availability, the state of the Mediterranean, etc., which if we didn't act immediately would have meant a postponement of a year. So Jeanne and everyone else was contracted and committed. In the rush to finalize production facilities, the one thing forgotten was the script. Again *auteurisme* was in the air, and the script, instead of being the first of problems, seemed the last.

The next mistake was the casting, but how disastrous it was I didn't realize for a while. I had wanted everyone from Paul Newman to Albert Finney, but none of them was interested and available. Finally I came round to Ian Bannen, an actor whose stage experience was impressive—he'd played leading roles at the Royal Court and at Stratford-upon-Avon. I'd worked with him on television, but I never knew that he had deep psychological problems—especially when dealing with sexual and emotional scenes, where he would often relapse into a psychotic infantilism so profound that it was impossible to reach him in any way.

The first hint of what was to come happened about two weeks into shooting. We were to do a scene where Ian's character—after he has broken with his girlfriend—picks up an Italian girl at a little Felliniesque village dance and wanders into the sand dunes to make love to her. We were working French hours—starting at noon—and during the morning I was combing the beach to decide exactly where I wanted to shoot. Christian de Chalonge, the acute French assisant, said, "I don't know why you have to decide now—after all, Ian'll never shoot this scene today." I thought Christian had gone crazy, and said so. "You'll see," he replied. When we got down to work, Ian was completely incapable. He couldn't remember a line, couldn't light a match. I'd never seen an actor like that on a set before. I immediately decided he must have drunk too much. I publicly abused and humiliated him (which I almost never do to an actor), told the assistants to throw him in the sea to sober him up, and finally announced a break for four hours. When we resumed later, I came back on the set determined to be gentleness and support itself after my earlier harshness. Then I heard Ian telling some of the crew that the stoppage had been because "Tony wasn't happy with the actress" (who was superb), and I realized that this was from neither embarrassment nor self-protection but because Ian had quite genuinely blotted the whole incident out as if it had never happened. Far from being hurt by my treatment, he was buoyant and exuberant—he didn't remember anything. Nor was he much better at playing the scene—we had to shoot it almost entirely on the actress.

On a personal level, too, I complicated everything hopelessly. Vanessa, still trying to keep our relationship going, had wanted to be part of the production and was playing the role of the girlfriend. Artistically it was perfect; personally—and this was what had been motivating me—it was disastrous. But I was delighted to have her: Vanessa is always wonderful in her generosities, her impulsiveness, and her mistakes.

There were, I think, only about six weeks between the end of *Mademoiselle* and the start of *Sailor*—with a mountain of preparation to do in several countries. We shifted our office and operation to

Rome. I rented a huge old villa on the via Appia Antica, owned by a decaying contessa and full of furniture that collapsed every time you touched or sat on it. We installed ourselves there—chauffeur, English nanny, local cooks, etc., and my parents came out to stay and babysit. (It was one of the sweetest footnotes to the experience that the old contessa fell for my father. He had never met anyone like her, nor imagined, I think, that he would ever have that kind of attention again. She used to arrive in a large convertible and inveigle him into long drives. Mother didn't mind, and Father—though bemused—was charmingly flattered.)

Vanessa was begging me to try for a "reconciliation." I knew it wasn't going to happen, but I felt guilty and so I agreed to put two weeks aside when we would be totally together. But Vanessa had also been planning a trip to China—at that time it was almost impossible to go there—and this trip finally coincided with the planned reconciliation. This summed up the reality of our state, and I was grateful for the extra time to plan with all our crews, whom we were leap-frogging from location to location. Off Vanessa went. Two days later I was due to leave with about twenty of our people. They rendezvoused at my house on the way to the airport, early in the morning. As the cavalcade drove away, a taxi arrived from the opposite direction. Out stepped Vanessa. In those days there was no Sino-Soviet split and the route to Beijing was through Moscow. On the plane, Vanessa had decided to disembark in Moscow. The Russians were baffled—she had no visa—so they locked her up for thirty-six hours in a prison cell until there was another plane back to Rome. So here she was for the reconciliation. I pointed to the cars and explained that now it was a machine working. "Why can't you just send them all away?" Vanessa said. How can you not love her?

The first ten days of shooting in Florence went well. The scenes didn't expose Ian, and Vanessa was in top form—her scenes scurrying up Giotto's tower and round sights of Florence are probably the best parts of the movie. We then moved south to Paestum, with its wonderful Hellenic temples. Jeanne joined us there, and we had a very uneasy few days of the kind that only I could have created. Vanessa knew everything, but I no intention of openly embarrassing her. We were staying in a little provincial hotel. Vanessa and the girls were on one floor, I was on another, Jeanne on a third, and there were no visits. Through this awkwardness, a new character entered.

Actually he'd entered earlier, during the preparation period. Neil Hartley had a great friend from his navy days, Henry McIlhenny, the Philadelphian millionaire and art collector. During his frequent Greek cruises, Henry had met a young Greek cadet—Theo—from, I think, the naval academy of Hydra, and had sponsored his education in America. During the week Theo studied acting in New York, organized by Neil, and allegedy obliged many rich ladies; at weekends he danced to the bouzouki in Henry's elegant Philadelphia drawing room in Rittenhouse Square. Theo had to return to Athens for military service, and during our initial scouting trips he'd escorted us around Athens and the islands. Dark and Macedonian in looks—almost Spartan—he had a vital and intoxicating personality. It was the time of that extraordinary moment of spring in Greece when flowers seem to burst out of the white rocks. Theo would leap down from a fiacre, tear up great bundles of asphodels, lilies, and poppies, and shower us with the fresh blooms. He was helpful in every way and, as he had aspirations toward acting, I thought he'd be ideal as one of the crew on the movie's boat. We engaged him. He was young, lively, attentive. As, inexplicably to Jeanne, I had involved Vanessa in our venture, I was pointedly ignoring Jeanne outside work while Vanessa was still completing her role. The inevitable happened.

Athens was our next stop. Vanessa and the girls had returned to England. I had either ignored the Theo situation or had thought it would go away. As soon as we got to Athens, Jeanne said that we'd been a seagull with a broken wing up until then, but now we were flying. But Theo didn't go away. On the boat between shots he'd be in Jeanne's dressing room, and in the Grande-Bretagne hotel we'd cross in the elevators. I behaved shamefully. I fired Theo. I became insanely, humiliatingly jealous. I raged, ranted, tried to trail Jeanne and Theo in the evenings. Jeanne denied to me the depth of her involvement. Meanwhile, every day, Theo was on the phone to Philadelphia; Philadelphia was on the phone to Neil— Theo and Jeanne were to get married. There was to be a huge public ceremony in which the couple were to be drawn by white horses in a carriage around Constitution Square and the whole Philadelphia social world was to arrive. Even Jeanne's French agent heard the rumors and arrived with a friend, the Contessa Marina

Cicogna, determined to prevent the union. They discovered that the document of divorce from Jeanne's earlier marriage wasn't in order.

I was becoming more and more miserable (Vanessa, generous as ever, flew out as a gesture of sympathy and support), and even more despondent at realizing how utterly the film was collapsing. I was indecisive; I couldn't think or work. Ian was becoming worse, almost gaga, in his intimate scenes with Jeanne—there was no sense of emotion or sex between them. The cameraman was Godard's famous collaborator Raoul Coutard. I had admired him before and had looked forward to working with him, but it hadn't worked out. He had a tough crew of vets from the Indo-Chinese war whom I thought were almost fascists. Coutard sensed my own uncertainty about the film and despised me for it—and for the Jeanne situation too. At the end he apologized for his attitude and behavior, but really I couldn't blame him—I knew that what I was doing was artistically bad. I was bitterly disappointed in myself but, as when stuck in a bad groove playing tennis, I didn't know how to pull myself out of it. I was worn out and crazed. There were quite a lot of cameo roles, including one for Orson Welles. I admired Orson as a director enormously, but as an actor he was nervous, drunk, and irresponsible. We were working against deadlines to get the boat over to Alexandria before the winter storms. Everything was going wrong and was wrong.

In India I'd seen poverty on a much vaster scale—millions sleeping and dying on the pavements of Calcutta and Bombay—but for sheer brutishness I'd never seen anything like Alexandria. The whole 1930s façade of the city was cracked and battered like old stucco, a neglect mirroring the contempt for human life that was evident on all the streets. On my first walk through the city I saw an autistic boy, senselessly punched by a casual passerby, fall under speeding traffic, to be instantly killed and then left to be repeatedly knocked from side to side by oncoming cars. I saw a petty thief almost lynched by a mob. We were shooting in a café near the harbor and had police to control the crowd. The police started with their fists, then brought out bullwhips, then splintered planks with long protruding nails which they smashed in the crowd's faces.

The viciousness was not confined to those in authority (the Brechtian effects of poverty with a vengeance). It was early December. Though cool, the weather was sunny, and some production manager suggested that the crew take their lunch—a few dried-up sandwiches in a cardboard box—onto the wall of the harbor. Unfortunately the girls in the crew—script, makeup, hair, etc.—went first. There was a crowd of urchins round them and at the sight of the food the kids rushed for it and, maddened by hunger and temptation, those who didn't succeed in grabbing a mouthful began literally biting into our girls' flesh. It was exactly the scene described in Tennessee William's *Suddenly Last Summer*.

Relations betwen everyone were at the lowest ebb. Outside of work, Jeanne had retreated to a villa at the far end of town. Theo was secreted there briefly. After a few sleepless nights in a fleabitten hotel, I began sleeping on the boat. The worst moment came during a night shoot. Owing to Orson Welles's vagaries, we had an uncompleted night scene. The boat had to return next day. It was one of those occasions when crew and cast, suddenly knowing something has to be finished, rally marvelously. That day someone had flown in from France and had brought Jeanne a Camembert cheese. Typically, she divided it into tiny morsels and distributed it among the crew. Ian, who was now avoided by everyone because his table manners were as atrocious as his acting, grabbed several pieces. Jeanne said sweetly, "Ian, there's only one bit for everyone—there isn't enough to go round." Ian struck her hard in the face. It was all quite unbelievable. After that, Jeanne had to go on and play a relaxed night love scene with him. No one except Jeanne with her absolute and consummate professionalism could have got through the night, but, knowing our problems, she did.

Two days later we had to go on to Ethiopia. The air schedules were complicated, so we took hotel rooms at the Pyramids for everyone to rest in before departing in the middle of the night for Addis Ababa. Ian, left alone in the hotel because no one wanted to ride camels with him, proceeded to smash up his room. Later, in the early hours, we were driving to the airport. I was in a car with Jeanne and Oscar Lewenstein. Suddenly we saw a taxi skid and swerve in front of us, almost going off a bridge. The car braked. The Arab driver leaped out and started screaming. This was clearly Ian's doing. He had been in the front of the car—with John Hurt, who was playing a small role, behind. At some point he had grabbed the driver's genitals—hence the incident. John and I managed to get him into the back and, pinioning his arms behind him, we got him to the airport. At the airport, Hugh Griffith, playing a role in the final scenes, had arrived from Iran. He was wearing about six kinds of hat and solar topi, one on top of another, and four pairs of sunglasses. He was so drunk that the airline refused to take him. Neil somehow got him on another plane. At a middle-of-the-night stop in Khartoum, Ian tried to destroy the airport gift shop before he was overpowered by the assistants.

It was the first major film to shoot in Ethiopia, and there was to be a reception at Addis Ababa airport. We arrived at 6:30 in the morning, sick and exhausted. Jeanne and I were asked to disembark first for pictures with the minister, a relation of Emperor Haile Selassie, and his guard of honor. We freshened up as best we could and stepped down the stairway. A band struck up, photographers crowded round, and a mangy lion from the emperor's collection was led to us to pose for pictures. Suddenly we heard a whoop from the top of the plane steps. Ian, who was paranoid about being denied publicity, leaped down on to the tarmac, emptied his briefcase and, upending it, tried to put it over the lion's muzzle as if he were giving a feed bag to a horse. The gesture was so startling that the band, photographers, and minister all froze. I'm afraid that as Ian was kneeling at our feet, my one thought was if the lion would take one good mouthful we could call in the insurers and the whole mess would be ended there and then.

When we finally arrived at our hotel, Hugh was already there and announced he was throwing a champagne-and-caviar party for the crew. He'd brought several pounds of caviar with him. No one went except Ian. They both passed out. Next day Hugh woke up, stark naked, to discover that Ian, who'd disappeared, had covered his body with caviar in intricate patterns like the body designs of a Maori warrior. Even for Hugh this was going a bit too far.

From Addis Ababa we moved to Gambeila, a jungle region near the frontier with Sudan. Most of the crew were under canvas. The conditions were tough, but Jeanne and I had made up our differences and were happy. The tribes around were pure Stone Age people. Because of their diets they had a very short lifespan, though the one thing their diet lacked, vitamin C, was everywhere around them on bushes of wild limes, which the crew practically lived on (it was swelteringly hot, as we were almost on the equator), but which the natives wouldn't touch despite all the efforts of local officials.

For the final denouement of the movie we needed a native girl. On an earlier recce I'd seen a stunning-looking girl standing bare-breasted in the long grass of the airstrip. I assumed then that we'd have no difficulty in casting a local, though as a precaution I took a lovely African actress with us. It was clear, however, that to mix the actress with the tribespeople would be as incongruous as putting a model in this season's Paris fashions on the production line of a Soviet commune. A search for girls began. It was hopeless. Girl after girl was paraded in, giggling or terrified. They were usually accompanied by their husbands, fathers, or brothers, and it was clear from their attitudes that they thought our purpose was to purchase a bed-partner on a temporary or permanent basis. A wife for life would probably have cost five dollars. By now we were getting desperate. Eventually, however, the original girl I'd seen (though how anyone knew she was the original I'll never know) was located in a neighboring village, which was feuding with our village. Some truce deal was struck and the girl admitted. But, when the girl was handed over, it was firmly explained to us that we had to keep her locked up until we'd finished with her, otherwise with her billionaire's riches of a dollar a day she would be carried off by some new suitor and would disappear for ever.

It must have been a terrifying experience for the poor girl. Hugh, to everyone's fury, managed to get her drunk and sick on the first day, until we got his flask of brandy away from her. Food was another problem. Realizing that our food would be unfamiliar, we got the local people to prepare the paste of water and manioc on which they survived. She still wouldn't eat. Then Jeanne realized the problem: She was intimidated by our cutlery and dishes. Jeanne started to feed the girl by hand, and she soon became happy. Directing her was something else. Not only did interpreters have to go from French to Amharic, to local dialect, to local dialect, there was also the problem of relating to someone who has not merely never heard of anything to do with film or cameras or acting, but whose language doesn't include such concepts as "like," "love," or any value adjective at all. With children, you can usually find some way to relate on a play level, but any such idea here was as remote as another galaxy. However, somehow we finally got through the scenes.

It was Christmas when we wrapped. I'd promised to spend it with Vanessa and the girls in London. This didn't please Jeanne much, but as soon as Christmas was over I was to return to her house in La Garde-Freinet. On the plane going home she suddenly became fidgety and nervous. I was playing bridge in the front cabin; she was sitting beside me, arranging my hands after each shuffle. We were on the leg between Cairo and Athens and, knowing her well, I knew something was up. In the end she confessed: Theo was waiting at the airport with all his family and friends, to receive her for the great marriage. What was she to do? Once we had landed I explained a version of the problem to the captain and got his permission for the two of us to remain on board during the stopover while Jeanne's dresser, Anna, an Italian peasant of great loyalty and sensitivity, was dispatched with a note calling the ceremony off.

After Christmas I returned to Jeanne and spent a fortnight being spoiled and kept by her. It's the only time that's happened to me, and Jeanne made it marvelously comfortable and exciting, although from time to time mysterious telephone calls came—Anna had a code word for them—obviously from Theo. I was feeling guilty about my marriage (I'd asked Vanessa for a divorce) and worried and ashamed about the film, and at bottom I couldn't give myself completely to Jeanne. I needed to escape from all the emotions and the stress. I flew off, as far away as I could get—to Tahiti and Bora Bora—knowing that Jeanne would take this, rightly, as rejection and that our closeness would almost certainly be over.

The Theo episode had a sweet ending. It's not part of this story, but I can't resist including it. He arrived in France, unannounced, and Anna, concealing Jeanne, dispatched him back to Greece. A little later, his old patron Henry McIlhenny started one of his Greek cruises. Theo was invited. On the boat was Lady Sarah Churchill, recovering from a recent divorce. Theo and Sarah soothed each other's wounds, ended up marrying, and living happily if not forever, then at least for several years. Sarah was the daughter of the Duke of Marlborough and a relative of Winston Churchill. It is said that when Theo phoned the duke and asked him for his daughter's hand, the duke replied, "You've had all the rest so you might as well have her hand too."

16

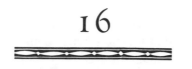

Red and Blue

The new year—1966—started as gloomily as it could: George Devine died while I was away in Bora Bora. I didn't get the news until ten days after the event. The previous summer he had been playing Baron von Epp in John Osborne's *A Patriot for Me*. Characteristically, with his total humility, George had accepted having to audition for the director, Anthony Page, who'd been an assistant at the Court and, also characteristically, had forced George to submit to this humiliating ordeal. During the run he'd had a massive heart attack. He was rushed by an emergency ambulance to St. George's Hospital. Due to some bureaucratic muddle, the absence of his and my doctor on holiday, he was stuck in a noisy public ward and then subsequently was too ill to be moved. It was a day or two before the end of the shooting of *Mademoiselle*, and as soon as I could be free I flew straight to London. I was appalled by what I saw.

Wonderful as the British National Health Service may be as a social policy, its care leaves everything to be desired. Jocelyn and all her family were camped out in a tiny adjacent waiting room without anywhere to stretch out or sleep, living on junk food the kids brought in. Jocelyn was distraught and almost in collapse. Our doctor had a silly inept partner. I upbraided him for not having taken care of Jocelyn—sent her home, seen she had some sleep, and so on. I demanded to know what could be done for George. He said, "Nothing," then admitted, reluctantly, that there was one new drug—experimental and a risk—that might prolong his life, though he had little hope. Knowing what Jocelyn would wish, I ordered him to administer it immediately. Jocelyn was sent home to rest, and some kind of order was achieved.

George did subsequently recover partially—enough to be sent home to the studio Jocelyn and he shared in Chelsea. He managed to write the first few pages of his autobiography, and Jocelyn was able to care for him and adjust to the inevitable end. Later I met our doctor. He'd always been a great friend before, but now he attacked me violently, saying, how dared I interfere: It would have been better if George had died there and then. Maybe, but I know what Jocelyn's reply would have been. I never spoke to Dr. Henderson again.

I had moved offices and living to Paris. There was to be a memorial meeting in the theatre. I flew in with, ironically, Harry Salzman sitting next to me. Memorials tend to be both ghoulish and hysterical—nearly always grotesque. Christopher Isherwood insisted he was to have none—how wise he was: I remember too many horrors. The most ludicrous moment of all was during a service for Ken Tynan, when Shirley MacLaine—hands together in prayer, eyes and head skyward—in a kind of Saint Joan whisper addressed Ken in heaven while the whole congregation doubled up, squirmed, pinched themselves in a desperate effort to prevent a breakout of riotous giggling. George's occasion was glum and spiritless. Jocelyn had asked me to speak. Public address is something I've developed a shyness about, so this was an extra dread. I'd prepared a few remarks based on Dorn's lines in *The Seagull*. John Osborne, who I could tell had developed some mysterious antagonism to me, was to speak before me. He used exactly the same thing, so I was totally confused as to what to say.

The occasion was, however, redeemed for me by two things. In the course of his short address, John said of George, "He spoke French." Three words: To many they're an inconsequential statement of fact, but to me—and I suspect anyone who, like Jocelyn, knew George well—they said everything. They spoke of George's striving for a world and values outside his own, of his reverence for Michel Saint-Denis, of his joy in all those sensual and physical pleasures—the wine, the food—with which, for anyone of his time, France was synonymous. They spoke of his pride in his very good French. And they were a generous acknowledgment on John's part of a side of George of which he would normally have been suspicious. Only John could have found that exact and spare eloquence, which for me is as resonant today as when John spoke. The other moment came from Edith Evans. Throughout my knowledge of her she had an unnerving quality. You never knew how she arrived at what she said, but when she said it it was devastating in its simplicity. She got up and said, "I am seventy-eight. I have never admitted this in public before." And she sat down.

It's easy to eulogize certain great men—they walked on the moon, cured cancer, painted the Sistine ceiling. It's much less easy when someone's greatness (and George was great) consists not in his monuments but in his anonymity. George was great in the way that those master masons of the great medieval cathedrals were great. Their names are unknown, but they taught, they inspired, they built. But George's monument was not the Royal Court Theatre— that had achieved and almost outlived its purpose. George's cathedral was not in stone but in the blood and flesh and minds and spirits of all the people who throughout his career he inspired and invigorated, and who through him glimpsed an attitude to theatre that they themselves could never have conceived: "For me, the theatre is really a religion or way of life . . . A theatre must have a recognizable attitude. It will have one whether one likes it or not." And George quoted John's *Look Back in Anger:* "If you can't bear the thought of messing up your nice, clean soul, you'd better give up the whole idea of life, and become a saint. Because you'll never make it as a human being." Today I often feel George has become praised as a kind of pietistic don, but he always had the cement and truck dust and sweat on his hands—that's why the hod carriers would follow him to the top of the scaffolding. And all of us who do or try to do better work today are his monuments. Of how many people can you say that?

Back in Paris, work went on. For *Mademoiselle*, in keeping with the austerity of the concept, we used no music—just natural sound effects. The finishing went quickly, and the film was premiered at the Cannes Festival. Cannes, which is a flesh and critics market, was the worst place for it to open. On top of that, the French attacked me for tackling a "French" subject. It is a film I'm proud of, though at the time I was destroyed by the violence of its reception. The only compensation of that particular festival was becoming friends with Jack Nicholson, who was peddling the Westerns he made with Monte Hellmann on the fringes of the festival. I liked his movies, was able to get them seen, and I think probably helped Jack in making some deals.

I was still half in love with Jeanne in a pathetic kind of way—knowing it wasn't any good, but not quite prepared to let go. She, naturally and rightly, had already moved on. I didn't know who I wanted to be or where I wanted to be. At moments I was even suicidal. Jocelyn Herbert came over from London and helped me. I had no place in London; I looked at apartments in Paris and at property in the south of France. Jeanne showed me a deserted, Sleeping Beauty–type hamlet—Le Nid du Duc—near her. It had a dreamlike beauty, but it was in total ruins and the prospect of renovating it seemed like a life's work in a quagmire. I became more and more restless and depressed.

I had no theatre prospects or interests. Woodfall had projects happening. *The Charge of the Light Brigade* was in the future: The only concrete project was an idea of making a portmanteau film of three Shelagh Delaney short stories. Lindsay Anderson, Peter Brook, and I were each to direct one. Somehow the project got derailed, and only Lindsay kept to the original plan with *The White Bus*—a funny poetic fantasy which I sometimes think may be the best movie he ever made. I think Peter went off first. Instead of a Delaney story he wanted to do a little farce he'd written about a Wagnerian diva trying to get to the theatre for a performance. Zero Mostel starred, and I think he was the reason Peter decided to do it. It was unshowable.

For a long time I'd been obsessed with doing a musical. I loved the songs of a Persian-Frenchman, Cyrus Bassiak, a friend of Jeanne's who'd written the song *"Le Tourbillon"* for *Jules et Jim* and whose song *"Jo le Rouge"* I'd used in *Sailor*. A great friend of Julian More's who had translated the lyrics for Peter's stage production of *Irma La Douce* and with whom I'd worked on several never-produced musicals was equally passionate about Cyrus's songs. He had a huge collection that occasionally he could be prevailed on to sing to his own guitar accompaniment. From his repertoire we concocted some kind of narrative. I think originally it was probably designed for Jeanne, who had sung all Cyrus's songs, but Vanessa loved them too and was determined to do the film. So in October 1996 I made *Red and Blue*, a thirty-minute musical with quite a stellar cast, including, besides Vanessa, Michael York, Douglas Fairbanks, Jr. (who pursued Vanessa and slipped sonnets under her door at night when we were on location), and a circusful of elephants. It's an oddity, and the music—extraordinarily personal—doesn't really fit into any category.

The weird triple bill was supposed to have been released under the title of *Red, White and Zero*. It never was. *The White Bus* and *Red and Blue* have been screened intermittently, but by now I think they have disappeared.

Preparation for *The Charge*—both in scouting trips in Turkey and in assembling a big crew for design and research—had been going on intermittently throughout the year. But there was another event, which was to lead to one of the closest and most valued relationships of my life. It took place at the Aqua Club, a beach restaurant in St. Tropez, and was almost like the meeting of Stanley and Livingstone. There was a figure standing at the bar, about my age, looking at me as if he knew me but wasn't quite sure—and I was looking at him in exactly the same way. "Aren't you—er—Tony Richardson?" "Aren't you—er—Jeremy Fry?"

Jeremy and I went back in a curious way. In the early days of the Royal Court most of our front-of-house photos were taken by Anthony Armstrong-Jones. I even knew him earlier, as he was a friend of the early supposed patroness of the Court, at whose parties he danced energetically and spectacularly. A little later he began his courtship of Princess Margaret. It was all strictly under wraps. Soon he started to give little supper parties at a studio house he had on the Thames at Rotherhithe, for HRH and his friends to get to know each other. These evenings were rather stilted and stiff. Having got to know her later, I know that Princess Margaret has great wit and mischief and a genuine loyalty to and concern for her friends, but she wasn't at ease at the time, nor was anyone else, much. There were also awkward questions of protocol—no one was supposed to leave before the princess, which, as I was rehearsing early, was impossible for me. Also, as I was the least respectful personality there, I felt I had to try to make the evenings go. I didn't enjoy them and soon stopped attending. Among the regulars were Jeremy—(a longtime friend of Tony's), very handsome, with wavy black hair—and his beautiful blond wife, Camilla. He never spoke, but I remember thinking that he was the one person there I felt instinctively I could be friends with and communicate with easily. The only time I remember our talking at all was when we had to travel together (the Secret Service always told us to arrive by different routes). Jeremy had been commissioned to bring ice. He'd forgotten, so had to stop in an East End pub to persuade the barman to split a chunk off the blocks on which beer is chilled at the bar. The ice was dirty and yellowish—stained from the bottles' labels—but, giggling, we figured we could get the drinks poured before the princess noticed the quality of the ice, and after her no one would dare object.

Knowing how stratified English life is, it seemed unlikely that our paths would cross again. I heard of Jeremy very briefly from time to time; he'd drifted in and out of the headlines. Forced by pressures in England and the breakup of his marriage, he'd lived in Sausalito, California, for a year. He returned to Bath, his home-town. (The Frys were well-known eighteenth-century chocolate merchants and were Quakers. Camilla and Jeremy had had a beautiful William and Mary house, Widcombe Manor, just outside the city). Jeremy was an architect, engineer, inventor, with all the mechanical skills I've never had. He'd invented an actuator—a valve controlling oil pipelines. With a little capital from friends, he started a business based on his invention which gradually became a success all over the world wherever there are pipelines. He later diversified into boatbuilding (earlier he'd been a racing-car enthusiast) and other products. His company was recognized as one of the most successful and best designed in England. In a way, though in a totally different sphere, it was a parallel to Woodfall.

Jeremy had just bought a deserted hamlet, Le Grand Banc, in the Basses-Alpes; I was still eyeing the Nid du Duc hamlet that Jeanne had shown me, which was still unsold. We were both getting divorced—on the same day. We talked and talked, and found that, although we were totally different in our approaches, we had almost everything in common. I have been very lucky in the number of close, close friends I've made all my life and who, I don't know why, have tolerated me through the years. But my friendship with Jeremy is something quite different. It was like finding the brother I never had. If I don't see Jeremy for months, when we meet again it's as if we've had breakfast that morning. There is a continuity of intercourse, as if there are no gaps to be filled in, unlike when you normally catch up with friends. Perhaps it's because we work in such different worlds. I can understand nothing about his, and I don't think Jeremy likes the world of entertainment much. But if you want your plumbing fixed, the telephones, the light switches, or plans for a new building . . . He instantly suggested people who could help if I decided to buy in France. And, confident in his talents, I plunged and bought Le Nid du Duc.

Again, the spirit of Le Grand Banc and Le Nid du Duc were the same, though all the details were the opposite. Le Grand Banc stood on open, exposed white hills; it had no trees and no water, but it did have electricity. Le Nid du Duc was buried in a valley, looking out on hills covered with cork oaks and pines and sweet chestnuts; there was a stream and waterfalls, but no electricity. Around both places are wild country and deserted farms, untouched since time began, where you can roam for days. Land, gardening, and plants are interests Jeremy and I share—and travel.

We have traveled all over the world—always just the two of us, in little rented cars, staying in everything from the most luxurious hotels to the filthiest and most fetid rooming houses. Our first trip together took us to Bombay and Delhi, to Agra and the Taj Mahal, en route for Sri Lanka, where we rode working elephants in the forests, were garlanded by smelly monks in the incensed darkness of the Temple of the Tooth in Kandy, and had vast teak bedrooms opened for us in a hill-station hotel which hadn't been used since the visit of the Prince of Wales in the early 1920s. The hotel was now used by German package tours. We were thought to be genuine sahibs and therefore got special treatment. We have been in a riot, quelled with water cannons, in Oaxaca, and in an earthquake in the ruins of Antigua in Guatemala, and we have climbed the pyramids of that most magical of the Mayan ruins, Tikal, buried under its rainforest cover, alive with toucans and coatis. We have sailed and slept on native feluccas in Egypt, descended into the tombs of the Valley of the Kings and stared at the grandiose temples at Karnak and Abu Simble, and at Baalbek in Lebanon.

We have stayed in freezing little Japanese hotels in the mountains and lakes outside Tokyo and have contemplated the Zen gardens in Kyoto, which is like a sixteenth-century Beverly Hills gone mad. (Japan was one of the few places to which we responded differently: Jeremy loved it and all the attention poured on you; I didn't). We have climbed up Jean-Christophe's Palace at Cap-Haïtien and had cocktails in the wicker theatricality of the Olafsen Hotel. Jeremy was nearly locked up in Bangkok, and I was refused a visa for Saigon during the Vietnam War. We have been menaced and robbed by the thuggish soldiers guarding Mobutu's palace in Kinshasa. We have chased hookers in Phnom Penh and glided in *pousse-cyclettes*— wicker chairs suspended in front of tricycles so that you seem to be drifting with an easy silent pace a foot or two off the ground, like lazy butterflies—round the ruins of the Khmer temples and forests at Angkor Wat, the most magical of all places and now tragically shut off by the horrors of the Cambodian devastation. I think we were some of the last tourists there.

We have bargained for carpets in the souks of Tashkent and watched the blue people in the camel market of Goulimime. Recently we have sat in an *Alice in Wonderland* ring, literally side by side with the silver-backed gorillas in the volcanic forests off Rwanda, have seen the pygmies hunting and performing in the far-off interior of Haut-Zaïre, and we have traveled the length of the Ruwenzori—the Mountains of the Moon—which Ptolemy called the greatest wonder on earth. And the journeys will go on.

Christmas brought another kind of joining. Vanessa was shooting *Camelot* in California, and she had persuaded me to spend Christmas there with the girls. Was this another attempt at reconciliation? She had rented Gladys Cooper's house in Pacific Palisades, and from the moment I got off the plane she proceeded to rush me from industry party to industry party, of the kind she knew I detested. I never quite understood the thinking behind this, but I decided just to go along with whatever she'd arranged. There were a lot of Brits in town, as *Doctor Doolittle* was also shooting. I had been in discussion with Rex Harrison about the possibility of his playing Lord Cardigan in *The Charge*. He was married at the time to Rachel

Roberts, an old acquaintance who'd been in *Saturday Night and Sunday Morning*, so we were thrown together a lot. Rachel had her fun moments (there was one wonderful dinner at a famous director's house, where there were first- and second-class guest tables. First got French champagne; second got Californian. Rachel and I had been relegated to second-class, and we proceeded to snatch bottles of the good champagne and behave as badly as we could) but there was a deep bitterness in her attitudes.

Vanessa had decided to give a British party for the Brits: "I know you think I can't organize anything, but I'll show you." Her idea was to hold the party at the British pub in Santa Monica. Next door was a fish-and-chips shop where they could be purchased and eaten Brit-style in newspaper. The guests then could drink Bass and Guinness and play darts in the pub. I suggested that several of the guests might want something else to drink, but then decided to shut up and just go along. When we got there, Vanessa had not checked and the fish-and-chips shop was closed. The locals at the pub had no desire to give up their dartboard to a load of Hollywood actors and resented our presence, and the guests did want more than beer. To avert total disaster I rushed over to a local restaurant— Chez Jay—and told the accommodating Jay the problem. He fixed up a dining table in a back room. The evening finished with Rachel denouncing Rex for trying to make a play for Vanessa and Vanessa for making a play for her, ending at midnight with her screaming to phone Lindsay Anderson in England, the only person who understood her.

The nightmare ten days climaxed on New Year's Eve with a round of several parties. I'd insisted on hiring a limo, knowing the night would be a heavy one. First stop was to be an intimate supper *chez* Rex and Rachel—pre-festivities and for some business discussion. We arrived at their Bel Air house. I told the limo to report back in an hour. Rex opened the door and launched into a tirade of insults and vituperation. He'd read, in one of the gossip columns, that I'd discussed the Cardigan role with George C. Scott. It was absolutely untrue, but his abuse was such that I was determined to leave—except we were carless in the hills. The evening wore on like that, through one of the first psychedelic parties given—screens on every wall and three competing rock-and-roll bands—and ending with a bash at the old Selznick home. There we started another inexplicable row, with Jane Fonda and Roger Vadim, with more embarrassment from Rex, who had become fulsomely apologetic. Then, at about 3 A.M., Richard Harris, who was starring opposite Vanessa, arrived with his son Damien on his shoulders. (Recently Damien has become a friend and tennis partner.) David Hemmings, who had a great rapport with kids, started sparring with Damien. Richard took this wrong and punched David in the face, cutting his lip. Vanessa burst into tears and swore she would not go on acting with Richard.

We got home at about 5:00. I couldn't wait to get on the plane home four hours later. Just as I was leaving for the airport, a crate of Dom Perignon arrived from Rex as an apology. It was good-bye to Hollywood for several years.

17

"O the Wild Charge
They Made!"

The Charge of the Light Brigade had been in the works for a long time. John Osborne had been as passionate about the subject as I was, and we had worked together on the script. One of the great problems was Cecil Woodham-Smith's *The Reason Why*. This brilliant piece of historical writing had been popular and critical success and had led to several film projects, none of which had come to fruition. The rights had been passed from, among others, Michael Balcon to the current owner, Laurence Harvey.

The original feature of Mrs. Woodham-Smith's concept and scholarship was the juxtaposition of the careers of Lords Cardigan and Lucan from birth, showing how their antagonisms led to their final confrontation over the disastrous orders and misunderstandings that led to the destruction of the famous regiment. We wanted to do something different, to concentrate on the charge itself, on the mixture of heroism, romance, farce, and horror embodied in the actions of a much more panoramic group of characters, using as our central figure the enigmatic and dashing Captain Nolan, who alone foresaw the mistake that had been made and who tried desperately to reverse the fatal decision to loose the six hundred horsemen into the Russian gun batteries, only to be killed at the last moment by a stray bullet. It was to be a film about the ironies of war.

There have, of course, been many other accounts of the famous charge (and an earlier film, a Warner Brothers vehicle for Errol Flynn which, set in India or Afghanistan, had nothing much to do with history). All these accounts are based, more or less, on Alexander Kinglake's *Invasion of the Crimea*, the first masterpiece of historical journalism. For this reason we saw no reason to burden the budget by negotiating the rights to a book whose emphasis was on different aspects of the story. To protect ourselves further we had set up a research department under John Mollo, a student of military history, whose brief was to ensure that any incident John Osborne employed in the screenplay would be amply documented elsewhere, to avoid trespassing on the original digging Mrs. Woodham-Smith had done. Everything was checked and rechecked, and we felt protected. We had also a great responsibility to United Artists, which was financing the film, its big-budget production for the year, and one of the biggest budgets of all time (at that time) for a British movie. John produced his script. It had many splendid and poetic things in it—especially in its evocation of English society before the Crimean War—but it still needed a lot of work, and finally Charles Wood, a brilliant and eccentric comic writer with a passion for all things military, came in to rework it. Charles stayed with us and contributed an extraordinary amount throughout the shooting.

Then a bombshell broke. Laurence Harvey, who was naturally miffed that his own project had never got off the ground, had obtained a copy of John's script and was suing him for plagiarism. I thought he had no case. We engaged top counsel. A week or two later the experienced QC we'd hired asked to see me urgently. He and his people had been analyzing the script and had come to the conclusion that John was clearly in the wrong. It wasn't that he had used any scene or incident that wasn't either invented or documented elsewhere, but he had helped himself liberally to stylistic phrases and descriptions in *The Reason Why*. The list of incidences was very long and devastating. When confronted, John murmured something about Brecht helping himself to Shakespeare, but the situation was disastrous.

In February 1967 there was a preliminary judicial hearing which went absolutely against us. John could in fact be liable to criminal prosecution. He had used the book; he was in breach of his writing contract with Woodfall; and Woodfall, of which he was a director, was clearly in breach of its contract with United Artists. A lot of money had already been spent, and the lives of many people would have been disrupted if the production were canceled now. Some kind of deal had to be struck to acquire *The Reason Why.* United Artists was forgiving and understanding. It agreed that if the film made money the rights could go on the budget; if not, it would offset the expense against other Woodfall projects. Laurence Harvey—to his credit—behaved as fairly as he could, when he could have asked for much more as blackmail. Laurence Harvey's lawyer, Lord Goodman (the-then Mr. Fix-it of Harold Wilson's Labour government, which was afraid of the film's collapse and its repercussions on the industry), met with me and, in a series of meetings that took place in London and, for some reason, late at night in Paris, we arranged terms.

There was one sticking point: Laurence Harvey, convinced that the movie couldn't be a financial success without his name on the marquee (in this he may have been proved to be right!), insisted he must be given a little role. There was nothing for him, but then I thought of a one-day scene—an incident among incidents before the charge, when Prince Radziwill, a peacock-uniformed Polish dandy attached to the French and British forces, is surrounded by a group of wild Cossacks but by his dash escapes them. Originally John himself was to have played the role, but replacing him seemed a small price to pay to avoid the threatened prosecution. Not to John. He accused me of complete betrayal, and it led to a total breach between us. Except for past projects, we split all the Woodfall companies, and never collaborated again. And it took many years to mend our friendship—which, I'm glad to say, out of old association, affection, and real admiration, we have now revived.

I didn't have much time to dwell on all this, because the exigencies of the production—much vaster than anything I'd previously undertaken—were acute and overwhelming. The most important problem of all had always been obtaining the necessary cavalry. We had in fact no options: Turkey was the only country we could work in that had a sufficient number of horsemen still in service. The only reason they still existed was that the Russians also still kept up largish numbers of cavalry on the Turkish borders, so there was a typical NATO standoff. In fact many of the horses were old hacks from Hollywood westerns, shipped out to Turkey in an American aid package. And of course the terrain in northern Turkey, the opposite side of the Black Sea from the Crimea, was perfect. Neil started negotiations with the Turkish government, helped by the American and, I think, French ambassadors—during all our different projects and locations we always found understanding and help from the Americans and the French, never from the British.

The only British diplomatic contribution to this whole enterprise—from which all the proceeds were going into the UK—was to complain 1. that I didn't go to sign the visitor's book at the embassy in Ankara and 2. that we refused to cancel shooting on the Queen's birthday so that our stars could attend the embassy party.

The negotiations with the Turks were tricky. Traditionally the president of Turkey is the former head of the armed forces. His former second-in-command becomes the head of the army until he in turn succeeds to the presidency. Between the two there is often tacit opposition and resistance, so that a policy implemented by one may later be reversed, and is probably resented by the lower echelons. We concluded a deal with the government whereby it would lend us the cavalry in return only for their upkeep. But we realized that the deal was fragile and that if it was changed we would have little recourse. Luckily the colonel of the cavalry, which also acted as the presidential bodyguard and had been employed just before our shooting in defusing a coup, became devoted to me and a great supporter of our project. We brought him to London and provided lots of cigars for him and black frilly whaleboned corsets and underwear for his girlfriend.

The valley itself was another big issue. After a lot of looking we found a valley some twenty miles from Ankara which was almost identical to the original valley of death and was accessible enough for the government to agree that we could move all its horses and men out from their permanent barracks to quarters under canvas. The valley was owned by two different villages. (The villages themselves are astonishingly unchanged from centuries ago—in many of them you could shoot scenes for a biblical epic without changing anything but the star and crescent on the local mosque.) The village councils are, surprisingly, democratically administered, and every one of the elders had a voice and a veto over any deal concluded. We wanted the villagers to agree to leave the valley unplanted for the months we needed it. In return, after government advice and negotiations, we offered three times the price their harvest could ever have fetched. However, negotiating with the local mullahs was for Neil similar to negotiating with the Ayatollah Khomeini and involved listening to a lot of denunciations of us as infidels and blasphemers. Finally the deal was done. But it wasn't respected: The villagers would secretly plow up the ground at night, making it dangerous for our horses, or would destroy the wooden forts we built on the hills. The army, or rather the cavalry, was on our side, and there were frequent and unpleasant clashes. We felt we were living under a state of siege.

Every day brought some new emergency. We had persuaded the authorities to let the young recruits grow mustaches and beards, to give them a period look. One evening a general arrived who understood nothing of the film and ordered everyone to shave. Next day we were desperately phoning Rome, Paris, and London for hairdressers and supplies to replace the night's devastation.

There were other, more dangerous, situations. We had engaged a British stunt coordinator to be master of the horse. He had gone out weeks earlier to start training the men. When I arrived, he gave me a demonstration of his methods. He had been getting the men to charge each other with wooden lanches. It wasn't called for in the script, and it was totally ineffectual—it looked like a silly parade-ground exercise. In an attempt to see what kind of expressiveness could be got out of the troops, I asked one of the officers to ask the men to repeat the exercise, yelling war cries. The effect was electric and lethal. Two of the men crashed into each other. Blood spurted with that frightening rush that no special effects can produce; their eyes were bursting and staring as if in a nineteenth-century battle painting. I thought both men had been killed. It was a disgusting and horrible moment. The two horses had to be shot. The men—one with a broken collarbone, the other a broken ankle—were taken to a hospital and recovered, but the Turkish press denounced us and claimed we had killed about ten soldiers. We nearly lost the cavalry there and then. But in another way it taught us all a lesson. We got rid of the stuntman and his lunatic maneuvers, and we never injured another man or, despite all the difficulties of guns and effects, another horse. The care everyone took of our horses—never using a trip wire, never overstraining them—was something we were all very proud of.

Relations with the Turks were always on a knife-edge. In making movies you have to respect the customs of the country you are in, but there is still an uneasy feeling (for us liberals) when, in the service of your work, your partners use methods of behavior which, normal to them, are repugnant to you. All kinds of violence went on within the army, and when the village whose labor we used to work on our construction went on strike, an officer publicly beat up the village mayor with his whip.

When the crew and cast finally assembled, in May 1967, I made a speech to them. We were there to make a film. We were not there to judge and criticize a society and mores radically different from our own. We had to close our eyes and mouths and get on with our work.

There wasn't much to do in Ankara at the best of times. It was still a cold spring. On the ponds in one of the lakes, the ice was breaking up and the frogs were spawning. One of our leading actors had gone to spend his time off in the park. A youngish man and his girlfriend were amusing themselves by throwing stones at the frogs. The English actor spoke up: "Stop it, you rotten bastard." The young man was one of the cavalry officers, out of uniform, and understood English. There was a major row. The officer claimed his birth and family's honor had been impugned. The colonel took his officer's side and expected me to order the actor flogged, literally. It took a lot of explanation and charm to settle for a public apology in front of the troops.

We were always in danger of being trapped in disputes between the various factions of the Turks themselves. The cavalry had moved into their quarters at the valley for several months, and their specifications for their quarters had, naturally enough, taken account of their length of stay. For the battle of Alma we needed a large contingent of infantry—about four thousand, I think. They were to be with us for only about five days and of course needed no training. But as soon as the infantry saw the cavalry barracks they demanded exactly the same. It was a question of inter-service rivalry. We had neither the time nor the resources to be able to oblige, and it took a lot of diplomacy to sort it all out.

I'd never quite understood one of the cavalry's demands. We had built their huge temporary barracks exactly to the government's specifications—which by and large meant luxury and space for the horses, confinement and squalor for the men. The men were housed in double bunks with hardly a foot of space separating them. They ate in the open, washed at communal sinks, and used communal latrines—little more than trenches in the ground. But the cavalry insisted on hot showers with separate enclosed cubicles. It seemed out of character. I asked the colonel to explain. He told me that once or twice a month the army provided a pathetic little show for their isolated troops—acrobats, clowns, sword-swallowers, etc. The show always ended with a belly dancer who stripped to her last G-string. The recruits were then rushed individually into the curtained-off showers to enjoy their one moment of sexual satisfaction.

Relations got even worse when we went to Istanbul to shoot the Crimean landing. There was a very small unit of cavalry there, due to be permanently disbanded and held over only until shooting was finished. The officers concerned resented the whole affair: They wanted to be off on leave or to their new jobs. The Bosporus is a treacherous place whose combination of tides and winds made it hard to coordinate the boats and the craft on which cameras were placed. As with all these big action scenes, you have to spend days planning and calculating positions—exactly as in a military operation—before you turn a foot of film. Finally the day came. The men were dressed and made up. The horses and guns were loaded from a jetty some two miles away from our beach. The barges had simply to approach the shore, load up the soldiers who were waiting in the costumes, steam back a few hundred yards, and come back in with the cameras rolling and the troops acting the disembarkment. Despite a lot of surliness from the cavalry officers, all went well until, as the boats were going back out to sea, all the young recruits, who'd never been on a boat before, got seasick and started to throw up. There should have appeared barges each loaded with a hundred or so men, but everyone was lying out of sight writhing on the boats' decks, awash with vomit, and assistant directors had to desperately try to prop up the odd shoulder in a camera lens to conceal the lack of numbers.

In the end we made it, without losing our troops and horses, although on one of our last days we nearly lost all our cast in a sudden earthquake which almost brought down our hotel and drove many of our famous names naked in panic onto the promenade. Neil had insisted from the beginning that we should shoot the difficult parts of the film—the battles and the charge—first, while our energy and determination were at their peak. That way, if problems did arise, we would have had time to work out some solutions. He was proved perfectly right, and returning to England and the lush soft summer was like a holiday after a long and nervy campaign.

We had assembled an exceptionally gifted crew. David Watkin was again the cinematographer. We had discussed trying to get a very soft period look, like the nineteenth-century photos of David Octavius Hill. He came up with the idea of resuscitating old, less precisely focused lenses. After a lot of hunting, he found two sets of these Ross lenses which his crew then worked on to make them functional and to adapt them to a Panavision wide-screen format.

The production design of the film was in the hands of Lila de Nobili, whose work in the theatre and in opera, notably for Visconti and Zeffirelli, I had long admired. Designers are the great unsung and underpaid heroes of the theatre. They work longer and more conscientiously, need more background, and have more responsibility than anyone else. There is usually very little recompense for all this. In films, of course, there's more, but then they don't have the satisfaction of the audience seeing their work as they've imagined or designed it—the greatest set in the world is nothing if it's shot with a close-up lens. Although she hadn't worked much in movies, Lila instinctively understood the problems. She, together with our military experts under John Mollo, researched the period for two years in advance, and with her knowledge of costume houses (mainly Italian, where the standard of design and costume-making was and still is higher than anywhere else in the world) and of existing stock throughout Europe we were able to achieve standards of accuracy that normally would have been impossible.

With her shawl, basket, one skirt, and black stockings (usually with holes in them), Lila looked like a figure out of *La Bohème*. When she first arrived in our offices in London, Neil thought she was the cleaning woman and handed her a broom and a bucket. But, though she seems so frail and vulnerable, she has a constitution that can outlast the strongest of production men and prop men, quell the authority of the biggest stars, and, if necessary, out-shoot the prima donnas among the ladies of the opera couture world. Her detail and her meticulousness meant she could never achieve a thousandth of what she envisaged, but what she did achieve was awesome.

Another remarkable contributer was the Canadian-born Richard Williams, who makes, designs, and illustrates cartoon films. To provide all the background history leading up to an event like the charge is impossible, and especially difficult in film terms. To make it lively and entertaining, I had the idea of framing the action with information provided through the kind of contemporary satirical cartoons that newspapers of the time would have printed. Dick responded perfectly, but until we started I had no idea how monumental the work of producing animation on film is—requiring hundreds and thousands of precise sketches to be designed. We discussed and scripted all this, and Dick started work at least two years in advance, but, despite all the efforts of his big studio, which worked entirely on the project during those two years, we were adding images right up to the day of the premiere and we never finished all we had hoped for.

Finally came the editing. The first cut was I don't know how many hours long. I've always been a fanatical cutter, believing that everything in the movies or theatre is too long. (I've never understood those purists who insist on playing every word, including the unplayable ones, of classics). I junked whole scenes, subplots, and sequences—like the charge of the Heavy Brigade. Kevin Brownlow, the editor (and now a renowned film historian), wanted to make a four-and-a-half-hour version of the film to release later in special situations. We never got around to it, and most of the material has now been destroyed.

The premiere, in April 1968, was notable for two things. I'd long had a feud with the British film critics, so I decided, with the backing of United Artists, to cancel all press screenings, refuse any cooperation, and, if the critics insisted on reviewing the film, make them pay for their seats. The outcry was predictable and violent. All critics resent being criticized themselves, displaying a sensitivity they would recognize in no artist: They scream like stuck pigs. The press followed up my gesture with headlines and cartoons, and, with the critics on the defensive, the movie probably got better notices than it might otherwise have done, knowing the critics' prejudices. My only regret, looking back, is that we didn't use the title *The Reason Why* instead of the more obvious box-office heroics of *The Charge of the Light Brigade*.

The other incident connected with the premiere was, alas, also typical of what happens to the projection of films. The soundtrack is vital to the impact of a film, and in this case we went to the extent of bringing our talented dubbing engineer and editor, Gerry Humphreys, to rehearse the finished product in the theatre, the Odeon Leicester Square. We set all the levels to our satisfaction, but when the premiere began, to our horror the sound was at a quite different and much lower level. Gerry rushed to the projection booth and asked the projectionist what was happening. The owner of the Rank circuit, Sir John Davis, was in attendance, as it was a royal premiere, with the Duke of Edinburgh. At any performance at which he was present, he refused to have sound beyond a certain level. "But it's Mr. Richardson's film," protested Gerry. "It may be Mr. Richardson's film," replied the projectionist, "but it's Sir John's theatre."

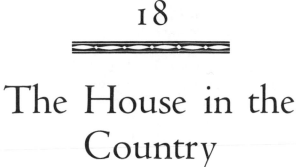

18

The House in the Country

As soon as the shooting of *The Charge* was finished, a group of friends and workers on the film went to camp out at my new French hideaway. Le Nid du Duc, "the nest of the night owl," is a traditional name, and tradition still rules the pace and style of the whole region. It is near La Garde-Freinet, at the top of the range of mountains which runs unbroken from Cannes to Toulon. In one direction the mountains look out to sea, in the other they look over the great valley which extends from the Alps to Avignon, through which the Roman armies and the false popes marched, and where Cézanne painted. Here, high on the mountains, the conquering Saracens built fortresses and walled towns so they could survey the approach of any enemy by sea or land. Nowadays a huge cross has replaced the Saracen citadel at La Garde, but the town still retains something of its Moorish character, and it's not difficult to see traces of Arab ancestry in the faces of some of the peasant families. The hills are harsh and tough. Nothing really survives but the cork oak, which was the main source of revenue for the inhabitants in the nineteenth century. It was for the women cork-oak workers that the first trade unions in France were founded, and La Garde-Freinet has until recently always been a center of radicals and anarchists. Even today in the village itself there's no gendarmerie—only an amiable village *garde de champêtre*, more like an Elizabethan constable than a modern policeman—though a triangle of the area stretching down to Toulon was for a long time a refuge for criminals.

Le Nid du Duc is a hamlet, a collection of dwellings where two or three families lived more or less together and scratched a living from these tough and hard hills. The climate is extreme—one year floods, another frosts; one year a plague of locusts or wasps, another a disease of the vegetation—and always, each summer, there is the threat or the fact of sweeping forest fires which can ravage hundreds of thousands of acres. The buildings are traditional. It's impossible to tell when they were begun, and each generation added, rebuilt, or let collapse whatever was necessary or superfluous to its needs. How fragile its economy was I realized acutely when studying the map of the property. All the hillsides are a patchwork of peasant holdings surrounded by the vast national forests. A peasant might have hung on to one tiny patch of land, no more than a few square yards cut off from the rest and with access only by a communal footpath, because there two streams cross and, shored up by stone walls against the steep inclines on the hills, there was a flat plot sufficiently damp for salad greens to be grown all year round, except in exceptional drought. That made those few square yards infinitely more precious than all the surrounding mountain lands, whose only produce was cork and chestnuts, requiring transport by mule or ox, and which were always exposed to the Mistral or the Vent d'Est.

But the somber gray-green of the foliage on the pines and cork is relieved by the lightness of the chestnut trees—which attract a large population of wild boar, keenly hunted by the locals—and by the endless, changing profusion of wildflowers. From the start of the year, when the wild mimosa bursts out, sometimes under the snow, season succeeds season with another brilliant crop and color: the wild tree heather, white and purple; the scarlet poppies; the violets and the blue periwinkles; the purple and yellow flags; orchids of every color; white starwort and daisies; gold celandine and ragwort; green spurge; the red and orange berries of the arbutus. Badgers, hares, foxes, martens, dormice, squirrels, tortoises, lizards, and salamanders fill the woods, despite the constant depredation of the *chasse* and the blood-lust of the peasantry, who will fire at anything that flies or moves. And in the sky are eagles and buzzards, jays, hoopoes, and the great night owls themselves. From

April to June the woods are filled day and night with the sound of cuckoos and the song of nightingales, and the summer evenings are full of swallows and whistling bats, with crickets and cicadas and the deep notes of the tree frogs.

When I first bought the property it was more or less in ruins. The last peasants had moved out in the 1950s—the last old lady now lives in another hamlet, La Tourre, a couple of miles below, where the climate and land are kinder, in a house whose main façade is completely covered in spring by a sheet of wisteria. Le Nid du Duc had been bought from the peasants by an upstanding Establishment Parisian (who local rumor alleged to be the illegitimate son of President De Gaulle, whom physically he resembled perfectly). He had obviously had an initial enthusiasm for the place and had planted some cypresses and a few eucalypti, but he kept it mainly as a summer vacation spot for this wife and young children. As he had become more embroiled in politics he had lost interest, so that by the time I bought it roofs had fallen in, walls had collapsed, and the forest had invaded all the terraces surrounding the houses, so that it was like a place asleep, like Sleeping Beauty's castle. Even the mounds of garbage that campers had left couldn't spoil its magical aspect.

When we first camped out there, there was only one outside tap for cold water, by the old *lavoir* where the peasants had washed their laundry. Beside the *lavoir* was a big oven where most of the communal cooking had been done. There was another oven in the main house, above what was now the sitting room, which had been the ox stable. We had nothing but sleeping bags and mattresses on the floor, but in the wonderful dry heat of the Côte d'Azur summer, with the beach and the blue sea only twenty-five minutes away, we didn't need anything else. With the crew that Jeremy had found, I set to planning the restoration of the place. I had decided from the beginning to try to restore what there was, except some of the barns and outbuildings, which had collapsed so completely that they had to be rebuilt from scratch. Among the first jobs were restoring water (we had several springs), clearing the land, and cutting down the invading forest. Until then I'd always thought it a crime to fell trees, but with the help of another friend of Jeremy's, Hiram Winterbotham, a great gardener, I began to learn how to landscape.

Traditional craftsmen—the kind who could build walls without concrete, mix the traditional Provençal colors and roughcast—were already disappearing, but after a search we located in Marseilles a family of woodcutters. They agreed they would come for a month in the autumn. When they arrived—old gnarled men, looking exactly like six of the Snow White's seven dwarfs—they brought their food, their wine, their oil, and their guns and hunting dogs. They had been tempted to come only by the prospect of hunting the wild boar. They moved in, sleeping on bare wood floors, and at the end of two weeks had made a huge difference.

At times the whole enterprise seemed out of control—like a movie gone mad and wildly over budget—and I would get panicky and regret I had ever started it. I saw bankruptcy looming. More and more workers seemed to arrive every day. One of them was a skinny little sparrow of a boy who looked as if he had been on a breadline all his life. I asked the boss—Jean-François Lefort—what he needed the boy for. He said, "Oh, he can do anything—he'll be very useful." The boy, Jean-Pierre Herbert, was the illegitimate son of a German soldier, born during the Second World War, and to a Frenchman, therefore, marked with shame for life.

He'd subsisted, barely, by being a pavement artist on the streets of Toulon. He stayed on with us and finally took over the management and running of the whole place. He became a member of the family, and almost like some impossible son. Sadly, after some years he became an alcoholic and increasingly violent and irresponsible. Like many alcoholics, he refused to acknowledge his terrible disease. Eventually he became too dangerous to keep on and I had to fire him. After several years during which, despite lots of financial help, he became a street bum, a *clochard*, he finally went to a clinic and we hoped for a cure for his alcoholism. We took him back, because he loved Le Nid du Duc more than anything else on earth, and in his prime he had made it vibrant and blooming. He hadn't, however, beaten his malady, and in the summer of 1985, after more and more violence, he finally shot his girlfriend and killed himself. That destructiveness is part of Le Nid du Duc too— or rather of the humans who have passed and will pass through it.

It took about a year to get the place more or less into shape. By then we had six houses habitable—though two of them are nothing more than cabanas; one room with a fireplace. We'd built a big cistern to store water. From an old cow-shed we'd created a large studio where we could put on shows and hold parties.

Le Nid du Duc lies in a cleft in the hills, looking down a long valley to ranges of lower purple hills in the mountains (which David Hockney has often painted); so, although it is high compared with the rest of the district, it is relatively sheltered, and certain trees can, if not thrive, at least survive there (until last winter, when a drought decimated everything). My first symbolic act had been to put a big palm tree in the center of the hamlet, on top of what had been an open rubbish dump. I followed it with oranges and lemons, olives, cypresses, wisterias, more palms, lavender, mimosas, honeysuckles, roses. The following year I installed a swimming pool. This was a major work, as it had to be cantilevered out from the sloping hillside. A famous swimming pool contractor came to design it, but it's pretty hard to answer the question "What kind of pool and what size do you want?" when you've never built a pool before. I knew I wanted it to be big enough to do lengths in, but not so big as to overwhelm the whole place. Finally I solved my part of the problem by going to all the pools I'd swum in in the district, and then, after swimming in them again, measuring them and deciding which sizes and features I liked and which I didn't.

The pool was delayed for months during the 1968 "student revolution," when the whole of the south of France was shut down. It was an exciting time. We would spend hours in the village trying to explain the student situation to the locals. It was like being in a war zone. Nice airport was full of rubble, and deserted: The only flights were an occasional one from England and a plane full of the inmates of a Swedish lunatic asylum—like something out of a Bergman movie. But this was nothing to some of the warlike conditions during the summer fires. Being in a valley, we had always thought that fires would leap over Le Nid du Duc, but one summer—the worst of all for fires—we were caught and forced to evacuate at a moment's notice. It was the middle of the summer season; the hotels were all full. I had about twenty-five people staying, from babies to sixty-year-olds. We were forced to the beach, where we scavenged for beach-mats and slept between them on the sand. Then, with the forests cruelly devastated around us, we were under siege for a week, the roads blocked by the army and all access forbidden except for fetching supplies. But in the end the forests endured.

The cork oak, burned black on the outside, put out a crop of tiny, very light green leaves, like hair on babies' heads, and once again life in the Var went on.

The Nid du Duc then became my country house. It was an ideal place to hole up and work. Writers on a project would come down and we could be free to argue, discuss, plan without any of the normal interruptions. Less than a couple of hours from London, it was easy for friends to come down to feel the first break of the weather after the gloom of English winters or to steep in the long sun-baked summers. The conditions were simple, unluxurious, but the food and climate were marvelous. In summer, the diversity of Provence—from the hinterland, untouched since the eighteenth century and before, to the raffishness of Cannes, to the snobbery of Cap d'Antibes and Monte Carlo, to the freedom and casualness of St. Tropez—is unlike anywhere else I know. And outside of the summer the seasons bring their own flavor and beauty. The surprises are endless, from the simplest to the most sophisticated. And there is the great pleasure of becoming part of a place, of a society— to know that this is your village street, to recognize every storekeeper, to discover new lifestyles, new friends, all united by a passion for the region. Contrary to many Anglo-Saxons' prejudices, once the language barrier is overcome the French are welcoming and accepting—certainly in the Var. I can't imagine the kind of friendliness I take for granted in La Garde-Freinet being found in any English village—let alone if you were a foreigner. So learning the ropes and exploring is just a constant delight, whether it's which *cooperatif* has the best *vin blanc* this year, which fishmonger has the freshest fish, or which stall in the market has the most interesting pots or the widest variety of salads.

Le Nid du Duc became a center of family life, filling up the hole of marriage. The girls spent all their vacation there and, growing up with the local village women in the kitchen, Natasha got the taste for cooking and has become an excellent cook, with the ability to be completely unfazed when told that there'd be an extra twenty for lunch. We kept a virtually open house—easily sleeping twenty, and even going up to thirty. Le Nid du Duc was perfect for kids: They could explore the woods and waterfalls for hours; they could commandeer their own house and create their own world in it; they could swim and play in the pool. Games became part of the ritual—strenuous Easter hunts (with clues written in rhyme, usually by John Mortimer), charades, "Murder in the Dark" at night, and all manner of parlor games.

Shows also became part of the tradition. They started with an Italian friend, a transvestite, who wanted to sing and act all the great operatic roles—Carmen, Tosca, Norma, Manon—but they developed into American musicals and original scripts, one of which—"The Legend of Le Nid du Duc"—ended with the entire cast and audience in the swimming pool with their clothes on. *Gypsy* was one of the standouts. Our Italian star, for whom the show had originally been chosen, decided that the clothes for the Ethel Merman role weren't glamorous enough: He refused to perform anything but the stripper—"the strumpet with the trumpet." Tasha, aged all of twelve, had to learn all the songs in three days. Joely, who was then very shy, was to perform Gypsy Rose Lee, but the strip-tease (it consisted in taking her long gloves off) terrified and shocked her. Unfortunately she overheard me say to some guest, who'd inquired how the show was going, "Oh, it all depends on whether Joely can make it." This brought on a *crise de nerfs*—but also great determination. When she descended the staircase, slowly peeling off her black gloves, trembling with fear, but set in courage, it was one of the most genuinely erotic moments I've ever seen.

By then the whole place was bursting with life. A chance visit to Toulon with David Hockney led me to buy some whippets (there'd already been another dog) and afterward I brought other champions from England. Whippets were rare in the south of France at the time, and our stock began gradually to spread all over the district. A few years ago I went to an improvised track where some breeders were racing them. They didn't know of my involvement. When we asked the name of the winner of the biggest race, they said "Vanessa"—though they had no idea why. Then we had aviaries full of birds, a flock of two hundred pigeons, a dozen or so peacocks, whose cries the guests surprisingly soon adjusted to, and several scarlet and blue and yellow macaws flying free. There was, alas, a constant toll taken by foxes, eagles, and hunting dogs.

Of course, some people hated the place—couldn't understand why I didn't pave the mile-long rough rocky dirt road which trailed down the hill, why I didn't install central heating or decorate in luxurious Provençal style—but most people saw the point, loved it as much as we did, and came back again and again.

During *The Charge* my father had seen a house in Knightsbridge which he thought I would like and had bought it for me. It was in Egerton Crescent, near Harrods. It was a commodious and comfortable house but I never warmed to it as I had to a similar house in St. Peter's Square. It was one of my regrets about Le Nid du Duc that my father was never able to see it. He'd been planning to come when he died suddenly one morning of a heart attack. My mother, who soon afterward began her long and sad withdrawal from life, came for visits, though she found the uneven surfaces and floors and the winding steps too dangerous, and she preferred to stay in a hotel on the nearby coast.

I began to spend more and more time in France. Being more and more committed to movies, it became increasingly difficult to plan theatre productions, as the vagaries of schedules and stars' commitments made the kind of long-term undertaking you have to give to serious theatre more and more problematic. And fewer and fewer new scripts of the kind that I could feel passionate about were being produced. London seemed less and less exciting, while the French countryside beckoned. I had by now a great circle of friends in the district and an established routine for doing large-scale entertaining. Le Nid du Duc was the center of my life.

It isn't now. It's a place that needs to be filled—with kids, with animals, with planting and projects. When I moved finally to California it became less easy to get there. Often I resented making an enforced pilgrimage once or twice a year. Friends come less often because it's far away and expensive for anyone living in America, and when you don't live a life of formal invitations and fixed dates, friends are never sure you'll be there and can't rely on it for holiday plans. There is no longer the guaranteed family gathering of the girls' annual school holiday. There are problems and lots of expenses. Often I just feel burdened with the responsibilities of ownership: I hate it and want to get rid of it. And then I return, and the Var begins to work its magic. The hills—with their colors and scents, the light and dusk always metamorphosing them into new subtleties and atmosphere—calm and heal. The lunches outside under the lime trees and the dinners lit by circus garlands begin, and, despite all the ravages and the many heartbreaks there have been, I know it is the place I have loved more than anywhere else on earth. It is a place of happiness, and of wisdom too. I know we will pass one day, as the peasants have passed, as the fires have passed, as all the dramas have subsided; but the crumbling houses of stone and plaster and the hills and the cork oaks and the winds will endure. As Ellie says in Shaw's play, "This silly house, this strangely happy house, this agonizing house, this house without foundations. I shall call it Heartbreak House."

19

Wanton Boys

Woodfall was in a period of retrenchment. Neil's main interest was in physical production. Oscar Lewenstein, who had tried to originate projects on his own, had departed. There were no other active producers. I wanted to be less involved in other directors' films: Instead of being a facilitator and catalyst, I kept finding myself involved in strictly directorial decisions that should have been theirs. I have always found business committee meetings tedious and boring, and, although I tried to get a mixed bag of other people's projects to work, I wanted to concentrate solely on directing. In the future I had a project, among others, of doing the story of Ned Kelly, the Australian outlaw. Then my friend and agent Robin Fox brought me a project for filming *Laughter in the Dark* (the only time an agent has ever brought me anything). Much as I loved Nabokov as a writer, and that particular novella, I was at first resistant. Robin persisted.

Robin had been one of the early members of the board of the English Stage Company and our most loyal and supportive ally. He was a most extraordinary man; half Jewish, half upper-class English establishment, he could move between the two worlds with consummate ease. He could swap Yiddish jokes with the Markses and Sieffs, and was purportedly the lover of Marina, the Duchess of Kent. He was a partner in commercial theatre with Robert Morley, but he was just as much at home with us at the Royal Court. We only ever had one quarrel, when he forbade me to offer his son "Willie" James Fox a small role in *The Loneliness of the Long Distance Runner*, saying his son had no talent and that for him to quit his job in a bank would be to disrupt his life. Willie did take my offer and went on to become a remarkable movie actor—in *The Servant*, *Performance*, and *The Chase*. Robin was then proud to represent him.

The Nabokov book began to intrigue me. I wanted to do something in the present after the long re-creation problems of *The Charge*. Making a period film is like both shooting a normal movie and having all the stresses of a theatre dress rehearsal each and every day. I began to see a way in which *Laughter* could be set in the "swinging" contemporary art world, and maybe something of its cynicism and cruelty correspond to my own mood of emotional depletion: "As flies to wanton boys, are we to the Gods;/They kill us for their sport."

Then the casting began to intrigue me too. There was talk of Richard Burton, who'd remained a friend since *Look Back*. I'd also done a television play with him in which he'd been remarkable. *A Subject of Scandal and Concern* was set in the nineteenth century and was about a labor martyr prosecuted for blasphemy. He has a speech defect which makes him unable to defend himself. John Osborne's drama builds up to a trial in which the character at last breaks through his impediment in a long and impassioned speech. Nevertheless, because of the establishment's rigging of the jury, he is convicted. The play was produced in 1960, in the primitive days of TV tape recording when it wasn't possible to cut or edit tape—you could only record as if it was a live performance. The foreman of the jury, a bit-role actor, had only one line—"Guilty, my lord"—but during the shoot he was so carried away by the magnificence of Richard's performance that he shouted, "Not guilty." And we had to reshoot the whole play.

There was also the possibility of casting Anna Karina, the beautiful and sexy Danish heroine of some of Godard's greatest movies, and his ex-wife. It is said Jean-Luc had put in a newspaper an ad saying "Wanted: movie star to live with the director," and that Anna had answered and her subsequent career resulted. I believe the story.

The project was owned by the American producer Elliott Kastner. He had negotiated a dubious deal for the rights with an Arab-French producer. He had also done a deal with Richard for a million dollars. I thought both were way out of line for the story, but as it was his property it wasn't my business. I started work on a screenplay with the British dramatist Edward Bond, of *Saved* fame. We then discovered that Elliott didn't have the backing he claimed. Woodfall was forced to step in and ask United Artists to finance the movie. They agreed to, but we were saddled with the huge deals already made. UA also insisted we guaranteed completion. Richard had a stop date because of another commitment, but, on the basis of past experience, this didn't worry me too much, as Richard had always been very professional and disciplined before and a pleasure to work with. This time it was very different.

Before the shooting, everything was fine. Richard was now married to Elizabeth Taylor. They were drinking a lot, but again no one was worried. At first they had a suite at the Dorchester, then they retreated to their yacht. Elizabeth had brought her dogs, which weren't allowed to land because of quarantine regulations, so the Burtons elected to stay on board.

One of the first scenes was to be shot with concealed cameras at an important auction of Impressionist paintings at Sotheby's in July 1968. Elizabeth decided she wanted to be an extra. It was all part of the old-friends-together atmosphere and we were all delighted. Then suddenly she demanded £10,000 for the day's work, arguing it was worth it for the publicity. I pointed out we didn't have it in the budget. Then she agreed to do it for free, but wanted an outfit made at some Paris couturier with trips for fittings, etc. Again I had to say no. She refused to appear, but in the end she upstaged the whole event by appearing in a dazzling white outfit with a high white toque. No one had much of an eye for the Monets and Renoirs after her entrance, but Richard bought her some picture as a gift.

What I'd been totally unprepared for was Richard's own behavior. He was hours late, unpleasant to the crew and other actors, sneering about the script. He'd take hours off for lunch: He and Elizabeth would disappear into his caravan or dressing room and abuse the first assistant when he called them. Then he would insist on leaving at 5:20, which was studio hours, not location. It was degrading and miserable to work with his attitude. One day he gave his makeup man the morning off to pick up a relative at the airport, then he refused to work or be made up by the other makeup artist we had on the shoot, even though he'd been Elizabeth's. He was surrounded by a huge entourage of yes-men and sycophants, who would appear before him and gossip about which way "the wind was blowing." Underneath the behavior was an incomprehensible rivalry as to which of the Burtons was entitled to more attention and personnel. It was a kind of movie world I'd never had to deal with before—though a precursor of a world of stars to come. What was most damaging was that every day we were falling more and more behind schedule—Richard, by his attitude, endangering his own stop date with which he kept threatening us. The second half of the film was to be shot on the island of Majorca, and with boat and Burtons I could see the production spinning out of any kind of control. Every day going to the set was a humiliation, and the crew were practically mutinous.

Two weeks into the shoot we had a particularly difficult production problem. We needed an exclusive art gallery. We tried to persuade one Bond Street firm to let us use its gallery on a Sunday. It finally agreed, stipulating that it was a strictly one-shot agreement and that, whatever went wrong, we couldn't ever go back. I went to Richard myself the day before, explained the gravity of the problem, and begged him not to be late that day. He promised. Rehearsals were called for 7:30 (it was a key scene) and shooting at 8:30. Despite nonstop calls, Richard didn't show until noon, eliminating any chance of completing the scene with him. I exploded with rage. He'd brought one of Elizabeth's children with him, almost as a shield to protect him. Faced with my anger, he turned around and walked off the set, ruling out any possibility of work that day. He was in breach of contract. I fired him.

Two days of chaos ensued. Richard was part of the contract, but he was clearly in the wrong. We had shot for two weeks. Much of United Artists' investment had been expended and we had no immediate replacement. UA was as supportive as it could be—making a new deal. It ominously called for me personally to guarantee a million dollars if the movie lost money, but we weren't in any position to quibble. For casting, it agreed to accept Nicol Williamson as a replacement for Richard, but he'd gone to the south of

France on holiday and no one knew where he was or how to contact him. Meanwhile, lawsuits were being threatened on every side. The news broke and, with Richard's career at its zenith, there were headlines in the next morning's newspapers and lead stories on TV. We had already lost the day's shooting on Sunday, and on Monday it was difficult enough to piece together bits to make up a day's work.

During all this, Elizabeth behaved sensibly and admirably. She telephoned me several times, sure that the breach could be saved. I didn't see how, but at her persuasion I agreed to meet with Richard after shooting on Monday. A launch was to meet me at some obscure Thames pier to avoid the TV cameras, now hot on the trail. One of the minions who was on our payroll, formally clad in a dark suit, met me stiffly. On board the yacht I met a subdued and sober Richard. We reminisced a bit about the past. Richard's only amazement was that either of us had ever worked for so little financially! I tried to return him to the present situation, explaining that the only way we could get back together was if he would agree to make up the time he'd cost us and in the future stick to the hours he was contracted to.

Elizabeth appeared—resplendently dressed but, I thought, having been drinking. She outlined a fantastic reconciliation scene, to be staged the next morning for all the TV channels, in which Richard and I were to apologize publicly to each other and then go back to work. I explained that I wasn't interested in apologies, only in discovering whether we could find a way of working together. This led to a long discussion of directors having begged Elizabeth to do this or that. I talked about agreements and stop dates. We weren't getting anywhere. Finally Elizabeth came right up to me and began to yell in that piercing-to-the-point-of-pain scream of hers, "Do you want Richard back or not? YESSS or NOOH? YESSS or NOOH?" Richard sat there, saying nothing. I finally left the cabin and went on deck, with Elizabeth still shrieking below. And then I had the problem of getting off the yacht! It was the end of our collaboration, and I never saw Richard again except across crowded restaurants.

Meanwhile, everyone I could appeal to was combing the south of France for Nicol. One of the spies spotted a group of obvious Englishmen sitting at a café on a terrace in Tamatuelle, and asked the most prominent of them if he'd heard of an actor called Nicol

Williamson. It was Nicol. We spoke, and he agreed to take over immediately.

I'd known Nicol for a long time. He'd been Flute in my abortive *A Midsummer Night's Dream* in 1962, and he'd played in several other plays at the Court. Above all, in 1964 he'd given an extraordinary performance as Bill Maitland in *Inadmissible Evidence*, conveying the very heart and mind of John's grubby and bitter solicitor. He is a brilliant actor, especially on stage. For film he has great technique, and sharp intelligence. The only thing the gods didn't give him is the quality of empathy on camera. Onstage it doesn't matter, because his pyrotechnics are so dazzling and so true that they're more than sufficient. It was, however, a damaging flaw for portraying Sir Edward More in *Laughter*, though I didn't realize it at the time. The character needed someone whom an audience could desperately feel for, though Nicol played all the gradations of the personality, from smooth art dealer to vulnerable blind man, brilliantly.

We had to reshoot much of the Burton footage, but afterward all went well. In Majorca we had found a villa belonging to a talented Italian stage designer, with a beautiful flight of stairs and huge collection of eighteenth-century balloon paintings. It was near the village of Deyá, whose local prophet and sage was Robert Graves. I had long wanted to make a movie of *I, Claudius*, which had tantalized many people after Korda's incomplete version, and with Lila de Nibili and Renzo Mongiardino I was doing immense research on how to re-create ancient Rome. (Only one film has ever made Rome look as it was—Fellini's fabulous *Satyricon*).

Getting to know Robert was wonderful—he had a far-ranging mind, with inexhaustible instincts, the charm of an Irish wizard, a sly raconteur's wit, and the battered jauntiness of the rake he would have been if he hadn't been a romantic. Edward Bond, who had accompanied the crew to Majorca and was reworking scenes daily, shared my passion for *I, Claudius*. He wanted to write the script. I was very pleased. He wanted to meet Robert. I arranged it. Edward then took an instant dislike to him, saying he was senile. (How anyone could not be captivated by Robert was incomprehensible to me). The book which had been Edward's favorite became a piece of trash. He wrote a screenplay which, scene by scene, consisted of just saying the opposite of what Robert had said. It was pathetic and unusable.

I had several other goes at getting a screenplay. I even did a stage adaptation with John Mortimer, which Michael White presented with David Warner in the West End. None of them ever worked. The ambiguity of the central character, which Robert could convey by interior monologues, defeated us. The movie was abandoned. Eventually the BBC made a TV series of it as an old-fashioned soap opera.

Laughter was not a commercial success. Since Woodfall had been set up there had been a big shift in the showing of movies. It had started when the US Monopolies Act had separated exhibition from production and distribution. Power had shifted to the exhibitors. It was more and more difficult for studios to make offbeat movies, because they could no longer guarantee they would be shown at all. The exhibitors looked for some kind of guarantee, but there is no guarantee at all for movies or movie investment. The nearest thing was a star name. This led to the escalation of star salaries (the Burtons were forerunners of this) and to star power, and with the stars came their agents. In the 1950s and 1960s there had, however, been an alternative chain of exhibition, the "art houses." The distributors—like the Walter Reade organization—that worked the art houses were content with a more modest profit, and didn't give up on the less successful films. The more successful of the Woodfall films—like *A Taste of Honey* and *Saturday Night*—didn't make vast sums, but then the others didn't lose much either. It was basically a healthier economy. I suppose the change affected us as soon as we moved to a big company, but it was partly disguised by the phenomenal success of *Tom Jones*. By the time of *Laughter*, however, United Artists had quite definitely changed. Advertising and promotion costs had risen dramatically, and the management had decided that, if there wasn't a clear prediction of success, it was better not "to throw good money after bad." So the long-term promotion of some finished movies began to be abandoned after a quick testing of the waters. *Laughter* was the first time we realized fully what was happening; now the jackpot mentality is universal.

My guarantee of *Laughter* compounded the pain for me, and I have been paying back the million ever since. I was urged to litigate. I went to see Oliver Poole, a top London QC who later became Lord Poole and a Privy Counsellor. He had looked at the case. He said he would undertake it, and could almost certainly guarantee collecting, but he explained that it would be three or four years before the case could be heard. "Is litigating what you're really about? Aren't you really about filmmaking? And won't you in three of four years be very bored by it?" I thought it was the smartest legal advice I'd ever been given. I've tried to avoid litigation ever since.

Ironically, *Laughter* did lead to a commercial success, albeit limited and inadvertent. One of the most talented of all British directors, Ken Loach, together with his producer Tony Garnett, had been trying without success to get finance for *Kes*, a story of a working-class boy who trains a kestrel. I persuaded UA to finance it and cross-collateralize *Laughter* (then with Richard) with what they regarded as a hopeless little British film. Ken Loach made a beautiful movie, but UA's distribution was nervous of it and handled it very badly, insisting on opening the film in the North, with the result that the national reviews (which were all raves) didn't synchronize with the possibility of seeing it in London or elsewhere in the South. However, it still did well and more than paid back its costs in British receipts. This was getting to be a rarity then; now it's a virtual impossibility. *Kes* didn't do so well in the USA, as it got buried in the New York Film Festival, and despite a careful redubbing under UA's supervision, audiences were alienated by the northern accents. It's a film I loved, and I was very pleased to have helped make it happen.

Laughter also led to another consequence. Admiring Nicol, I wanted to do something with him in the theatre. I had never staged *Hamlet*. I felt there had been no major reevaluation of the character since the legendary "poetic" Hamlet of John Gielgud's in the 1930s. It seemed an ideal role for Nicol, and I longed to explore the play. Although I practically knew it by heart before we began rehearsals, I knew that whatever I might say or theorize about it from a literary and critical point of view, there is no way to examine a play so deeply as by presenting it.

Silly as the game of playing superlatives is, *Hamlet* seems to me the seminal work for all Western European culture. *Lear* touches darker, deeper notes, creating a range of suffering, cruelty, and endurance that we in this century recognize only too well. *Antony and Cleopatra*, in its juxtaposition of the sublime speeches with the ridiculousness of the characters of its principals, creates a more resplendent mirror of the extremes of human behavior. But *Hamlet* encompasses the greater variety of life and people. It relates, reflects, comments on every aspect of action and of choice, of thought and of humor. For all its revenge-theatre setting, its world is the everyday world of power: the forum, the marketplace, the palace—today you'd also say the media—and its limits are the limits of political endeavors and possibilties. Its poetry is not the poetry of "O! wither'd is the garland of the war,/The soldier's pole is fall'n; young boys and girls/Are level now with men; the odds is gone,/And there is nothing left remarkable/Beneath the visiting moon"; not the poetry of "I will do such things,—/what they are yet I know not,—but they shall be/The terrors of the earth"; it is the poetry of "The pangs of dispriz'd love, the law's delay,/The insolence of office, and the spurns/That patient merit of the unworthy takes,/When he himself might his quietus make/With a bare bodkin." And, for me, the key to any really successful interpretation of Hamlet himself is in understanding his sense of irony—irony of mind, thought, feeling, language, action. Other great characters engulf us in their feelings; Hamlet makes us always assess, reexamine, our choices. And his irony is pure—not born out of bitterness, or overcolored by emotion, but the result of an ability to stand back and detach himself; to see clearly even when he acts willfully, violently, playfully; to assess not under some lightning- and thunderstruck sky but in the cool daylight. It's a quality many great leaders have. Many people have written about President Kennedy having it, and certainly Churchill, for all his penchant for dramatic action, had it. It was this irony I believed Nicol could embody as Hamlet.

I didn't want to do a conventional proscenium production; I wanted to find a space that would permit a simple and free staging. In Camden Town was the Roundhouse, a nineteenth-century locomotive repair shed. It was a fascinating space, with a vaulted ceiling and an upper gallery raised on thin iron columns which created a circle within the circle of the building itself. Various theatre people had been tempted by its possibilities. Arnold Wesker had tried to launch an all-purpose arts center (disastrous concept) there, and, more notably, Peter Brook had staged a partially experimental *Tempest* in it. No one had solved its acoustic and seating problems.

I asked Jocelyn to design the production. It wasn't just designing a show—it was really designing a theatre. Together with Neil, we decided to confine ourselves to the inner circle. We hung thick black drapes from the gallery down between the columns. We built a low semicircular stage and curving seats on three sides, so that it was like a half–circus ring within a circle, and we suspended baffle-boards above the stage and audience to confine the sound. It all began to come together. It was an exciting space that needed no scenery as such. With entrances possible from all sides, and a few raised blocks if we needed sitting areas, action could be swift, and angles and acting areas could change constantly. Jocelyn designed glowing orange and yellow costumes, German-medieval in feeling but rich and sensual—except, of course, for Hamlet in his black and Horatio in his scholar's gown. Our approach was to do a classic performance that allowed total freedom to the actors and the text. As usual, there was the exhilaration of discovering how work revealed possibilities and truth unimaginable before rehearsals.

The supporting cast was very strong—Mark Dignam, Anthony Hopkins, Judy Parfitt, Gordon Jackson, Roger Livesey, Michael Pennington. Even the bit parts had actors who have since gone on to important careers. Angelica Huston, in her first stage job, was one of them and understudied Ophelia. Ophelia was played by Marianne Faithfull—beautiful, sensuous, and totally vulnerable. She made complete sense of this astonishingly difficult role, with its combination of worldliness and innocence combusting into madness. She was unfortunately often off, but, when she was on, to me she was perfection.

When it opened in March 1969, *Hamlet* was an enormous hit and received international plaudits (even *Time* reviewed the show). Nicol was recognized as his generation's Hamlet; without illusions, yet humorous and ironic, capable of instant rage and mockery, and with a sad, existential resignation. He too was erratic in performances and walked off or interrupted the show several times—to the consternation of the stage management and company, but to the titillation of audiences, who loved to participate in these kinds of drama of temperament. Worse, he soon was way over the top in his own acting and reckless of other people's feelings. Soon after the opening he was already overacting shamelessly, although he didn't know it. I attacked him for it. He never forgave me, and our relations have been strained ever since.

We had been invited to do the show in the USA. Buoyed by the success, the company were eager to go. I agreed. It was a big mistake. The production had been conceived for the unique space of the Roundhouse; had I been doing it for a proscenium stage I would have had Jocelyn design the play very differently. As after many first enthusiasms, family pressures and other jobs forced a number of the original cast to drop out. Their replacements—like Constance Cummings as Gertrude and Anjelica Huston as Ophelia—gave good performances, but the American show didn't have the same cohesiveness of spirit. The set was a mock-up of features of the Roundhouse and, though adequate, seemed skimpy.

Notices were okay; so was business. But Nicol walked off once too often. On the first night in Boston he walked out during the play scene—not exactly a difficult scene for Hamlet—leaving the whole company with "egg on their faces." (Before he had always walked off when he was on stage alone.) Roger Livesey said to the audience, "This is where we'd bring the curtain down, only in this production we don't have a curtain," and Connie Cummings said, "Poor boy, he's so tired." Nicol's contempt for their feelings led most of the older, senior, members of the company to leave the show at the end of the Boston run. The producer and Nicol replaced them, without consulting me, and, I'm sure, without adequate rehearsals. I dread to think what kind of standards prevailed, and the production finally ended ignominiously in Los Angeles after Nicol had crashed his car, when drunk, and was taken to the hospital. But in the early days, when he was good, he was terrific.

Earlier, in London, there had been another interesting development. I have always been frustrated by movies of Shakespeare. Not that some of them, like Zeffirelli's *Romeo and Juliet* and Olivier's *Hamlet* and *Henry V*, don't have wonderful moments and performances, but the conflict between the power of the cinematic image and the rhythms of the speech has always seemed to me divisive. "Think when we talk of horses that you see them./Printing their proud hooves i'th' receiving earth" is a totally different experience if you actually do see them. On the other hand, just photographing an existing stage production—however successful—is bad cinema, and usually the acting is not adjusted for the screen. I thought it would be an interesting experiment to try to make a movie of *Hamlet* in which in a way you would *devalue* the power of the image and let the text and performance speak uninterruptedly, scaling the production down and staging it for cameras.

We found backing (through Marty Ransohoff of *The Loved One*) and set out to film while the show was still playing. The Roundhouse gave us a unique opportunity to do this because of its physical possibilities. Each night a crew came in after the show, pulled out the seating and stage, and set up new sets and lit them. Although I'd conceived of shooting the film mainly in close-up, and in long takes, Jocelyn knew we needed more realistic pieces, if only furniture and backdrops, to hint at the world we were showing on camera. The show, though cut, was three hours long, and I wanted the movie to be no more than two, so I gave the actors a cut-down version of whatever scene we were to shoot the next day. This gave them time to study it before they came to the film set in the morning. I then restaged the scene in the new setting and for the cameras, making the actors play much more intimately. Sometimes we used features of the Roundhouse like the cellars, which we couldn't have used in the theatre, or brought in a few horses to give a glimpse of Fortinbras's army. We shot until about 4:00 P.M. each day, then the actors went to rest and the crew came in and transformed the Roundhouse back into a theatre for the evening performance.

It took us about ten days to shoot the two-hour film. Of course it was a great strain on the actors, especially Nicol, who had no time off at all. On the other hand, it brought its own rewards, even to the stage show. By forcing the actors to go back to the text, to rethink precisely their thoughts, it made the text constantly fresh in the evening, for the danger of all Shakespeare is that the music of the iambic pentameter carries and lulls the performance, and its sound obliterates thought. That's why, traditionally, older actors in Shakespeare could always disguise forgetting their lines by murmuring sounds that were gibberish but scanned. For what it is, I think the movie *Hamlet* is not unsuccessful. And with Jocelyn's sets and costumes and Gerry Fisher's lighting it looks amazingly sumptuous for something that cost in all only $350,000. It went into profit immediately, as Marty was able to sell it next day for $500,000. It has obviously made a lot more than that, as it plays constantly, but, as with so many movies, we've never had any accounting.

20

The Wild Colonial Boy

Sydney Nolan, the Australian painter, had made a series of paintings of the famous Australian outlaw Ned Kelly which were widely exhibited in London in the early 1960s, and perhaps it's due to him that this enigmatic mythic personality started to haunt our imagination. I say "our" because Karel Reisz also toyed for a while with doing a movie about Ned Kelly. After Karel dropped it, I took up the idea. Ned Kelly was a natural anti-authority hero—a bank robber and thief to some; a kind of Robin Hood of the bush to others. His story—with its strange image of the homemade suit of armor he fashioned for his final shoot-out with the combined forces of constabulary and army—was a natural for a movie. The more I worked on it, the more I thought I could make it by adopting a ballad, almost country-and-western, formula. Neil and I made an extended scouting trip to Australia, with stop-offs in Singapore and the still-idyllic Bali, hardly awakened from its long no-tourist sleep of the previous thirty years.

Australia seemed a mysterious and unsympathetic land. The most striking impression was the monotony of the ubiquitous eucalyptus trees, broken only where the forests had been ring-barked and burned, the result like great black scars on the dull green land. Sydney, despite its natural harbor and the conch-like curiosity of the opera house—the exterior designed by one architect, who was then fired, and the interior redesigned as a conventional Viennese opera house and concert hall (with a committee perpetually squabbling about which was which and switching them over)—seemed to combine the worst elements of Glasgow and San Francisco. I wanted desperately to see the "bush" in the raw. We had a local contact who could arrange it, so one weekend we hired a plane and flew to the ranch of a friend of his deep in Queensland and about one hundred miles from an opal-mining town.

This young good-looking man was the son of the powerful governor of, I think, Northern Australia province. He had been given the ranch and a herd of prize cattle to make enough of a personal fortune before he was twenty-five to finance a political career. The nineteenth-century ranch house was vast, with wide verandas and French doors. It was in the British colonial style of architecture, and was designed to accommodate a big family and staff. Now all farming tasks were done on a contractural basis and all necessity for live-in labor had disappeared, though one Aborigine and his family lived in a cabin somewhere on the property. The Aborigine himself had gone walkabout, having disappeared to wander the bush. The ranch house itself had only its one inhabitant (his girl-friend visited on alternate weekends and stocked the refrigerator with frozen food). It was dilapidated and run-down—the wood burnt and buckled by the sun, the shutters half-off and creaking, the rooms with leaves and sand in the corners—but wonderfully evocative of a way of life long gone. In the acres around the house were birds and parrots of every kind, wallabies, emus, and kangeroos, including the rare great red. The light burned down on the desert vegetation and sparse pasture.

It was announced that we would visit the opal town that afternoon, in time for the opening of the bar at four o'clock. Our hosts' nearest neighbors, a couple of huge lubberly brothers who owned an adjoining sheep farm, joined us for the expedition. The drive took about an hour and a half on the straight red-dirt roads. The opal town consisted of two or three dirt streets lined with shacks. The mines, dotted around the small hills, were individually owned, with narrow shafts hacked out of the dusty earth and the sides supported with bits of corrugated iron on rough wooden boards. The miners—all very much their own men—ranged from exsurfers to old-timer derelicts. The nickname of the oldest was "Hanoi"—because he was bombed every night. That was the best joke in nine months in Australia.

Social activity for the whole district, an area of probably a thousand square miles, was centered in this one bar from four o'clock on Saturday onward. There was a tiny band—1940s knees-up— who bawled "Roll Out the Barrel" with dirty lyrics to the roars and leers of the clientele, who poured beer after beer down until they went outside to throw up and then returned to the bar. The girls were all to one side. It was one of the more unpleasant features of Australia at the time that there was complete sexual segregation. In many pubs and bars women were forbidden altogether, and even at what might be thought the more elegant Sydney cocktail parties men talked to men, women to women. Here the only contact was that one of the louts would stagger over to the group of local nurses and teachers, grab one of them, and drag her off to have her outside. Our politician mingled, glad-handing everyone, and intermittently disappeared.

The hours blurred on, stale with beer and dirty ditties. There was nothing to eat, and the nearest café was apparently two hundred miles away. There was nothing to do except drink. As both Neil and our contact were on the wagon (as was our pilot, for professional reasons), they got even more restless than I did. Finally I found our host and persuaded him to let us have his truck so we could drive back to the ranch. About three miles out of town we had a flat tire. There was no spare. I decided to walk back, and stumbled awkwardly along as the night was vast and black and the road hardly marked. When I got back to the bar, the band and the bar were still swinging soggily. Our host had disappeared, but finally I found the two sheep-farming brothers. I had a tough time persuading them to leave, and finally had to shove them outside physically. They'd picked up two nurses, and their VW was already packed before we got to the other three, but somehow, lying across each other, we all sandwiched in. They hurtled off at about 120 mph. Big kangaroos leaped across the road in front of us, startled by the headlights. Each time they saw one, the brothers whooped and gunned forward, trying to hit the animal; often the kangaroo was mesmerized by the lights, so at the last minute in order to protect the VW they'd brake sharply—often skidding off the road, several times just missing gum-trees. Just as we finally got home, our host turned up in a truck with yet another girl. To our surprise the three girls were told to "fuck off home"—another hundred miles away—and we set out to devour all that remained in the freezer—frozen French fries.

Drunkenness was endemic in Australia; one or two beers were enough to set anyone off in a violent and destructive way. Quite literally it was dangerous to invite people to the house. During the shoot we rented a very beautiful 1820s sheep ranch near Bungendore, outside Canberra. With its cool, wood-paneled rooms, it was too lovely to risk beer bottles flying at moldings or into mirrors. At the end of the movie we were to give the obligatory party for the crew and the locals who had helped us. After a lot of thought we built a barbed-wire compound about ten feet high to contain the revelers. The party was to start at ten in the morning, so that with luck the guests would depart sometime before night. The next morning there were still people passed out and bleeding, lying in the shards of broken glasses and plates covering the earth. Not a single cup or glass or other receptacle had survived. Even so, we considered ourselves lucky, as a local gunning club whom we'd used in the film brought their nineteenth-century cannon and tried to lob shells at the house—one of the few authentic period houses remaining and a famous landmark. This time the alcohol was on our side and their aim was off.

The customs of the country were just as strange about food. We'd hired all the horses and cattle from a local rancher, who owned much land, with big herds, and was a millionaire many times over. I was riding back from location one day with his wife, a lovely and sympathetic lady, grateful as all Australian women were for any word from a man. She enthused about the quality of the food provided by the location caterers. I thought it was inedible and disgusting, and said so. "But you see," she said, "I never get to eat any beef." The butchers were full of the best steak at giveaway prices, so I asked how come she, with her family's resources, never had steak. "Oh," she said, "we're only allowed to eat lamb. My husband says his father only killed the old rams for their table; he's willing to kill ewes. That, he says, is enough progress for him." I sent the gentleman several pounds of steak (it cost probably about five dollars). He didn't see any irony in the gift.

Back in England, the problem was casting. Albert Finney wasn't interested and had gone off around the world. I tested some very good actors; none of them was bankable (this was before the word was in vogue). Then Mick Jagger was suggested. Mick was sniffing at a career as an actor. I'd always been a fan of the Stones and was excited by the prospect: the wicked, battered, "Irish" face was perfect for Ned. We met, got on. Mick talked of how he wanted an acting career, how he would work. We discussed the problem the role would present in terms of its physical demands. He would have to be able to handle horses and guns. He was sure it was only a question of practice, and, astonished by his magnetism, energy, and freedom on stage, I persuaded myself there was a way that his body, with the speed of an urban street cobra, could be transformed into that of an outdoor bushman. It was a mistake. The face was great, but the body seemed frail and at times spastic. Though fire and energy snakes out of Mick like electricity in concert, he can't produce them cold as an actor. It's a problem with many rock performers. Another problem is that great artists in another medium—singers, dancers, sportsmen—don't carry their public with them when they cross over into a different, often alien, situation. But the mistake was mine.

Having gone for Mick, I should have made a very different kind of film—maybe a kind of collage that capitalized on the striking contrasts of his talent, instead of trying to push Mick into being an incipient John Wayne. He did try for a while. He rode, he shot guns, he learned how to improvise. But, for all his exceptional intelligence (I often thought he was far too intelligent to be an actor) and imagination, he couldn't understand the dues he would have to pay to look at ease in the saddle—or maybe he just got bored. He couldn't suspend himself and become a character. And probably if I'd tried to tailor the character more to him he'd have resisted it. I tried to include him in the musical side of the film—where he could have contributed and built in more songs—but apart from his very true performance of "The Wild Colonial Boy," he would have nothing to do with any of it. And after a number of false hopes—I wanted either the Band, Johnny Cash, or Van Morrison—the music was something we failed in, except for the performance of the great country-and-western singer (at that time almost unknown) Waylon Jennings. But to be with Mick was always a pleasure—stimulating, rewarding, and often, in his passions and loyalties, very touching. I like him a lot.

The production began in crisis and went from crisis to crisis throughout—some of them funny; some nearly tragic. The near-tragic hit us at the start of shooting, in July 1969. Marianne Faithfull, who was then Mick's girlfriend in real life, was to play his girlfriend in the movie. Their relationship was under strain. She was very unhappy. The evening she arrived she took a massive overdose of sleeping pills. She was rushed to the hospital. She lapsed into a coma. She wasn't expected to survive. The Australian press behaved like a ravening pack of hunting dogs. The hotel where we were staying had to have massive security to prevent them breaking into Mick's suite, and there had to be massive security at the intensive-care ward. The security was eventually broken by a pressman who disguised himself in a white coat as an intern. Escaping when discovered, he managed to knock over the IV equipment of several dying patients. Nevertheless, in triumph, one of the local papers boasted its scoop—a huge, front-page, out-of-focus photo of an unrecognizable Marianne with blurred tubes in her mouth and nostrils. Even the complaint to the Australian Press Council about the medical damage done was ignored. To everyone's relief and surprise, Marianne did pull through enough to come to our house outside Canberra for a frail and uneasy convalescence until her mother transported her back to England.

We had a brief stay in gloomy Melbourne, made gloomier by our using the original gallows in the jail where Ned himself was executed. Then, arriving in Bungendore, we were told it was the rag week of Canberra College. During this spree, the students were on out-of-control rampages, smashing and destroying local stores, terrorizing shopkeepers, and getting up to other semiserious pranks like kidnapping and burglaries. That year they announced their goal of holding United Artists to ransom by kidnapping Mick and me. Consequently we lived for ten days in a state of siege—exactly like in a western. At night the students were encamped in the hills and pastures around the house, their fires flickering in the darkness. We were guarded by six or so huge burly policemen who slept in the corridors and hallways and over whose recumbent bodies you had to clamber for coffee in the morning or if you wanted to sneak a joint in the dining room in the evening. Going to location, we had to have a car full of police both in front and behind, to prevent hold-ups. It worked: We weren't kidnapped—though the conditions, if we had been, might have been preferable to our stifling guests. Then, when we were on a remote location, the caravan with our wardrobe, most of which came from London and much of which had already been used and was therefore a continuity matter, was burned out. Jocelyn had somehow to improvise and make replacements.

Worse was a gunfight battle during the final battle, when the government forces surround Ned's hideout. In the normal way, we had had gunsmiths convert period rifles and pistols to take blanks. These were rigorously tested and inspected, as regulations required. Suddenly, during a take, Mick yelled and dropped his revolver. His hand was bleeding. We thought somehow his pistol had exploded, or the blank had backfired. On examination in hospital, we found that a piece of jagged metal from one of the guns that had been firing at him had, just like a bullet, pierced his hand, which had been only a few centimeters away from his eye, and had also threatened his forefinger, the most crucial for his guitar playing. Mick behaved impeccably and courageously, but it was two weeks before we could start shooting with him again. We had a lengthy investigation into the cause, but we never really found it. To convert the guns, an inner casing of metal had been poured, and the best hypothesis anyone produced was that one of the gunsmiths had topped up a casing with some molten metal at the wrong temperature and part of the casing had come away when the gun was fired.

I never look back or try to judge any movie when it's finished. What you achieved, you achieved. Where you failed, you failed. *Ned Kelly* is a case apart for me—it was like having a stillborn child. The shape and features were all there, but without a breath of life.

Although I'd planned originally to visit other parts of Australia— the Barrier Reef, Alice Springs, the Northern Territory—I couldn't wait to get out of the country and away from the sound of Australian accents. The nearest non-Australian–speaking place was New Caledonia. I flew there with Jocelyn and Will Chandler, a friend and a Woodfall associate. After a day or two in Nouméa, we went to a deserted beach hotel on the Île des Pins. Every day we went out in a boat, swam and fished in the coral reefs. We made fires out of driftwood and cooked our morning's catch in big conch shells on little sandy atolls so deserted that the birds and the landed sea snakes would gather round us, so ignorant of humans that we could gather them in our hands. It was just the rest and peace we needed after the production, and after two weeks we felt restored enough to fly off to New Guinea.

New Guinea is fascinating still because of its mountainous terrain; it is one of the last unexplored regions on earth, where isolated villages and communities have developed their own customs, rituals, and religions unlike anything anywhere else in the world. These religions, called cargo cults, include eating the people's own dead or venerating President Johnson as a god. In a modern little inland capital with architecture like the 1950s British new towns you would see bare-breasted native women suckling piglets at their breasts while their babies were strapped on their face. Pigs have an almost totemic value and as such get priority over human babies until every four months they're slaughtered for a feast. In the country outside we saw a census taking place. A young white colonial officer lolled insolently, feet up on a table, while the natives in an array of grass and leaf skirts and caps of fur and feathers patiently lined up to record their existence, until our arrival disrupted the business—to our delight and the fury of the officer.

We were on our way to a bird of paradise sanctuary. The roads had become impassable and eventually we had to ford a river on foot to arrive at our destination. It was at the edge of the jungle. Giant hornbills flew playfully around us. There were a lot of birds of paradise flying free, and many rare species in elaborate, well-planted aviaries. A group of dedicated bird-lovers was fighting for the existence of the sanctuary, which, like so many wildlife reserves, was becoming increasingly endangered as scientific farming and industrialization encroached.

After the highlands we flew to the lowlands, to the Sepik river. The Sepik is one of the great rivers of the world, and still unexplored. It curves its sluggish way through Papua New Guinea to the borders of West Irian, where Michael Rockefeller was purportedly eaten by cannibals. We'd heard of a trader who had a boat we could rent. We hired a little Cessna to fly to him, but, as the jungles had flooded, it was hard to distinguish the course of the river from the newly created swamps and, running out of fuel, we nearly had a disaster. The boat, when we found it, was a tin rectangular box strapped on top of two outrigger canoes. It worked very well, and we spent a week gliding down the river and visiting the villages, which in their beauty and elegance and in the originality of their artifacts—each village has its own speciality: masks, shields, decorated oars, figurines—was like visiting the towns of pre-Renaissance Italy with their individual styles of carving or painting.

Each village is dominated by its *haus tambaran*, a collective meetingplace for the males, for councils and puberty rites. Built on stilts, with long, slender, curved roofs sloping up as high as the trees, these buildings have an amazing elegance of line. The main pillars, roof beams, and doorways are painted—amber and yellow and rust—and decorated. Inside and around the entrances are hung the artifacts, their function becoming more and more decorative. Building the *haus tambaran* is a communal effort. The tribesmen converge on the village from the surrounding jungle, live together for several months, and then, once the house is finished, after the kind of community effort of an Amish barn-building, disappear back into the jungle to farm or hunt. This has to be repeated every four or five years, as the humidity is so great and the jungle timber so green that the lovely structures simply rot back into the earth like trees that have fallen in the rain forest.

During the ten days we were on the river we saw no one except the villagers and one mission boat piloted by two white nuns. It was a Seatruck designed and made by Jeremy Fry.

After New Guinea we flew to Manila and canoed down mountain gorges, then to Singapore and back to Bali—now swarming with jets and tourists. The growth of tourism had led to a big revival in native crafts and dances—always edgily balanced between historic tradition and commerciality. At the hotel where we were staying, the managers were fans of the Balinese dance and had become specialists. Each village was now developing its own troupe, hoping for an engagement at the Balinese Hilton or Sheraton. The managers had been invited to advise on some new spectacle in a remote village and invited us to come along. We drove for maybe two hours, deep into the hills, sculpted exquisitely with their terraces of rice paddies. Finally we arrived in a field where there were the carved remains of a stone temple. Seats of honor had been prepared for us under palm umbrellas, with touching little gifts of a five-pack of cigarettes and bananas.

Like most Balinese dances, the dance we were to see was based on the Hindu epic of the *Ramayana*, an odd mixture of romance, religion, and popular humor, as if Chaucer, *Pilgrim's Progress*, and *Gammer Gurton's Needle* were all intercut. Gods, maidens, monkeys, and dragons followed one another for three hours, until we were almost nodding asleep in the hot sun. Each dance had the same theme and was almost identical to what you could see in the Hilton except that the setting and the faces of the enthralled villagers gave it an atmosphere that a Western hotel completely precluded.

Suddenly there was a change of pace. A group of young men erupted onto the scene, each carrying a kris—a short sacred dagger with a wavy blade like a beaten-out corkscrew. Unlike most of the other performers, they were unmasked. Dilated eyes and quivering muscles gave them an intensity as if they were on drugs. In the story they were to be the followers of the Barong, a big, long dragon that was the symbol of beneficence or evil (it's hard, in the *Ramayana*, to be sure which). They began to stamp and advance like a group of drilled and aggressive bullfighters advancing in formation on their antagonist. They uttered hard thudding cries. Suddenly, as their fury climaxed, they began to stab themselves with their krises so that blood spurted everywhere. Immediately priests emerged from between the old stone columns, showering incense and petals. Chickens were swirled round and their heads were lopped off; goats were dragged out and had their throats slit in sacrifice. Animal and human blood mingled.

The excitement subsided; the young men, still bleeding, began to calm down. The boundary between "art" and some primitive mythic rite had been crossed. Christ whipped and on the Cross, the Aztec human sacrifices, the immolation of suttee: All tap into some deep need to debase the human and offer humans up on the overwhelming altar of a destructive fate. The bullfight has something of this horror, sublimity, and obscenity—the indoctrinated suicide squad combined with the tackiness of a tattoo parlor. But from such stomach-churning violence came Oedipus's blinding and Lear's suffering in the storm. What we had witnessed was at once the clarification of all the writings of the theorists of theatre as ritual, of theatre as cruelty, and at the same time their refutation. It was certainly not for twice-nightly repeats at the Hilton. It was the strangest and most disturbing performance I've ever seen, made stranger, as we drove away in the early evening, by seeing some of the young men at work again with their rhythmic scythes in the rice fields, their arms and bodies covered with plasters.

After Bali, Jocelyn had to go home. Will and I continued on to southern India, and then up to Calcutta and Benares, with a side trip to some fraudulent game sanctuary on the Burmese border, where, in the course of a long evening's hunt for tigers or elephants, we saw one rabbit. We then went on to Kathmandu and explored Nepal, the land where, until something like sixty years ago, no one knew what a wheel was. At the time, Nepal was a hippie paradise— there were cafés that had hash tea, grass cookies, and acid soup on the menu. Just as we were about to leave, someone slipped some acid on whatever I'd ordered, and after going to sleep I awoke again in the most terrifying trip I'd ever imagined. I called up Will and he came into my room. He'd also taken the drug inadvertently, but it hadn't started to work on him as quickly. I was fighting it hard, which is fatal once you're gone; he was able to prepare himself and go with it. Sometime during the long night a doctor appeared, but two aspirin aren't much good against a strong rush of LSD. We had to cancel plane reservations and sweat it out for twenty-four hours. Then, going back through Agra, Fatehpur, Sikar, and Delhi, we headed back to London.

21

Balancing Acts

All life is a series of journeys, and the wonder of the best of them is that you end up somewhere other than where you started. Two different and abortive projects led to major changes in my life, and they were both unexpected. Oscar Lewenstein, now an ex-partner, had become involved in developing a script of the Canadian novelist Margaret ("Peggy") Atwood's *The Edible Woman*. Peggy was virtually unknown at the time. Oscar showed me the book, and I liked it a lot.

The Edible Woman is a slight oddball comedy about a group of people just out of university, growing up and coping with or developing that dread subject, feminism. The comedy is on the edge of fantasy. The heroine is in the middle of a relationship with a man you'd now call a jock yuppie. She starts to be unable to eat one thing after another, until even a raw carrot seems too much. Finally she makes a big iced cake of herself and presents it to her fiancé. That, she feels, is how he wanted her, and by that gesture she liberates herself. Meanwhile she has been falling for a hopeless mathematician who spends his time watching clothes turn in the machines of a laundromat. Art Garfunkel was to play this role. We got to the stage of testing people for all the other parts. Peggy and

I had worked on the script, which, though slight, could have been very funny. Then the bottom fell out of the project.

Canada is a difficult country to deal with—full of all kinds of activity designed to cover up Canadians' inferiority complex *vis-à-vis* the States and their feeling of being second-class citizens (which, with the exception of the Quebecois, they are). They want to promote film financing, then they hedge it in with various quotas and point systems—points being awarded for "Canadianness." Many companies have been hooked by the lower dollar and the cheaper rates, but they've often found them a mirage that traps them in the loss of quality enforced by the regulations. *The Edible Woman*, being Canadian, should have been a natural project. Oscar overplayed his hand, however, and, using my name, behaved to the financier like a colonialist out slumming. We had an offer from some mystery banker to finance everything. Then, in the course of a party, our Maecenas made a few innocuous remarks about casting. Oscar berated him in front of the man's wife: How dare he open his mouth?—it was privilege enough to have the chance of mere association with the likes of us. That was the gist of it. Our money disappeared in a flash, and our financier turned out to be the controller of the consortium that regulated all film financing. We were blackballed by all the other producers, and *The Edible Woman* never got off the ground.

It had, however, been fun and rewarding working with Peggy, though she had her eccentricities. One day, near a lake cabin belonging to her family, she stood in a bed of nettles, facing a broken-down wooden shack, and—tears running down her face—communicated with the devil. "What the devil does she mean by 'the devil'?" Oscar asked furiously. She also did my horoscope, in great detail and with beautiful illustrations. I wish I had it now—it might have saved me writing all this.

But the importance for me of the project was someone else. Oscar had a knack for finding himself attractive girls. He usually had one hardworking secretary who did all his work and "another" for social, decorative purposes—a sinecure called, I think, play-reading, with excuses for intellectual discussions and long lunches. In the Woodfall days this latter role was filled by the lovely Diana Dare (now Mrs. Terence Donovan); now it was Grizelda Grimond. In the beginning she was kept well away from me. As a director I could be tolerated, but socially I was "mad, bad, and dangerous to know."

How do you ever describe someone you love? Grizelda was the daughter of Jo Grimond, who before he resigned had been the head of the Liberal Party, and his wife, Laura Bonham-Carter, the granddaughter of the prime minister Herbert Asquith and a niece of the film director Anthony Asquith. Jo was extraordinarily handsome and charming, with a wide range of culture and an immediate gift of sympathetic contact. A native of Orkney, he has an underlying deep Celtic melancholy, like "the prophetic soul/Of the wide world dreaming on things to come." Thus caught between the past and the present, he hadn't been able to make use of all his talents. He would be ideal casting for Brutus—or the real-life model of John Gielgud's Hamlet. Laura belongs to that wonderful tradition of English upper-class ladies: forthright, opinionated, humorous, full of vigor, and on the surface no-nonsense practicality. Grizelda has much of both of them in her. My first impression was of her vitality, her energy, her merriment. It was as if she was in rustling taffeta tartan skirts, turning, twisting, laughing in a Highland fling with her wild dark hair swishing round her head. Dancing, dancing, dancing—that was what I loved. She was full of adventure and joy and excitement, physical and intellectual. She was always great fun. She is loyal and generous and passionate, willing to work to the point of martyrdom for those she loves. We loved the same things: the country, books, old musicals, songs, flowers. As soon as she saw Le Nid du Duc she fell for it as no one else has ever done. She saw the point of everything, and—sometimes too much, I think—would like never to change a thing.

There was one big gulf: Grizelda has never liked (though she would probably deny this) nor understood show business. Her attitude is a kind of non-malicious contempt for an activity she sees as essentially frivolous. This is a fairly universal attitude in England and is come at by the different classes in ways that are superficially different though essentially the same. With Grizelda there was a touch of its being fit only for children and servants on wet Saturdays and at Christmas, but deeper than that is the sense of Celtic sadness—that such distractions are only frivolities to be swallowed, only to disappear in the great gray sea of the past. My own lifestyle was well-defined and I was set in it in some ways that were difficult for Grizelda. I think too that I expected her to make a bigger attempt to link the different parts of her life and bring them together, whereas she may have deliberately wanted to keep them separate.

Rilke wrote of a "love which consists in this, that two solitudes protect and limit and greet each other." I had always thought the quote pretentious, but now I think that's maybe what I have in mind. One thing that made for an absolute link was the birth of our daughter Katharine on January 8, 1973 (curiously enough, within a day of Joely's birth eight years earlier). Katharine has much of both of us in her, not least in her love of animals and living things. More than a friendship, less than a marriage, my relationship with Grizelda now has lasted some fifteen years. Maybe that's what Le Nid du Duc does too.

Early in 1972 I had done a production of which I was quite proud—*The Threepenny Opera*. With its combination of pastiche John Gay with capitalist politics, fairground humor, and Kurt Weill's cabaret songs, this is one of the seminal works of this century's theatre. Brecht wrote several versions of it, including one for the Pabst film, and we combined them all—very successfully, I think. We played the rarely used "Lucy Aria"—a satire on Puccini, wonderfully sung by the *Carry On* comedienne Barbara Windsor—and the tea party from Brecht's steal of *The Importance of Being Earnest*, which is again rarely performed. We also used extensively some of the material from *The Threepenny Novel*, where Polly, the sweet ingenue, gradually becomes a capitalist and takes over as president of the company. I still think it's the most powerful version I've ever seen.

I was pleased too with the staging. In combination with the designers Patrick Robertson and Rosemary Vercoe, we took a real carousel from a fairground and staged everything on it as though it were part of its carvings and paintings. Then, for the happy ending, everything was lit and turned and the fairground music played.

Michael White, the boldest and most interesting of all British producers, presented the play. We had planned it as a big popular musical, and because of that Michael had hired one of the musicals houses in London with a "pop" tradition of vaudeville and pantomime. We had discussions and got, we thought, a commitment from an actor who had some popular following and was excellent casting to play Macheath. At the last moment he reneged. Michael was faced with a huge commitment to a theatre but a production without a "top" name, though the cast included such solid talents as Annie Ross (who sang Jenny), Hermione Baddeley, Joe Melia, and Ronald Radd. We were both desperate; then Vanessa, knowing our problems, offered to play Polly for six weeks. We were delighted, as it meant six weeks' solid business, and she was quite wonderful. (Polly is, of course, the secondary role, even in our expanded version. Note for all directors and producers of *The Threepenny Opera:* Go for a strong Macheath and a real heavyweight as Peachum.)

At our first public preview, the whole technical side was in chaos, the carousel not working, the orchestral timings and balance all over the place, the choruses ragged. I said to Vanessa, "You've got to go in and make it work." Which, for that performance, with a will of iron she did. She dominated the show with an incandescence that made the technical mishaps unnoticeable—a true star. Unhappily, after several weeks Michael had to transfer the show to another theatre, and Vanessa wasn't willing to go. Inevitably the public interest drops whenever a star leaves. The transferred production did well, but if Vanessa had stayed we would probably have run forever. Perhaps after all the advice should be for presenters of *The Threepenny Opera* to have a strong Polly—or maybe just hire Vanessa.

The following year I did a sketch production of *Antony and Cleopatra*—treating it as work in progress, if you like, since the resources available were slight. For several years Sam Wanamaker had run a small festival in a tent on the site of the original Globe theatre on London's South Bank. That year he had plans to turn it into a more permanent building, but in the end the development didn't happen and it was back to the tent. This didn't bother me too much, as I've always had a dread of reconstructed Shakespearian theatres—however much the features of the contemporary stage may have influenced the plays' construction, there are better ways of staging them now.

Antony has some of the most magnificent poetry in the whole canon, and it combines an epic sweep of dramatization—worlds colliding—with an equally reckless presentation of human character in squalor and sublimity. Antony and Cleopatra are monsters—

mean, shabby, drunken, cowardly, indulgent of their own pleasures and vanities to the point that they're willing to sacrifice their pasts, their honors, and their countries, and yet made glorious by their passion and greed for each other and the style in which they can express them. You can think of many, many parallels today. They are, if you like, the first great stars of history, as concerned with show as with achievement, and so wonderfully unconcerned about revealing their desires so shamelessly and so despicably that they become purged by them.

I think we served the play very well. On an abstract set of scaffolding, with a sort of Elizabethan structure underneath, we could transform the setting easily from Egyptian court to ship, Rome, tomb, and monument. We set it vaguely in the 1930s. Cleopatra was like a Hollywood star—Theda Bara, Tallulah Bankhead, and Bette Davis all in one. Antony was a dashing Errol Flynn aviator. The Romans, in Mao-Stalin jackets and uniforms, were the style of the world to come, as Pompey, the buccaneer, was the world gone by. There was no pageantry, and every one of the twenty in the cast contributed as individuals, not extras. Vanessa by her daring was able to explore sides of the character with a harshness and truthfulness unparalleled in any other Cleopatra I've ever seen. Julian Glover, Bob Hoskins, Dave King, and Julia Covington were also in the cast.

Unfortunately, the English weather is not conducive to performing outside or in tents. After the play opened I went to France, and a storm lasting several days raged in London. When the performance wasn't totally stopped, the actors had to compete with the noise of the rain on canvas. Finally the storm was such that the tent was completely blown away. It was the end of *Antony and Cleopatra*. Grizelda thought it quite a joke, but I loved the show too much to see the funny side—maybe when I've done the *Antony* of my dreams I will. *Antony* is perhaps my favorite play, and I long someday to be able to realize fully the production that Vanessa and I started on the South Bank. Few people saw the show, but those who did loved it—even, to my surprise and delight, John Gielgud.

That same year, 1973, the earlier experiment of filming *Hamlet* led me to try a development of this. A group under the auspices of the producer Ely Landau had launched an enterprise called American Film Theater. The idea was to shoot a number of properties of the kind that weren't snapped up for the "big-screen" treatment and to show them in special screenings for limited performances. Tickets were to be sold on a subscription basis, and publicized together, and the concept was that an audience would be attracted to seeing the whole series. It didn't seem a very good idea, and when they had offered me several of the group—including, I think, John Osborne's *Luther* and Ionesco's *Rhinoceros*—I had said no. Then they came back with Edward Albee's *A Delicate Balance*.

I had always been a great admirer of Edward's. I produced (at the Court) his first double bill in England with *The American Dream* and *The Death of Bessie Smith*. For these I got Peter Yates his first theatre assignments as director. Then later I had a marvelous experience with Edward on a film script about Nijinsky. This was a project of Harry Salzman's. Harry had tried to make it work with many combinations. None was successful and, reluctantly, he came to me. I longed to do the subject and produced a treatment for the story. On the basis of this, Rudolf Nureyev and Paul Scofield accepted the roles of the dancer and Diaghilev. Edward and I met. He'd refused to get involved in some of the earlier attempts, but this time he accepted.

He came to Le Nid du Duc, and for about a week we worked through and expanded on my outline. It was a week when there was a lot of hard thinking. After my experience with John Osborne, I was frankly dubious about a dramatist of Edward's caliber providing a workable screenplay. However, on the called-for day of delivery it was stunning. Without being slavish, he'd filled out, remolded, and yet remained faithful to all the work we'd done together. It was better than my hopes and would have made an extraordinary film, but Harry, who had overcommitted himself in his usual way to some financial system to take over Technicolor, didn't agree—or rather, he needed to find a way out of his commitment to make the movie, although we were only six weeks away from shooting. Edward had written some silent scenes. Harry claimed that these were amateurish and unprofessional and reneged on the deal. Many years later he was responsible for a travesty of the subject.

The more I thought about *A Delicate Balance*, the more I liked the idea of working with Edward's dialogue. I began to think of it not as a film but as a recorded play, like *Hamlet*. Some of the casting ideas were exciting—Henry Fonda or Paul Scofield and Kate Hepburn. They were all people I'd idolized and wanted to work with. But beyond that there was another reason—Kim Stanley. At first I'd kept in touch with her after *Natural Affection;* then, as with most of her friends, contact had been less. Occasionally there'd be snippets through the grapevine—she'd retired to Taos, New Mexico; she was teaching autistic chidren; she was better. The role of the alcoholic sister was perfect for her. Quixotically, I saw the project as a rescue operation, a spectacular comeback for her. I started to track her down, and Neil and I set off for Taos. It was wonderful to see her again, and, though overweight, she seemed in good form and with a positive attitude: She wanted to get back to work. I accepted the project, stipulating only that my price was Kim in the role of the alcoholic sister. Dubiously, the Landau organization agreed. Paul Scofield had said yes, so all that was left was to woo Kate. The role of the imperious matriarch was ideal for her, but she resisted it. She didn't understand the play. She also resisted Kim, feeling that their styles would be too different. (There may have been an old trouper's smell of competition.) But eventually she succumbed.

The film was to be shot in England, mainly for budgetary reasons. During the preparation there were complaints of erratic phone calls with Kim and pressures to recast her, but I took them all as lies and gossip—an attempt by the production office to alter a piece of casting it didn't like. I was adamant. And so finally the cast assembled in England. Lee Remick, Joseph Cotten, and Betsy Blair (now Karel Reisz's wife) completed it. Kim arrived a few days ahead. She had not lost her excess weight as she had promised but she was otherwise fine. She stayed with me and always refused drinks when offered.

The cast came together at my house for the first reading. The idea was to have the most relaxed setting possible. I asked them to read the play through lightly, at the kind of pace they might imagine finally playing it, but without trying to perform. That way, I told them, we might get a rough timing for the whole thing. The first act more or less proceeded like that. Then we came to Kim's scenes. Gradually she started to act, not read. She began to improvise on Edward's text, she crawled on the floor, she sputtered, she cried.

Looked on one way it was a parody of the stereotypical view of Method acting. In a London first-floor drawing-room, expressing her emotions, her flesh, her bulk, it was almost obscene. "How could you have let that happen to us?" Paul—whom I didn't know—hissed violently at me when we finally broke up. But it was magnificent—its reality so compelling, so violently and truthfully exposed, that there was more knowledge of the depths of human experience and of alcoholism than I've seen in any other performance. It transcended anything I'd ever imagined could be in the play, and I knew instantly how to direct it. It had the ugliness, the truth, the understanding of great art. But it was clear that Kim's truth was at the expense of everything else—the other performers, the text of the play, and the exigencies of the production. If we had had a year to shoot I could have got something so disturbing on film it might have been unwatchable. We had two weeks' rehearsals and then four weeks to shoot.

At the end of the day, in which everyone had been shattered—all in different ways, and without being able to articulate it—Kate announced she was withdrawing. She couldn't go on with Kim. I was furious and accused her bitterly of trying to wreck the production by a kind of cheap blackmail. In this Kate was right and I was wrong. Kate had had long experiences of Kim's condition and, without diagnosing it, she saw that, given our conditions (and probably—Kate's aversion was so great—given *any* conditions), there was no practical way we could go on. Kim had partly collapsed; she knew what the situation was and wanted to try to talk to Kate. Kate wouldn't see her. In the crisis, everyone behaved impeccably. Ely Landau, who had worked with Kate before and adored her, refused to take sides and generously left the decision entirely to me. Paul, whatever his hidden feelings were, said he would continue to work with whomever I chose.

I'd brought in my doctor, Patrick Woodcock, a great personal friend with an enormous experience in dealing with show-people. He examined Kim. Then quite brutally he explained to me what the disease of alcoholism is and how it manifests itself. He exposed the telltale quarts of vodka buried in a closet. In one sense Patrick's firmness and openness was invaluable, and I understood for the first time the difference between an alcoholic and a drunk. This needs widespread publicizing, because, until the disease is understood and acknowledged by anyone unfortunate enough to be infected by it, only suffering and danger can result. It was the hardest decision I've ever had to make. It meant turning away my friend, my idol, the only reason I undertook the enterprise; it also meant denying that one possibility of artistic greatness. But on any responsible level there wasn't a choice: Kim had to go. The Landau organization was generous again in paying her fully as if she'd done the show. There were no recriminations.

Rehearsals started on a sour note. I was still feeling hurt, thwarted, guilty. I had been very hard to Kate, but in her generous and upbeat way she helped to heal the break. There was a lot to do, as the rehearsal time was so short and as we were rehearsing as if we were rehearsing a play, but a play staged in reality, not with audience and stage. It was a continuation of the method of *Hamlet*, except in this case, instead of having small sets, we had an entire house, arranged and dressed as if it were the family house. We were going to work in long-sustained takes, some of them nine to twenty minutes long—as long, almost, as a reel of film would last. Given the nature of the play and the production limitations, it was an idea that worked quite well.

I found the play itself, the more we worked on it, unsatisfying in its emotional underpinnings. Edward's mandarin dialogue is fascinating, and modulated with impeccable rhythms—satisfying for performers to handle—but the moral dilemmas at the core seem small in comparison with the intricacy of the trappings (excepting the portrait of the alcoholic sister). The central "betrayal" is that the husband has grown away from his wife—no longer wants her physically. That's not the greatest sin in the world. To me, the effect of the play is similar to the effect of Henry James. When I was an adolescent, I used to think he was the greatest novelist ever; now I find him unreadable—the surface is just too elaborate for the amount of life underneath; the characters become etiolated, and finally the manner becomes tiresome. But you can go off works of art in different ways. Later, in 1976, while working on a stage production of Ibsen's *The Lady From the Sea*—a play I imagined I loved; with Vanessa, who gave one of her greatest performances and had a fabulous success in the role that was Duse's favorite—I became disillusioned with the play because of the clumsiness of its construction and because the key scene—when the husband has to

persuade his wife, Ellida, to abandon her real or phantom lover—
is underwritten to the point of extinction. No one, however, could
accuse Edward of clumsiness—his piece was as well worked-out as
a baroque concerto.

After, as she described it, our bad beginning, I found Kate a
total delight to work with, above all because she has a great sense
of humor and takes nothing too seriously (which is not to say that
she isn't the complete professional). Shooting became a kind of
Punch and Judy show between us. We would insult each other in
such an open and outrageous way that even up to the end, and after
witnessing the fencing match every day, the crew still imagined we
were for real and that there'd been a complete breach between us.
And, Paul, I'm sure, thought we were hopelessly frivolous and silly.
But we loved our sparring, and it helped Kate to ignore her other
anxieties about the production. I think she found working in real
spaces cramping, and she didn't like David Watkin's lighting. She
wanted, or imagined she wanted, the old-fashioned star-flattering
treatment, but David and I both thought her too beautiful and too
expressive to need that kind of softening.

At some time or another it's every film director's ambition to make
a thriller. Thrillers are naturals for movies. Many fine directors
make nothing else, and others turn to thrillers to fill the gaps between projects that they feel more intensely about. Which was my
case. I wanted very much to do something commercial, and in
looking for material I hit on the idea of filming one of the Dick
Francis novels, which, if successful, could lead to a series of films.
An ex-jockey whose most famous moment came when his mount
owned by the Queen Mother, stopped a few yards before the Grand
National winning-post when it was way ahead of the rest of the
field, Dick Francis turned to writing when his active career was
over, and he continued to produce a series of novels which are
wonderful reads and which have a large and devoted series of fans.
As I always loved horses, and was fascinated by the horse world
(though never quite in it), the books seemed a natural for me. I
settled on *Dead Cert*, his first novel.

Unfortunately, wonderful reads don't necessarily make wonderful scripts, and as I worked on the script with (Lord) John Oaksey—
the racing correspondent of the *Daily Telegraph* and the most famous

amateur rider in England—we found more and more that the story, which reads so smoothly, didn't have the underpinnings of character that alone can give a script life. I thought that casting could compensate and that the twists of the story would carry us along, but even with the casting I made mistakes—settling for good and realistic actors rather than more obvious larger-than-life thriller types. And the actor I chose for the hero, though he looked and rode well, wasn't engaging enough to make anyone care for him.

We shot the film in July and August 1973. The sequences with the horses themselves were fascinating. The problems were almost the opposite of those in *The Charge of the Light Brigade*. Here we were using valuable thoroughbreds (John Oaksey coordinated all the horse production problems, and Merrick Francis, another charmer like his father, was the horse master), so we could get only one or at the most two takes before they became exhausted. They were nervous and skittish. It was very hard to accustom them to helicopters, which I needed to get close enough to the action, and it was difficult to coordinate helicopter flights to the oval and irregular courses. We used cameras everywhere, even 8mm cameras concealed in jockey's helmets and boots, and we trained professional jockeys to handle cameras while in the race. At the end of the first showing of the film to United Artists, one of the executives said, "Well, the horses were great." Which summed it all up. And the film was made incomprehensible to American audiences (which by now were our biggest market, the bottom having dropped out of whatever public Britain once had) by the gap between racing practices in the two countries. The laxity and the lack of surveillance on many British racecourses, especially in steeplechasing, is unbelievable across the Atlantic—as are the carnage and violence of the Grand National.

Dead Cert brought me a big personal loss too. Jan, my driver and friend, died of a heart attack during one day's shooting. He had watched and looked after me, and fought for me and the children and my parents for nearly twenty years. He had seen me through marriages, relationships, plays and films, new houses, parties; had catered to everyone's welfare, and attended to every guest and friend's wishes. His was a loyalty and care that was beyond any kind of service. It was a way of life for him. He had been born in that part of Poland which the Russians invaded at the beginning of the Second World War. He was sent to Siberia, and there—often living on only a handful of potato peelings a day—he learned how to improvise and how to service. Later, when Stalin switched sides, Churchill made a deal to finance the training of the men in the camps. Then, as they were moved out of the USSR, in a gesture not officially recognized, Churchill unequivocally offered them all British citizenship—which was how Jan came to England. With me he found the family he'd never had (he adored and loved children) and he sustained us throughout his life—even though he nearly killed us all by the spectacular recklessness of his driving. His death was one of the things—as was the ambience of *Dead Cert*—that led to another major change in my life. My mother, whom Jan and his wife and a Polish nurse had cared for in her withdrawn years, died about two years later.

22

A Place in the Sun

Sam Shepard, the playwright, was living in London at this time—writing and attending the greyhound-racing tracks (he owned two dogs himself, I think). From the start I'd been one of his great admirers and, though I was no longer part of the Royal Court, I was instrumental in getting his work presented there, where the plays were directed by Jim Sharman, an Australian who had worked for me on *Ned Kelly*.

I asked Sam to work on a film script. I wanted to take the classic themes of *The Changeling*—of sex, not desire; of murder, and paying the price—and translate them to today's jet-set world. He became enthusiastic about the commission, and we were helped by Micky Howard, the Earl of Suffolk, a racehorse breeder who'd become a friend on *Dead Cert*, and whose ruined ancestral home we used as an image in the last part of the script. Sam started work, and then we went to Le Nid du Duc to finish it. We called the script *The Bodyguard*. It's a very powerful piece of imaginative writing (though it needed more work, and Sam too shied away from rewrites); I was excited about its possibilities—and have been ever since. It needed an American star, so I decided to go off to Los Angeles to talk to people. And, without intending to at the outset, I've stayed there ever since.

Business takes four or five times as long in Los Angeles as in New York or London or Paris. Days go by before calls are returned; weeks pass before scripts are read; work stops completely during holidays. Life is just too easy and pleasant. Neil and I arrived and started to have meetings and discussions, firstly with that perennial flirt Warren Beatty and then with Steve McQueen, who had somehow got hold of the script, had become fascinated by it, and wanted to invest in developing it.

It was clear we were likely to be in Los Angeles for some time, so we decided to rent a house instead of staying on in the Beverly Wilshire. After looking at various possibilities, we settled on a house on Kings Road. It belonged to Linda Lovelace, star of *Deep Throat*, or rather to her boyfriend, David Winter. It was beat-up, dirty, dilapidated. The walls were dingy redwood, and there were holes in the roof. Built in 1927, it was one of the cabins that people retreated to when downtown LA was still a working show biz district. Linda and David had crammed it full of nineteenth-century junk—unwieldy carved thrones with scalloped velvet seats, iron escutcheons and shields on the walls, china angels, smudged tapestries, what-nots loaded with cute bibelots, paralyzed turtledoves in a rotting cage—the accumulation of rubbish you'd find in an old prop-room. There were also a couple of suitably equipped waterbeds. I asked Linda if some of her previous objects could be stored away, on the grounds of safety. But no. As I was British and cultured, she knew I'd appreciate them and wanted me to enjoy them. All I wanted to do was to junk the whole lot.

The house had the advantage of two floors like separate apartments, so Neil and I could function separately. What we didn't know when we rented it was that the house was under foreclosure and David Winter had declared himself bankrupt. Almost immediately, all the service companies arrived—phone, gas, electricity—to switch everything off, while the bank informed us we'd no right to be living there. Luckily Jeremy Fry arrived for the weekend, crawled under the house, and reconnected all the switched-off services. Then quickly I began to develop a feeling for the house itself. A great window looked east to downtown, where the dawn breaks over a city that seems like Brecht's Mahagonny. In homes buried in the canyons of sunny California the sun is often absent except for a brief hour or two, but here it moved around the house all day until it set beyond Catalina and Santa Monica in the west. The light was gorgeous and magnificent, and strong light has always been wonderful to me. The chiaroscuro of mists and softnesses are best for the camera, for atmosphere, but give me the clarity of the light of Cézanne and Picasso. The light convinced me to buy the house.

A few weeks earlier, if anyone had suggested I would be thinking of living in Los Angeles I'd have laughed at them. Despite all the fun I'd had there before, I'd never liked any of the places I'd lived in and I wasn't attuned to the magic and rhythm of the city. But I didn't like my house in London either, and I didn't like the world of London itself. The girls didn't need me there as much, and deep down was some instinctive desire to change my whole life-style—to become freer, more self-reliant, to get away from the coziness and setness of London society and the ministrations of servants. I knew how quickly this wreck could change with a clean-up and a coat of white paint, so I bought the house and became a Los Angeleno. Michael White, just breaking up from his first marriage, had been living in my London house. He wanted it, and so I let it go.

Work on the script went slowly. Inevitably, when the next draft was finished, Steve rejected it, thinking Ali MacGraw's role was too important. At this point I went to Jack Nicholson—I can never understand why I didn't go to him in the first place: It was one of those aberrations. We'd always wanted to work together, and he, with certain reservations (he was never as keen on Sam's work as I was) accepted the script. I started to work again, with new writers—including John Byrum, now a director. I got stuck on the treadmill of cosmetic Hollywood changes. It was a big mistake, and one mistake led to another.

John Byrum was also working on or rewriting the script of *Mahogany* for Berry Gordy of Motown. It was to be the next vehicle for Diana Ross, after her screen debut in *Lady Sings the Blues*. As John and I were getting on extremely well, the producer, Rob Cohen, suggested that I might collaborate with John on the improvements. This meant additional money at a time when I was financing *The Bodyguard* rewrites myself, so I agreed. Then, after I met with Berry and Diana, they asked me to direct the film. I explained my other commitment. They then suggested that I give them an option on my directing *Mahogany* if my own film got delayed. Secure, as I stupidly thought, in my own dates and therefore in no danger of having to do this film, I agreed.

Jack had always wanted to do *One Flew Over the Cuckoo's Nest*, but he hadn't been able to come together with the producers over dates. Suddenly the *Cuckoo* situation changed. Jack phoned me and asked me to go back in the queue so that he could do the other movie—arguing that it was Milos Forman's first chance to direct in several years. But the worst was that he was already signed up to do a film immediately after *Cuckoo*, so it meant going back two in line. (In the end Jack was tired of working and the project had gone stale on him, so he never did *The Bodyguard*). It left me unprotected from the *Mahogany* deal.

Berry Gordy's world was intriguing. The first rendezvous was elaborately planned. Two cars were waiting at the west gate of Bel Air, filled with guards. One drove in front and another behind us as we proceeded to his house. Once inside the gates, you were immediately under closed-circuit TV surveillance. The house itself has once belonged to Red Skelton and was a rather bad imitation of an English Tudor manor house that looked as if it belonged on the MGM back lot. Berry was in the process of transforming it into part *Playboy* mansion and part fortress—the walls, floor, and ceiling of the corridor leading to his bedroom were all quarter-inch steel, and all the glass in the room was bulletproof. An elaborate zoo meant to rival Hugh Hefner's was being installed. All the work was being done by acquaintances of mine, and it was being done all wrong. A range of aviaries was being built on the slope exposed to the north wind, which is fatal to birds. Llamas, suitably shampooed and deshitted, were escorted regularly onto the lawns. Beautiful little Asian deer were wandering in and consuming the flower beds and contracting from the plants diarrhoea, which soon decimated them; they were then cast as bronze statues. Splendid Egyptian geese and peacocks were scattered about; they'd all been operated on to remove their vocal cords. We conferred around a table on the lawn, surrounded by the llamas, and a butler (white) brought out tape recorders on silver salvers to preserve all our brilliant thoughts. At intervals, members of the family, girlfriends, or various Motown functionaries came to present their respects and pay obeisance. Berry used to call Rob Cohen "my little white nigger." The atmosphere was exactly that of *The Godfather*, and I loved observing it.

The same atmosphere was sustained even when we were shooting in Chicago, where Berry was always surrounded by guards with guns and an entourage ready to protect the *capo di capi* from any attack, slight, or insult. Once, after dailies, a brash young projectionist yelled at Berry and me to jump out of the way in a parking lot. Berry did a slow burn, and that evening minions were dispatched to break the man's legs as a lesson. I was accused of shielding him, but luckily he had apparently gone on vacation with a girlfriend and so he never knew what kind of retribution he'd escaped. Another time one of the workmen told me they were moving a safe and by some chance touched off the combination so that it sprang open and hundreds of thousands, maybe millions, of dollars fell out. They had to quickly erect a wall around it and guard it until next day, when accountants could check the amount. Senior members of his entourage used literally to kiss Berry's ring, and one of our stars who was discovered smoking grass had henchmen assigned to sleep in his room to prevent any further transgression. Personally I liked Berry enormously, and he was fascinated by me. He used to say, during the few days I was shooting, "Man, I just can't understand you. You're so calm."

When we started, the script was still in the process of being rewritten and the improvements were at best problematical. I'd somehow psyched myself up to imagining that there was in it a subject I could feel about and "do": the naïveté of the young designer dreaming Erté dreams in the Chicago ghetto and then being exposed to the corruption and ludicrousness of a Felliniesque European world seemed like the classic story of the American innocent. But it was tenuous, and more and more I felt I was kidding myself. Berry was dabbling in the scouts and production—not ostentatiously, but I could feel him looking over my shoulder, often with respect, but with a clear itch to meddle and control. He would become obsessed by this or that detail and would behave as if the success or failure of the project hung on that one preoccupation.

His relationship with Diana was very complex. She had started as his secretary before becoming part of the Supremes, and they had a long past together. He felt he owned her, and he would often humiliate her openly. (I remember him once saying, "Tony, you've gotta understand—Diana isn't a personality, she's a product.") He could be unfairly critical of her (Diana was in all her behavior a total professional and at bottom always loyal to Berry), and yet at the same time he was protective and even at moments in awe of her, for, despite her loyalty, she could attack him in a gut way no one else would.

It became clear that I was much less pliant than he had hoped and didn't take his suggestions or obsessions very seriously, though we never quarreled outright. I could sense how much Berry wanted to be controlling the show. That's what his whole life had been about, and now—cut off from his power base in Motown, kicked upstairs by whoever the now-ruling Motown powers were, and indulged in such whims as being allowed to make movies—he was becoming more and more frustrated. As I would have been only too happy to relinquish a project in which I'd no belief, I teased him about his directorial ambitions and suggested he should take over. Berry refused, but a few nights later nemesis struck.

We were doing a fairly small and unimportant scene in which Diana, on her way home, is accosted by some drunk who grabs at her. (Berry had elevated this attack into a warning about how all American women should combat rape.) We had been casting small roles out of the Chicago area. I'd been unhappy with the first choice and didn't think the actor frightening or formidable enough for the incident, so, though we held him, I made our casting assistants go on looking. At the last moment they came up with someone much bigger and more threatening. Unknown to me, Berry had been rehearsing the original choice (he was an average character performer) and trying out various makeups on him. He was so carried away by the guy that he promised, I'm told, to star him in a TV series. When Berry heard I'd replaced the actor he was devastated. He couldn't believe I wouldn't yield to him, but I stuck to my contractural right of casting. It was a stand-off. The production was shut down. Then Berry ordered some other shots done. Most of the crew, whom I'd engaged and who were loyal to me, went on strike. It was in the middle of a cold rainy night in the ghetto of Chicago. Diana stuck by Berry, although she wasn't working, and sat by the camera in a raincoat, as a sign of loyalty for which I admired her enormously. I repeated my suggestion that he take over, in which case I would persuade the crew to continue. (With

Neil and David Watkin and my first assistant, Andrew Grieve, they couldn't have been better able to give Berry the protection and support that he needed—even if he didn't know it.)

Negotiations went on all night, I think, and in the end my suggestion was accepted. Berry went on to direct (which was what he wanted), I left (which was what I wanted), and the crew went on at increased salaries (which made them happy). Only Diana was aggrieved, and probably felt betrayed by everyone. There wasn't any animosity, and I'm as happy to see Berry today as I was when I first met him. He is one of the great originals and doers.

I returned to California and further frustration over *The Bodyguard*. Not expecting to be back, I'd loaned the house to Vanessa, who was playing *Macbeth* at the Ahmanson, and nannies and secretaries were installed in it with the girls. When I could finally move back in, I got involved in something which is of no public importance and probably no interest to anyone but me but which nevertheless has so absorbed me and in many ways conditioned my life in Los Angeles—and which is perhaps the key to some hopeless Don Quixote side of me—that I have to write about it.

Next to my house was a fenced-off, boarded-up property which was under some sort of slide—not mud; decomposed granite. I think I first went exploring it with Kate Hepburn, who'd been an adviser and friend and help during my acquisition of the house. Under a steep cliff, where houses were precariously cantilevered out from the shifting earth, was a derelict acre and a half with corroding automobiles (Dual Ghias, coveted by the rat pack in the 1950s) buried up to the car doors. There was a derelict tennis court with the fences all collapsed and strewn with broken trees. There was a guest cabin whose roof had caved in and whose inside was black and silver early-1960s psychedelic, the floor covered with foam rubber for the orgies for which it had been designed. There was a swimming pool of indeterminate size, as only a few feet of tiling could be glimpsed at one end, but a high diving board suggested it might be extensive. There were brick terraces and steps all broken and covered with sand. There were piles of trash and old appliances—washing machines, stoves, TVs. There was a miniature children's house. The trees, bushes, and other vegetation had taken over, concealing some of the squalor with hibiscus flowers. There were hummingbirds. It was a kind of Pompeii on the Strip, and I decided I would find out who owned it. It took time. The owner was a tough little sixty-year-old real estate operator, like an ex-flyweight boxer, called Mo Mancourth. He wore two-piece linen suits in brick red and apple green and a wig. He hung out in a Mafia resaurant on Sunset. He was charming. It took time, but we did a deal. I bought the land; he had to clear it. Then I restored it—including the tennis court.

After a life of loathing sports and all they stood for, I decided I would try to learn to play tennis. I suppose there's some appalling lesson in this about how possessions take over your life, because if I hadn't bought the court I'd have never attempted to play, which maybe would have been much smarter. Anyway, I started to plunge, pathetically, into an adolescence I'd never had.

My first teacher wasn't even a professional, but I figured that as I would be so completely hopeless, so irredeemably uncoordinated, it didn't really matter who tried to teach me. He was hopeless—mouthing phrases like "Take your racket back" and "Bend your knees" so mechanically that sometimes I would stop and watch him continuing without realizing that I wasn't even trying to return the ball. I started to try to direct him into teaching—I'd say, "Watch me—tell me what I'm doing." It made me more aware than ever of the gap between teaching and directing. There are lots of fabulous teachers who can't direct at all, yet they try to be directors; and there are a lot of directors who can't teach at all (like me). How I envy those people who can stand up in front of a group or class and say, "This is how you do it"—for me it would just be a nightmare. Anyway, at the end of three or four months of much humiliation I ended up with acute tennis elbow. As I was going to France for the summer, I thought it didn't matter much as I wouldn't be playing over there. But at the end of the summer the elbow was just as painful. It was time, I thought, to put away childish things and reconcile myself to a sportless life.

Unfortunately I've never been good at taking no for an answer: "No" immediately challenges me. I started thinking about ways to change things, and all those childish adages like "If at first you don't succeed, try, try again" came into play. Dumbo me. But there I was and there the court was. Someone told me of another coach. He was a laid-back, red-haired, red-bearded Californian, perpetually stoned. I explained my elbow problem. In one hour he'd made it disappear, and so I started again on the longest, most grueling, most self-exposing journey of any I've ever undertaken. As someone who has never been introspective, never for one moment contemplated psychotherapy or analysis, I'd embarked on a trip that would make me more aware of myself, my limitations, my monstrosities, my indulgences than anything I've ever done. Donne's "No man is an Island, entire of itself" is just not true when you're on the court—there's just you and nothing else. You become aware of every limitation, both physical and psychological: your hopeless physical equipment and your rotten personality. Presumably if you play sports earlier none of this happens. It's a physical appetite, but nevertheless applauded, in which thought and self-consciousness don't enter into the calculations. Probably that's why team sports are so valued. Life becomes simple and released. But I came to it late and, though willing, "The time is out of joint; O cursed spite,/ That ever I was born to set it right!"

The tennis court has become the stage for my own psychodrama. I am as hooked on it as anyone is on their analyst's couch. I progressed from my California redhead to a crazed and quirky Australian with almost as much determination and lack of self-ridicule as I have myself (coming for a stay at Le Nid du Duc, he tried to hunt wild boars with sharpened gardening forks) and finally to a dedicated Irish Chinaman with an absolute knowledge of the physical techniques required and the patience of Job. I'm not sure Job would be quite the role model for a teacher, though, because the patience becomes psychotic and the relationship between us becomes at times an adversarial battle royal, with me testing his tolerance and acceptance to the absolute limit and allowing myself to wallow in self-pity and petulance to a monumental degree.

Playing tennis isn't just compensating for what you didn't do; it's indulging every whim and tyranny that you shouldn't have been allowed anyway. I regress like that. I become a caricature of all that those encounter groups and *est* and those other horrible freak shows are advocating. And as often as I say, "No more—it's all rubbish," as often, Don Quixote–like, I go on. I waste hours and hours in sulks. I don't try, when with trying I maybe could progress. And for what? The impossibility of accepting failure, though your body and mind and spirit tell you that you can never achieve—probably never could have achieved—what you want. A perpetual masochism, like probing an aching tooth. The refusal to admit that what you want to do is win—"I only want to play as well as I can. I don't care about the result." The constant defiance of what Tennessee Williams once called "our great enemy, time." It's all this, and yet more.

It's certainly led to a much greater understanding of myself and, through me, my family and the traits of their characters. Joely at about thirteen decided she wanted to become a tennis professional. Today, of course, it's almost impossible to become an athlete—certainly a tennis player (that's the only sport I know anything about)—unless you're conditioned to it from birth, or at least from three years old. Anyway, as she wanted to do something of her own we let her go to the Hopman Institute in Florida, set up by the mentor of that great sportsman John McEnroe, one of the key heroes of our time in the way he has revaluated thinking about his sport and has tried to strip it of some of the humbug and accretions that have stuck to it (which is why he has been so vilified). She stayed there for two years, and through being able to relate my own fumbling experience to hers, and seeing her strengths and weaknesses both of ability and of character, I learned to reassess my own and to look back at members of our family and see a continuity of both the good and the bad in things. Once again something has been reached unexpectedly by an unlikely route. Without my hours of experience and self-knowledge on the court, I doubt I could have ever written this account. I think tennis made me interesting to myself. And I will go out tomorrow and tomorrow and tomorrow and test my nonexistent skills for hitting a yellow ball with a racket as French aristocrats did in the fifteenth century. Perhaps in California, where activity is not so frenetic, tennis has filled some void for me. "They also serve who only stand and wait."

23

Border Crossings

You'd have thought I felt ambivalently about California, as the next movie I made took me straight back to the English countryside. I decided to film another novel by Henry Fielding—*Joseph Andrews*. I'd always thought I'd make a movie of it some day, and now seemed a propitious moment. I'd just met Peter Firth, who had scored a big success on stage in *Equus*. I thought he'd be a perfect Joseph. But what really attracted me to the book was not its satirical aspect (*Joseph Andrews* started out as a parody of Samuel Richardson's *Pamela*): It was the possibility of making a love story set in pre–eighteenth-century England—an England with its rituals, paganism, and lyricism still intact; the England that first the rationalism of the eighteenth century and then the industrialization of the nineteenth century would destroy.

It was a film that was very smooth and easy to make—after we had got over the weather hazards of the opening May sequences. Michael Annals, an established stage designer, did wonderfully in his first film assignment. The cast, which included the lovely Ann-Margret as Lady Booby, with a perfect British accent, the matchless comedienne Beryl Reid as Mrs. Slipslop, Michael Horden as Parson Adams, and Jim Dale as a fortune-telling peddler, were all a joy to work with. Old friends like John Gielgud, Peggy Ashcroft, Peter

Bull, and Murray Melvin came up for odd cameos, and the English countryside was as ravishing as ever to be in. David Watkin was the cameraman. You couldn't have asked for better working conditions.

The film commercially was a flop. Unlike many directors and producers, I rarely complain about distribution methods, but in this case they were bad. Despite all our pleadings, *Joseph Andrews* was sold as a son of *Tom Jones*—long forgotten by 1977—and was first launched in the South and the Middle West instead of trying to get the prestige of New York and big-city reviews. These reviews eventually were mixed—though some, like that in *The New York Times*, were very good. But even had the film been handled better I doubt if the results would have been more than marginally different: The public today seems to have antennae of extraordinary sensitivity to what it wants to see, and *Joseph Andrews* was simply not to the taste of the time. I believe it to be a much better-made film than *Tom Jones*, but, coming after it, it was inevitably judged in comparison. There was a determined sense of *déjà vu*, and the film wasn't judged on its own merits. That, of course, could be said to be my fault too, as I couldn't ignore the comparison. I also made some mistakes. I've always had a horror of length and indulgence—I prefer quick spare timing—and in editing I probably hacked down the opening sequences (which I think are very beautiful) in the interests of launching into the story. And, again in retrospect (which I don't usually waste time on), the music could have been fresher and less "movie." But, apart from the box-office results, the experience was a satisfying one.

My next venture couldn't have been more of a contrast. I was sent a book, *A Death in Canaan* by Joan Barthel, which Warners wanted to make into a TV movie. The story was riveting. A boy of seventeen had been persuaded by police interrogation and the skillful use of a lie-detector test to confess to the violent murder of his mother. Subsequently the locals in Connecticut, where the real-life drama had been enacted, banded together, knowing the family and believing the boy to be innocent. Finally the verdict was reversed. I said yes immediately, and began reading everything I could about the subject.

The producers, Bob Christiansen and Rick Rosenberg, were very sympathetic and efficient, but Warners had imposed on them a

writer, Tommy Thompson, who had reduced the real-life events
to pulp drama. We had a couple of abortive meetings when he
announced he would "fix" the script on a weekend. All I wanted
to do was to go back to the original transcripts—both of the lie-
detector test and of the court hearing themselves—which were
staggering in their richness. With the help of Joan Barthel and
others, that's more or less what we did.

I did a quick scouting trip with her to see the real places. (The
budget didn't allow us to shoot on them.) In the course of the trip,
Joan arranged for me to meet the boy himself, who was now working
as a paramedic. We spent a morning pursuing him from place to
place and finally had to wait in a temporary fire station where he
was meant to arrive for lunch. Suddenly I got in a panic. Suppose
when I saw him face-to-face I thought he was guilty? How was I
going to do the show? (I was already totally convinced he'd been
framed and coerced.) When finally he appeared, luckily I didn't
think him guilty—he had the kind of passive, non-defined personality into which any suggestion could be poured.

We were fortunate in *A Death in Canaan* that we didn't confront
any of the main frustrations of working for American TV. The
production limitations, the small budgets, the short schedules have
never been a problem for me—I even like and respond to them.
What is much harder to deal with is the caution and fear within
the networks and the production companies themselves. This generalized fear is compounded by bureaucratic infighting between the
different personalities involved, whose concern is not the quality
of the individual shows but their positions and ambitions within
the hierarchy. It makes working for TV worse than dealing with
the studio moguls at their most horrendous. At least the latter
have the courage of their own monstrosities. This isn't true of the
sneaky and craven personalities who collect in television and whose
collective front prevents the public having the entertainment it de-
serves. (Though the style may be different, this is just as true for
British as for American TV. Americans self-deprecatingly often
deny this, but it's a fact.)

In our case we were dealing with public records and not challenging any of the major taboos like explicit sex or threatening
politics. This made life comparatively easy, and the subject's confined spaces (the tiny cell-like detector room specifically designed

to block out all associations), its necessity for close-ups and to see the drama in changing facial expressions, made it ideal for television. This kind of thing is something unique to TV, and the captive audience is prepared to relax into a slower time-scheme than would ever be possible in movie houses.

The only concession demanded by the production company and/ or the network was a fabricated subplot to give the television name Stefanie Powers something to justify her involvement. This wasn't, let me add, something that Stefanie, who is a very sweet lady, had demanded—there was simply nothing for her to do. It is one of the many follies of TV companies that they cling to what they consider their "names." If you walked into many TV network offices and offered them, say, Clint Eastwood, Barbra Streisand, Meryl Streep, or Robert Redford, they'd say they were worthless and quote back at you names that many film and theatre people, and I suspect a large proportion of TV viewers, have never heard of. Yet at the same time they are ridiculously petty about their own concerns. In a desperate attempt to give some interest to the concocted subplot, I decided to shoot one scene against the spectacular coastline of rocks in the part of nothern California, near Eureka, where we were working. At least it gave a visual injection to the dead material. Next day an executive who had a house in Connecticut was on the phone, begging me to reshoot the scene. "There are no rocks in Connecticut," he said. "They're driven up to Maine," I countered. "But Mike Nichols [he was a neighbor in Connecticut] will know there are no rocks on the Connecticut coast!"

The heroes of American TV are the actors. The speed of TV production, or perhaps the competitiveness for roles, the hunger to work, has made them into a group who arrive prepared, resourceful, imaginative in a way I've never encountered elsewhere. They know they have a very limited time to achieve what is wanted, and they give themselves absolutely. Once they recognize a certain seriousness of purpose, they'll give up anything to accomplish what you outline. On *Canaan* I started working directly from the transcripts with Kenneth McMillan, who played the lie-detector operator, and Paul Clemens, who played the boy. Then we edited the original for length, and the scenes were shot untouched like that. But the whole cast—which included Brian Dennehy, Conchita Farrell, and Jacqueline Brookes—all had the same attitude. These actors produce a truth and nakedness that you could never find in a similar group of actors in England, where reality is soon lost in technique and laziness. It was the kind of honest but not brilliant work that is very satisfying. Alas, most TV productions involve working methods, subjects, and producers (Bob and Rick were bright exceptions) that militate against achieving their potentials.

There still exist many people who try to make a distinction between TV and cinema. Such a distinction is totally false. Of course TV can present certain events—like sports, a launch-off, or a political speech—at the time when they're happening, and the nature of its audience—a small group in the home—requires certain emphases; but ultimately the basis of film and TV is the same— an image on a screen. Beyond that, the only difference is audience response and tolerance. Movies are going to be made more and more for TV, and should be. In one night *A Death in Canaan* was probably seen by more people than have ever seen many of my most successful and acclaimed movies. That's why it's so important that TV should be freed from the corporations and bureaucracies that have seized it. This is probably one of the most important issues of our times, but it is one that most people are hardly aware of. TV is the future, but the future has at present been captured by the worst ideologists and entrepreneurs of the past.

An opportunity to visit China came up soon after *A Death in Canaan*. China was just beginning to open up, but tours were still allowed only on a very organized basis. You had to go in a group. Our group was part Beverly Hills—record producers and film people, show biz lawyers—and part New York old lefties. The leader was Harold Leventhal, who'd been in China with General Stilwell during the Second World War. Subsequently he became Woody Guthrie's producer. Mrs. Marjorie Guthrie was along too. Harold was perfect and discreet in his role of group leader, but the Beverly Hills contingent—especially the wives—were unhappy—there were constant complaints about plumbing and hotel accommodations, generating the feeling they would have been happier staying back on Rodeo Drive.

Once inside China, the tours were organized like this. There was a group of permanent guides assigned to supervise the whole tour, then in each city or town we visited locals were recuited to supplement the others. Aware of the regimentation ahead, I was already getting prepared to escape as much as I could.

Beijing was our first stop. It was extraordinarily impressive. The Imperial Palace and the Forbidden City are to me the most satisfying and varied architectural complex in the world, amazing in the breadth of their vistas, the richness of their colors, and their amalgam of the theatrical with the precisely domestic, as if everything had been perfectly planned to the needs of the inhabitants. I delighted in the visual rhythms as each gateway and arch leads to a small enclosure, a minutely organized garden off a great open public square, and in the decoration ranging from the most ornate of silk hangings, carvings, and lanterns to the simplicity of a vast terracotta wall.

We were staying, luckily, in one of the hotels just off Tiananmen Square, so it was very easy to go back again by myself at any time of the day. (Early morning always presented the ghost ballet of thousands of elderly citizens doing slow-motion t'ai chi.) Tiananmen Square also contains Mao's tomb, and visits there were governed by the utmost decorum. Groups from all over the world lined up in silence, observing each other and performing as it were to each other in a monumental feat of stage management, so that the presence of each reinforced the tomb's overwhelming effect on the others. And not a joke or a laugh or any raggedness of formation was allowed to spoil the solemnity. Finally we were escorted into the vast air-conditioned funeral hall itself, where the bier of Mao rests behind banks of flowers and in front of great red banners bearing quotations from his works. Silence is insisted on, heads are half-lowered, all the world pays obeisance. No pharaoh had it so good, and Mao had upstaged all the other emperors of his own great people, including the famous Dowager Empress of the nineteenth century, whose peaks and palaces outside the city we visited and in whose favorite tea-house we were given an endless lunch by the film community, who were just beginning to come out of the woodwork after the Cultural Revolution. They all seemed very old and like sleazy B-feature Hollywood producers of the 1940s. "Bottoms up" was their only English as they downed cup after cup of tsing tao, the Chinese liquor.

Beijing was easy to get about in if you persisted, and there were no restrictions as far as I could make out. Taxis were available, and if you got the hotel desk to write out addresses—which, after a bit of resistance, they always would—you could get taken anywhere. I'd brought along with me a lot of pre-Revolution guide books I'd found in second-hand stores (this is a good tip for all serious travelers). They would list temples, monasteries, and ruins that had long been neglected or, out of the way, weren't deemed worthy to be put on the normal tourist route. This took me to odd parts of the city that I wouldn't otherwise have visited. Sometimes buildings had almost collapsed, or were wired off and disintegrating, but often you could find surprising old relics in the middle of new developments. This applied too to all the other towns we visited. Often, by consulting the old books, I would discover that such and such a building existed that even the local guides had forgotten, ignored, or never knew about. Occasionally you'd run into other odd remains of the pre-Revolutionary world—an old, old gardener with his own pagoda in a public park where he was allowed to go on cultivating an almost private bonsai collection which had obviously once been the personal hobby of some mandarin, or a collection in tubs and pools of fancy overbred koi and goldfish with swollen eyes and long silken fins.

What fascinated me most of all—outside Beijing—was the life of the rivers. They are everywhere in China and are still the major routes of transport and commerce, with the incredible variety of craft, from steel tankers and huge barges to broken-down dhows and canoes, reflecting every facet of Chinese life. Wandering along the riverbank in one village, I even found some old whores, like figures out of *Mother Courage*, who drifted from barge to barge. Now hiding, obscene, grinning, but with the grace of survivors, they had outlasted dynasties and revolutions and ideologies and still plied their trade on the barges that were poled incessantly down the gray and yellow streams.

I spent more and more time walking the streets or fields. We used to be transported everywhere by bus, usually being deposited at some commune or factory or public works where the group would be given tea, a pep talk, and a statistical lecture. I would just ask the time when we had to leave and then skip out of the formalities. This started to cause a lot of resentment. "What if we all behaved like you?" the good liberals would say. "The Chinese would have to change their policy," I'd reply. I found an ally in Bob Caputo, a young photographer from *Life*. We would go off together and buy breakfast in the local bakeries and wander the markets. In Nanking we were stuck in some sterile hostelry way out of town, but we discovered that some of the buses had Roman numerals on them and, quickly deciphering them, we could then find our own way on local transport into the city at night. And, as always, even though we couldn't speak a word of each other's language, there were always people who would help and guide us back home.

There was always the fascination of watching barriers being broken down (which is why there should always be travel and contact and more travel). In Canton, Marjorie Guthrie, who was a trained Martha Graham dancer, was asked to give a class to the classical-ballet school. We had become great friends and, as she knew I understood dance, she asked me to go with her. The whole school and company was assembled to meet her. Kicking her shoes off, Marjorie demonstrated some basic Graham steps, then she invited the kids to join in. They all refused. They were terrified of taking off their ballet slippers, terrified of not being on points, and, despite all the encouragement of their teachers, obviously felt that this dignified and gentle old lady was some kind of foreign devil. Then some of the senior members of the professional company kicked off their shoes and started to try out the technique; then, one by one, gradually the whole room joined in. It was a moment of triumph of some kind.

Bob Newman, a friend whom I'd asked to come on the holiday, inadvertently stabbed himself in opening some package in a small town. A tourniquet had been applied, but by the time we arrived by train in Shanghai some hours later, he was still bleeding badly. He had to be rushed to a hospital early in the morning. Conditions were primitive; all the lighting seemed to be by twenty-five-watt bulbs, but the concern of the staff and interns roused in the middle of the night was touching and impressive. Driving back from the hospital at 3:00 A.M. in a taxi through the deserted streets of the commercial district, with the warehouses and original bank buildings all looking as if they came from the middle of Glasgow, was an eerie and strange experience.

Eventually all our permanent guides got together to complain about my lack of cooperation with group programs and my determination to go off everywhere by myself. I was turning it into an

individual tour, they said. They were right. They demanded that
Harold Leventhal reprimand me for such antisocial behavior. Harold did his best, but I explained that I wasn't going to change; I
didn't know when I would be back in China, and I wanted to do
and see as much as I could. On being told this, the interpreters
had another meeting. Encountering a fixed obstacle, they found a
way of coping—dialectically. I was right after all; I had been following Chairman Mao's advice about seeking contact with the people. And, having squared me with the Party line and got their
consciences reconciled, I got nothing but praise thereafter and was
nicknamed "Marco Polo."

To live in southern California is to live near a stretch of the most
dramatic border in the world, along which the richest, most successful society on earth confronts for thousands of miles one of the
poorest. Passage between the USA and Mexico has of course gone
on for centuries, but with the accumulation of wealth to the north
and the steep rise in population to the south of the border the
numbers involved have mounted dramatically. Twenty years ago,
when I was first living in California, one heard very little of the
problem. On the simplest level, all the gardeners were then Japanese; now practically all domestic help is from Mexico or Central
America. And with the population influx have come all kinds of
rackets and exploitation—most of all in the transport of human
beings fighting desperately for a grasp on a livelihood.

Que Viva Mexico, Eisenstein's fragmentary movie, which I'd seen
many times in its different versions, had made me fall in love with
Mexico long before I could ever imagine the possibility of traveling
there. Admittedly Eisenstein's was a much more exotic and aesthetic Mexico than the grit and smog and squalor of much of the
overcrowded Mexico of today, but I've never failed to be enthralled
by this wonderful country and what to me are still its brooding
and mysterious people. Living in Los Angeles, where the papers
were full every day of stories of the cross-border traffic, the Border
Patrol, the smuggling, the tragedies, I became more and more fascinated by the subject. (It's a very keen contrast to the lack of
awareness you find on the East Coast and in the East Coast press,
where the problem is at best academic and addressed through cold
statistics.) I studied everything I could. I tried to find a "hook" on

it. I collected information and paid visits to Tijuana, and made contacts in the Border Patrol. I had lots of notes and ideas and stories but though the subject obsessed me, nothing so far had jelled.

Somehow I got involved in a project to remake Graham Greene's *A Gun for Sale*, which had already been filmed twice—the second version having been directed by James Cagney. By the sale of various film libraries, the rights had passed from Parmount to Universal. Universal was interested enough to agree to finance a screenplay. After discussions with Thom Mount, then the head of development, I met with Deric Washburn, an imaginative but wilful writer who had collaborated on the screenplay of *The Deer Hunter* (to an extent that is disputed by all parties). At first we seemed to be of the same mind. We were to do an updated version of *A Gun for Sale*, using as our reference the Bolles murder, a car blown up by a bomb in Phoenix, Arizona, which had then been very much in the news.

In the course of our work together, Deric mentioned that he had been commissioned to write a screenplay by Universal and by Edgar Bronfman, Jr., the heir-apparent of the Seagram family, who at the time was ambitious to make a career in show business. The project had been designed to star the actor Robert Blake, who, because of the success of a TV series, was under contract to Universal. It was said that the contract with Blake was for life, and, in exchange for mounting increments, he was to have films written for him as well as further TV work. If these were successful, there were elaborate clauses that specified what his future should be; if not, Universal had the right to put him in this and that, down to game-show hosting and even supermarket-promotion appearances, though all the time his remuneration was rising as if his star status prevailed. Deric had already done two drafts of the material but felt it was regressing, and he asked me to read them, especially when he learned of my interest in its subject—the Border Patrol.

I agreed with him: The rewrite had weakened what was potentially an interesting if overblown character and idea. He conveyed my interest to the studio and to Edgar. They asked me to come into the project. There was, however, a big problem which no one would admit to and which took me quite a while to understand. The top authorities seemed to love and believe in Robert Blake (they had installed him in a luxurious bungalow on the lot which in the darkness of its raw wood decor was like the cave of a mountain man—a role that Robert, who in reality was a child of Los Angeles show biz, loved to play to the hilt, even to liberal use of the spittoons strewed around the floor). The film division, under Ned Tanen, did not—they loathed him and had no intention of doing anything for him. The farce played on: New versions of the script were prepared.

Deric and I began to differ. He wanted the mythic and monumental; I believed in the precise and the realistic—the human scale. We parted. Another writer, David Freeman, came in. We worked and worked, but the top office always came back with "No." Finally we arrived at a version which I felt was near enough finished for a final decision to be made, one way or another. Robert claimed to like it. (My own relationship with him had always been friendly, and I didn't have the problems that all the others had with him— their emotions ranged from terror to disgust to ridicule.) However, after assuring us of his loyalty to the project (and God knows we had been loyal enough to him), he telephoned everyone to say that not only did he think the script dreadful and want no part of it, he also thought the film should never be made. In a heated defense to me—swearing "on the heads of my children"—he denied all this. But it was true. To everyone's relief, it was the end of Robert.

I immediately took the script to Jack Nicholson. He read it immediately and agreed to do it. We'd always wanted to work together, and perhaps he felt unconsciously some residual guilt for his abortive encouragement of *The Bodyguard*. I went back to Ned Tanen. He was weary of the project until he heard the magic name; then the script, which a few days ago had been the worst ever, became "great" in an instant. The budget, which had always been modest for Robert, instantaneously tripled and finally increased prodigiously.

Some of the old studios were cost-conscious in the worst way, cutting where it harmed the quality of the product. Universal has gone the other way. Charging an enormous overhead (25 percent of the budget), its complacent bureaucrats are interested only in protecting themselves. Its equipment is outmoded and won't be used by any competent technician, so that when outsiders insist on bringing in their own equipment, to the squeals of the establishment, you're paying probably twice for everything. Its workshops, whether they're building scenery, casting plasterwork, or fabricating a piece of breakaway glass, are totally non-competitive in their prices but the budget is stuck with them. If the work is botched or unsatisfactory, you have no recourse—you are charged anyway. And if you're basically maverick-minded, as we were, it's hard not to get the paranoid feeling that the home base wants to foul you up anyway. Simply, they haven't learned the lessons. The first is that if the directors and producers aren't trusted to be responsible themselves, then they'll behave irresponsibly because there's no pressure not to. Second, they're still stuck with the dinosaurian concept of a studio, when years ago companies like United Artists learned to discard all the real estate and to put the emphasis of moviemaking where it belongs—on each individual film with its unique problems. Admittedly Universal had tried to protect its flanks with its Disneyland-type studio tours, its amphitheatre, and its hotel. But it could still have done all that and just kept its stage settings, without its vast bureaucracy. It's rather like the situation in the Soviet Union and needs the same kind of hard rethinking.

Some of the propositions that Universal personnel made in the early preparation of *The Border* were mind-boggling. They included building whole shantytowns and cathedrals. The cost would have been in the millions of dollars. It would easily have been approved. When we proposed simpler and to me much more effective solutions, for a fifth of the cost, all the house experts fought us. For the earthquake at the beginning of the film, I remembered my trip to Antigua with Jeremy and described how easy it would be to rig things to create the effect on location. We were told it was impossible—there were no paved roads in Guatemala. In the end the whole opening sequence cost about $350,000 instead of the studio's $1,500,000, and it would have cost even less if we hadn't had to transport and carry some useless executives who had to supervise us poor amateurs.

The Border got off to a rocky start as an official actors' strike began two weeks after we began shooting in El Paso in July 1980. We'd all been aware of the risk before we started but until the very day the strike happened everyone had believed that some settlement would be reached. The period of the strike was a very unsettling limbo. It wasn't like a postponement. It wasn't a period when you could work on aspects of the production or script (at least I found

I couldn't), because every day there was new speculation and pro-jections about when we could go to work again. It lasted about eleven weeks. In the end it cost us our talented director of photog-raphy, Vilmos Zsigmond. Vilmos is an infuriating mixture of re-sourceful artist, roguish Hungarian gypsy, and demanding prima donna, but at least he was with us long enough to establish the basic style of the movie and he came back again when we reshot the ending. We went from a parched desert, with temperature readings in the hundreds and a crew living on salt, tomatoes, and soft drinks, to gray skies, green scrub, and morning temperatures often below freezing. And Natasha, who'd come out to work as a runner—arriving in a British picture hat and fitted skirts and meta-morphosing into jeans and Texas workshirts as she instructed extras to arrive in their most beaten-down clothes—had to return to school before we began again.

Besides Jack, the cast included Valerie Perrine, Harvey Keitel, the impeccable Warren Oates (whose last but one movie this was to be), and an unknown Mexican actress, Elpidia Carrillo, whom I'd found in Mexico City after an exhaustive search among Chicana or Latina (the preferred term was changing all the time) actresses. Walon Green, who was to become a great friend, came in to help with rewrites and commuted throughout the shooting, and with his exact ear he contributed a lot to the texture of many scenes.

Relationships among the cast were checkered, however, and they all tended to work on different wavelenths. Valerie is a fine actress but a difficult and needlessly bitchy and offensive woman to most of the people working around her. She was always fine with me and skillful and responsive in rehearsal, but she isolated herself from the company, and her relationship with Jack, who'd started out with great enthusiasm for her, deteriorated—which was not totally Valerie's fault, as Jack's own entourage disliked Valerie and whipped him up against her so that in the end he behaved callously toward her. Nevertheless, Valerie does everything she can to let the least attractive sides of her personality swamp her talent. Harvey is an obsessive worrier—some would say a caricature Method actor—but he's endearing and effective because he is so transpar-ently honest in his work. He's the kind of actor who's only good in take ten (or thinks he's only good in take ten and next day is still worrying about yesterday's take ten). He needs reassurance like a baby needs a bottle. He would want more and more rehearsals, yet when we rehearsed he would never go all-out in case he peaked too soon and some magic essence, never to be recovered, was lost forever.

Working with Jack was totally different from what I had imagined as a longtime friend and fan. I had expected, I suppose, that our collaboration would be much closer, his involvement much more complete—more on the lines of many of the theatre stars I worked with. I had expected more challenge, more dialectic, more dis-agreement. What I got was a different kind of total star: Someone who once he arrived on the set was always meticulously prepared, who liked to be told where to be and what to do, and who could instantly deliver the goods required. In terms of stating or playing a scene, Jack didn't want to experiment or to try different ideas, but whatever I asked he would do—and with great authority. He was also wonderfully flexible on each take. He would do one thing, and for the next take I'd ask him to stress some other value, and again he would understand and deliver another color or nuance instantly. Where he was marvelously helpful and more collaborative in the way I imagined was on details of physical action and staging (which I've never been particularly good at). His experience and skill in making this side of things work is extraordinary, and it was fascinating for me to see as great a master with the revolver and the shoot-out as Olivier was with a sword, a cloak, and a crown.

Our first rehearsal was also fascinating. I was overchoreographing a group scene—thinking in terms more of image than of reality. Jack was uneasy and muttered to me, "More Kazan and less Josh Logan." I knew exactly what he meant and stuck by it afterward. All our communication was like this—at its most successful when at its most fragmentary and oblique. Scenes that required the most difficult and delicate emotional shading were to me the most sat-isfying to work on with Jack, because once I probed him there was no color I couldn't get him to produce. On the other hand, I have always felt making a movie to be the kind of collaborative process where everyone has to give everything critically and constructively, and often I felt Jack could have contributed more to the whole.

The other aspect of Jack I could never understand was his de-termination to provoke me to rage and anger—to test how far he could go. He used to say to others that he fed on anger and wanted to find my break-point. But my own temperament is too violent to have let that breach ever happen; I would probably have split the movie apart and finished our relationship forever, so I determined that it was a battle Jack could never win.

Once I'd edited the movie I was still dissatisfied with it. After a lot of thought I proposed a new ending. Ned Tanen was very supportive of this and let us go back to reshoot. I liked and still like the new ending better, but who's to say if I'm right? *The Border* was never a tidy movie. It's a kind of documentary fresco of an enormous subject of which we touched on a lot of different aspects, and maybe not complete. Perhaps the border is just too big and too living a situation to be contained in the form of any story. I am very proud to have been able to wrestle with it, and grateful to Jack for making it happen.

24

The Hotel New Hampshire

The dichotomy between making movies and getting the money to make them has never been as evident for me as on *The Hotel New Hampshire*. I had loved John Irving's work from the first time I read him. He seems to me one of the most original and towering of contemporary writers. He is a born storyteller in the tradition of Fielding and Dickens, with, like them, an ability to see his characters physically from the outside (he needs a contemporary "Phiz") as well as depicting their feelings and passions from within.

At a time when the fashion of contemporary novelists is for the stream of consciousness and internal monologue, John stands out against the general trend and so arouses critical resentment and even vilification. He is accused of being bizarre, sensational, and oversentimental. The "bizarre" charge has always seemed to me, well, bizarre. The lives of my family and friends; families—the lives reflected in every day's newspaper—leave John's wildest fancies limping behind. Life goes further than art, every day—as Cleopatra says of Anthony, it's "nature's piece 'gainst fancy, condemning shadows quite." True sentiment and sentimentality are always, as in Dickens, close sisters, and what belongs to one and what to the other is largely a personal distinction. Again, it takes courage today not to fight sentiment. I predict that John's courage and the range of his universe will still be durable when many of his more intellectually acclaimed rivals will have dwindled away.

My response to John's work was much more as an admirer and reader than as a filmmaker hungry for material. Some of his early books could be made into films, but I had never thought for instance of *The World According to Garp* as a movie (until, of course, it had been made). With *The Hotel New Hampshire* it was the opposite. It sprang off the pages to me. I could visualize and identify with all the characters. Its magical juxtaposition of the foreign and the familiar throbbed with life. I didn't, however, imagine that it would easily come my way. I knew the rights would be costly and, although John Irving was no easy sell in the world of the studios, there would be a lot of proposals and offers. I think I found out the asking price—which was high—and for the moment I waited. I was anyway dickering with other projects.

On cue entered another character from the past, a none-too-successful theatrical producer, Norman Twain. He had been involved in the Broadway presentation of John Osborne and Anthony Creighton's *Epitaph for George Dillon*, in the increasingly shameful tour of my *Hamlet*, and in a production of *As You Like It* I had done at Long Beach in 1979. Norman was something of a bus-and-truck version of Harry Salzman. He'd spent his life hustling, mainly in the theatre (for which he had a genuine passion), without ever making too much of himself. There were many horror stories about Norman from most people who'd been involved with him at one time or another. He'd been banned from the producers' association. There were accusations of actors being unpaid and "betrayed." He was unscrupulous both in financial dealings and with artistic standards.

For a long time I'd defended Norman from his many detractors, aware of how difficult it is to promote any live theatre and believing that real enthusiasm often outweighs propriety, in my book at least. Of course Norman lived in his fantasies, and he bent the truth to realize them, but that's part of the necessary infectiousness of the hustler. He had the vigor and challenge of a mad horse that you'd set off charging while knowing you'd have trouble keeping the reins. So over the years I'd thought of Norman as a friend, and I'd often been pleased to encounter him in different places and had had good times with him. He was commuting at this time between New York and LA, always full of some new enterprise. He called in for a drink, and over it I happened to rave about *The Hotel New Hampshire*, which I'd just finished reading.

A few weeks later I got a wild phone call. By coincidence, Norman had run into John Irving at his agent's office and had told him of my enthusiasm. John was interested. I flew to New York and met with John. We clicked immediately. John approved of my making the film, and we started to have serious discussions with his agent about the rights. Norman got, or rather was, involved in all this because of his initial luck in bringing the two of us together. Neil and I were anxious about his participation, knowing his past behavior, and knowing that the tricks that might pass in some hanging-on-by-the-teeth theatrical operation were totally unacceptable in the larger world of movies. Not, of course, that there isn't just as much (in fact much more) finagling and impropriety involved in movies, but that was something that we had from the beginning scrupulously kept Woodfall out of: Though it sounds holier-than-thou, we had an impeccable record in our dealings and weren't about to change. Eventually we worked out a deal—not without a few stormy clashes with Norman on the negotiations. Try as we might to explain to him the necessity of absolutely open dealing, hard reality in thinking, and complete probity, these weren't in the nature of the beast and he was always in danger of being lured into the traps of his own pipe dreams.

We still, of course, had no money to make the film and we were holding the rights on loan from an old associate of Neil's. Norman suddenly introduced two new characters. One of them was a pizza king from Kansas; the other, his associate, was a so-called lawyer. Mr. Pizza Parlor—Gene Bicknell—had acting aspirations (although he was long past the age when he could have fulfilled them, even if he had talent) and had financed two or three films in which he played the principal role. These were done on quite a scale, so we had every reason to believe that money was about. According to Norman and to the "lawyer," Gene wanted seriously to get into film production in the midst of his other business activities (which included the recent acquisition of a baseball team). The "lawyer" claimed that he too had independent resources of several million from a family trust fund. They proposed we form a company to produce the film. It was agreed that Gene would have no other role in the project beyond being one of the producers and that they would learn the business from our expertise. (The "lawyer" also claimed that he had worked for Twentieth Century-Fox and was therefore one ahead of Gene in terms of knowledge.) They guaranteed that if we couldn't find the budget (which was then I think about twelve million dollars) through normal sources, they (or specifically Gene) would raise the money from the many private investors they had. We were to form a company. We called it the Group of Five (Group Five Productions). As a token of their seriousness, Gene and the "lawyer" agreed to advance the money we had paid for the rights (it was about two hundred thousand dollars) and to advance an additional sum for scouting trips and expenses. They did. They would often advance additional sums as the production required it, to be returned when the final financing was in place. An attorney was hired and agreements were drawn up. So far everything seemed to be completely above board, and we had no reason to distrust them—although Norman's presence in the middle, trying to manipulate everyone, and being manipulated himself, made us uneasy.

Neil and I went about preparing in the normal way. I had written a script with John's advice and participation. (At the very outset the material seemed so rich that I'd had the idea of doing two films, which could be made back-to-back and shown back-to-back, though the impracticalities of this and the lack of solid artistic logic soon overruled whatever novelty that idea had.) We started casting, and we began to approach technicians. We visited New Hampshire and Maine, saw the original hotel that John had used as a reference, and worked out a whole production plan for doing the movie on the original location. We began to think of how we were going to do the scenes in Vienna. Neil and I knew the city quite well, but on revisiting it we found that the Vienna of John's earlier experience had been obliterated in a face-lift. Everywhere had been cleaned up and "boutiqued." The area where he'd lived was now a pedestrian zone where smart shops alternated with period restoration, and the whores and whorehouses had gone to the suburbs (though we did find them there). We went on to Budapest, thinking that we might find a better (and cheaper) approximation to old Vienna there. But once again the oppression of an Iron Curtain country overwhelmed me. There was a bitter contrast between the business and Party types who were hustling for hard currency and wooed and dined us and the idealism of the technicians who would have loved to work on the film but who had no control over their lives. Physically we could have created a very good illusion there (if an overgrim one, because the destruction and bullet marks of the 1956 revolution are still everywhere), but, like many deals which Iron Curtain countries offer, it seemed that the deal was more advantageous on the surface than the organization (with its regulation and lack of flexibility) could really live up to. So we rejected it.

We were in negotiations with a series of actors—although our wires were often crossed by Norman's meddling to the point at which I'd decided it was impossible to continue with him as a working producer on a day-to-day basis. Meanwhile it was becoming clearer that *The Hotel New Hampshire* was not going to be an easy sell to the studios, though we were constantly reassured about our backup financing. No further funds for the mounting costs were emerging, however, and as far as we could tell no one was approaching the so-called private investors. I had already talked to Orion Pictures (the original United Artists), and my old friend and mentor Arthur Krim had indicated that Orion would be prepared to put up two thirds of the budget in return for the North American rights. The "lawyer" had come along on this particular trip, and on meeting Arthur Krim (one of the most distinguished and long-lived studio heads) had behaved with such familiarity and bad manners (he kept calling Arthur "Art") that it was embarrassing. On our return together to Los Angeles, the plane had been overbooked. Our seats were confirmed but the airline was offering virtually free tickets to anyone who would be prepared to give up his place and take a later reservation. The "lawyer," who was suffering from some kind of stomach upset, jumped at the offer and stayed behind. It didn't seem quite the action of a self-proclaimed millionaire.

Similar omens piled up. The "lawyer" rushed to the Cannes Festival, where he was soliciting the last reliable sources of finance. Even then his personal contacts were obviously on the least effective level. God knows what information he'd been feeding his partner during this time. On his return, a showdown was precipitated. Unbeknownst to Neil and me, the attorney who'd been appointed representative to the Group of Five had been instructed to draw up some company document that gave control of the rights and the whole project to Gene Bicknell. When challenged, the attorney nervously began to withdraw. The "lawyer" then demanded we transfer the rights to Bicknell. The Group of Five collapsed.

The "lawyer" made a final appearance at my house, bringing along some strong-arm goon who tried to stare me down. There had been some unexplained expenses for him in the company's joint account and he wanted to recover the checkbook from our secretary, Sandy Maltz, obviously to suppress them. I ordered him and his sidekick out of the house. They finally retreated through my office, overturning the furniture and my desk and vandalizing it in a feeble kind of way. We followed them out, and the goon made a number of physical threats—breaking my legs, throwing me down the hill, etc. That was the last I saw of them.

I wrote to Bicknell, who was still obviously under the "lawyer's" spell, as was Norman in some muddled kind of way. Later the real facts emerged. It was all a scam. The "lawyer" had enticed the naive Bicknell into believing that his relatively small original investment would enable him, without further exposure, to gain possession of a twelve-million-dollar film. (I believe a similar scam had been proposed over the acquisition of the baseball team.) Subsequently it also emerged that the "lawyer" had never been a member of the California bar, as he had claimed. Bicknell's eyes were opened, eventually. We repaid him his original advance, and he admitted that he had been conned by the "lawyer" as we had—although, it must be said, he had obviously gone along with the scam himself. Norman, as far as I know, persisted in thinking that millions of Kansas dollars would have been poured into the project but for my intransigence, and his only concern was to try to blackmail us for as much as he could (now that our money people's lawyers were understandably anxious about ownership of the rights) to compensate for his wounded *amour propre*.

Financially we were back to square one—minus. The project had already been announced as funded, and once money is known to have disappeared it becomes doubly difficult within the industry to revive something—there is an atmosphere of threat over it. We still had Orion's offer—Arthur Krim's word, once given, is always honored—and now we had a deal with Jodie Foster to play Franny and commitments to many crew members. We attacked the problem

in two ways: one by trying to reduce the budget, and the other by
seeking foreign financing. The first proved easier. On scouting trips
we'd considered Canada, especially Quebec province, which adjoins
New Hampshire. Quebec had a lot of other advantages besides
being considerably cheaper than the USA, and it was possible to
bring in technicians from wherever without union restrictions. I
had already got commitments from David Watkin for camera, and
from Bob Lambert and Bill Scott, editor and assistant from *The
Border*, and my dear friend Jocelyn Herbert fell in love with the
script and agreed to design a film again. The old part of Montreal
was a good base on which to recreate the Vienna of John's time
there, and by a piece of absolute luck I'd found, far up along the
St. Lawrence, an old hotel built early in the nineteenth century
which in its bright red, green, and white pop colors seemed perfectly to embody the spirit of the book. By deciding to shoot there,
we were eventually able to reduce the budget by half.

I'd hoped that Orion would now fund everything, because for
less than what it had originally agreed to spend it could now have
the rights for the whole world. But there was strong opposition to
the project within the company, and it would only stick to the
original offer of two thirds of the budget whatever it was. So we
had a shortfall of about $2 million to find somehow.

The only possibility seemed to be to sell off foreign territories.
We'd never financed a film in this way before, and it was a nightmare. What happens in this process is that the selling company
auctions off the local distribution rights for a guaranteed sum, part
of which is an advance, most of it coming later. Initially the scheme
looked fine, as the worldwide rights predictions exceeded easily the
necessary sum. But it's not as simple as that. In order to have the
money available for production, you have to discount the money
with a bank. The banks and brokers who arrange this all take a
cut, thus further reducing what's available. The territories themselves divide into hard and soft currencies, the latter being defined
roughly as those that are politically and economically unstable, so
that any advances promised are either useless or minimal as far as
the discounting banks are concerned. Add to that that deals are
reneged on and currencies fluctuate, then stir in the swarms of
lawyers that proliferate from everywhere, and the soup gets thinner

and thinner. We reckoned on *Hotel* that lawyers' and brokers' fees were more than double the cost of the cast. It was a far cry from when Woodfall began.

As the gap between expectations and reality widened, and as there was no flexibility from Orion, we had to scramble to plug the shortfall with private money—my own and that of various investors. This led to even more negotiations. Often promises were made, sometimes well-intentioned, sometimes not, but were unfulfilled. Meanwhile, production dates were getting closer and closer. Neil and I spent most of our days and nights (because of the time differences) telephoning London, New York, and Australia. Key figures would disappear inexplicably. Contracts would be drafted, then their wording was disputed. It was becoming clear that except for Arthur Krim, Orion wanted out of the picture. The financing collapsed.

I took the redeye to New York and, as first light was breaking, somehow evolved a formula which, if it could be made to work, would satisfy the original agreements. My solution was distorted in presentation and Orion now felt I was too tired and overwhelmed by the business deals to be fresh enough to direct, but Arthur Krim stuck to his word. In Montreal, a whole crew was working—building and converting sets and making costumes. The cast was due to arrive within days for rehearsals. The all-night telephoning went on. Jocelyn, who was as always rock supportive, used to keep vigils with us. Again and again everything broke down or wasn't consummated. Anxiety was rife among the crew. We were behind in salaries. We didn't want them to lose their jobs if we folded, but in order to sustain morale we had to keep up a front of optimism that it would all work out, sick as we were inside. The last days came. By then we didn't have enough money left in the account to buy air tickets back from Montreal. Then, on the very last day, the final cornerstone was slowly eased into place and we knew we could go on.

The relief gave us absolute release. The tension and the tiredness disappeared overnight, and the lovefest began. Because that's what *The Hotel New Hampshire* was. It started with Jodie Foster—so bright, so gifted, and so amazingly sane after all that had been unloaded on her. I remember the first time she came to see me at the Algonquin. It was at the time of the Hinckley trial, and more or less nude pictures of her from *Taxi Driver* were plastered all over the New York papers. She was working as an assistant at *Esquire*, and she walked along the streets to meet me. I asked her if she wasn't alarmed by all that was going on. She told me that at first she'd been traumatized by the experience, but then she'd thought, "I wasn't responsible anyway for what happened, and then I decided if I went on letting it get to me I'd be nuts for life. I decided I just had to live a life as normal as if nothing had happened, to survive." But to do that required great endurance, and often during the preparation period, when she'd come up to New York to have dinner and talk with me, I'd walk her back to Grand Central for the last train home and as she walked away from me—alone and vulnerable—I'd marvel at her calm, knowing that there could be a crazy with a gun behind any pillar. Nastassja Kinski, the finest and most joyous of spirits, was a wonderful alchemist too. But so were all the family—Rob Lowe, Jennie Dundas, Beau Bridges, Paul McCrane, Wilford Brimley, and Lisa Banes.

Before shooting, we rehearsed for a week. I feel very ambivalent about the use of rehearsals for filming. What working on film offers actors is the opportunity to use their first impulses freely, to respond to each other, the situation, the circumstances of shooting, the weather—in contrast to theatre rehearsals, where you consider, build slowly, go forward and back, regurgitate, until some architecture emerges that is defined and strong enough to be capable of repetition. But sometimes rehearsals can be valuable for films— when the basic material has theatrical antecedents, is strongly rooted in dialogue, or deals, as here, with longtime relationships, which need to be clear in everyone's mind. During rehearsals we improvised the whole family background and played at family games and discussions. Making the group relate and expose themselves to each other as they would have done in a family situation was, I think, invaluable in creating a familiarity that would have been less easy if it had had to work immediately under the strain of shooting. Except—and it was equivalent—for *A Taste of Honey*, I've never directed a film with a whole cast who worked so spontaneously together.

The group feeling was strengthened by the reduced circumstances of the production. There were no trailers or limousines, and we were all living more or less in the same hotel. Some of the kids talked of it as being like summer camp or a slumber party—except that there wasn't much slumber. And when we got to the final locations of the hotel, we were all subject to the same black flies. Though smaller than gnats, these are the most irritating and painful insect phenomena I've ever experienced. When they sting, a stream of blood can spurt out like a small fountain on someone's cheek in the middle of a take. Or they can bite so deep that the area attacked becomes infected for weeks. The art department was particularly vulnerable: spraying, creams, nets, pills—nothing much worked for them. As the old wooden hotel was only open during the black-fly season—the rest of the year, with the St. Lawrence being frozen, it was much too cold and inaccessible—I could never understand how it could have survived its 150 or so years. But—apart from the flies—the rough hills and forests, the river with its tidal estuary and steep sand dunes plunging down hundreds of feet so that you could become a human toboggan, and the long summer nights were magical. It was my favorite location and favorite cast ever.

The end of shooting, in Sepember 1983, brought another unresolved problem: the music. How and when I decide on music varies as widely as does the number of people I see or don't see for casting. (In the case of *Hotel*, Jodie was my instantaneous choice for Franny as soon as I met her, whereas I saw hundreds of boys and tested several before I found an ideal John in Rob Lowe.) Sometimes I know who I want before I go into the movie—as, for example, I did with Ry Cooder for *The Border*. Afterward we met and worked splendidly together. On *Laughter in the Dark*—another example of, to me, an incredibly positive use of music—the idea of using Monteverdi's *L'Incoronazione di Poppea* came from Raymond Leppard, with whom I'd worked in the theatre. For *Hotel* I was vaguely thinking of using some pop composer, and several groups were interested. We talked. In one case songs were even written. But something wasn't quite working for me with any of the possibilities.

While we were shooting one of the climactic scenes in the movie, where John's father takes him to the bar of his dreams and then breaks down and confesses his failures to his son, we hired a local harpist to provide some kind of atmosphere. On the day, I asked her what she could play. She suggested three pieces, none of which

I thought really suitable. Then she said she probably could get through the barcarole from *The Tales of Hoffman*. It was exactly right in feeling, so I told her to play that. Ever since, it had haunted me in connection with the movie. I began to think more and more about Offenbach. His work embodied a parallel to the comic and serious that's quintessentially John Irving. I began to research and play some of Offenbach's less well-known pieces and experimented with playing passages alongside cut parts of the movie. The two seemed to mesh together perfectly. I abandoned all my earlier ideas and plumped for Offenbach. Raymond Leppard then came in and reorchestrated and arranged the selections, and to me they worked amazingly. John kept on saying, "Make it less real, more fairy-tale," and the barcarole itself was to me the dream fantasy of the hotel, and the dreams and aspirations of the characters of his wonderful family.

The film was not a success with the American critics—they tore it apart as if it was something obscene and filthy. Much of the abuse was directed toward John, whose very success—the fact that his writing works popularly—seemed to them to be the ultimate insult. This kind of outright hatred is always surprising, but it's something that with different authors—like John Osborne and Bertolt Brecht—I've experienced over and again. Finally, of course, critics end up in the trash cans with yesterday's newspapers, however momentarily wounding they may be. Curiously enough, the notices were the most perceptive and the warmest in England, where I least expect any kind of friendly treatment and where the critics are my old enemies. Perhaps this was because John Irving isn't dancing on their sacred ground. I've never figured out what critics must feel when they've killed something commercially or publicly. Have they never thought that the only time critics are remembered—whether it's Hazlitt on Kean, Bernard Shaw on Wagner, or Roger Fry on Cézanne—is when they have been enthusiasts, not when they've slated? As Flaubert said, "Criticism occupies the lowest rung on the hierarchy of literature as regards form, almost always, and as regards moral worth, incontestably."

Like all my other movies, *The Hotel New Hampshire* is dead for me now. Once I've made a movie, it's over—it's flown the nest. People often ask me (as they do all directors), "Which is your favorite movie?" It's a question impossible to answer. You've assessed the movie's achievements and its failures and flaws during its making. There's nothing more to be said or done about them afterward. Looking back would be futile. A critical attitude belongs essentially to the outsider, to the one who hasn't participated. Often I think that when the world asks you to comment on your own work it's asking you to kneel down and make your *mea culpa* so that the confessor can then slip home smug in his superiority. All a creator can feel about the past, I think, is a more or less generalized affection. And purely on that level I've never loved any movie more than *The Hotel New Hampshire*.

25

Coda

On all the many trips I've embarked on, I've never taken photos. I never wanted to be encumbered with the apparatus, and I wanted to snap everything in memory. Perhaps it's a pity, though I don't think so. But sometimes I happen on a photo someone else took that records one of those moments, and I get an odd, sharp, sometimes exciting sensation—not as unpleasant as the mild electric jolt you get from a defective lead to a coffeepot, but similar. Was that me? Was I really like that? Is that how and where "it" was? In my head, these places, those times, are already sunk and overlaid by new layers of memory, as Lillian Hellman described in *Pentimento*, or disappearing beneath the sediment and embellishments of time. Why, then, am I now trying to project my mental snapshots onto the wall? This seems to me a very legitimate question for any autobiographer to ask himself. Is it to erect a monument, the shards and pebbles of one individual existence piled on the shore of time; or a publicist's act of self-glorification; or to attempt a late self-understanding similar—and probably as self-indulgent—to entering analysis, a probe into the interior where all the other journeys have been external; or to provide amusement for a while in the way that old photo albums can fill some awkward moment in a social visit between unequals?

It's certainly not to attempt to instruct, to pass on received knowledge or experienced wisdom. As you grow older, you realize how little you know that's worth knowing. "Travel for enjoyment,/Follow your own nose," Auden wrote. Nigel Dennis once told me that Auden had said to him, "All problems are technical." This seemed meaningless to me at first, then Nigel explained. If you think of all the problems, no matter how emotional or passionate or engulfing they are, as technical problems to be solved, then at least there's hope you might crack them. It's a bit fancy, and none too memorable, but not bad. Best of all is Auden's birthday wish, which I've quoted many times and still seems to me the best twenty-first birthday wish you can make for anyone:

> So I wish you first a
> Sense of theatre; only
> Those who love illusion
> And know it will go far:
> Otherwise we spend our
> Lives in a confusion
> Of what we say and do with
> Who we really are.

I always thought Auden should have underlined "And know it," but it would have spoiled the rhythm.

What, then, have I learned about myself—what discernible patterns are there in these fifty-seven years of existence? A constant drift to America, and all things American—to the promised land where you can be accepted but never enter without that high school education and all that led up to it? But that I knew already. Perhaps I've a clearer perception of myself as traveler—"for my purpose holds/To sail beyond the sunset, and the baths/Of all the western stars, until I die." That certainly. And maybe that is the only pattern; that I have gone on to new places and undertakings, each different from those already familiar to me. ("Oh, where is that sense of unifying style?" the critic would say, trying to lasso one out as a cowboy does a steer in a corral.) Why? Out of a sense of dissatisfaction, of restlessness, of unfulfilment? "No," I must answer, because each time I've pushed off it has not been from the necessity or wish to get away but because the newer world held the promise of a positive and glowing thing which I wanted to experience or create.

I remember recently reading some book which listed the names of things that have disappeared this century which the author was either fond of or remembered precisely. Anyone who has lived any time at all can make such a list, but what struck me was not how I lamented the old but how much I welcomed the new, even if I was often baffled by the skills necessary to make use of the newest inventions.

Before starting to write this, I glanced again at books by some of the theatrical heroes I most admired, like Tyrone Guthrie and Peter Brook. Even when these books were written recently, the problems, the controversies, the arguments—for or against the proscenium stage, the theatre of illusion, the theatre of representation, the theatre of myth, the theatre of cruelty, etc.—all seemed to be about battles long ago, wars and revolutions won, barriers already broken. We have the luck to be living in an exceptionally free time when all kinds of ways of hearing, doing, and seeing coexist and are available to be used. And none of them seems inherently better than the others.

During the early years of the century, form was broken and dissolved by giants like Joyce, Picasso, Pound, and Schoenberg, and even deep down with an unseen hand by blues and jazz and the art of the silent screen. This was a time when the basic intellectual steps were taken, the big reevaluations of perception. The 1920s and 1930s were a kind of period of suspension. The bulldozers had done their work subterraneanly and, apart from odd outcroppings, the surface looked more or less placidly unchanged. It was only when the world had recovered from the exhaustion and depletion of the Second World War that everyone could see that the whole landscape had fundamentally and universally changed—as was confirmed most significantly by the advent of rock and roll and of TV advertising. (I say TV advertising because it is a superficial version of what the *nouvelle vague* film critics were calling for, which was the original freedom of the silent movies that had slept for a while during the introduction of sound and the doldrums of the studio system.)

Of course this is not to say that the new products were or are necessarily any better than the old. The bottles have still to be filled each season with fresh and original life, but now the shelves of every supermarket have bottles, barrels, and containers in a variety that was previously available only in the back rooms of some sheltered specialized store, if at all. And the same is true politically, sexually, morally. This is not to condone the abuses of the system, not to ignore the huge wave of neo-conformism which is always either building up offshore or crashing on to the beachheads already won: It is merely to record where I'm at, or believe I'm at, in this one moment of history. For, as Carson McCullers said, "This minute is passing. And it will never come again."

Snapshots of my three daughters look directly at me from a bulletin-board as I'm writing. As each of their gazes makes contact, they seem to be asking the one question—what's ahead? In the theatre, just as there's a well-known superstition that you can never quote or mention "the Scottish play"—*Macbeth*—without bringing bad luck, there's also a superstition that you should never say the last word or the last couplet of a Restoration play until the first night. I'm finding this as hard to finish as to get to that last word. I can say to Natasha and Joely and Katharine that I love them very much, but I sense they want more. So I think of what I will say to myself for the future, which is exactly the same as what I want to say to them. There's a story of a rehearsal (wonderfully enough, at the Royal Court). An actor was having great difficulty performing a scene. "I can't do it," he moaned. "I'm failing, I'm failing." The play was by Sam Beckett. He was watching. Quietly he said, "That's all right. Go on failing. Go on. Only next time try to fail better."

Tony Richardson's Theatre and Film Work

For stage work, all theatres are in London unless otherwise stated, and pre-London or pre-Broadway tours are generally omitted. For films, the date cited is the release date in the film's country of origin. Timings may vary with different cuts. An asterisk after "CAST:" denotes a selective cast list.

PROFESSIONAL STAGE WORK

The Changeling

AUTHORS:	Thomas Middleton and William Rowley
DIRECTOR:	Tony Richardson
OPENED:	Wyndham's Theatre, 16 May 1954
CAST:*	Leo Ciceri *(Alonzo de Piracquo)*, Russell Enoch *(Alsemero)*, Martin Benson *(De Flores)*, Lore Ross *(Beatrice-Joanna)*, Diane Cilento *(Diaphanta)*, Heather Stannard *(Isabella)*

The Country Wife

AUTHOR:	William Wycherley
DIRECTORS:	Tony Richardson and William Gaskill
DESIGNER:	Clare Jeffery
OPENED:	Theatre Royal, Stratford East, 28 June 1955
CAST:	Nigel Davenport *(Horner)*, William Gaskill *(Quack)*, Thomas Foulkes *(Sir Jasper Fidget)*, Margaret Vines *(Lady Fidget)*, Marriott

327

Longman *(Mrs. Dainty Fidget)*, Jon Rollason *(Harcourt)*, Colin Jeavons *(Sparkish)*, Julian Somers *(Pinchwife)*, Barbara Fishwick *(Mrs. Pinchwife)*, Denyse de Mauny *(Alithea)*, Fanny Carby *(Mrs. Squeamish)*, Margherita Parry *(Lucy)*

Mr. Kettle and Mrs. Moon

AUTHOR: J. B. Priestley

DIRECTORS: Tony Richardson and J. B. Priestley

OPENED: Duchess Theatre, 1 September 1955

CAST: Phyllis Morris *(Mrs. Twigg)*, Clive Morton *(George Kettle)*, Wendy Craig *(Monica Twigg)*, Julian Somers *(Alderman Hardacre)*, Richard Warner *(Superintendent Street)*, Frances Rowe *(Delia Moon)*, Raymond Francis *(Henry Moon)*, Beckett Bould *(Clinton)*, John Moffatt *(Dr. Grenock)*

Look Back in Anger

AUTHOR: John Osborne

DIRECTOR: Tony Richardson

DESIGNER: Alan Tagg

MUSIC: Thomas Eastwood

OPENED: Royal Court Theatre, 8 May 1956

CAST: Kenneth Haigh *(Jimmy Porter)*, Alan Bates *(Cliff Lewis)*, Mary Ure *(Alison Porter)*, Helena Hughes *(Helena Charles)*, John Welsh *(Colonel Redfern)*

REVIVED: Lyric Theatre, Hammersmith, 5 November 1956, with Richard Pasco *(Jimmy Porter)*, Alan Bates *(Cliff Lewis)*, Doreen Aris *(Alison Porter)*, Vivienne Drummond *(Helena Charles)*, and Kenneth Edwards *(Colonel Redfern)*; Royal Court Theatre, 11 March 1957, with the same cast except Heather Sears *(Alison Porter)* and Deering Wells *(Colonel Redfern)*

TRANSFERRED: Lyceum Theatre, New York, 1 October 1957, with costumes by Motley and with Kenneth Haigh *(Jimmy Porter)*, Alan Bates *(Cliff Lewis)*, Mary Ure *(Alison Porter)*, Vivienne Drummond *(Helena Charles)*, and Jack Livesey *(Colonel Redfern)*

Cards of Identity

AUTHOR: Nigel Dennis
DIRECTOR: Tony Richardson
DESIGNER: Alan Tagg
COSTUMES: Motley
MUSIC: Thomas Eastwood
OPENED: Royal Court Theatre, 26 June 1956
CAST: Kenneth Haigh *(Beaufort)*, Agnes Lauchlan *(Mrs. Paradise)*, Michael Gwynn *(Captain Mallett)*, Nigel Davenport *(Jellicoe)*, Joan Greenwood *(Mrs. Mallett)*, Peter Duguid *(Dr. Towzer)*, Alan Bates *(Stapleton)*, Joan Plowright *(Miss Tray)*, John Welsh *(President)*, John Moffatt *(Dr. Bitterling)*, Rachel Kempson *(Miss Black Planorbis)*, John Osborne *(Dr. Scavenger, An Aunt,* and *Custodian)*, Colin Jeavons *(Youth)*, George Selway *(Mother* and *A Radio Commentator)*, Christopher Fettes *(Vinson)*, Stephen Dartnell *(An Aunt)*, George Devine *(Father Golden Orfe)*, Robert Stephens *(Bank Manager, An Aunt,* and *A Radio Commentator)*

The Member of the Wedding

AUTHOR: Carson McCullers
DIRECTOR: Tony Richardson
DESIGNER: Alan Tagg
COSTUMES: Stephen Doncaster
OPENED: Royal Court Theatre, 5 February 1957
CAST: Richard Pasco *(Jarvis)*, Geraldine McEwan *(Frankie Addams)*, Greta Watson *(Janice)*, Bertice Reading *(Berenice Sadie Brown)*,

James Dyrenforth *(Royal Addams)*, John Hall *(John Henry West)*, Vivienne Drummond *(Mrs. West)*, Anthony Richmond *(Schoolboy)*, Susan Westerby *(Helen Fletcher)*, Dudy Nimmo *(Doris)*, Ann Dickins *(Schoolgirl)*, Connie Smith *(Sis Laura)*, Orlando Martins *(T. T. Williams)*, Errol John *(Honey Camden Brown)*, Neville Jacobson *(Soldier)*, Garry Nesbitt *(Barney McKean)*

The Entertainer

AUTHOR:	John Osborne
DIRECTOR:	Tony Richardson
DESIGNER:	Alan Tagg
COSTUMES:	Clare Jeffery
MUSIC:	John Addison
OPENED:	Royal Court Theatre, 10 April 1957
CAST:	George Relph *(Billie Rice)*, Dorothy Tutin *(Jean Rice)*, Brenda de Banzie *(Phoebe Rice)*, Laurence Olivier *(Archie Rice)*, Richard Pasco *(Frank Rice)*, Vivienne Drummond *(Gorgeous Gladys)*, Aubrey Dexter *(William Rice)*, Stanley Meadows *(Graham)*
REVIVED:	Palace Theatre, 10 September 1957, with George Relph *(Billie Rice)*, Joan Plowright *(Jean Rice)*, Brenda de Banzie *(Phoebe Rice)*, Laurence Olivier *(Archie Rice)*, Richard Pasco *(Frank Rice)*, Jennifer Wallace *(Britannia)*, Albert Chevalier *(William [Brother Bill] Rice)*, Robert Stephens *(Graham)*
TRANSFERRED:	Royale Theatre, New York, 12 February 1958, with Jeri Archer, Guy Spaull, and Peter Donat replacing Jennifer Wallace, Albert Chevalier, and Robert Stephens

The Apollo of Bellac

AUTHOR:	Jean Giraudoux
TRANSLATOR/ADAPTER:	Ronald Duncan

DIRECTOR:	Tony Richardson
DESIGNER:	Carl Toms
MUSIC:	John Addison
OPENED:	Royal Court Theatre, 14 May 1957, in a double-bill with *The Chairs* by Eugène Ionesco
CAST:	Richard Pasco *(The Man from Bellac)*, Heather Sears *(Agnes)*, John Osborne *(Commissionaire)*, John Moffatt *(Secretary)*, Alan Bates *(M. le Cracheton)*, Robert Stephens *(M. Lepedura)*, Anthony Creighton *(M. Rasemutte)*, Stephen Dartnell *(M. Schulze)*, Esmé Percy *(Principal)*, Margaret Ashcroft *(Mlle. Chevredent)*, Vivienne Drummond *(Thérèse)*

The Chairs

AUTHOR:	Eugène Ionesco
TRANSLATOR:	Donald Watson
DIRECTOR:	Tony Richardson
DESIGNER:	Jocelyn Herbert
OPENED:	Royal Court Theatre, 14 May 1957, in a double-bill with *The Apollo of Bellac*, by Jean Giraudoux (see above)
CAST:	George Devine *(Old Man)*, Joan Plowright *(Old Woman)*, Richard Pasco *(The Orator)*
REVIVED:	Royal Court Theatre, 5 August 1957, with the same cast in a double-bill with *How Can We Save Father*, by Oliver Marlow Wilkinson, directed by Clare Jeffery; Royal Court Theatre, 18 June 1958, in a double-bill with *The Lesson* by Eugène Ionesco (see below), with Jeremy Kemp replacing Richard Pasco
TRANSFERRED:	Phoenix Theatre, New York, 9 January 1958, in a double-bill with *The Lesson* by Eugène Ionesco (see below), with Eli Wallach *(Old Man)*, Joan Plowright *(Old Woman)*, and Kelton Garwood *(The Orator)*

The Making of Moo

AUTHOR:	Nigel Dennis
DIRECTOR:	Tony Richardson
DESIGNER:	Audrey Cruddas
OPENED:	Royal Court Theatre, 25 June 1957
CAST:	George Devine *(Frederick Compton)*, John Osborne *(Donald Blake)*, James Villiers *(Constable)*, Joan Plowright *(Elizabeth Compton)*, Martin Miller *(William)*, Nicholas Brady *(Sergeant)*, John Moffatt *(Fairbrother)*, Stephen Dartnell *(Willis)*, Robert Stephens *(Mr. Fosdick* and *A Native)*, John Wood *(Walter* and *A Native)*, Anthony Creighton *(A Native)*

Requiem for a Nun

AUTHOR:	William Faulkner
DIRECTOR:	Tony Richardson
DESIGNER:	Motley
OPENED:	Royal Court Theatre, 26 November 1957
CAST:	Bertice Reading *(Nancy Mannigoe)*, Ruth Ford *(Temple)*, John Crawford *(Gowan Stevens)*, Zachary Scott *(Gavin Stevens)*, David Gardner *(Governor)*, John McCarthy *(Pete)*, Mark Baker *(Mr. Tubbs)*
TRANSFERRED:	John Golden Theatre, New York, 30 January 1959, with Scott McKay, House Jameson, Christian Flanders, and John Dorman replacing John Crawford, David Gardner, John McCarthy, and Mark Baker

The Lesson

AUTHOR:	Eugène Ionesco
TRANSLATOR:	Donald Watson
DIRECTOR:	Tony Richardson
DESIGNER:	Jesse Beers
OPENED:	Phoenix Theatre, New York, 9 January 1958, in a double-bill with *The Chairs* by Eugène Ionesco

CAST: Paula Bauersmith *(The Maid)*, Joan Plowright *(The Pupil)*, Max Adrian *(The Professor)*

TRANSFERRED: Royal Court Theatre, 18 June 1958, in a double-bill with *The Chairs* by Eugène Ionesco, designed by Jocelyn Herbert and with Phyllis Morris *(The Maid)*, Joan Plowright *(The Pupil)*, and Edgar Wreford *(The Professor)*

Flesh to a Tiger

AUTHOR: Barry Reckord
DIRECTOR: Tony Richardson
DESIGNER: Loudon Sainthill
MUSIC: Geoffrey Wright
OPENED: Royal Court Theatre, 21 May 1958
CAST:* Tamba Allen *(Joshie)*, Pearl Prescod *(Lal)*, Cleo Laine *(Della)*, James Clarke *(Shepherd Aaron)*, Dorothy Blondel-Francis *(Vie)*, Lloyd Reckford *(George)*, Edmundo Otero *(Papa G.)*, Johnny Sekka *(Ruddy)*, Nadia Cattouse *(Gloria)*, Connie Smith *(Grannie)*, Edgar Wreford *(Doctor)*

Pericles

AUTHOR: William Shakespeare
DIRECTOR: Tony Richardson
DESIGNER: Loudon Sainthill
MUSIC: Roberto Gerhard
OPENED: Shakespeare Memorial Theatre, Stratford, 8 July 1958
CAST:* Edric Connor *(Gower)*, Paul Hardwick *(Antiochus)*, Zoe Caldwell *(Daughter of Antiochus)*, Richard Johnson *(Pericles)*, Cyril Luckham *(Helicanus)*, Donald Eccles *(Cleon)*, Rachel Kempson *(Dionyza)*, Mark Dignam *(Simonides)*, Stephanie Bidmead *(Thaisa)*, Geraldine McEwan *(Marina)*, Michael Meacham *(Lysimachus)*

Othello

AUTHOR: William Shakespeare
DIRECTOR: Tony Richardson
DESIGNER: Loudon Sainthill
MUSIC: Leslie Bridgewater
OPENED: Shakespeare Memorial Theatre, Stratford,
                    7 April 1959
CAST:*   Peter Woodthorpe *(Roderigo)*, Sam
                    Wanamaker *(Iago)*, Paul Hardwick
                    (Brabantio), Paul Robeson *(Othello)*, Albert
                    Finney *(Cassio)*, Ian Holm *(Duke of Venice)*,
                    Edward de Souza *(Lodovico)*, Donald Layne-
                    Smith *(Gratiano)*, Mary Ure *(Desdemona)*,
                    Angela Baddeley *(Emilia)*, Julian Glover
                    (Montano), Zoe Caldwell *(Bianca)*

Orpheus Descending

AUTHOR: Tennessee Williams
DIRECTOR: Tony Richardson
DESIGNER: Loudon Sainthill
OPENED: Royal Court Theatre, 14 May 1959
CAST: Diana Beaumont *(Dolly Hammer)*, Mavis
                    Villers *(Beulah Binnings)*, Larry Taylor
                    (Pee Wee Binnings), Ivor Salter *(Dog Hamma)*,
                    Diane Cilento *(Carol Cutrere)*, Catherine
                    Wilmer *(Eva Temple)*, May Hallatt *(Sister
                    Temple)*, John Harrison *(Uncle Pleasant)*, Gary
                    Cockrell *(Val Xavier)*, Bee Duffell *(Vee
                    Talbot)*, Isa Miranda *(Lady Torrance)*, Fred
                    Johnson *(Jabe Torrance)*, Robert Cawdron
                    (Sheriff Talbot), Maria Britneva *(Woman)*,
                    David Airey *(David Cutrere)*, Bessie Love
                    (Nurse Porter), Michael Seaver *(Clown)*,
                    Richard Wilding *(Man)*

Look After Lulu

AUTHOR: Noël Coward, after *Occupe-toi d'Amélie* by
                    Georges Feydeau
DIRECTOR: Tony Richardson

DESIGNER:	Roger Furse
OPENED:	Royal Court Theatre, 29 July 1959
CAST:	Vivien Leigh *(Lulu d'Arville)*, Peter Stephens *(Bomba)*, Shirley Cameron *(Yvonne)*, Fanny Carby *(Paulette)*, Jeanne Watts *(Gaby)*, John Gatrell *(Valery)*, Cecil Brock *(Emile)*, Robert Stephens *(Philippe de Croze)*, Sean Kelly *(Adonis)*, Peter Sallis *(Gigot)*, Meriel Forbes *(Claire, Duchess of Claussones)*, Anthony Quayle *(Marcel Blanchard)*, Lawrence Davidson *(General Koschnadieff)*, George Devine *(Herr van Putzeboum)*, Max Adrian *(Prince of Salestria)*, Ann Bishop *(Rose)*, Bitsa *(Roger, the dog)*, Arnold Yarrow *(Oudatte* and *A Florist's Boy)*, Peter Wyatt *(Cornette)*, David Ryder *(Photographer* and *A Florist's Boy)*, Richard Goolden *(Mayor of the District)*, Barbara Hicks *(Aunt Gabrielle)*, Elaine Millar *(Little Girl)*, Michael Bates *(Inspector of Police)*
REVIVED:	New Theatre, 8 September 1959, with the same cast except for Peter Sallis replacing George Devine

A Taste of Honey

AUTHOR:	Shelagh Delaney
DIRECTORS:	Tony Richardson and George Devine
DESIGNER:	Oliver Smith
COSTUMES:	Dorothy Jeakins
MUSIC:	Bobby Scott
OPENED:	Lyceum Theatre, New York, 4 October 1960
CAST:	Angela Lansbury *(Helen)*, Joan Plowright *(Josephine)*, Nigel Davenport *(Peter)*, Billie Dee Williams *(The Boy)*, Andrew Ray *(Geoffrey)*

The Changeling

| AUTHORS: | Thomas Middleton and William Rowley |
| DIRECTOR: | Tony Richardson |

DESIGNER: Jocelyn Herbert
COSTUMES: David Walker
MUSIC: Raymond Leppard
OPENED: Royal Court Theatre, 21 February 1961
CAST:*   Alan Howard *(Alonzo de Piracquo)*, Jeremy
               Brett *(Alsemero)*, Robert Shaw *(De Flores)*,
               Mary Ure *(Beatrice-Joanna)*, Annette Crosbie
               (Diaphanta), Zoe Caldwell *(Isabella)*

Luther

AUTHOR: John Osborne
DIRECTOR: Tony Richardson
DESIGNER: Jocelyn Herbert
MUSIC: John Addison
OPENED: Theatre Royal, Nottingham, 26 June 1961
CAST: Julian Glover *(Knight)*, James Cairncross
               (Prior), Albert Finney *(Martin)*, Bill Owen
               (Hans), Peter Duguid *(Lucas)*, Dan Meaden
               (Weinand), Peter Bull *(Tetzel)*, George Devine
               (Staupitz), John Moffatt *(Cajetan)*, Robert
               Robinson *(Miltitz)*, Charles Kay *(Leo)*, James
               Cairncross *(Eck)*, Meryl Gourley *(Katherine)*
TRANSFERRED: Royal Court Theatre, 27 July 1961, and
               Phoenix Theatre, 5 September 1961, with
               the same cast; St. James Theatre, New York,
               25 September 1963, with Glyn Owen
               (Knight), Ted Thurston *(Prior)*, Albert
               Finney *(Martin)*, Kenneth J. Warren *(Hans)*,
               Luis Van Rooten *(Lucas)*, Alfred Sandor
               (Reader), John Heffernan *(Weinand)*, Peter
               Bull *(Tetzel)*, Frank Shelley *(Staupitz)*, John
               Moffatt *(Cajetan)*, Robert Burr *(Miltitz)*,
               Michael Egan *(Leo)*, Martin Rudy *(Eck)*,
               Lorna Lewis *(Katherine)*

A Midsummer Night's Dream

AUTHOR: William Shakespeare
DIRECTOR: Tony Richarson
DESIGNER: Jocelyn Herbert

MUSIC:	John Addison
OPENED:	Royal Court Theatre, 24 January 1962
CAST:*	Robert Lang *(Theseus)*, Morris Perry *(Egeus)*, Corin Redgrave *(Lysander)*, Kenneth McReddie *(Demetrius)*, Ronnie Barker *(Quince)*, Stuart Harris *(Snug)*, Colin Blakely *(Bottom)*, Nicol Williamson *(Flute)*, David Warner *(Snout)*, James Bolam *(Starveling)*, Yolande Bavan *(Hippolyta)*, Rita Tushingham *(Hermia)*, Lynn Redgrave *(Helena)*, Colin Jeavons *(Oberon)*, Samantha Eggar *(Titania)*, Alfred Lynch *(Puck)*

Semi-Detached

AUTHOR:	David Turner
DIRECTOR:	Tony Richardson
DESIGNER:	Loudon Sainthill
OPENED:	Saville Theatre, 5 December 1962
CAST:	Laurence Olivier *(Fred Midway)*, James Bolam *(Tom Midway)*, Mona Washbourne *(Hilda Midway)*, John Thaw *(Robert Freeman)*, Eileen Atkins *(Eileen Midway)*, Patsy Rowlands *(Avril Hadfield)*, Kenneth Fortescue *(Nigel Hadfield)*, Joan Young *(Garnet Hadfield)*, Newton Blick *(Arnold Makepiece)*

Natural Affection

AUTHOR:	William Inge
DIRECTOR:	Tony Richardson
DESIGNER:	Oliver Smith
COSTUMES:	Ann Roth
MUSIC:	John Lewis
OPENED:	Booth Theatre, New York, 31 January 1963
CAST:	Kim Stanley *(Sue Barker)*, Harry Guardino *(Bernie Slovenk)*, Tom Bosley *(Vince Brinkman)*, Monica May *(Claire Brinkman)*, Gregory Rozakis *(Donnie Barker)*, John Horn *(Gil)*, Robert Baines *(The Superintendent)*, Bonnie Bartlett *(Sal)*, Gerald Covell *(Max)*

The Resistible Rise of Arturo Ui

AUTHOR: Bertolt Brecht
TRANSLATOR/ADAPTER: George Tabori
DIRECTOR: Tony Richardson
DESIGNER: Rouben Ter-Arutunian
MUSIC: Jule Styne
OPENED: Lunt-Fontanne Theatre, New York,
                         11 November 1963
CAST:*   Paul Michael *(The Barker)*, Michael
                         Constantine *(Dogsborough)*, Elisha Cook
                         (Giuseppe Givola), Lionel Stander *(Manuele
                         Giri)*, Christopher Plummer *(Arturo Ui)*,
                         George Cotton *(Mulberry)*, James Coco
                         (O'Casey), Madeleine Sherwood *(Betty
                         Dullfeet)*

The Milk Train Doesn't Stop Here Anymore

AUTHOR: Tennessee Williams
DIRECTOR: Tony Richardson
DESIGNER: Rouben Ter-Arutunian
MUSIC: Ned Rorem
OPENED: Brooks Atkinson Theatre, New York,
                         1 January 1964
CAST: Bobby Dean Hooks and Konrad Matthaei
                         (Stage Assistants), Tallulah Bankhead *(Mrs.
                         Goforth)*, Marian Seldes *(Blackie)*, Ralph
                         Roberts *(Rudy)*, Tab Hunter *(Christopher
                         Flanders)*, Ruth Ford *(The Witch of Capri)*

The Seagull

AUTHOR: Anton Chekhov
TRANSLATOR: Ann Jellicoe
DIRECTOR: Tony Richardson
DESIGNER: Jocelyn Herbert
MUSIC: John Addison
OPENED: Queen's Theatre, 12 March 1964
CAST:*   Malcolm Taylor *(Yakov)*, Philip Locke
                         (Semyon), Ann Beach *(Masha)*, Paul Rogers
                         (Sorin), Peter McEnery *(Konstantin)*, Vanessa

Redgrave *(Nina)*, Rachel Kempson *(Polina)*, George Devine *(Dorn)*, Peggy Ashcroft *(Arkadina)*, Peter Finch *(Trigorin)*, Mark Dignam *(Shamrayev)*

Saint Joan of the Stockyards

AUTHOR: Bertolt Brecht
TRANSLATORS: Charlotte and A. L. Lloyd
DIRECTOR: Tony Richardson
DESIGNER: Jocelyn Herbert
MUSIC: John Addison
OPENED: Queen's Theatre, 11 June 1964
CAST: Lionel Stander *(J. Pierpont Mauler)*, Dervis Ward *(Cridle)*, Siobhan McKenna *(Joan Dark)*, Rachel Kempson *(Martha)*, Nicholas Smith *(Jackson)*, Mark Dignam *(Graham)*, Bruce Boa *(Lennox* and *Workers' Leader)*, Denis Shaw *(Meyers)*, Michael Medwin *(Sullivan Slift)*, Thick Wilson *(Detective 1)*, Derek Fuke *(Detective 2)*, Roy Pattison *(Foreman* and *Second Leader)*, Dudley Hunte *(Young Lad)*, Patricia Connolly *(Mrs. Luckerniddle)*, Hal Galili *(Gloomb)*, Brian Anderson *(Other Man)*, Clive Endersby *(Waiter)*, Robert Ayres *(Paul Snyder)*, Malcolm Taylor *(Mulberry)*, Katie Fitzroy *(Reporter 1)*, Desmond Stokes *(Reporter 2)*

Hamlet

AUTHOR: William Shakespeare
DIRECTOR: Tony Richardson
DESIGNER: Jocelyn Herbert
MUSIC: Patrick Gowers
OPENED: The Roundhouse, 17 February 1969
CAST:* Gordon Jackson *(Horatio)*, Anthony Hopkins *(Claudius)*, Judy Parfitt *(Gertrude)*, Mark Dignam *(Polonius)*, Michael Pennington *(Laertes)*, Nicol Williamson *(Hamlet)*, Marianne Faithfull *(Ophelia)*, John Carney *(Player King)*, Roger Livesey *(Gravedigger)*

TRANSFERRED:	Lunt-Fontanne Theatre, New York, 1 May 1969, with Patrick Wymark, Constance Cummings, and Francesca Annis replacing Anthony Hopkins, Judy Parfit, and Marianne Faithfull

The Threepenny Opera

AUTHOR:	Bertolt Brecht, based on *The Beggar's Opera* by John Gay
TRANSLATOR:	Hugh McDiarmid
MUSIC:	Kurt Weill
DIRECTOR:	Tony Richardson
DESIGNER:	Patrick Robertson
COSTUMES:	Rosemary Vercoe
CHOREOGRAPHY:	Eleanor Fazan
OPENED:	Prince of Wales Theatre, 10 February 1972
CAST:*	Lon Satton *(Narrator)*, Ronald Radd *(Mr. Peachum)*, Hermione Baddeley *(Mrs. Peachum)*, Joe Melia *(Macheath)*, Vanessa Redgrave *(Polly Peachum)*, Arthur Mullard *(Jake)*, Annie Ross *(Jenny)*, Barbara Windsor *(Lucy Brown)*
TRANSFERRED:	Piccadilly Theatre, 10 April 1972, with Helen Cotterill replacing Vanessa Redgrave

I, Claudius

AUTHOR:	John Mortimer, based on *I, Claudius* and *Claudius the God* by Robert Graves
DIRECTOR:	Tony Richardson
DESIGNER:	William Dudley
COSTUMES:	Sue Plummer
OPENED:	Queen's Theatre, 11 July 1972
CAST:*	David Warner *(Claudius)*, Charles Lloyd Pack *(Augustus)*, Freda Jackson *(Livia)*, Rosalind Ayres *(Calpurnia)*, Warren Clarke *(Caligula)*, Sara Kestelman *(Messalina)*

Antony and Cleopatra

AUTHOR:	William Shakespeare
DIRECTOR:	Tony Richardson

DESIGNER: Brian Thomson
COSTUMES: Maria Björnson
OPENED: Bankside Globe Playhouse, 9 August 1973
CAST:* Julian Glover *(Antony)*, David Schofield *(Octavius)*, Bob Hoskins *(Sextus Pompeius)*, Dave King *(Enobarbus)*, Vanessa Redgrave *(Cleopatra)*, Lorna Edwards *(Octavia)*, Julie Covington *(Charmian)*

The Lady from the Sea
AUTHOR: Henrik Ibsen
TRANSLATOR: Michael Meyer
DIRECTOR: Tony Richardson
DESIGNER: Rouben Ter-Arutunian
MUSIC: Richard Peaslee
OPENED: Circle in the Square Theatre, New York, 18 March 1976
CAST: George Ede *(Ballested)*, Kimberly Farr *(Bolette)*, Kipp Osborne *(Lyngstrand)*, Allison Argo *(Hilde)*, Pat Hingle *(Dr. Wangel)*, John Heffernan *(Professor Arnholm)*, Vanessa Redgrave *(Ellida)*, Richard Lynch *(The Stranger)*

As You Like It
AUTHOR: William Shakespeare
DIRECTOR: Tony Richardson
DESIGNER: Rouben Ter-Arutunian
COSTUMES: Cara Benedetti
OPENED: Center Theatre, Long Beach, Los Angeles, 1 August 1976
CAST: Jonelle Allen *(Phoebe)*, Stockard Channing *(Rosalind)*, Bruce Davison *(Orlando)*, Michael Keenan *(Touchstone)*, Ian McShane *(Jacques)*, Arthur David Roberts *(Oliver)*, Sarah Rush *(Celia)*

Toyer
AUTHOR: Gardner McKay
DIRECTOR: Tony Richardson

DESIGNER: Rouben Ter-Arutunian
OPENED: Kennedy Center, Eisenhower Theatre,
                        Washington, D.C., 1 February 1983
CAST: Kathleen Turner *(Maude)*, Brad Davis *(Peter)*

Dreamhouse
AUTHOR: Stewart Duckworth
DIRECTOR: Tony Richardson
DESIGNER: Richard Hernandes
OPENED: L.A. Stage Company, Hollywood, 21 March
                        1984
CAST: Nina Axelrod *(Marilyn)*, Alyson Croft
                        (Denise), Matthew Laurance *(Bob)*, Lewis Van
                        Bergen *(Dennis)*, Lesley Ann Warren *(Wanda)*

FILMS

Momma Don't Allow

UK, 1956
PRODUCTION COMPANY: BFI Production Fund
DIRECTORS: Karel Reisz and Tony Richardson
CAMERA: Walter Lassally
EDITING AND SOUND: John Fletcher
CAST: The film is a documentary featuring the
                        Chris Barber Band—Chris Barber
                        (trombone), Pat Halcox *(trumpet)*, Monty
                        Sunshine *(clarinet)*, Lonnie Donnegan
                        (guitar), Jim Bray *(bass)*, Ron Bowden
                        (drums), and Ottilie Patterson *(vocals)*—and
                        their audience at the Wood Green Jazz Club
                        22 mins

Look Back in Anger

UK, 1959
PRODUCTION COMPANY: Woodfall
PRODUCER: Harry Saltzman

DIRECTOR: Tony Richardson
SCREENPLAY: Nigel Kneale and John Osborne
PHOTOGRAPHY: Oswald Morris
MUSIC: Chris Barber
EDITOR: Richard Best
MUSICAL DIRECTOR: John Addison
ART DIRECTOR: Peter Glazier
COSTUMES: Jocelyn Rickards
CAST:*   Richard Burton *(Jimmy Porter)*, Claire Bloom *(Helena Charles)*, Mary Ure *(Alison Porter)*, Edith Evans *(Mrs. Tanner)*, Gary Redmond *(Cliff Lewis)*, Glen Byam Shaw *(Colonel Redfern)*
    101 mins

The Entertainer

UK, 1960

PRODUCTION COMPANY: Woodfall/Holly
PRODUCER: Harry Saltzman
DIRECTOR: Tony Richardson
SCREENPLAY: John Osborne and Nigel Kneale
PHOTOGRAPHY: Oswald Morris
MUSIC: John Addison
EDITOR: Alan Osbiston
ART DIRECTORS: Ralph Brinton and Ted Marshall
COSTUMES: Barbara Gillette
CAST:*   Laurence Olivier *(Archie Rice)*, Brenda de Banzie *(Phoebe Rice)*, Joan Plowright *(Jean Rice)*, Roger Livesey *(Billy Rice)*, Alan Bates *(Frank Rice)*, Daniel Massey *(Graham)*, Albert Finney *(Mick Rice)*, Shirley Ann Field *(Tina)*, Thora Hird *(Mrs. Lapford)*
    96 mins

A Subject of Scandal and Concern

UK, 1960

PRODUCTION COMPANY: BBC TV
DIRECTOR: Tony Richardson
SCRIPT: John Osborne

ART DIRECTOR:	Tony Abbott
CAST:*	John Freeman, *(Narrator)*, Richard Burton *(George Holyoake)*, Rachel Roberts *(Mrs. Holyoake)*, George Devine *(Mr. Justice Erskine)*, Nicholas Meredith *(Mr. Alexander)*, Nigel Davenport *(Mr. Bartram)*

Saturday Night and Sunday Morning

UK, 1960

PRODUCTION COMPANY:	Woodfall
PRODUCER:	Tony Richardson
DIRECTOR:	Karel Reisz
SCREENPLAY:	Alan Sillitoe
PHOTOGRAPHY:	Freddie Francis
MUSIC:	John Dankworth
EDITOR:	Seth Holt
ART DIRECTOR:	Ted Marshall
CAST:*	Albert Finney *(Arthur Seaton)*, Shirley Ann Field *(Doreen Gretton)*, Rachel Roberts *(Brenda)*, Hylda Baker *(Aunt Ada)*, Norman Rossington *(Bert)*, Bryan Pringle *(Jack)* 89 mins

Sanctuary

USA, 1961

PRODUCTION COMPANY:	Darryl F. Zanuck/Twentieth Century Fox
PRODUCER:	Richard D. Zanuck
DIRECTOR:	Tony Richardson
SCREENPLAY:	James Poe, based on *Sanctuary* and *Requiem for a Nun* by William Faulkner
PHOTOGRAPHY:	Ellsworth Fredricks (Cinemascope)
MUSIC:	Alex North
EDITOR:	Robert Simpson
ART DIRECTORS:	Duncan Cramer and Jack Martin Smith
SET DIRECTORS:	Walter M. Scott and Fred Maclean
COSTUMES:	Donfeld
CAST:*	Lee Remick *(Temple Drake)*, Yves Montand *(Candy Man)*, Bradford Dillman *(Gowan*

Stevens), Harry Townes *(Ira Bobbitt)*, Odetta
(Nancy Mannigoe), Howard St. John *(Governor
Drake)*, Reta Shaw *(Miss Reba)*, Strother
Martin *(Dog Boy)*, Wyatt Cooper *(Tommy)*
90 mins

A Taste of Honey

UK, 1961

PRODUCTION COMPANY:	British Lion/Woodfall
PRODUCER AND DIRECTOR:	Tony Richardson
SCREENPLAY:	Shelagh Delaney and Tony Richardson
PHOTOGRAPHY:	Walter Lassally
MUSIC:	John Addison
EDITOR:	Anthony Gibbs
MUSICAL DIRECTOR:	John Addison
ART DIRECTOR:	Ralph Brinton
COSTUMES:	Sophie Harris
CAST:*	Dora Bryan *(Helen)*, Rita Tushingham *(Jo)*, Robert Stephens *(Peter)*, Murray Melvin *(Geoffrey)*, Paul Danquah *(Jimmy)* 100 mins

The Loneliness of the Long Distance Runner

UK, 1962

PRODUCTION COMPANY:	British Lion/Woodfall
PRODUCER AND DIRECTOR:	Tony Richardson
SCREENPLAY:	Alan Sillitoe
PHOTOGRAPHY:	Walter Lassally
MUSIC:	John Addison
EDITOR:	Anthony Gibbs
PRODUCTION DIRECTOR:	Ralph Brinton
ART DIRECTOR:	Ted Marshall
SET DESIGNER:	Josie MacAvin
COSTUMES:	Sophie Harris
CAST:*	Tom Courtenay *(Colin Smith)*, Michael Redgrave *(The Governor)*, Avis Bunnage *(Mrs.*

Smith), James Bolam *(Mike)*, Julia Foster *(Gladys)*, Alec McCowen *(Brown)*, Joe Robinson *(Roach)*
104 mins

Tom Jones

UK, 1963

PRODUCTION COMPANY:	Woodfall
PRODUCER AND DIRECTOR:	Tony Richardson
SCREENPLAY:	John Osborne, based on the novel by Henry Fielding
PHOTOGRAPHY:	Walter Lassally (Eastmancolor)
MUSIC:	John Addison
EDITOR:	Anthony Gibbs
COLOR CONSULTANT:	Jocelyn Herbert
PRODUCTION DIRECTOR:	Ralph Brinton
ART DIRECTOR:	Ted Marshall
SET DESIGNER:	Josie MacAvin
COSTUMES:	John McCorry
CAST:*	Albert Finney *(Tom Jones)*, Susannah York *(Sophie Western)*, Hugh Griffith *(Squire Western)*, Edith Evans *(Miss Western)*, Joan Greenwood *(Lady Bellaston)*, Diane Cilento *(Molly Seagrim)*, George Devine *(Squire Allworthy)*, Joyce Redman *(Mrs. Waters* and *Jenny Jones)*, Rachel Kempson *(Bridget Allworthy)*, Wilfred Lawson *(Black George)*, David Warner *(Blifil)*, Micheál MacLiammóir *(Narrator)*
	128 mins

Girl with Green Eyes

UK, 1964

PRODUCTION COMPANY:	Woodfall
PRODUCERS:	Oscar Lewenstein and Tony Richardson
DIRECTOR:	Desmond Davis

SCREENPLAY:	Edna O'Brien
PHOTOGRAPHY:	Manny Wynn
MUSIC:	John Addison
EDITORS:	Anthony Gibbs and Brian Smedley-Aston
ART DIRECTOR:	Ted Marshall
CAST:*	Peter Finch *(Eugene Galliard)*, Rita Tushingham *(Kate Brady)*, Lynn Redgrave *(Baba Brenan)*, Marie Kean *(Josie Hannigan)*, Julian Glover *(Malachi Sullivan)*, T. P. McKenna *(Priest)*
	91 mins

The Loved One

USA, 1965

PRODUCTION COMPANY:	MGM
PRODUCERS:	John Calley and Haskell Wexler
DIRECTOR:	Tony Richardson
SCREENPLAY:	Terry Southern and Christopher Isherwood, based on the novel by Evelyn Waugh
PHOTOGRAPHY:	Haskell Wexler
MUSIC:	John Addison
EDITOR:	Anthony Gibbs
PRODUCTION DIRECTOR:	Rouben Ter-Arutunian
ART DIRECTOR:	Sydney Z. Litwack
SET DESIGNER:	James Payne
COSTUMES:	Nat Tolmach, Rouben Ter-Arutunian, James Kelly, and Marie T. Harris
SPECIAL EFFECTS:	Geza Gaspar
CHOREOGRAPHY:	Tony Charmoli
MAKEUP:	Emile La Vigne and Bunny Armstrong
CAST:*	Robert Morse *(Dennis Barlow)*, Jonathan Winters *(Wilber Glenworthy* and *Harry Glenworthy)*, Anjanette Comer *(Aimee Thanatogenos)*, Rod Steiger *(Mr. Joyboy)*, Dana Andrews *(General Brinkman)*, Milton Berle *(Mr. Kenton)*, James Coburn *(Immigration Officer)*, John Gielgud *(Sir Francis Hinsley)*, Tab Hunter *(Guide)*, Margaret Leighton *(Mrs.*

Kenton), Liberace *(Mr. Starker)*, Roddy McDowall *(D.J. Jr.)*, Robert Morley *(Sir Ambrose Abercrombie)*, Lionel Stander *(Guru Brahmin)*, Ayllene Gibbons *(Joyboy's Mother)*, Martin Ransohoff *(Lorenzo Medici)*, Paul H. Williams *(Gunther Fry)*
116 mins

Mademoiselle

UK/France, 1966

PRODUCTION COMPANY:	Woodfall-Procinex
PRODUCER:	Oscar Lewenstein
DIRECTOR:	Tony Richardson
SCREENPLAY:	Jean Genet (English translation by Bernard Frechtman)
PHOTOGRAPHY:	David Watkin (Panavision) (French version, Philippe Brun)
EDITOR:	Anthony Gibbs (French version, Sophie Coussein)
ART DIRECTOR:	Jacques Saulnier
SET DESIGNER:	Charles Merangel
COSTUMES:	Jocelyn Rickards
CAST:*	Jeanne Moreau *(Mademoiselle)*, Ettore Manni *(Manou)*, Keith Skinner *(Bruno)*, Jane Berretta *(Annette)*, Mony Rey *(Vievotte)*, Umberto Orsini *(Antonio)*
	103 mins

The Sailor from Gibraltar

UK, 1967

PRODUCTION COMPANY:	Woodfall
PRODUCERS:	Oscar Lewenstein and Neil Hartley
DIRECTOR:	Tony Richardson
SCREENPLAY:	Tony Richardson, Christopher Isherwood, and Don Magner, based on the novel *Le Marin de Gibraltar* by Marguerite Duras
PHOTOGRAPHY:	Raoul Coutard
MUSIC:	Antoine Duhamel and Bassiak

EDITOR:	Anthony Gibbs
SET DESIGNER:	Marilena Aravantinou
COSTUMES:	Jocelyn Rickards
CAST:*	Jeanne Moreau *(Anna)*, Ian Bannen *(Alan)*, Vanessa Redgrave *(Sheila)*, Zia Mohyeddin *(Noori)*, Hugh Griffith *(Legrand)*, Orson Welles *(Louis of Mozambique)*, Gabriella Pallotta *(Girl at a Dance)*, John Hurt *(John)*, Theo Roubanis *(Theo)*
	91 mins

Red and Blue

UK, 1967

PRODUCTION COMPANY:	Woodfall
PRODUCERS:	Oscar Lewenstein and Lindsay Anderson
DIRECTOR:	Tony Richardson
SCREENPLAY:	Tony Richardson and Julian More
PHOTOGRAPHY:	Billy Williams (Eastmancolor)
SONGS:	Cyrus Bassiak
EDITOR:	Kevin Brownlow
ART DIRECTOR:	Assheton Gorton
CAST:	Vanessa Redgrave *(Jacky)*, John Bird *(Man on Train)*, Gary Raymond *(Songwriter)*, William Sylvester *(Trumpeter)*, Michael York *(Acrobat)*, Amaryllis Garnet *(Songwriter's Girl)*, Douglas Fairbanks, Jr. *(Millionaire)*
	35 mins

The Charge of the Light Brigade

UK, 1968

PRODUCTION COMPANY:	United Artists
PRODUCER:	Neil Hartley
DIRECTOR:	Tony Richardson
SCREENPLAY:	Charles Wood
PHOTOGRAPHY:	David Watkin (Panavision/DeLuxe Color)
MUSIC:	John Addison
EDITORS:	Kevin Brownlow and Hugh Raggett
ART DIRECTOR:	Edward Marshall

COSTUMES:	David Walker
SPECIAL EFFECTS:	Robert MacDonald
ANIMATION:	Richard Williams
CAST:*	Trevor Howard *(Lord Cardigan)*, Vanessa Redgrave *(Clarissa)*, John Gielgud *(Lord Raglan)*, Harry Andrews *(Lord Lucan)*, Jill Bennett *(Mrs. Duberly)*, David Hemmings (Captain Nolan), Peter Bowles *(Paymaster Duberly)*, Mark Burns *(Captain Morris)* 141 mins

Hamlet

UK, 1969

PRODUCTION COMPANY:	Woodfall/Filmways
PRODUCER:	Neil Hartley
DIRECTOR:	Tony Richardson
SCREENPLAY:	From the play by William Shakespeare
PHOTOGRAPHY:	Gerry Fisher (Technicolor)
MUSIC:	Patrick Gowers
EDITOR:	Charles Rees
DESIGNER:	Jocelyn Herbert
CAST:*	Gordon Jackson *(Horatio)*, Anthony Hopkins *(Claudius)*, Judy Parfitt *(Gertrude)*, Mark Dignam *(Polonius)*, Michael Pennington *(Laertes)*, Nicol Williamson *(Hamlet)*, Marianne Faithfull *(Ophelia)*, John Carney *(Player King)*, Roger Livesey *(Gravedigger)* 119 mins

Laughter in the Dark

UK/France, 1969

PRODUCTION COMPANY:	Gershwin-Kastner/Marceau/Woodfall
PRODUCER:	Neil Hartley
DIRECTOR:	Tony Richardson
SCREENPLAY:	Edward Bond, based on the novel by Vladimir Nabokov
PHOTOGRAPHY:	Dick Bush (DeLuxe Color)

MUSIC:	Raymond Leppard
EDITOR:	Charles Rees
ART DIRECTOR:	Julia Trevelyan Oman
CAST:*	Nicol Williams *(Sir Edward More)*, Anna Karina *(Margot)*, Jean-Claude Drouot *(Hervé Tourace)*, Peter Bowles *(Paul)*, Sian Phillips *(Lady Elizabeth More)*
	104 mins

Ned Kelly

UK, 1970

PRODUCTION COMPANY:	Woodfall
PRODUCER:	Neil Hartley
DIRECTOR:	Tony Richardson
SCREENPLAY:	Tony Richardson and Ian Jones
PHOTOGRAPHY:	Gerry Fisher (Technicolor)
MUSIC:	Shel Silverstein
EDITOR:	Charles Rees
PRODUCTION DIRECTOR AND COSTUMES:	Jocelyn Herbert
ART DIRECTOR:	Andrew Sanders
CAST:*	Mick Jagger *(Ned Kelly)*, Allen Bickford *(Dan Kelly)*, Geoff Gilmour *(Steve Hart)*, Mark McManus *(Joe Byrne)*, Clarissa Kaye *(Mrs. Kelly)*, Diana Craig *(Maggie Kelly)*, Frank Thring *(Judge Barry)*
	103 mins

A Delicate Balance

USA, 1973

PRODUCTION COMPANY:	American Film Theatre
PRODUCER:	Ely Landau
DIRECTOR:	Tony Richardson
SCREENPLAY:	Edward Albee
PHOTOGRAPHY:	David Watkin
EDITOR:	John Victor Smith
ART DIRECTOR:	David Brockhurst
COSTUMES:	Margaret Furse

CAST:* Katharine Hepburn *(Agnes)*, Paul Scofield *(Tobias)*, Lee Remick *(Julia)*, Kate Reid *(Claire)*, Joseph Cotten *(Harry)*, Betsy Blair *(Edna)*
132 mins

Dead Cert

UK, 1974

PRODUCTION COMPANY: Woodfall
PRODUCER: Neil Hartley
DIRECTOR: Tony Richardson
SCREENPLAY: Tony Richardson and John Oaksey, based on the novel by Dick Francis
PHOTOGRAPHY: Freddie Cooper (Eastmancolor)
MUSIC: John Addison
EDITOR: John Glen
ART DIRECTOR: David Brockhurst
CAST:* Scott Antony *(Alan)*, Judi Dench *(Laura)*, Michael Williams *(Sandy)*, Mark Dignam *(Tudor)*, Julian Glover *(Lodge)*, Joe Blatchley *(Joe)*
99 mins

Joseph Andrews

UK, 1977

PRODUCTION COMPANY: Woodfall
PRODUCER: Neil Hartley
DIRECTOR: Tony Richardson
SCREENPLAY: Allan Scott and Chris Bryant, based on a story by Tony Richardson and the novel by Henry Fielding
PHOTOGRAPHY: David Watkin (Movielab Color)
MUSIC: John Addison
EDITOR: Thom Noble

PRODUCTION DIRECTOR:	Michael Annals
ART DIRECTOR:	Bill Brosie
SET DECORATION:	Ian Whittaker
COSTUMES:	Michael Annals, Arthur Davey, Jean Hunnisett, and Patrick Wheatley
CAST:*	Ann-Margret *(Lady Booby)*, Peter Firth *(Joseph Andrews)*, Michael Hordern *(Parson Adams)*, Beryl Reid *(Mrs. Slipshod)*, Jim Dale *(Peddler)*, Peter Bull *(Sir Thomas Booby)*, Karen Dotrice *(Pamela)*, John Gielgud *(Doctor)*, Hugh Griffith *(Squire Western)*, Peggy Ashcroft *(Lady Tattle)*, Timothy West *(Mr. Tow-Wouse)*, Wendy Craig *(Mrs. Tow-Wouse)*, James Villiers *(Mr. Booby)*, Ronald Pickup *(Mr. Wilson)*, Murray Melvin *(Beau Didapper)* 104 mins

A Death in Canaan

USA, 1978

PRODUCTION COMPANY:	Chris-Rose Productions/Warner Bros. TV
PRODUCERS:	Robert W. Christiansen and Rick Rosenberg
DIRECTOR:	Tony Richardson
SCREENPLAY:	Thomas Thompson and Spencer Eastman, based on the book by Joan Barthel
PHOTOGRAPHY:	James Crabe
EDITOR:	Bud Smith
ART DIRECTOR:	Bob Jillson
COSTUMES:	Dick La Motte and Nancy McArdle
CAST:*	Stefanie Powers *(Joan Barthel)*, Paul Clemens *(Peter Reilly)*, Tom Atkins and Kenneth McMillan *(Police Officers)*, Jacqueline Brookes *(Defense Attorney)*, Brian Dennehy and Conchita Farrell *(Neighbors)*, William Bronder *(Judge)* 150 mins

The Border

USA, 1982

PRODUCTION COMPANY:	Universal/RKO/Efer
PRODUCER:	Edgar Bronfman, Jr.
DIRECTOR:	Tony Richardson
SCREENPLAY:	Deric Washburn, Walon Green, and David Freeman
PHOTOGRAPHY:	Ric Waite and Vilmos Zsigmond (Technicolor)
MUSIC:	Ry Cooder
EDITOR:	Robert K. Lambert
ART DIRECTOR:	Toby Rafelson
COSTUMES:	Vicki Sanchez
CAST:*	Jack Nicholson *(Charlie)*, Harvey Keitel *(Cat)*, Valerie Perrine *(Marcy)*, Warren Oates *(Red)*, Elpidia Carrillo *(Maria)*, Shannon Wilcox *(Savannah)*
	107 mins

The Hotel New Hampshire

USA, 1984

PRODUCTION COMPANY:	Orion
PRODUCERS:	Neil Hartley and James Beach
DIRECTOR:	Tony Richardson
SCREENPLAY:	Tony Richardson, based on the novel by John Irving
PHOTOGRAPHY:	David Watkin (DeLuxe Color)
MUSIC:	Jacques Offenbach
EDITOR:	Robert K. Lambert
MUSICAL DIRECTOR:	Raymond Leppard
PRODUCTION DIRECTOR:	Jocelyn Herbert
ART DIRECTOR:	John Meighen
COSTUMES:	Jocelyn Herbert
CAST:*	Rob Lowe *(John)*, Jodie Foster *(Franny)*, Paul McCrane *(Frank)*, Beau Bridges *(Father)*, Lisa Banes *(Mother)*, Jennie Dundas *(Lilly)*,

Wallace Shawn *(Freud)*, Wilford Brimley
(Iowa Bob), Nastassja Kinski *(Susie the Bear)*
110 mins

Penalty Phase

USA, 1986

PRODUCTION COMPANY:	Tamara Asseyev Productions
PRODUCER:	Tamara Asseyev
DIRECTOR:	Tony Richardson
SCREENPLAY:	Gale Patrick Hickman
PHOTOGRAPHY:	Steve Yaconelli
MUSIC:	Ralph Burns
EDITOR:	David Simmons
ART DIRECTOR:	Steve Karatzas
COSTUMES:	Ron Talsky
CAST:*	Peter Strauss *(Judge Kenneth Hoffman)*, Jonelle Allen *(Susan Jansen)*, Karen Austin *(Julie)*, Melissa Gilbert *(Leah Furman)*

Shadow on the Sun

USA, 1988

PRODUCTION COMPANY:	Tamara Asseyev Productions/New World Television
PRODUCERS:	Tamara Asseyev and Stefanie Powers
DIRECTOR:	Tony Richardson
SCREENPLAY:	Allan Scott
PHOTOGRAPHY:	Steve Yaconelli
MUSIC:	John Addison
EDITOR:	Robert K. Lambert
ART DIRECTORS:	Bob Cartwright and Gary Constable
COSTUMES:	Jane Robinson
CAST:*	Stefanie Powers *(Beryl Markham)*, James Fox *(Mansfield Markham)*, Timothy West *(Charles Clutterbuck)*, Claire Bloom *(Lady Delamere)*, Nicola Paget *(Amanda Orchardson)*, Trevor Eve *(Denys Finch Hatton)*

240 mins

The Phantom of the Opera

USA, *1990*

PRODUCTION COMPANY:	Saban/Scherick Productions
PRODUCER:	Ross Milloy
DIRECTOR:	Tony Richardson
SCREENPLAY:	Arthur Kopit, based on the novel by Gaston Leroux
PHOTOGRAPHY:	Steve Yaconelli
MUSIC:	John Addison
EDITOR:	Robert K. Lambert
SOUND:	Jean-Philippe Le Roux
ART DIRECTORS:	Timian Alsaker and Jacques Bufnoir
CAST:*	Charles Dance *(Erik—the Phantom)*, Burt Lancaster *(Carriere)*, Ian Richardson *(Cholet)*, Andrea Ferreol *(Carlotta)*, Teri Polo *(Christine)*, Adam Storke *(Count Philippe)*
	240 mins

Hills Like White Elephants

USA, *1990*

PRODUCTION COMPANY:	David Brown/HBO Showcase
PRODUCERS:	David Brown and William S. Gilmore
DIRECTOR:	Tony Richardson
SCREENPLAY:	Joan Didion and John Gregory Dunne, based on the story by Ernest Hemingway
PHOTOGRAPHY:	Steve Yaconelli
MUSIC:	Marvin Hamlisch
EDITOR:	Robert K. Lambert
ART DIRECTOR:	Timian Alsaker
CAST:*	Melanie Griffith *(The Girl)*, James Woods *(The Man)*

Part of a trilogy, *Women and Men: Stories of Seduction*, with *The Man in the Brooks Brothers Shirt*, directed by Frederic Raphael, and *Dusk Before Fireworks*, directed by Ken Russell.

90 mins (total running time)

Blue Sky

USA, not yet released

PRODUCTION COMPANY:	Orion
PRODUCER:	Robert H. Solo
DIRECTOR:	Tony Richardson
SCREENPLAY:	Rama Laurie Stagner, Arlene Sarner, and Jerry Leichtling
PHOTOGRAPHY:	Steve Yaconelli
MUSIC:	Jack Nitzsche
EDITOR:	Robert K. Lambert
ART DIRECTOR:	Gary Jóhn Constable
COSTUMES:	Jane Robinson
CAST:*	Jessica Lange *(Carly Marshall)*, Tommy Lee Jones *(Hank Marshall)*, Powers Boothe *(Vince Johnson)*, Chris O'Donnell *(Glenn Johnson)*, Amy Locane *(Alex Marshall)*, Carrie Snodgrass *(Vera Johnson)*

Index